9·28·81

ENGLISH PLAYS OF THE NINETEENTH CENTURY

ENGLISH PLAYS

OF THE

NINETEENTH CENTURY

III. *Comedies*

EDITED BY MICHAEL R. BOOTH

OXFORD
AT THE CLARENDON PRESS
1973

Oxford University Press, Ely House, London W. 1

GLASGOW NEW YORK TORONTO MELBOURNE WELLINGTON
CAPE TOWN IBADAN NAIROBI DAR ES SALAAM LUSAKA ADDIS ABABA
DELHI BOMBAY CALCUTTA MADRAS KARACHI LAHORE DACCA
KUALA LUMPUR SINGAPORE HONG KONG TOKYO

*Printed in Great Britain
at the University Press, Oxford
by Vivian Ridler
Printer to the University*

FOREWORD

THE editorial principles and criteria of selection employed for these two volumes of Comedies and Farces are the same as those outlined in the Foreword to the two volumes of Dramas that have already appeared. There is, and has been, some overlapping with plays contained in other selections; this is to some degree inevitable since *English Plays of the Nineteenth Century* is intended—with the exception of the plays of Shaw and Wilde —to illustrate the century's drama in its own right rather than supplement what is already available in print. Certain plays, important because of their merit, popularity in their own time, or their expression of a noteworthy dramatic trend in a more interesting and significant way than other possible choices, cannot readily be omitted without impairing the representative value of the edition.

It is heartening to see a growing interest in nineteenth-century drama, both in the theatre and among scholars and students. Certainly, if the number of anthologies of nineteenth-century plays that have been published in the last few years is anything to go by, this interest is deepening. Such publication does, however, make the problem of avoiding duplication more difficult. As far as I know, only two of the fourteen plays in Volumes Three and Four are available elsewhere; indeed, when it comes to farce the indifference and contempt of the anthologist and critic for one of the most popular forms of nineteenth-century drama has been so great that it is virtually impossible to read an English farce of this period in any twentieth-century collection, and almost as difficult to read *about* nineteenth-century farce.

One more volume remains to complete this edition, and this will contain pantomimes, extravaganzas, and burlesques. Acknowledgements are due to Samuel French for permission to print *The Magistrate*, to Methuen for material incorporated from my article 'Early Victorian Farce: Dionysus Domesticated' in *Nineteenth Century British Theatre*, and to the Victoria and

Albert Museum for all illustrations except those otherwise acknowledged. I am also most thankful for personal assistance valuably supplied by Professor William Appleton, Professor Jane Stedman, the Edinburgh Public Library, and the always helpful staff at the Enthoven Collection in the Victoria and Albert Museum. I must express my gratitude to the University of Guelph for generously providing research leave to enable me to complete these two volumes, and to the Canada Council for its continued support and assistance, which has been so vital since I began work on this edition.

MICHAEL R. BOOTH

University of Guelph
Guelph, Ontario

CONTENTS

ILLUSTRATIONS

INTRODUCTION TO VOLUME THREE

In 1821, a critic reviewing *The School for Scandal* at Drury Lane was moved to reflect, not only upon the performance itself, but also upon the comedy of Sheridan and the Restoration, and its place upon the modern stage:

> It is the bustle and stage incident alone of these pieces which bear them up in the present day, aided possibly by a reading interest in a small portion of the audience. . . . We suspect, indeed, that the composition of a modern audience differs essentially from that of one of half a century ago. At the latter period, the prosperity of a theatre depended mainly on people of rank, and a critical Pit. . . . All this is swept away by the enlargement of theatres, and the immense alteration produced by the commercial intoxication of the last thirty years— nine-tenths of an audience will not come to listen to what is chiefly interesting to the other tenth. This simple fact alone will account for the non-attraction of some of our very best comedies . . . they are not sufficiently *frappant* for the multitude, upon whom their wit, humour, and antithesis descend like lightning upon an iceberg.[1]

Complaints about the taste of audiences and the 'decline' of comedy are legion among critics in the first half of the nineteenth century; this reviewer's remarks can serve as a starting-point for an introduction to a selection of nineteenth-century comedies.

Sentiment, morality, and the coexistence of the comic with the serious and pathetic, all significant aspects of eighteenth-century comedy, survive and are intensified in early nineteenth-century comedy, but the sense in the former of refinement, grace, and social elegance is weakened to the point of vanishing. Virtually gone also is any strong feeling of social norms and proprieties. The relatively stable social order and often narrow social focus of comedy disappeared in a theatre that no longer expressed, either in its drama or in the character of its audience, the superiority, disciplined restraint, and social control of the fashionable aristocracy and the educated middle class. Social and political change, the enlarging of the patent theatres, the

---

[1] The review, in an unidentified newspaper clipping, is signed 'G.'

broadening and inevitable coarsening of audience tastes—all this brought with it a demand for a new kind of comedy, incorporating the most favoured elements of the old but discarding much in order to make room for what appealed to contemporary taste. Yet one element of eighteenth-century comedy remained stable all through the nineteenth century. Despite the changing composition of audiences and fluctuations in taste, comedy was centred in the middle class: its social settings and domestic concerns were those of the middle class, its characters and viewpoints predominantly middle-class characters and middle-class viewpoints. This is not true of melodrama, farce, and pantomime, and a study of the repertory of East End theatres after 1843 (the date when 'legitimate' comedy could legally be played outside the major theatres) shows that three- or five-act comedy played an infinitesimal part; its world was irrelevant to the lower-class audiences of these theatres.

Writers early in the century noticed aspects of comedy that they found disagreeable. Elizabeth Inchbald was more restrained than most: admitting that her *To Marry or Not to Marry* (1805) was too refined for the new taste, she remarked:

The stage delights the eye far oftener than the ear. Various personages of the drama, however disunited, amuse the looker-on; whilst one little compact family presents a sameness to the view, like unity of place; and wearies the sight of a British auditor fully as much. Incidents, too, must be numerous, however unconnected, to please a London audience: they seem, of late, to expect a certain number, whether good or bad. Quality they are judges of—but quantity they *must have*.[1]

Leigh Hunt, one of the most determined foes of the new comedy, accused dramatists of 'an inveterate love of punning', 'a deformed alteration of common character and incidents', and 'a dialogue either extremely flowery or extremely familiar'.[2] He declared that it was impossible for the town to relish delicacy and graceful sentiment while indulging their current taste for buffoonery, since 'we have been like those unfortunate youths, who having got among frivolous acquaintances, place all their enjoyment and idea of social wit in horse-laughter and a certain

---

[1] 'Remarks' on *To Marry or Not to Marry*, in *The British Theatre*, ed. Elizabeth Inchbald (1808), xxiii.

[2] *Critical Essays on the Performers of the London Theatres* (1807), p. 52.

noisy nonsense, removed from all that is elegant, rational, and respectable.'[1] A German visitor lamented that 'most English comedies, although bustling, witty, and humorous, do not possess that refinement and delicacy of the best French comedies',[2] and grew indignant about English dramatists 'who disarm the rage of the critics by entering the lists with Joe Miller. Wit never was more shamelessly prostituted or more casually maltreated than by these unlucky *bon-mot* hunters. Indeed, it appears most extraordinary how these buffooneries are permitted to disgrace a stage where the majesty of Shakespeare commands veneration.'[3]

The drama of the first half of the nineteenth century was the favourite game of angry and contemptuous critics, who flushed comedy, tragedy, spectacle, and melodrama alike from the dark woods of 'decline' and 'illegitimacy', and pursued them energetically in repeated but vain attempts to hunt the quarry to a death that would rid the theatrical land of impure and noisome beasts and restore it to the exiled monarch of legitimacy and the rule of taste. It is more helpful for us to accept that drama on its own terms, illustrate its constituent elements, and with hindsight denied to the early nineteenth-century critic relate it to the drama that was to follow.

An initial impression of the comedy of the period 1790–1820, the comedy written by Colman, Frederic Reynolds, Thomas Dibdin, Andrew Cherry, Thomas Holcroft, Thomas Morton (its chief authors), and others, is of a lack of aim and a deficiency of form, of an uncertainty of comic purpose, of a bustling attempt to please everybody by any available means. A closer look, however, reveals a pattern of writing and subject-matter which was surprisingly repetitive and homogeneous over the short time when this kind of comedy was in full flower. It was bourgeois and anti-aristocratic, strongly sentimental and heavily moralistic. It endlessly proclaimed the beauty of virtue.

[1] *The Examiner*, 21 January 1810.

[2] C. A. G. Goede, *The Stranger in England* (1807), ii. 220.

[3] Ibid., ii. 198. Half a century later George Vandenhoff was complaining about comedy in almost the same terms as these earlier critics: 'Vulgar familiarity passes for easy elegance; strut and swagger for dignity and grace. Buffoonery is more welcome to the general audience than humour; practical jokes than the most sparkling wit; and everything is sacrificed to the bringing down a round of applause, or the raising a boisterous laugh.' (*Dramatic Reminiscences* (1860), p. 310.)

It idealized the simple, the rustic, and the domestic. It was strongly patriotic, including in praise of native land the glories of commerce, agriculture, the soldier and sailor. Although it indulged extensively in heavy drama, its villains were remarkably weak and susceptible to reform. Oddly coexisting with intensely melodramatic elements were equally strong components of low comedy and eccentric characterization that provided most of its humour. The best of it dashed breathlessly towards a fifth act, unhampered by all this lumber of content and untroubled by any thought of a well-made plot, in a style that did not so much communicate speeches as hurl great chunks of rhetoric, melodrama, farce, and pseudo-wit at audiences which responded with delight because of the brilliance of actors who had thoroughly mastered seemingly impossible material. Such a comedy defies definition: calling it a middle-class marriage between farce and melodrama would be near enough for our purposes.

Indeed, one of the most striking features of this comedy is the mixture of the pathetic and potentially tragic with the comic and farcical; frequently the two elements are quite unrelated. A pattern of this type is, of course, nearly as old as English drama. Comic elements appear in otherwise serious miracle and morality plays: tragi-comedy established itself early on the stage, and Shakespearean tragedy is not without ingredients of low comedy. Comedy itself could contain elements of tragedy and pathos. To go back no further than the eighteenth century, the immediate ancestor of the serio-comic drama now under consideration is the sentimental comedy of Cibber, Steele, Kelly, and Cumberland (an author still writing in the first decade of the nineteenth century). The reviewer of *The School for Scandal* quoted above said that 'the truth cannot be concealed— we have become a melodramatic people'. Melodrama alternates the violent and pathetic with the absurdly farcical with no consciousness of incongruity; such a pattern was essential to the melodramatic form.

The most melodramatic comic dramatist writing around the turn of the century was Thomas Morton. In *Speed the Plough* (1800) the fearful secret of Sir Philip Blandford is revealed— years ago he found the woman he was to marry embracing his own brother. Stabbing him to the heart, he fled the country and gambled away his estates, which fell into the hands of the mysterious Morrington, who did not seek to possess them. He lives broodingly in a Gothic castle with a secret chamber in which is hidden the bloody knife used in the stabbing. As it turns out, Morrington is Sir Philip's perfectly recovered brother, protectively watching over him and the estate. Both men suffer acutely from bad consciences. The virtuous young hero, Henry, is the offspring of Morrington's illicit love. The play ends emotionally, to say the least:

MORRINGTON. Kneel with me, my boy, lift up thy innocent hands with those of thy guilty father, and beg for mercy from that injured saint. [HENRY *kneels with him.*]

SIR PHILIP. O God! How infinite are thy mercies! Henry, forgive me —Emma, plead for me. There! There! [*Joining their hands.*]

HENRY. But, my father—

SIR PHILIP. [*Approaching.*] Charles!

MORRINGTON. Philip!

SIR PHILIP. Brother, I forgive thee.

MORRINGTON. Then let me die—blest, most blest!

SIR PHILIP. No, no! [*Striking his breast.*] Here—I want thee here. Raise him to my heart. [*They raise* MORRINGTON. *In the effort to embrace he falls into their arms exhausted.*] Again! [*They sink into each other's arms.*]

HANDY JUNIOR. [*Comes forward.*] If forgiveness be an attribute which ennobles our nature, may we not hope to find pardon for our errors—here? [*The Curtain falls.*]

Similarly, in Morton's *The School for Reform* (1805), Lord Avondale, about to marry Julia, is confronted by a wife whom he abandoned twenty years ago to further his career as a diplomat. Their son Frederick, who loves Julia, discovers his parents, and his own identity is revealed by a mark on his neck, put there by the Yorkshire countryman Tyke, in whose care Frederick was placed when an infant. Towards the end of the play Avondale, disguised in mask and cloak, seizes evidence of his past and flees; in order to save him Frederick assumes his disguise, is taken for the mysterious robber, and sent to prison, where Tyke recognizes him from the mark on his neck. All are reconciled in the happy ending. Tyke himself is a tragi-comic figure with a criminal past who reforms through a chance encounter with his old father. The stage directions for Tyke indicate the intensely emotional nature of his part. He *'speaks with difficulty and sighs heavily'*, *'looks with a vacant stare of horror'*, *'tears his hair in agony'*, *'groaning, strikes his Breast'*, *'laughs hysterically'*, and, recognizing his father, *'by Degrees he tremblingly falls on his Knees, and clasps his Hands in energetic Devotion'*.

Obviously influenced by the Gothic novel and Gothic tragedy, French and German sentimental drama, melodrama, and plays like Colman's *The Iron Chest* (1796), *Speed the Plough* and *The School of Reform* would hardly seem to qualify as comedies. Yet the first two acts of *Speed the Plough* are mainly humorous, with excellent comic characterizations in Ashfield, a Hampshire farmer, Sir Abel Handy, whose inventions are always going wrong, and his son Bob, who fancies he can do things better than anybody else and fails miserably. Five characters out of twelve are comic. In *The School of Reform* the pure comedy devolves upon Ferment, furious because his wife will not talk to him, and his silent spouse. In both plays, as in almost all comedy of this kind, there is little attempt to integrate the comic with the serious plot. The two blithely coexist, as they do in melodrama.

The comedy is stronger in Reynolds than in Morton, although the mixture is much as before. In *Life* (1800) the penurious Marchmont, living humbly with his adoring daughter Rosa and persecuted for non-payment of rent by the evil Craftly, finds—in a scene of wild emotional abandon—the mysterious Mrs. Belford to be the wife whom he left and believed dead years before. The wealthy Primitive, who deserted a daughter as Marchmont deserted a wife, discovers her in the person of the same Mrs. Belford. If Marchmont is subjected to the half-hearted villainy of Craftly, Mrs. Belford endures an abduction attempt from Clifford, who pursues her feebly throughout the play. Together with these characters are the stupid Lackbrain, Primitive's adopted son, and Sir Harry Torpid, a jaded elegant consumed with boredom unless agitated by events that create in him intense feeling and the desire to dash about helping the suffering virtuous. Thus melodramatic plot lines and melo-dramatic emotions are mingled with feverish comedy and a great deal of sentiment and goodheartedness. Like all the good characters in Morton's plays and their near relations in a dozen other Reynolds comedies, Primitive, Rosa, Marchmont, Mrs. Belford, and Sir Harry Torpid trail clouds of virtue behind them and exude endless worthy sentiments, typical of which is Sir Harry's 'Let a man make virtue his pursuit, and he'll find life a very pleasant spree, I'll promise him.' 'None but madmen would forsake that peace which virtue yields—preserve it—cling to it. Fortified with that, you boast a bulwark may defy the world' is one sentiment of many like it from Reynolds's *The Delinquent* (1805). Here the mysterious Delinquent (Sir Arthur Courcy, as he really is) is in the power of the villain Sir Edward Specious and reluctantly aids him in a plot to abduct the beautiful Olivia. It transpires that not only is the Delinquent Olivia's father, but also the husband of Olivia's governess, Mrs. Aubrey, who long ago had so plunged him into debt with her extravagances that he was forced to flee his creditors into exile; however, she is atoning by tenderly watching over her daughter Olivia, who does not know her real identity.[1] In the end Sir Arthur forgives his wife and Sir Edward relents, declaring, 'To persist in plunging in despair parent and child, long parted and thus found, demands that daring and ferocious spirit which still, thank heaven, your coward master needs'—a speech which alone demonstrates that *The Delinquent* is not true melodrama, since it would make any genuine melodramatic villain turn wrathfully in his grave.[2] Alongside this incredible and casually motivated plot—Reynolds took less trouble with his plots than his contemporaries, who themselves took very little—is a comic plot in which the dashing rake young Doric makes up to his rich uncle and falls in love with Olivia. There is also the hypocritical

[1] It can easily be seen how much Reynolds owed to his borrowings: not only from an enormously popular play like Kotzebue's *The Stranger* (1798), with Kemble in a part much like the Delinquent (which he also played), and from other dramatists such as Morton (*Life* and *The Delinquent* strongly resemble *Speed the Plough* and *The School of Reform*), but also from himself.

[2] Sir Edward Specious in this play, and Craftly and Clifford in *Life*, are examples of the debilitated villains, frequently aristocrats, common to this school of comedy. Others are Malcour in Reynolds's *Folly As It Flies*, Sir Charles Cropland in Colman's *The Poor Gentleman*, and Squire Chevy Chase in Thomas Dibdin's *The School for Prejudice*. These three also make ineffective attempts upon a woman's virtue and are easily foiled. True villainy could not exist in the excessive benevolence and sentimentalism of these plays; the melodrama in them is therefore not nearly as dark as in real melodrama.

Miss Stoic, who pretends to love country seclusion, and the blustery, good-hearted Major Tornado, Olivia's guardian.[1]

No matter, then, how strong were the serious parts of their plays, authors were careful to justify the title of comedy by a generous proportion of comic material. To create humour, they relied—apart from verbal wit—upon eccentricity and low comedy in which Irishmen and countrymen abound. Major Tornado, Sir Abel Handy in *Speed the Plough*, Sir Harry Torpid in *Life*, Sir Solomon Cynic in Reynolds's *The Will* (1797), Colman's energetic philanthropists Sir Robert Bramble in *The Poor Gentleman* (1801), and Torrent in *Who Wants a Guinea?* (1805), are all eccentrics and 'humours' characters of one kind or another. The list of low comedy characters is longer, and since they are often the heart of a dramatist's comic appeal they spend a great deal of time on stage. Colman is especially rich in them: Stephen Harrowby in *The Poor Gentleman*, a farmer's son obsessed with soldiering; Dennis Brulgruddery and Dan in *John Bull*; and the Yorkshire servants Solomon Gundy and Andrew Bang in *Who Wants a Guinea?* Selfish, shrewd, stupid, silly, sentimental, drunken, virtuous, and loyal, they sometimes serve higher purposes than low comedy, and bear a burden of morality and sentiment as well. Sharing characteristics of both eccentric humour and low comedy are such imaginative creations as the pedantic, money-hunting tutor Pangloss in Colman's *The Heir-at-Law* (1797) and the apothecary Ollapod in *The Poor Gentleman*, whose vocabulary is a strange blend of medicine and hunting.

These comic ingredients were much in demand, and playwrights ignored them at their peril. Reflecting on the failure of her *To Marry or Not to Marry*, an elegant but rather grave comedy, Elizabeth Inchbald said that 'it appears as if the writer of this comedy had said, previous to the commencement of the task, "I will shun the faults imputed by the critics to modern dramatists; I will avoid farcical incidents, broad jests, the introduction of broken English, whether Hibernian or provincial".' The result, she confessed, was unsatisfactory. 'In the dearth of

[1] Tornado comes from India, Primitive in *Life* from the West Indies. In comedy of this period, and in earlier and later comedy as well, these geographical areas were guarantees of a good, albeit careless heart, an abrupt though kindly manner, an innate sense of justice and fair play, and a disposition to relieve distress.

wit, an audience will gladly accept of humour; but the author who shall dare to exclude from his comedy the last, without being able to furnish the first, assuredly must incur the rigorous, though just sentence of dulness.'[1] To be pleasantly amused was not enough for an English audience; it wanted to laugh, and laugh loudly, as well as shed tears at the pathetic parts. Of the success of *John Bull* and the hostility of the critics to comedy, Mrs. Inchbald noted:

The introduction of farces into the entertainments of the theatre has been one cause of destroying that legitimate comedy which such critics require. The eye, which has been accustomed to delight in paintings of caricature, regards a picture from real life as an insipid work. The extravagance of farce has given to the town a taste for the pleasant convulsion of hearty laughter, and smiles are contemned as the token of insipid amusement.[2]

The pathetic, the sensational, the eccentric, and the farcical were not the only essentials of turn-of-the-century comedy. The strong expression of sentiments on all possible occasions—again a characteristic of melodrama—together with the impregnable virtue of nearly every major character, raised comedy to ethical heights it never reached even in its most fervently righteous moments later in the century. More interesting than the energetic pronouncements of a general morality is the subject-matter of particular sentiments, or 'claptraps', as objecting critics called them.[3] In Reynolds's *Folly As It Flies* (1801) the repentant Lady Melmoth, who has ruined her kindly husband with her thoughtless extravagance, addressing herself to the ladies in the boxes ('ye votaries of dissipation'), declares, 'I know, I'm sure, that in the splendid equipage and dazzling dress ye never taste one moment of substantial joy. Then seek it in your husbands' and your children's hearts—make home a shelter 'gainst the storm; and, let it roar around, still shall you find domestic life the scene of peace!' Here sounded one of the major themes of the nineteenth century, not in comedy alone but in all forms of drama, as well as in the novel. 'Domestic life the scene

---

[1] 'Remarks' on *To Marry or Not to Marry*.

[2] 'Remarks' on *John Bull* in *The British Theatre*, xxi.

[3] 'The moral point is everything', Charles Lamb remarked wearily of the comedy of his time. (*The Dramatic Essays of Charles Lamb*, ed. Brander Matthews (1891), p. 149.)

of peace' was an ideal that burned brightly on the stage throughout the century. Reynolds, Colman, Morton, and their colleagues
depicted relationships between father and son, father and daughter, and husband and wife, with intense feeling. Old Dornton in
Holcroft's *The Road to Ruin* (1792) dotes passionately on his
profligate son Harry, and with equal passion tries to repress
this love and drive him from home for his follies. But he cannot
bring himself to do it, and there is a final reconciliation. The
scenes between father and son, powerfully written, are the emotional core of the play. Father–daughter relationships aroused
the maximum domestic emotion: the brooding protectiveness of
Worthington for Emily in *The Poor Gentleman*, the outbursts of
emotion when long-lost daughters are restored to their fathers in
Who Wants a Guinea?, *The Will*, *Life*, *The Delinquent*, and *To
Marry or Not to Marry*. The reconciliation of erring wives
with now forgiving husbands is important in many comedies
written after *The Stranger* and the reunion in that play of
the repentant Mrs. Haller with the proud and mysterious
Stranger.

Together with the idealization of domestic bonds went the
accessory though subordinate idealization of various aspects of
English life and character, the virtues of a simple country
existence, the pursuit of agriculture, and the ownership of land.
John Grouse, the Yorkshire gamekeeper in Thomas Dibdin's
The School for Prejudice (1801), foils villainy and fulfils a moral
function that sometimes belonged to low-comedy countrymen.[1]
Sir Charles Cropland in *The Poor Gentleman*, a town man at
heart, is morally corrupt and contaminates the wholesome
Kentish countryside. His steward reminds him of his duty 'to
support the dignity of an English landholder, for the honour of
old England; to promote the welfare of his honest tenants; and
to succour the industrious poor, who naturally look up to him
for assistance'. (As in melodrama, the moral tone is hostile to
the aristocrat—but not to the landowner, generally a figure
of opprobrium in melodrama.) Looking forward to an idyllic

---

[1] The hero is named Frank Liberal, and behaves accordingly. Virtue is so
extensive that it possesses the Jewish money-lender Ephraim, idealized after the
manner of the do-gooding Sheva in Richard Cumberland's *The Jew* (1794).
Ephraim restores £10,000 he finds in the lining of an old coat to its owner, saying,
'Ten thousand pounds is no more recompence for de loss of a good conscience
than if it was a dwopenny bank-note.'

retirement in the country with his adopted son Lackbrain, Primitive in *Life* declares enthusiastically that 'the English cottage is, and ever will be, the seat of peace, industry, and virtue'. He is disappointed, not by the cottage, but by the hypocrisy of Lackbrain and his wife, who only pretend to love the country in order to secure Primitive's wealth, and actually lead a fashionably dissipated life. The simple rustics of *The Heir-at-Law*, Cicely and Zekiel Homespun, come to London in search of Cicely's sweetheart Dick Dowlas, who incidentally describes an English farmer as 'one who supports his family, and serves his country, by his own industry. In this land of commerce . . . such a character will be always respectable.' Dick tries to desert Cicely because he is now heir to a title and wishes to become a man of fashion, but conscience and love prove too much for him. The Homespuns, honest, affectionate, and worthy, are clearly the main repository of the play's virtues. Farmer Ashfield in *Speed the Plough* and Farmer Harrowby in *The Poor Gentleman*, characters partly sentimental and partly comic, upright and true men both, are idealized as the very soil of England.

The soldier, the sailor, and the man of commerce take their place beside the countryman and the farmer in comedy's hierarchy of values. Highly patriotic sentiments are frequently expressed, such as 'I wish I may be shot if I can give harsh treatment to an honest man in misfortune, under my thatch, who have wasted his strength and his youth in guarding the land which do give us English farmers a livelihood' and 'A gallant soldier's memory will flourish, though humble turf be osier-bound upon his grave. The tears of his country will moisten it, and vigorous laurel sprout among the cypress that shadows its remains.' A low-comedy servant who prides himself on his excruciating French refuses to take a farthing from a distressed English sailor, and is told, 'Whatever your proficiency may be in French, such language is pure English, and that of the best subjects in the British dominions.' The man of business is likewise elevated. Old Dornton in *The Road to Ruin* is a City merchant to be admired for his moral and financial integrity as well as his love for his son. In *The Heir-at-Law* Daniel Dowlas, a simple chandler, succeeds to the title and fortune of Lord Duberly and tries to improve his language and manners to fit his new position. However, he feels uncomfortable, cannot leave the chandler behind him, and for his attempt is satirically rebuked. In the play's value system, being an honest chandler is better than being a peer. The real heir turns up alive to claim the title, and Dowlas resumes his proper social and moral station. The social responsibility of the landowner and merchant is repeatedly emphasized. Endeavouring to persuade the miserly Hogmore to aid the victims of a village fire, Heartly in *Who Wants a Guinea?* tells him, 'The wealthy of this land forbid the drops of disappointment to fall from labour's eye and rust the ploughshare. Industry is the source of our country's riches; and English policy would teach opulence to dry the peasant's tear, if English justice and generosity did not continually prevent its flowing.' The philanthropist (a not uncommon figure in contemporary comedy) of the same play asks his friend to 'look at the commercial names that swell every list of national subscriptions, and then tell me whether men of the highest rank do not acknowledge, with pleasure, the merchant's kindred ardour in the country's welfare'.

The comedy of the late eighteenth and early nineteenth century is interesting and important, not only in its own right as the most flourishing 'legitimate' drama of its age, but also for what it led to, since it established a comic pattern that with some modification became in its essentials the comedy of the Victorians. To the idealizing of domestic ties the Victorians added what was peculiarly their own, a strong feeling for home and hearth. Marriage and domestic life, though no less sacred, were treated more prosaically and with more realistic detail. Eccentric character and low comedy remained major sources of humour for the early and mid Victorians, and most comedy still contained, in varying degrees of emphasis, pathetic and potentially tragic elements, melodramatic plots, and character types. Morality, sentiment, and the glories of virtue were adapted, as dramatic material, to differing social contexts and expressed with somewhat less *braggadocio*. The process of refinement and domestic realism that gradually occurred in comedy as in other forms of nineteenth-century theatre cannot disguise the fact that the Victorian playwright's basic material and his moral attitudes were in substantial part an inheritance from an earlier comedy and not his own invention.

For this reason alone the plays of Colman, Reynolds, Morton, and Holcroft are significant, and there are further grounds for rebutting the oft-repeated charge, made by contemporaries and later generations of critics, that their theatre was irrelevant to the world they lived in. Perhaps Dutton Cook stated the case most succinctly: these comedies 'belong exclusively to the play-house and the players. They reflect real life and manners in no way; as pictures of the period in which they were written they have no kind of value. They are mere theatrical contrivances for the display of the actors' peculiarities for winning laughter at any price from the audiences, and dismissing them amused with the slightest possible tax upon their reflective powers.'[1] This statement is true in so far as it pertains to the abilities of the actors.[2] But putting aside the question of the dramatists' intentions, which were certainly not to paint a faithful picture of the period, there is no doubt that the restlessness, the bustle, the structural carelessness, the sentimental liberalism, the idealization of the simple country life, the simplistic morality, and the heavy drama of the comedies pleased the taste of a public unlikely to favour a theatre that had nothing to do with the age in which it lived. In fact, these characteristics admirably reflect, in a manner that had to be non-political and socially harmless in order to satisfy the Examiner of Plays, the general sense of being unsettled, of restlessness and social unease after the French Revolution, the breakdown of traditional standards of gentility and graceful living, the fashionable liberal sentimentalism, the upthrust into a less stable society of a vulgar and poorly-educated class of people with flamboyant artistic tastes, and the developing moral sense that was to culminate in a Victorian ethic. Through the general rather than the particular the comedy of the age mirrored significant aspects of the times. When one realizes in how many ways another contemporary dramatic form, the melodrama, was socially and philosophically relevant to the age that gave it birth, the accusation that the

---

[1] *Nights at the Play* (1883), pp. 13–14. These comments come from a review of a revival of Morton's *The Way to Get Married* (1796) at the Olympic in 1867. Cook complained that 'everything is sacrificed to farcical incident and extravagance of character . . . the whole comedy hangs loosely together' (p. 14). The play had been cut, especially in its serious parts, and Cook thought that no modern audience would tolerate the original in its entirety.

[2] See the Appendix on the acting of early nineteenth-century comedy, pp. 145–53 below.

comedy of the early nineteenth century—or of any other period in the century, for that matter—was completely isolated from contemporary life and thought simply cannot be sustained.

After 1810 there was a decline in the vigour and humour of a comedy that had been pre-eminent for twenty years. Colman's last comedy was performed in 1805; Holcroft's in 1806; Reynolds's in 1808; after 1807 Morton wrote only three comedies in twenty-three remaining years of playwriting. Both Colman and Reynolds took up other dramatic forms, perhaps realizing that the five-act comedy with pretensions to legitimacy belonged to the past. Imitators were numerous and even more objectionable to critics than their masters, and no single playwright or group of dramatists was acknowledged as being at the head of comic writing. Although there were many excellent comic actors on the stage, by the 1820s the older generation that performed so brilliantly in Colman and Reynolds and Morton was passing away. Mrs. Mattocks retired in 1808; Lewis in 1809; Bannister in 1815; Johnstone in 1820; Emery died in 1822; Munden retired in 1824; Mrs. Davenport and Fawcett in 1830. The actual quantity of comedies performed appears smaller after 1810; success was doubtful in that area, and dramatists turned more and more to melodrama, spectacle, musical comedy, and farce. The growing number of minor theatres, confined by law to playing the 'illegitimate', increased their output, and the patent theatres, caught between the responsibility of presenting the traditional, legitimate drama and the dire financial necessity of cashing in on the popularity of the illegitimate, compromised by devising playbills made up of both.

Thus an increase in low comedy and farcical comedy, and the heightening of a strong tendency to vulgarity found in the earlier comedy, is not surprising. As the attendance of the fashionable classes at the theatre declined and managers began to cut prices to attract less select audiences, this trend accelerated. In William Moncrieff's *Wanted a Wife* (1819),[1] for instance, most of the humour arises from low-comedy characters and farcical plotting. Separately but simultaneously advertising in the Echo Office for a wife and a domestic place, Arthur Wildfire and his servant Frank are taken up by a young lady and her middle-

---

[1] Moncrieff complained in the preface to the printed play that Drury Lane was two-thirds empty on opening night.

aged aunt. The young lady believes that Wildfire is the servant she advertised for, whereas he believes that she answered his advertisement for a wife; the aunt understands that Frank, who thinks he has found a place as her servant, is actually replying to her advertisement for a husband. The quadruple misunderstanding lasts, quite incredibly, until the end of the play. The amusement here is provided by the farcical complications; additionally there is the low comedy of the proprietor of the Echo Office, an Irishman, M'Shift, and his Yorkshire servant, Jolt, parts played by Johnstone and Emery respectively. The full-blown sentiment has disappeared, and with it any sense of elegance or refinement; the serious interest has been reduced to the unimportant and extraneous story of a young orphan seeking her father.

Since audience taste in humour was moving towards the obvious and the farcical—a movement apparent in turn-of-the-century comedy, where nevertheless an older though debased tradition of wit and foppery lingered by its side—the growing emphasis on farce in comedy is unremarkable. Clearly the comedies which succeeded did so mainly or entirely because of low-comedy interest and the excellence of low-comedy acting. Two such plays featured Liston in low-comedy roles. In Theodore Hook's *Exchange No Robbery* (1820), the landlord of the Pig and Windmill tries to pass off his lubberly potboy son, Sam Swipes (played by Liston), as the rightful husband-to-be of a refined and wealthy heroine. The play centres on Sam Swipes's behaviour in this ridiculous situation. Several scenes are set in the Pig and Windmill, and Liston's performance—Sam became one of his best-known parts—must have been virtually the only source of humour in an otherwise weak comedy. Clumsy, vulgar, carousing in the servants' hall, and roaring out praises of his beloved kitchen-maid Polly, Sam of course looks quite ludicrous *'in the extreme of fashionable dress, except the head, which remains in the original plebeian style'*. In *Paul Pry* (1825), by John Poole, the social setting is more elegant, but it is typical of the comic dramatist's indifferent plotting and inability to express a variety of humour that the main interest of the play attaches to an incidental character who only becomes involved in the plot at the very end. Paul Pry, a thick-skinned vulgarian played by Liston (probably his most famous part), insatiably curious about private family matters, questioning, spying, infuriating everybody by intruding when quite unwanted, wanders around the fringes of a plot that is otherwise serious though relatively unemotional. Pry is threatened with violence when caught peeping through the keyhole of a garden door; he is also chased by dogs and gets his clothes torn when taken for a thief.

This kind of comedy possesses the same eccentricity of behaviour and helter-skelter extravagance as that of the previous generation, with the developments noted above. In 1844 Catherine Gore commented on her own comedy, *Quid Pro Quo*, which won the prize of £500 in a competition to determine the best comedy submitted to a panel of judges, and was performed at the Haymarket:

A general feeling of disappointment has arisen from the mistaken idea that the prize purported to produce what is termed a high-life comedy; a style of piece which the experience of the past twenty years proves to be wholly ineffective on the modern stage. No such object was suggested by the manager; and a bustling play of the Farquhar, or George Colman school, appeared far more available to the resources of the theatre, and the taste of the play-going public. Were the boxes often filled as I had the gratification of seeing them for the first representation of 'QUID PRO QUO', with those aristocratic and literary classes of the community who have absolutely withdrawn their patronage from the English stage, for *their* more refined pleasure, a new order of dramatic authors would be encouraged to write, and of performers to study. But no one familiar with the nightly aspect of our theatres will deny that they are supported by a class requiring a very different species of entertainment, for whose diversion, exaggeration in writing and acting is as essential, as daubing to the art of the scene-painter. Now that professional distinctions are extinct, and that the fusion of the educated classes has smoothed the surface of society to a rail-road level, a mere Daguerreotypic picture of the manners of the day would afford little satisfaction to the disproportion and caricature *established into the custom of the stage* by the exigencies of our colossal patent theatres.[1]

---

[1] Preface to *Quid Pro Quo*. From the 1840s there were many suggestions that the new conformity in manners and dress deprived dramatists of important comic material. As late as the 1880s Joseph Knight said, 'With the abolition of distinctions of costume, the chances of eccentric comedy were seriously impaired. Bob Acres or Tony Lumpkin would now be found in the stalls of a theatre in no wise distinguishable from the rest of the audience, and Dr. Pangloss, should he return, would discard wig, cocked hat, and cane, and appear in a black coat and waistcoat and subfusk continuations.' (*The Theatre*, September 1881, p. 171.)

Quid Pro Quo is socially a cut above comedies like *Wanted a Wife* and *Paul Pry*, and more a comedy of high life than 'a bustling play . . . of the George Colman school', despite Mrs. Gore's professed intention to write in 'a broader style as a dramatist, than as a novelist', a style that would be 'likely to provoke the greatest mirth of the greatest number'.[1] The relative refinement of *Quid Pro Quo* showed that some attempt was still being made to provide comic entertainment for the fashionable and educated classes of society.

There are other evidences of this attempt, and nothing could be more wrong than to believe that from about 1810 to Victoria's accession theatre audiences were a boorish rabble hungering only for farce, sensation, and jolly pantomime. A considerable audience—though not considerable enough for the financial comfort of most managers—was still interested in the legitimate drama and a theatre of taste. Not legitimate drama, because it was illegal to perform it in the minor theatres before 1843, but tasteful and elegant even in their illegitimacy, are the musical extravaganzas, burlesques, and burlettas performed under Madame Vestris's management of the Olympic from 1831 to 1839. A part of the Olympic's repertory consisted of short comedies, often in two acts, containing songs and written after French models by authors such as J. R. Planché, Charles Dance, and T. H. Bayly. The tone of these *petites comédies* can be restrained and even refined; some of them are notably free from the heavy emphasis on farcical situations, low comedy, and vulgar characterization common enough in comedies at other theatres. For instance, in Dance's *The Beulah Spa* (1833), Caroline Grantley wishes to push the hesitant Beauchamp into proposing to her. She disguises herself, first as a minstrel to sing him a love song, and then as a gypsy to tell his fortune. Finally she reveals herself and he does propose. The plot is simple and the general tone fairly elevated. Even simpler is the same author's *A Dream of the Future* (1837). Captain Lovelock and Dr. Mildmay arrive at the home of Mr. Harbottle to take his nieces, Georgina and Honoria, to a ball and to propose marriage. Honoria refuses the timid Mildmay and Georgina accepts the dashing Lovelock. After the ball, Honoria has a dream that she relates to her sister in song: forty years have

---

[1] Preface to *Quid Pro Quo*.

passed, and she is a dissatisfied old maid, mocked by a contemptuous and successful Mildmay and the unwilling observer of the philandering Lovelock's scurvy treatment of his wife Georgina. The relation of the dream has a salutary effect: when the men arrive Honoria accepts Mildmay and Georgina rejects Lovelock, who then reveals himself as the fortune-hunting scoundrel he really is. All this is rather delicately and quietly expressed; broad humour is confined to Harbottle's penchant for wine and the low comedy of an Irish servant with a muddled vocabulary. The parts of Caroline Grantley and Honoria in these two pieces were played by Vestris: sentimental, witty, and refined, her heroines set the mark of elegance and taste upon a comic style that at its best possessed considerable charm and grace, and whose plots were usually economical and deftly managed. The characteristics of charm, delicacy, a tender sentimentalism, and a restraint of expression often found in these *petites comédies* but hardly anywhere else in contemporary comedy, had to wait thirty years for further development, when they became key elements of Robertsonian comedy.

A direct attempt to perpetuate the most traditional kind of legitimate comedy and to appeal to a higher level of public taste than that catered for by the ordinary run of comic entertainment was the writing of poetic comedies after the manner of the Elizabethans. This was part of a larger effort to deflect the whole course of the drama from the channels in which it was inevitably running and to recapture the vanished glories of an Elizabethan drama that had received the accolade of 'literature'.[1] The main impetus of this movement was tragic, but comedies were also written; the most admired poetic comedies in their time were by John Tobin and Sheridan Knowles. Tobin's *The Honey Moon* (1805: posthumously produced), a skilful and not unpleasing mixture in blank verse and prose of the plots of *The Taming of the Shrew*, *Twelfth Night*, and *Much Ado about Nothing*, with other matter, was praised by George Daniel in the preface to the Cumberland edition (1827) in terms which clearly convey the literary movement's lofty rationale and haughty contempt for the enemy:

He [Tobin] had drank deep at the pure fountain-head of English Poetry —the works of our ancient dramatists. From them he acquired a

---

[1] For a brief mention of this effort, see Volume One, pp. 7–9.

correctness of taste, a fertility of thought, and a harmony of language, that none of his contemporaries have attained. . . . Farcical plot and sprightly nonsense, oaths and obscenity, he left to those authors who, for many years, monopolized the stage to the total exclusion of superior talent; had he descended to compound such base materials, he might, like them, have inherited temporary popularity and lasting contempt; but he adopted a wiser and more independent course, sacrificing present advantage for the nobler award of posterity. . . . Thus has the author of the Honey Moon, by *one* happy effort of taste and genius, attained a rank in literature, which the vapid and multifarious productions of his contemporaries shall in vain aspire to.

In the 1830s the name of Knowles was joined with that of Tobin. By the time he came to write comedies, Knowles's considerable reputation had already been achieved by tragedies and dramas like *Virginius* (1820), *William Tell* (1825), and *The Hunchback* (1832). His three comedies are set vaguely in Elizabethan times, two of them in London, and are written in a sometimes tolerable blank verse and a painfully laboured imitation of Shakespearean prose. The plots are romantic, the characters mostly high-born, and the idealization of domestic relationships intense. In *The Beggar of Bethnal Green* (1834) Lord Wilford sees Bess, the daughter of the blind beggar Albert (actually a nobleman), in the street, falls in love with her, discovers her again as the barmaid of an inn, and marries her. The Queen acts as *dea ex machina*, and Albert is restored to high estate. In a comic sub-plot the swollen-headed son of Old Small dresses as a lord and marries a chambermaid in the belief that she is a lady. The plot of *The Love-Chase* (1837) has echoes of *Much Ado about Nothing*: the reluctant Wildrake falls in love with the quarrelsome, witty, jealous Constance, and Waller pursues his love for Lydia, maid to the Widow Green, under the guise of wooing the complaisant Widow. Widow Green is in turn pursued by old Sir William Fondlove, who mistakenly believes that she dotes passionately upon him. Constance at last sees that Wildrake loves her; Wildrake's friend Trueworth discovers that Lydia is really his sister and therefore a lady;[1] Widow Green accepts Sir William because nobody else will

---

[1] Like Bess in *The Beggar of Bethnal Green* and Virginia in *Virginius*, Lydia is another of Knowles's impossibly sweet, ethereal, and morally perfect heroines, all of them intended as ideal types of young womanhood.

have her. *The Love-Chase* is Knowles's best comedy, and the most popular one in his day. It is certainly superior to *Old Maids* (1841), written for Vestris and Mathews at Covent Garden, in which Thomas Blount rises from journeyman jeweller in his father's shop to Colonel in the army and wins the heart of Lady Blanche. At the same time Sir Philip Brilliant, a fop with a good heart, falls in love with Blanche's friend Lady Anne, and becomes as a result a quieter, worthier man.

The plots of Knowles's comedies indicate his devotion to his sources and his approach to comic material. Yet he catches only something of the outward manner of Elizabethan comedy; the imitation of externals is clever, but there is little life or vitality within—the usual fault of the legitimate school. Knowles's verse and prose can be prolix and clumsy, and the comedies are without the vitality of the tragedies and dramas, which at least contain a degree of vigorous action and a tragic passion of sorts. As with the tragedies and dramas, however, Knowles was fortunate to find his comedies acted by the best players of the day, performers of the quality of Vestris, Mathews, Harley, Webster, Mrs. Nisbet, and Mrs. Glover. As in the tragedies and dramas too, Knowles's essentially domestic spirit is all-embracing. Parental love and the family relationship are at the emotional heart of *The Beggar of Bethnal Green*, for example, as they are in *Virginius* and *William Tell*. Bess loves Lord Wilford as soon as she lays eyes upon him because he resembles the miniature of her father. Albert's grief when his daughter is taken from him is intense; similarly, Old Small bewails the loss of his son:

> Sir, you see
> A poor old man that has an only son,
> Whom he, in evil hour, let go from him,
> Thinking that he could live without him, till
> The task he tried, but found too hard a one . . .
> Yet was my fault my love—
> My too fond love! So fond it could not see
> How duty could be harsh and yet be kind.

Knowles's preference for centring his plots upon the relationship between parent and child is more evident in the tragedies and dramas than the comedies, although it is obvious in *The*

Beggar of Bethnal Green. In his plays generally this theme is more prominent than in the comedies of Colman, Reynolds, Morton, and Holcroft. No matter how hard he tried to be Elizabethan and legitimate, in treating this subject at least Knowles could not avoid contemporaneity.

Since poetic comedy with Elizabethan settings was not attuned to an age much more interested in prosified images of daily life, it dwindled away.[1] Between 1810 and 1840 there was a curious thematic hiatus in comedy. Many years after 1810 were spent imitating Colman and Reynolds and their like, and a desire to say something about the modern world did not reach comedy for some time. In the 1830s Knowles's domestic themes were truly modern, but his style and setting were not; on another level the domesticity of Buckstone's three-act farces in the same decade is again contemporary.[2] With the 1840s a change came over comedy. Not only was it becoming gradually more domestic and realistic, though still with a strong admixture of rhetoric which it never wholly lost, but also thematically more significant. In sum, comedy was modernizing itself. In 1844 the prologue to *Quid Pro Quo* declared:

> 'Tis time to turn some newer page, and show
> Life as it is, and manners as they go . . .
> Tonight our cost and care
> Would picture—English manners as they are.

Mrs. Gore's play hardly fulfils this intention, but within the framework of ideals and fantasy in which they all operated, the comic dramatists of the 1840s and of succeeding decades did indeed treat of subject-matter relevant to modern life.

The major themes explored in comedy over the next thirty years were those of wealth and social ambition; the virtues of rustic and domestic simplicity; the artificiality and moral inferiority of Society; the idealization of womanhood, the marriage bond, and domestic harmony; and the assertion of the rightful authority of husband over wife. Such themes readily

---

[1] One of the better poetic comedies of the second half of the century is Westland Marston's *Donna Diana* (1863). Written in blank verse and set in Barcelona, the play is gracious, elegant, and correct, yet essentially lifeless. The verse, though rather flat, is simpler than Knowles's, and free of his laboured conceits and tortured syntax.

[2] See the Introduction to Volume Four, pp. 10–13.

interconnect, frequently two or three in the same play. Thus discussion of each one separately is somewhat artificial and a little difficult, especially since Victorian playwrights did not as a rule think out their ideas clearly and develop them carefully. George Henry Lewes, in urging English dramatists to follow French models of construction and character representation, complained of English comedy that 'any materials, however carelessly gathered, are thought good enough, so that the "jokes" be abundant. Constructing a story as the development of some idea—grouping around that the characters which will most clearly set it forth—and subordinating the *writer* to the *dramatist*—these are processes which, however necessary, our dramatists disdain or overlook.'[1] The method might have been sloppy and sometimes little different from the method of fifty years before, but the ideas were certainly there, no matter how awkwardly worked out.

Bulwer-Lytton's *Money* is a satirical examination of the importance of wealth, or the lack of it, in determining conduct and attitudes. The author may have known Douglas Jerrold's *The Golden Calf* (1832), a remarkably cogent and disciplined attack upon the corrupting power of wealth. A mysterious *deus ex machina*, Chrystal, forces the dissipated, ruined Mountney to see the folly of his ways and return to his father's honourable (but unspecified) trade, which the snobbish profligate had previously scorned. In one ironic scene, Chrystal invites Mountney's elegant and heartless 'friends', who think Chrystal enormously rich, to dinner in Theobald's Road at the unfashionable hour of one, makes them lay the table, tend to the fire, and cook the mutton chops, all the time relishing their discomfiture. He waxes eloquent on the play's main theme:

When 'tis not asked, 'What can a man do?' but 'What seems he to possess?' not 'What does he know?' but 'Where does he live?' and when this passion for appearance stays not with some hundred gilded nondescripts, but like one general social blight is at this moment found in every rank, in every walk—for a verity, we may not call the present age the age of gold or of silver; but, of all ages else, the AGE OF OUTSIDES!

So consistently ironic, bitter, and savage is the tone of *The Golden Calf* that, although called a comedy, it is more of a

---

[1] *The Leader*, 17 May 1851.

drama, a fact that again draws attention to the problem in this period of dramatic definitions and to the comfortable coexistence, in comedy after comedy, of the serious and the comic, the melodramatic and the farcical, the punning joke and the tender sentiment.

Jerrold continued his attack in *Bubbles of the Day* (1842), set specifically in '*London in 1842*'. The subjects of his wrath here are the aristocratic fool in Parliament, Lord Skindeep; the business adventurer ('the bandit of society—the brigand of a city') Smoke; the money-lender Shark; and the fawning hanger-on, Sir Phoenix Clearcake. The first act is promising, but thereafter Jerrold turns away from the themes he began with to trivial love and plot entanglements, although these are centred around money and property. A thematically significant first act that dribbles away into trivia occurs commonly in Victorian comedy, and in Jerrold more than once. His writing for the minor theatres (including *Black-Eyed Susan*, *Thomas à Becket*, and *The Golden Calf*) is more interesting, vital, and consequential than his later 'legitimate' work for more important theatres, represented by indifferent comedies like *Bubbles of the Day*, *Time Works Wonders* (1845), and *St. Cupid* (1853).

Dramatic satire upon wealth was hardly peculiar to the Victorians, and Jerrold's obvious anger in *The Golden Calf* is rather generalized. More particular in the sense of an immediate social context is the satire in Dion Boucicault's *The School for Scheming* (1847). Here all the plot lines develop the central idea of what people will do to attain position and fortune and whom they will sacrifice in order to achieve them. The aristocratic Claude Plantagenet schemes to escape his debts by marrying the seemingly wealthy Mrs. Fox-French, the headmistress of a finishing school that teaches girls the social arts necessary to ensnare rich and titled husbands, and she marries him for the same reasons. Each is actually ruined and trying to cheat the other; the mutual deception is revealed in an excellent and bitter scene conducted while the bailiffs wait offstage. Plantagenet's daughter Helen, dazzled by wealth and the prospect of a title, and callously manipulated by her father, rejects the man she really loves but in her turn is rejected by the aristocrats she pursues. Like Evelyn in *Money* and Chrystal in *The Golden Calf*, the mysterious Sykes, who finally reveals himself as the father of Helen's unsuccessful suitor, acts as chorus and comments savagely on the ways of the world.[1] The most interesting character in the play is the low-comedy Perkins, who assumes the name of The Macdunnum. He schemes feverishly to be a wealthy capitalist, floats companies, raises stock, apes the aristocracy, is exposed and ruined. 'Commerce' and 'progress' are the keynotes of this part of the play. The Macdunnum has an exchange on these topics with the girl who loves him but whom he discards after obtaining temporary wealth.

MACDUNNUM. This is the age of iron and locomotion.

SALLY. Say rather the age of paper and arrest.

MACDUNNUM. When England's aristocracy are ennobling her enterprise, making speculation fashionable.

SALLY. And England's merchants enriching her Gazette, making bankruptcy respectable.

MACDUNNUM. Oh, Sally! What a definition of our commercial progress!

Early in the play, The Macdunnum, bewildered by the web of pretence and speculation thickening around him, doubts the reality of existence:

There's no reality anywhere—the very age is electro-plated—figures on the top—humbug underneath. . . . It is the same everywhere—all unreal. Facts exist no more—they have dwindled into names—things have shrunk into words—words into air—cash into figures—reputation into nothing. This is the reign of NOTHING: to possess it is the surest foundation of fortune in every walk of life. Examine the pocket of the capitalist—*nothing*! Penetrate the skull of the politician—*nothing*! Value the credit of a free and enlightened state—*nothing*, or your own—*nothing*! Thus ridiculed, despised, calumniated, *nothing* is the philosopher's stone of our age; it turns all it touches into gold—to fame—to beauty—and all the other cardinal virtues. Scepticism is our faith, and this is our creed—trust a stranger never; your friend when you cannot help it, and yourself as little as possible. Even seeing is no longer believing.

Were it not for its fifth act, *The School for Scheming* would be one of the century's best comedies, but it collapses in a welter of improbable reconciliations and reunions, sudden financial windfalls, and platitudinous sentimentalizing. Boucicault was

---

[1] The drama of the day had a fondness for the protective fairy godfather, like Chrystal and Sykes, who makes everything come right in the end.

either unable or unwilling (given the demands of the conventional happy ending) to work out his plot in terms of the
irony and satirical strength of the first four acts.

Despite these flaws, *The School for Scheming* is a significant
comedy, and indeed Boucicault's only one. *Alma Mater* (1842)
and *Old Heads and Young Hearts* (1844) have nothing to say.
The former belongs to that class of nineteenth-century comedy
eschewing any serious matter, and presents an Oxford in which
drinking, racing, and love-making are the only approved occu-
pations of university students. The play is full of faded character
types of an older comedy and is extremely trivial in plot. The
love entanglements of *Old Heads and Young Hearts* are complicated to the point of incoherence. Here again are the familiar
marks of Boucicault's determined attempts to write legitimate
comedies: bustling plot activity of little consequence, excessive
dependence on eccentric characterization, forced plays of wit,
and a generous sprinkling of strained metaphors and similes.
His best-known comedy, *London Assurance* (1841), looks back
rather than forward, and has nothing in it of the new age except
surface manners and dress. The general rattle and bustle, the
gulled fop who ends as a moralist, the laboured rhetoric, the
fundamental decency, goodness, and kindness of its principal
characters—these qualities place *London Assurance* at the end of
the eighteenth century rather than in the middle of the nineteenth. In any case, Boucicault's métier was not comedy but
romantic drama and Irish melodrama with strong comic
elements, and he did not find it until the 1850s and 1860s.

The materialism of the age, its social ambition and self-
seeking drive towards status, wealth, and privilege, are topics
not really explored in pre-Victorian comedy. The Victorians
explored them at some length, and they also brought to comedy
a strong sense of class and a militancy about class that was not
there before. *Money* and *New Men and Old Acres* dramatize such
subject-matter, which also occurs in many plays of approxi-
mately the mid-century period. The ridiculousness of Daniel
Dowlas, chandler, trying to be Lord Duberly, and the folly of
his son's imitation of a man of fashion are ridiculed in Colman's
The Heir-at-Law; in Knowles's *The Beggar of Bethnal Green*
and *Old Maids* social-climbing sons are rewarded for their
efforts by being duped into marrying servants. However, an

acute class-consciousness, the theme of social ambition in a clearly defined class situation, and hostility to members of a lower order pressing upwards by means deemed vulgar, became common only in Victorian comedy.

In *Quid Pro Quo* a retired stationer, foolishly enamoured of the aristocracy, aspires to a seat in Parliament and a baronetcy; the Earl whom he so greatly admires dreams of a Garter and hypocritically spouts radical sentiments in support of his election interest. Both characters are satirically conceived, but the weight of condemnation falls more heavily on the former. The characters of Jerrold's *Retired from Business* (1851), set in the village of Pumpkinfield, include the Pennyweight family. Mrs. Pennyweight, the wife of a prosperous retired greengrocer who can see nothing wrong with his former trade, re-names the family Fitzpennyweight and changes the name of Candlemas Cottage to Torchlight Lodge, redecorating in the gaudiest *nouveau-riche* taste to the amazement of her husband. At all costs, she tells him, the secret of his trade must be kept from the village, for it is a terrible thing to have been a grocer. The neighbours begin to call, and Mrs. Fitzpennyweight, aided by Puffins, a snobbish retired Russia merchant, sorts out those who are socially acceptable from those who are not:

PUFFINS. To be plain. In Pumpkinfield, the gentry of previous whole-sale life do not associate with individuals of former retail existence. The counting-house knows not the shop. The wholesale merchant never crosses the till. . . . Thus, in Pumpkinfield, there is what we call the billers and the tillers; or, in a fuller word, the billocracy and the tillocracy. . .

PENNYWEIGHT. And wholesales don't mix with retails? I think I see. Raw wool doesn't speak to halfpenny ball of worsted—tallow in the cask looks down upon sixes to the pound, and pig iron turns up its nose at twopenny nails.

Both Puffins and his friend Creepmouse, a retired army tailor, try with disastrous results to save their children for marriages with rank, and they look down contemptuously upon neighbours like the good-hearted Jubilee, a retired pawnbroker. The Puffins doctrine is exploded, but unfortunately the social promise of Act I evaporates in later acts. Instead of developing the interesting ideas he begins with, Jerrold abandons them to concentrate upon a series of love affairs among the younger generation of Pumpkinfield; thus the play peters out disappointingly, with love conveniently solving class problems.

Pennyweight's clash with his wife points to another major theme of mid-century comedy: the domestic ideal and the proper relationship between wife and husband.[1] The text for this dramatic sermon could be taken from the pious utterance of a character in Edmund Falconer's *Extremes* (1858): 'Marriage is at once the most solemn and the most beautiful mystery of this life; and as among nations a reverence for its sacredness, as an indissoluble, an intransgressible bond between two beings, and *only* two, is the highest test of civilization, so the nobler the estimate individual man or woman forms of its obligations, the higher must each be lifted in the scale of humanity.' 'Do you not believe me?' he asks, and the woman replies, 'I do, I do, with all my heart and soul.' On both the comic and serious levels Victorian comedy worked out the secular implications of this speech, dwelling especially upon the marital obligations of the wife as well as enumerating her ideal attributes. *Masks and Faces* (1852), by Tom Taylor and Charles Reade, shows two women in sharp contrast: the gay, careless, immoral, generous Peg Woffington and the simple, timid, domestic Mabel Vane, newly married to a man infatuated with Woffington. The underlying pattern of the play is melodramatic, with a comic man in the distressed poet and painter Triplet, a suffering heroine in Mabel Vane, and a villain in the aristocrat Sir Charles Pomander, who pursues her. Woffington is the female lead, and with her wit, charm, and bubbling personality she easily captures masculine attention. But there is no doubt that Mabel Vane is meant to be the true heroine and that the audience saw her as one. Woffington in fact regards Mabel as her personal ideal and renounces Mabel's husband, telling her, 'Angel of truth and goodness, you have conquered.'[2] Another ideal wife is Mrs. Fitzherbert in Taylor's *Victims* (1857): devoted and hardworking, she earns just enough money by dressmaking to pay for the idle pleasures of a husband who aspires to literary fame, treats her indifferently, and even refuses to acknowledge her as

---

[1] See also Volume Two, pp. 10–13.

[2] The view of eighteenth-century actors taken by *Masks and Faces* is thoroughly sentimental: Cibber, Quin, and Mrs. Clive are basically decent and good-hearted, and Woffington is a fairy princess who pours money and food into the household of the penurious Triplet.

his wife in case it should damage his literary reputation for bohemianism. She is clearly intended as a contrast to the affected Mrs. Merryweather, who keeps a salon and neglects her husband so badly that he cannot get a decent breakfast in his own house. The ideal woman of a later comedy by J. S. Coyne, *The Woman of the World* (1868), is not the ambitious, intellectual, and brilliant Mrs. Eddystone of the first act, but the tender, gentle Mrs. Eddystone of the last, who now occupies herself with charities and dotes over a cradle.[1] She then accepts the hero, and the implications are that she has not been enough of a true woman to be worthy of him before.

Conflicts that arise in marriage are nearly always resolved in favour of the husband. The amiable City merchant in *Victims*, Merryweather, with his decent middle-class values, is the norm and anchor of sanity in a crazy world of literary and intellectual affectation. At the end of the play his values are triumphant, the outside forces that create domestic discord are in retreat, and the wife comes to her senses. Coyne's *My Wife's Daughter* (1850) begins interestingly with the struggle of a gay man-about-town of twenty-eight, newly married to a widow of forty, to adjust himself to a quiet domestic existence; once again this promising theme is not sufficiently developed. The wife, over-fond, jealous, and short-tempered, eventually perceives her folly (all the fault is on her side) and begs her husband's pardon:

MRS. ORMONDE. For this I have been justly punished—for this behold me humble and penitent—[*About to kneel.*]

ORMONDE. Not there, dear Marion! But here in my bosom! [*Raises and embraces her.*] The storm raised by your jealous fears is past; the heavens smile again upon us.

MRS. ORMONDE. Oh, joy, joy! Dear Arthur, am I forgiven—my errors and your wrongs—forgiven?

ORMONDE. Aye, all forgiven, and forgotten, in this kiss. [*Kisses her.*]

One of the most triumphant assertions of a husband's superiority and authority comes in Taylor's *Still Waters Run*

---

[1] Running parallel to the sentimental idealism of the play is a good vein of comedy. The first act begins with a dramatist reading his latest work to a company that has fallen asleep on him, and in one purely farcical scene there is much hiding behind screens and in cupboards and smashing of china; three men successively conceal themselves in Mrs. Eddystone's bathroom, with resultant uproar.

Deep (1855), another of those Victorian plays that were entitled comedies but in which comic elements are subordinated to serious ones. The quiet Mildmay, a retired businessman, allows himself to be dominated by his wife and her aunt because he values domestic peace. They treat him with open contempt and admire the dashing Captain Hawksley, who has been the aunt's lover and now pursues Mildmay's wife. Mildmay proves himself when he confounds Hawksley's scheme to sell the family shares in a fraudulent company, forces Hawksley to return private letters with which he was blackmailing the aunt, outfaces him courageously when he demands a duel, and has him arrested for forgery. This demonstration of power in the world of men and business, together with the sudden assertion of Mildmay's domestic rights, ensures absolute submission on the part of his womenfolk. He tells the repentant aunt, 'You shall never find me wanting in duty and respect, but from this day forth, remember, there's only one master in this house, and his name is John Mildmay.' His wife receives similar treatment:

MILDMAY. Trust to me, henceforth, to make you what a wife should be. I should prefer to win you by a lover's tenderness, but if I cannot do that I know how to make a husband's rights respected.

MRS. MILDMAY. Oh, thank you, dearest, thank you—tell me of my faults—I will try to correct them. I will honour and obey you, as a wife should.

The advantages of the simple, domestically minded girl over the sophisticated (meaning unfeminine) woman as a marriage partner are considered unassailable in Victorian comedy, and a further advantage is obtained if the girl is from the country.[1] The contrast between rural virtue and aristocratic vice is familiar in melodrama, and the emotional intensity with which the village heroine is depicted is a consecration of ideal feminine virtues as well as a dream exercise in nostalgic recreation for urban audiences of rural origins. This contrast is incidental in many comedies of the Colman–Reynolds school, but Taylor's *An Unequal Match* (1857) is constructed around it. In Act I, set in a Yorkshire dale, Arncliffe confirms his proposal to Hester

---

[1] A rural setting is not essential for the expression of this theme. For instance, the superiority in simplicity and femininity of Mabel Vane over Peg Woffington, of Mrs. Fitzherbert over Mrs. Merryweather, and of the later Mrs. Eddystone over the earlier Mrs. Eddystone, are demonstrated in a London setting.

Glazebrook, daughter of a blacksmith, despite the news that he has inherited wealth and a baronetcy. In Act II the newly married couple are in Arncliffe's Hampshire home, and the baronet, all memories of his country idyll extinguished, despairs of his wife's unaffected simplicities and rural enthusiasms (she rises at five in the morning to help with the harvest). In a house full of sneering aristocratic guests he is further embarrassed by a visit from her father. Hester is contrasted with the elegant and sophisticated Mrs. Montressor, whom Arncliffe had courted before his marriage and now begins to admire again. He lectures his wife on proper social conduct:

ARNCLIFFE. You must learn to repress your feelings when they are out of keeping with the tone of society, to trifle where you wish to be serious, to smile when a frown would better express your real sentiments, to be tolerant of bores and civil to rivals, to accept light attentions lightly, to forget your early life and its associations; in a word, to fit yourself for the artificial world in which my position now places you.

HESTER. In short, to be no longer the Hester you loved in Glaizedale, but a different and—forgive me, Harry, if I say—not a better woman.

Shortly after delivering this homily, Arncliffe follows Mrs. Montressor to Ems; there he discovers that he abhors the fashionable tedium of spa life and yearns for his wife's sweet innocence and unspoilt simplicity, rejecting the cold artificiality he finds around him. Hester arrives in Ems, pretends to have reformed her character, and poses as a woman of the world—insincere, coquettish, artificial—the very person Arncliffe urged her to be in Act II. Horrified by this change, he learns his lesson and gets his values right by the time Hester undeceives him and the play ends.

Another comedy dealing with the same theme is Falconer's *Extremes*, a popular and successful piece in its day. Here the innate virtue of Frank Hawthorne, of humble Lancashire origins (a character full of lengthy moral precepts and ringing sentiments), together with the rustic simplicity and honesty—despite the comedy of their dress and dialect—of the Wildbriar family, are favourably contrasted with the affected and cynical behaviour of the members of Society present in the elegant country house that is the setting of the play. The heroine Lucy tries to discourage Frank by pretending to be frivolous and unkind, but fails to carry it through because frivolity and unkindness are not part of her real feminine self. At one point Frank, rebuking Jenny Wildbriar for insincere flirting, says, 'Cousin of mine, that is not the pulse of the honest unsophisticated heart of girlhood as it should beat in the breast of an English farmer's daughter.'

Contrasts between simplicity and artificiality are also found in *All That Glitters Is Not Gold* (1851), by John Maddison Morton and Thomas Morton Jr. The setting is the master's house and cotton-spinning factory in Bristol. The master, Joseph Plum, has two sons. Frederick, the younger, has been well educated and socially polished; a marriage is arranged with his like, Valeria. The elder son Stephen, blunt and workmanlike, sticks to the factory and loves Martha, one of the work-girls. The contrasts are between the virtuous, devoted Martha and the refined but morally weak Valeria on the one hand, and the gentlemanly but ineffectual Frederick and the rough, hard-working Stephen on the other. Plum is torn between the two worlds these characters represent. The comedy of the first act changes to pure melodrama in the second: by compromising herself Martha saves Valeria from seduction by an aristocratic villain and is involved in intensely emotional scenes in which she demonstrates heroic virtue. Superficial plot complications again obscure the original themes, which quite disappear from view.

The comedy in which there are strong dramatic elements is the predominant kind of nineteenth-century comedy. The intensity of these elements and the importance attached to them in the general context of plot structure, characterization, and thematic material, is a matter of degree and varies widely. A minority of comedies have nothing or very little that is serious about them, such as *Exchange No Robbery*, *The Beulah Spa*, and *London Assurance*. A nineteenth-century play can be termed a comedy, I believe, when the pathetic and potentially tragic, or melodramatic elements do not overwhelm the comic and are kept at least in equal balance with them. *John Bull* and *Money* are rightly 'comedies', then, but *Still Waters Run Deep* and *All That Glitters Is Not Gold* are not, at least not by this rule-of-thumb definition. These two and others like them have been discussed here because their authors or publishers called them comedies, and it is difficult to ignore contemporary terminology. Nineteenth-century dramatic nomenclature was, however, imprecise and constantly changing; the subject-matter of the 'melodrama', the 'drama', the 'comedy', and the 'farce' was extraordinarily eclectic; and to formulate *genre* definitions rather than describe and characterize dramatic trends is almost impossible.

Perhaps enough has already been said to demonstrate the emotional and situational range of nineteenth-century comedy, but one further example may illustrate this range and the problem of framing definitions. R. B. Peake's *The Title Deeds*, performed at the Adelphi in 1847, is called a comedy on the title-page of all editions. It is set in the London and Somerset of the present day. Morant, the senior partner of Fustic, Morant, and Fustic, on his way to the docks to redeem the failing fortunes of the firm in the West Indies, leaves a box containing bags of sovereigns and title deeds to a valuable West Indian estate in the hackney carriage of Humphrey Haywhisp. The Haywhisp family (father, young wife, children, old mother), struggling desperately against poverty, keep quiet about their find and buy a house in Somerset. The involved and incident-packed plot concerns four main actions: the Haywhisps' growing guilt about the money, the dissipation and gambling debts of sporting Philip Fustic (old Fustic's nephew), old Fustic's efforts to arrange a match for his two sons with the daughters of Mrs. Evergay (to whom he is markedly attentive), and the search for the important title deeds after Morant returns from the West Indies. All the characters rally round old Fustic when he is arrested for his nephew's debts; Haywhisp comes clean about the box containing the deeds, which is at last found in the ruins of Glastonbury Abbey where the demented old mother had secretly buried it by moonlight; Philip Fustic renounces his past life; and all ends happily. Three of the plot lines are strongly melodramatic, and the emotional potential of a bad conscience, guilt, remorse, bankruptcy, and ruin is fully exploited. On the other hand, Haywhisp's crony Peter Hush is a low-comedy part, and Haywhisp himself is involved in low-comedy scenes, including an extremely comic meal at an inn where a sporting gentleman, Turfy Goodwood (another low comedian), misunderstands the conversation of Haywhisp and

Hush at table and believes that they are desperate villains scheming to murder him. A second level of more delicate comedy exists in the interplay between old Fustic and Mrs. Evergay, and a third, rather more farcical, in the arrival of Fustic's sons from Jamaica, who, to the horror of the ladies, are coloured.

Thus *The Title Deeds* could either be termed a comedy with strong dramatic components or a drama with strong comic components; distinctions of *genre* are meaningless. One must also remember that the play was written for an Adelphi audience, whose tastes inclined more to farce and sensationalism than did the tastes of, for example, the Haymarket audience for whom Taylor wrote the relatively upper middle-class *An Unequal Match*. The part of Humphrey Haywhisp was played by O. Smith, a melodramatic actor of some repute, whereas Hush and Goodwood were performed by the Adelphi's great low comedians, Wright and Bedford. The size of a low-comedy part in the text—Goodwood's, for instance, is fairly small—was often no indication of its stage prominence in the hands of an accomplished comedian. Purely theatrical factors are therefore also essential in a careful determination of the character of a nineteenth-century comedy: we must take into account the theatre at which it was played, the audience of that theatre, and the actors in the piece. An examination of this kind will go far to explain the variety and breadth of comic material and style.

From the vantage point of the 1860s one could look back at the evolution of comedy and trace a continuous line of thematic and stylistic development stretching from Colman to Robertson; a similar line can be perceived in the development of theatre itself and in conventions of staging, acting, furnishing, costuming, and lighting. There is no need to stop at the 1860s; in 1900 the same observations could be made of a whole century's growth and change in both drama and theatre. Thus it is necessary to place the comedies of Tom Robertson in proper perspective, and briefly to consider the generally held view that in combination with the stagecraft that presented them these comedies were really the beginnings of the modern theatre, that Robertson himself was 'first in time among the dramatic writers of the present'.[1]

Essentially what Robertson did was to use the theme

[1] Allardyce Nicoll, *A History of English Drama*, 2nd edn. (1959), v. 131.

material and some aspects of his predecessors' dramatic technique, and employing them in a style distinctively his own
gave unique satisfaction to a large middle-class audience whose
theatrical taste he had correctly analysed. He was certainly
fortunate to discover Marie Wilton and the Bancroft company,
and they were fortunate to discover him. Although he was not
paid munificently, he did better financially than any other
dramatist of the sixties except Boucicault and possibly F. C.
Burnand; in their turn the Bancrofts, after twenty years'
management at the Prince of Wales's and the Haymarket,
retired in 1885 with a net profit of £180,000.[1] A great deal of
this amount was realized from the comedies of Robertson, and
its size is hard proof of Robertson's popularity during these
twenty years. In fact the Bancrofts gave nearly 3,000 performances of his plays, 800 of *School* alone;[2] an average of 150
performances a year for the period of their management.

In his first comedy—excluding *David Garrick* (1864), which
is more drama than comedy—to achieve prominence, and the
first to be staged by the Bancrofts, *Society* (1865), one notices
the familiar preoccupations of Victorian dramatists. The poor
but well-born Sidney Daryl is contrasted with the vulgar
nouveau-riche Chodd Jr., who is trying to buy his way into
Society. Despite the obviousness of the satire, the scenes
involving the Chodds are excellently conceived. The younger
Chodd tells Daryl how he intends to get on in the world:

CHODD JUNIOR. The present age is—as you are aware—a practical
age. I come to the point—it's my way. Capital commands the world.
The capitalist commands capital; therefore the capitalist commands
the world.

SIDNEY. But you don't quite command the world, do you?

CHODD JUNIOR. Practically I do. I wish for the highest honours—I
bring out my cheque-book. I want to go into the House of Commons
—cheque-book. I want the best legal opinion in the House of Lords
—cheque-book. The best house—cheque-book. The best friends, the
best wife, the best-trained children—cheque-book, cheque-book,
and cheque-book.

---

[1] Squire and Marie Bancroft, *The Bancrofts* (1909), p. 275.
[2] Squire and Marie Bancroft, *Mr. and Mrs. Bancroft On and Off the Stage*,
4th edn. (1888), ii. 409.

SIDNEY. You mean to say with money you can purchase anything?

CHODD JUNIOR. Exactly. This life is a matter of bargain.[1]

Daryl and Chodd Jr. are rivals for Maud Hetherington, whose aunt, the snobbish Lady Ptarmigant, tries to push her into a marriage with the moneyed Chodd. Finally Daryl defeats Chodd in an election campaign in the former's family seat, inherits a baronetcy and a fortune, and is accepted by Maud and Lady Ptarmigant. What is conventional in *Society* is the concern with money, the satirical treatment of the foolish aristocrat and the vulgar rich, the reliance on eccentric comedy (in the person of Lord Ptarmigant, who dozes in a chair where others trip over him), the heavy drama—Daryl's wild despair when Maud initially rejects him—and the clumsy plot, in which the author can think of no better reason for Maud to refuse Daryl than her believing that a little child for whom Daryl is caring is his illegitimate daughter. After the fashion of these plots she never questions him about the child; even more incredibly the little girl is actually the child of Lady Ptarmigant's dead son. One feels that Robertson hedges his bets: Daryl does not win Lady Ptarmigant's and Maud's consent because he is a good man and now clear of suspicion on the child's account, but largely because he has just inherited wealth and a baronetcy by the convenient last-minute death of his brother. Values based solely upon fortune, property, and birth are satirized, but at the end of the play it just so happens that Daryl possesses all three. What is new is the delicate restraint of a quiet, gentle, simple love scene—Robertson never wrote a better—between Maud and Daryl in a London square at twilight, the genuine humour of a scene in a bohemian literary club, and the economy of the dialogue in those portions of the play not given over to intense emotion (Robertson could pen as purple a passage of prose as anybody if he had occasion to). From the evidence of *Society*, Robertson's strength as a dramatist lay in satire, light and unforced comedy, the depiction of mild eccentricity, the small quiet moments of human contact, and the gentle sentimentalism of deepening love. In later plays these remained his strengths and were part of his distinctive contribution to comedy. In other

---

[1] Digby Grant's 'little cheque' speech concluding the first act of Albery's *Two Roses* is surely inspired by the words of Chodd Jr.

areas, where he exceeded the relatively narrow limits of his talents, he could be a very indifferent dramatist. Unfortunately, he too often strayed from what he could do best.

Robertson's next comedy, *Ours* (1866), has an even weaker plot than *Society*, and a quite incredible serious sub-plot in which a wife believes that her husband is giving money to a mistress whereas he has actually been protecting her cheque-forging brother, who never appears in the play, from the consequence of his crime. Robertson makes his first use of a love scene with two couples in which the dialogue is contrapuntal. All the characters turn up in the Crimea in the last act (Robertson was always a patriot), which develops around the domestic and comic use of food: the heroine makes a roly-poly pudding on stage while the mutton roasts, and we see in use or hear discussed anchovies, bacon, marmalade, vegetables, sweets, game, flour, roasting, baking, boiling, and stewing. The play ends with the characters sitting down to eat what has been prepared. Thus the author ingeniously reduces the Crimean War to the proportions of a back parlour high tea; the domestication of the serious and dramatic could hardly go further.

Caste (1867) may also be analysed in terms of what preceded it; the merit of the play lies in the ability with which Robertson utilized familiar material and in the superiority of the result to so much comedy that attempted more or less the same kind of thing. The use of eccentricity and aberration is more apparent than in *Society* and *Ours*: Eccles, the Marquise, and to a lesser extent Hawtree provide this kind of humour. Amusement is again derived from the preparation and eating of food, and Sam and Polly indulge in much traditional and unrefined low-comedy business. Sam is also the man of commerce on the way up (though not, for the comfort of the Prince of Wales's audience, too far up), embodying as he does the ethic of hard work and 'go'; 'whatever's commercial is right', he says. In contrast the drunken Eccles—a splendid comic creation, perhaps the greatest in nineteenth-century drama—commands no respect because he does *not* work, and social agitation is ridiculous on his lips. The play is not in the least democratic and completely supports the *status quo*; the clash between classes is merely comic when the only militant representative of the lower orders is Eccles and the only standard-bearer of the aristocracy is the Marquise. From the moment that the relationship between George and Esther begins to operate on the emotional and pathetic level rather than the comic, and when it is isolated from the contrapuntal, undercutting comedy of Sam and Polly, Robertson in treating this relationship becomes almost indistinguishable from many a poorer playwright. It is worth noting that the heroine is the serious mother rather than the jolly actress full of life (the resemblance to *Masks and Faces* is close). Esther is the standard feminine ideal of nineteenth-century drama; she tells the Marquise, presumably in climactic order, 'I am a woman—I am a wife—a widow—a mother!'

After *Caste* Robertson's work deteriorated, and the narrowness of his achievement is more noticeable. *Play* (1868) is enfeebled by awkward misunderstandings and coincidental eavesdropping; away from an English domestic setting (the play is located in a German spa) Robertson seems uncomfortable, and unsure of himself in an attempt to be more romantic than usual. In obtaining strong curtains, a tradition Robertson found it hard to break away from, he repeatedly used tired, conventional stage business of a kind illustrated by the following example, where the deserted wife faints into the arms of the hero, thus precipitating a major misunderstanding with the heroine, Rosie:

Enter AMANDA *through arch, a smelling bottle in her hand, and almost falling.*

AMANDA. I understand all now! He loves another! I watched him; his looks, his manner, all confirm it! And she seems a mere child! Oh, why did I come hither?

[*Falls fainting on a stone seat.*

Enter PRICE, *by arch.*

PRICE. I left the lozenges somewhere here, and Rosie wants one. [*Sees* AMANDA.] Eh! What's this?

[AMANDA *reels backward and falls fainting into his arms.* MRS. KINPECK *sees all this from her perch, and gesticulates with her parasol to those above and below her.*

Enter FANQUEHERE, ROSIE, BROWNE, *and* TODDER, *from different points, to form picture.*

Eccentric comedy, in the persons of a peppery old gambler and a Prussian officer who can speak only one sentence of English, is much in evidence, and once again we find the vulgar and satirically treated *nouveau-riche* in Bodmin Todder of Todder's Original Patent Starch; once again, also, the juxtaposition of a sentimental love scene with a noisy quarrelsome one.

The faults of the Robertson style are magnified in *School* (1869), and it is a tribute to the Bancrofts that they made the play so popular in spite of their material. The plot concerns the love affairs of Bella and Naomi,[1] two girls in Dr. Sutcliffe's Academy, with Lord Beaufoy and Jack Poyntz. Because of its setting the *dramatis personae* include a large number of young girls, who are idealized *en masse* in a dreamy fantasy of English womanhood.[2] The langorous femininity of *School* and the utter fatuity of the young men give the love scenes, which are nevertheless written with some charm and skill, a sickly sweetness previously incipient in Robertson's sentimentality but now openly emergent. They can be compared unfavourably with the scene between Maud and Daryl in the first act of *Society*. It seems that, unable to develop as a dramatist after *Caste*, Robertson simply repeated himself; what was originally delicate and subtle coarsened through unvaried use.

Progress (1869) is thematically more significant than *School*, and begins promisingly. In Act I there is a confrontation between Arthur, son of Lord Mompesson, and Ferne, a railway engineer who has come to Mompesson Abbey to plan its demolition in order to make way for a railway and station. Arthur, the aristocratic traditionalist, stands for the old order and condemns 'progress':

That is the modern slang for the destruction of everything high and

---

[1] Clearly Mrs. Bancroft's playing of Naomi, her best-known and most popular Robertson part, was fundamentally escapist and idealist in appeal, in keeping with the author's conception of the character: 'The artless simplicity and sunny nature of "Nummy", the utter ignorance of the existence of any sadness in the whole world except what school discipline enforces, her fearless and open avowal of her romantic adoration for Jack Poyntz, make her a lovable thing... It was a delight to act Naomi Tighe; she is as fresh as country butter, and every word she utters breathes the unladen atmosphere of a bright, green spot "far from the madding crowd".' (*Mr. and Mrs. Bancroft On and Off the Stage*, ii. 413.)

[2] *School* concludes with an apostrophe to the 'true lady' as Dr. Sutcliffe and the eccentric old Farintosh sum up between them her qualities. They make an interesting list: 'nobility of feeling', 'a kind heart', 'a noble mind', 'modesty', 'gentleness', 'courage', 'truthfulness', 'birth', 'breeding', and—'above all'—'School'. This arrangement of ending a play with the consecutive enumeration of necessary qualities of character is taken directly from *Money*.

noble, and the substitution of everything base and degrading. . . . Horses, which in my youth were considered noble animals, are abolished for engines that smash, for trains that smash, for velocipedes that smash; and the débris of broken wheels, boilers, bones, and shattered human beings, you call progress! . . . As to manners, progress has indeed altered them. Everyone is much too occupied to think, to feel, to love, or to improve. Progress does not permit sleep, or sentiment, or accomplishment, or leisure. . . . Nowadays you eat rapidly, you drink rapidly, you make love rapidly, you marry rapidly, you go through the Divorce Court still more rapidly. Luxury everywhere, comfort nowhere.

Ferne replies with his *credo*:

We have changed from the worst to the better—we are changing still, from bad to best; and during this transition I am proud to know that it is I—the engineer, the motive-power—who leads the way. 'Tis I who bring industry, invention, and capital together; 'tis I who introduce demand to supply. 'Tis I who give the word—'tis I who direct the train that flies over valleys, through mountains, across rivers—that dominates the mighty Alps themselves. 'Tis I—the engineer—who exchanges the wealth of one country against the poverty of another. I am broad, breathing humanity, that whirls through the air on wings of smoke to a brighter future. I spread civilisation wherever I sit a-straddle of my steed of vapour, whom I guide with reins of iron and feed with flames. As for the tumbledown old ruins I knock down in passing, what matter? Where I halt towns rise and cities spring up into being. 'Tis the train that is the master of the hour. As it moves it shrieks out to the dull ear of prejudice, 'Make room for me! I must pass and I will, and those who dare oppose my progress shall be crushed!' Its tail of smoke is like the plume of a field-marshal; and the rattle and motion of its wheels are as the throb and pulsations of the progress of the whole world.

After the first act, however, there is little reference to the theme of progress. Arthur returns from London, having saved the Abbey from the railway but enthusiastic about the new joys of travelling by rail, wearing new clothes, and ordering new furniture. His niece Eva falls very ill and he curses because he cannot quickly obtain a medical consultant, since he has been all too successful in banishing the nearest railway and telegraph station to a distance of sixteen miles from the Abbey. The plot becomes involved with the ups and downs of Ferne's love affair with Eva, and by the end of the play 'progress' merely means the attainment of individual happiness. Eva says, 'My path must lead to happiness when love and hope conduct me, and affection and experience guide me—[*Smiling.*] that's Progress!' Prominent among the characters are the Bunnythornes, vulgarian father and tippling son; old Bunnythorne comically upholds traditional values. Robertson's predilection for melodramatic effect is again evident, notably at the Act II curtain when the ailing, lovesick Eva tries to kill herself by rushing out into the freezing wind and snow, and is carried fainting inside.

This tendency to heavy drama overwhelms *Birth* (1870), nominally a comedy, and like *Progress* not acted by the Bancrofts. The theme is class antagonism between the proud Earl of Eagleclyffe and the factory owner Paul Hewitt, whose works are contiguous to the Earl's estate. The Earl has been forced to sell his estate to Hewitt, piece by piece, until he is entirely dispossessed and Hewitt moves into the castle. Once again potential significance of theme is frittered away after the first act in trivial love complications and irrelevant melodramatic incidents. The author evades a real development of his theme by patching up the whole affair with an engagement between Hewitt and the Earl's sister and another between the Earl and Hewitt's sister. *M.P.* (1870), Robertson's last comedy to be performed by the Bancrofts, is also taken up by two love affairs. As in *School* there is a moonlight scene for two couples, but the love scenes between the Quaker girl Ruth and Chudleigh Dunscombe are feebly trivial and enervatingly sentimental. Again the well-bred gentleman defeats the *nouveau-riche* schemer; this time the schemer is a villain rather than a vulgar fool.

Robertson's success in adapting his drama to the taste of his middle-class audience, and the Bancrofts' skill in working with their playwright to find a performance style that exactly suited his comedies, reveals much about the plays themselves. Writing of *Society*, Bancroft said that Robertson 'rendered a public service by proving that the refined and educated classes were as ready as ever to crowd the playhouses, provided only that the' entertainment given there was suited to their sympathies and tastes. . . . The return to Nature was the great need of the stage, and happily he came to help supply it at the right moment.'[1] The smallness of the Prince of Wales's was a great

---

[1] *The Bancrofts*, p. 83.

advantage in the cultivation of an intimate, controlled acting style that so satisfactorily provided the illusion of domestic realism and a 'return to Nature'. Dutton Cook commented on the first presentation of *School*:

> A story gains in strength and significance by being brought so close to the view of the spectators; and the players are not constrained to unnatural shouting and grimacing in order that their speeches may be heard and the expression of their faces seen from the distant portions of the house. Both author and actors are thus enabled to avoid the exaggeration of language and manner which has long been a prominent failing in dramatic writing and representation.[1]

Writing in 1881, Henry James remembered the Prince of Wales's as 'a little theatre':

> The pieces produced there dealt mainly in little things—presupposing a great many chairs and tables, carpets, curtains, and knicknacks, and an audience placed close to the stage. They might, for the most part, have been written by a cleverish visitor at a country house, and acted in the drawing-room by his fellow inmates. The comedies of the late Mr. Robertson were of this number, and these certainly are among the most diminutive experiments ever attempted in the drama ... This gentleman's plays are infantile, and seem addressed to the comprehension of infants.[2]

Current critical opinion was much friendlier to Robertson than this, although there was some dissent, which grew in the 1880s and 1890s, from the general praise with which the comedies were received. 'Realism', 'truth', 'nature', and 'plausibility' were terms repeatedly used in this praise; there was a strong feeling that the comedies were a much-needed departure from contemporary practice, and critics quickly perceived how much Robertson was indebted to the Bancrofts and to the sizeable public ready and eager to support him.

After a perusal of Robertson's comedies one sees that he owed much more to previous dramatists than either his contemporaries or modern critics realized. His debt was in both theme and form. Wealth, the ideal woman, social ambition, the importance of privilege and birth, the aristocrat and the parvenu, the virtues of simplicity and domesticity—all this was inherited material.

---

[1] *Nights at the Play*, pp. 69–70. The Bancrofts' move to the larger Haymarket did not, however, adversely affect the popularity of Robertson's comedies.

[2] 'The London Theatres', *Scribner's Monthly*, xxi (January 1881), 363–4.

Similarly, the reliance on eccentric and even low comedy, the mingling of the intensely pathetic and serious with the lightly comic,[1] the recurrence of stumbling and often unbelievable plots, the pervasive sentimentalism—these too were familiar aspects of comic technique before the 1860s. One tends to forget that before he became prominent as an author of comedies Robertson had a long apprenticeship in melodrama and farce (his first play was performed in 1845, twenty years before *Society*), and even after fame reached him he continued to write lurid melodramas such as *The Nightingale* (1870); it was easy for him in his comedies to slip into traditionally melodramatic ways—and he did.

It is my opinion, then, that Robertson confirmed existing trends rather than created new ones, that his comedies represented the exhaustion of an established tradition of writing rather than a new approach to comedy. In comparison with the greatly varied, vigorous, and inventive comedy of his contemporary Taylor, Robertson's plays lack blood and spine. The erratic energy and bursting life of an older comedy was not Robertson's. Nevertheless, he was an important dramatist who made a most significant contribution to the development of nineteenth-century comedy, even though a large part of that contribution came already prepared to his hand. He had considerable talent in the creation of credible characters and dialogue, a genuine simplicity and freshness, and powers of restraint and economy—when he chose to exercise them. But much more important was his domestication of everything he touched; the romance, the rhetoric, the morality, the sentiment of nineteenth-century comedy became, in Charles Lamb's phrase, the 'fireside concerns' of Robertson. 'Domestic and commonplace, dealing only with the superficial phases of an over ripe civilisation, calling upon no great powers of genius in the actors, indeed, scarcely elevating them beyond the tame emotions of every-day existence' was the description H. Barton Baker applied to the theatre of Robertson.[2] The appeal of the domestic,

---

[1] Boucicault's well-known advice to Bancroft in 1868 that the public preferred broadly comic domestic drama, 'a sentimental, pathetic play, comically rendered' to pure comedy, could well describe Robertson's comedies, as Boucicault himself recognized. (*Mr. and Mrs. Bancroft On and Off the Stage*, i. 245–6.) But it was only what comic playwrights had been doing since the nineteenth century began.

[2] *Our Old Actors* (1878), ii. 370.

the appeal of the normal, the ordinary,[1] the quiet, the simple, the seemingly matter-of-fact, an appeal embodied in carefully chosen middle-class contexts; and attitudes, sentiments, and characters chosen with equal care for their attractiveness to middle-class sensibilities and homely but romantic ideals—this was the appeal that made Robertson so popular and the Bancrofts so rich. The results of Robertson's success in domestically taming and shrinking the content and scope of the older comedy was to impel comedy firmly in the direction of a commonplace domestic realism, a direction it has never entirely abandoned. After an uncertain interlude, the playwrights of the 1880s and 1890s strengthened and intensified this realism in better-made plot structures than Robertson could ever manage, and rooted it even more deeply in middle-class soil.

Robertson's influence on the comedy of the seventies was immediately evident. The only dramatist who stood quite apart from him and developed a different vein of comedy was Gilbert; on the other hand James Albery was a direct imitator. His first and best comedy, *Two Roses* (1870), carries Robertson's sentimental idealism to extreme lengths, and Albery's domestic romanticism is syrupy beyond anything seen before. The haughty but poor Digby Grant comes into a fortune, contemptuously pays off those who befriended him, and forbids his sweet and beautiful daughters Ida and Lotty (the two roses) to associate any more with their penurious young men, Wyatt and the sentimentally conceived Caleb Deecie, who is blind. Of course the girls continue to love them, and the old-fashioned dénouement employs melodramatic plot machinery: Deecie is discovered to be the lost heir to the fortune, and virtuous poverty is rewarded by beauty as well as riches. The first entrance of Lotty and Ida characterizes their appeal; they appear framed in a window counting roses: '*They smell first one, then the other, till at last they run their faces together, when they both laugh, throw their*

---

[1] For instance, when Hawtree in *Caste* says, 'I don't pretend to be a particularly good sort of fellow, nor a particularly bad sort of fellow. I suppose I'm about the average standard sort of thing', he must have gone right to the hearts of his audience. Naturally he is a sympathetic character, an ideal of quiet manliness, decency, good humour, and true friendship, a superior version of the mildly idiotic, eccentric 'swell' with a heart of gold who was so popular in the comedy of the seventies and eighties—the lineal descendant of the fops Lewis used to play at the turn of the century.

arms round each other's necks and kiss, then leave the window. . . .
The Girls come in, the bright light falling on them as they pause at
the door . . . both flushed with health.' Although Albery's sentimentalism is excessively sweet, it is skilfully counterpoised by
the richly comic figure of Digby Grant, simultaneously paternal,
tender, proud, hypocritical, posturing, and sybaritic. Low comedy
is present in Our Mr. Jenkins, a travelling salesman, and his
tyrannical wife.

The most prolific playwright of the decade was H. J. Byron,
who began to write in the fifties and had already achieved a
considerable reputation in extravaganza and burlesque. In the
1870s and 1880s he was the author of numerous comedies,
dramas, and farces; his output was so large and its quality so
generally poor that William Archer, a sworn enemy to Byron,
considered that 'he has done more than any other man to hinder
the development of a worthy modern drama in England, by
fostering a taste for frivolous and puerile work'.[1] Yet Byron
did attempt something more serious in several comedies, full
though they are of puns, jokes, and wildly improbable plots,
characters, and human relationships. Unlike Robertson, Byron
in these plays dealt with unhappily married couples rather than
sweet young lovers; he was not original in this, but such a shift
of focus became fundamental to the comedy of the 1890s.

In *Cyril's Success* (1868), a successful novelist and dramatist
pays little attention to his wife, and the well-written first act
vividly conveys her loneliness as she broods on being neglected,
her husband's preoccupation with writing and business, and the
tensions developing between them. After that, however, all is coincidence, unbelievable misunderstanding, and mistaken identity.
In *Partners for Life* (1871) a husband has separated from his wife
because he found his independence corrupted by her fortune. They
meet again and are reconciled. The play is of little interest,
but the ideal of home and hearth is strong even in their misery:

FANNY. I would rather lead a domestic life, if I had the opportunity
—the pleasant late dinner with the curtains closed and the gas
lighted—the music and the chat, and the cozy hour or two with
coffee, and one or two of my husband's old friends smoking a cigar
and talking of their old bachelor days—the calm pleasant close to
the long day; how charming is the picture if it could but be realized.

---

[1] *English Dramatists of To-day* (1882), p. 121.

TOM. [*Aside.*] By Jove, how true her words are! What a waste my
life is. What are *my* evenings? Soda and brandy, and bitter thoughts.

Married in Haste (1876), more drama than comedy, is concerned
with a young artist's jealousy of his wife's talent. Cut off by a
rich uncle, Vere resorts to painting for his living; but his wife is
the better painter and he will not permit her to sell her work.
Since he has quarrelled with the only potential purchaser of his
own paintings, the couple are reduced to poor circumstances and
the wife leaves, partly because she cannot stand bickering and
being in debt to tradesmen and partly because Vere has been
keeping feminine company. In the last act Byron evades the
issues in the credible and difficult domestic situation so far
portrayed. The rich uncle buys the wife's paintings and is
reconciled with his nephew, who has worked hard and attained
success by being hung in the Royal Academy. Husband and wife
are brought happily together again, and the problem of his
artistic jealousy is left unresolved and unmentioned.

Even a comedy like the immensely popular *Our Boys* (1875),
which ran for over four years, was built around contemporary
thematic material, as well as absorbing large quantities of
Robertsonian sentiment. Comic tension, slipshod and crude
though the presentation is, arises from class hostility between
the wealthy retired grocer Middlewick and the arrogant
baronet Sir Geoffrey Champneys. Their sons, Charles and
Talbot, have returned from a European tour together, and Sir
Geoffrey designs Talbot for the heiress Violet Melrose. But
Talbot loves poor Mary Melrose and Charles loves Violet.
Middlewick will not let Charles marry Violet because she des-
pises the butterman for his class. The sons defy their fathers and
retreat to London, where they live together in humble lodgings;
finally the fathers come after them and relent. Humour arises
from the contrast between the extreme haughtiness of Sir
Geoffrey and the profound cockney ignorance of Middlewick,
as well as the effete foppishness of Sir Geoffrey's son. Middlewick, a fine comic creation, is innately noble and golden-hearted
despite his ignorance, as indeed are Charles and Talbot and
almost everybody else in the play. Puns abound, and the
extremely banal and watery love scenes are patterned upon
Robertson's. *Our Boys* was despised by many critics for

farcical exaggeration, but it is right in the mainstream of Victorian comic development.

Talbot Champneys in *Our Boys* is dressed in 'velvet coat and vest, light pants, eye-glasses, blonde wig parted in centre, blonde side-whiskers and small blonde mustache'. Such a character, one of many modelled on the Lord Dundreary of E. A. Sothern in Taylor's *Our American Cousin* (1858)—and with another ancestor in Sir Frederick Blount of *Money*—is an example of the dependence on eccentric comedy in the 1860s and 1870s, a phenomenon worth noting. Robertson's fops and eccentrics are mild in conception compared to Byron's. These required appropriate acting techniques, and the joyful indulgence of many actors in comic excess easily toppled the comedies in which they appeared into purely external farce. Percy Fitzgerald objected that the taste for 'sensation' in comedy now meant that the characters, in order to 'draw', must be 'of that startling "raree-show" description popularized by burlesque, laid in such staring gaudy colours as all who run may read'.[1] Byron's performance of Sir Simon Simple in his own comedy, *Not Such a Fool as He Looks* (1868), drew Fitzgerald's fire:

Mr. Byron . . . worked on the surface, merely following to the established principles of the day. The first object was the creation of a purely eccentric character, who would stand alone, and whose oddities of dress, speech, and manner might cause laughter. A great deal of effect is produced by a dull sheepish manner, an eye-glass permanently fixed in the eye, sleek yellow hair, &.c. Nearly every speech he utters is written to produce a point and convey variety.[2]

To Fitzgerald such writing and acting was pernicious, and destructive of real characterization and true comedy; much of it, he thought, was the legacy of Robertson, not only of his characters but also of his inclination for 'forced quips' and epigrams for their own sake.

The actor introduces himself, his fun, his gags, and his vanity into the part, quite regardless of whether any be appropriate to, or at variance with, the character. In the same fashion, the writer only thinks of what he considers the 'good things' that will tell on the audience, never considering whether his 'sparkling epigrams' are suitable to the situation, or ridiculous in the mouth of the particular actor.[3]

[1] *Principles of Comedy and Dramatic Effect* (1870), p. 82.
[2] Ibid., pp. 83–4.   [3] Ibid., p. 103.

Thus the objection was to character fabricated out of external bits and pieces, 'strange-coloured hair, false forehead, comically cut coats, parti-coloured trousers; also out of tricks of elocution, of strange sounds, and jerks of manner. . . . These are what make up character-parts—strange beings formed on no human model, wearing clothes seen in no known street, talking as no human beings ever talked: and these are the creations that figure in the pieces where anything comic is required.'[1] What distressed Fitzgerald so much died away in the 1880s and 1890s, when dramatists depended far less on eccentric comedy and hardly at all on low comedy.[2] The last flowering of eccentric comedy in Robertson and Byron had its roots in the vigorous eccentricity of the Colman–Reynolds school, and this kind of humour had provided English comedy with essential material since the beginning of the nineteenth century.

Byron was still writing comedies in the eighties, but the best comic work of the decade was being done by Gilbert and Sullivan in the Savoy operas. Since opera and operetta are outside the bounds of these volumes because of their primarily musical content, we are left with dramatists of merit and reputation such as Sydney Grundy, Henry Arthur Jones, and Arthur Pinero. I am omitting Wilde and Shaw in the nineties (whose plays, because they are so generally available in print, are excluded from selection): Wilde because *Lady Windermere's Fan* (1892), *A Woman of No Importance* (1893), and *An Ideal Husband* (1895) are not comedies at all, but thoroughly conventional Society dramas with comic additions that one would say were uniquely Wilde's if one forgot how much he was influenced by Gilbert, even to the extent of his ironic viewpoint and dialogue. His famous epigrams are the ultimate refinement of an earlier comic technique (seen at its worst in Robertson and Byron); his wits, both male and female, are aristocratic developments of the comic men and women of an earlier drama. *The*

---

[1] Ibid., pp. 64–6. During the rehearsals of *Caste*, Bancroft surprised everybody by refusing to adopt the conventional fop's blonde wig and long flaxen whiskers for Hawtree, instead appearing as 'a pale-faced man with short, straight, black hair', dressed 'in the quietest of fashionable clothes'. (*Mr. and Mrs. Bancroft On and Off the Stage*, i. 230.) Thus even the extravagant 'swell' was tamed and quietly domesticated in productions of Robertson.

[2] The last traditional low comedian of repute, J. L. Toole, retired in 1895. He performed in new comedies by Byron until 1885.

Importance of Being Earnest (1895), Wilde's only comedy, is too well-known to require discussion. Undoubtedly it is a comic masterpiece, yet again one must point out its heavy debt to *Engaged* and the whole tone of the Savoy operas. Shaw, too, hardly needs comment; his work has received and continues to receive elaborate critical treatment. However, it is worth noting two things. Firstly, that the duality of the comic and the serious, basic in such plays as *Major Barbara* and *Heartbreak House* (to name only two), and clearly apparent in early comedies like *Arms and the Man* (1894) and *Candida* (1895), is of central importance in the development of nineteenth-century comedy. Secondly, and the point is a similar one, Shaw's material and techniques in his early plays—and not only the early ones—originated in existing traditions in the writing of nineteenth-century comedies.[1] Thus neither Wilde nor Shaw can be isolated from his immediate dramatic heritage.

The contrast between Grundy on the one hand and Jones and Pinero on the other is instructive. Grundy adapted widely from the French, and his best comedy, *A Pair of Spectacles* (1890), is one such adaptation. Jones and Pinero used French sources very little; the effort to be original was characteristic of authors in the last two decades of the century, in contrast to the wholesale and legally unrestricted pilfering from French and German plays that had gone on for many years, and in which Taylor and Robertson, for example, both indulged.[2] In structure and outlook *A Pair of Spectacles* is also of an older school of playwriting. The plot concerns the change of character that the philanthropic Goldfinch undergoes when he breaks his spectacles and borrows those of his flint-hearted brother Gregory. Previously generous to all in distress, he becomes suspicious and miserly. He is made himself again by the restoration of his mended spectacles, and his eyes are further opened by numerous offers of money and service from all those he treated badly, who mistakenly think him ruined. Even the miserable Gregory, shaken by the arrest for debt of his starving son, reforms to the point of liberality. The play has the appeal of a wholesome fairy tale: the good brother and the cruel brother, the rich son and

---

[1] This debt has been fully explored and documented in Martin Meisel, *Shaw and the Nineteenth Century Theatre* (1963).

[2] See Volume Two, pp. 14–15, 18–19.

the poor son, the magic spectacles, the procession of gift-givers in the last act. *A Pair of Spectacles* is suffused with goodness and benevolence, and its sentiment, unlike the delicate romantic sentiment of *Two Roses*, hearkens back to the strenuous, militant sentiment of Colman, Reynolds, and Morton.

That there was still a large audience for a good wallow in sentiment and the sunny side of human nature is indicated, not only by the success of *A Pair of Spectacles*, but also by the great popularity of Pinero's comedy-drama *Sweet Lavender* (1888). In this play, which relates the removal of obstacles to a union between a young barrister and the daughter of his laundress, and the reformation of his seedy, hard-drinking, but generous friend, every character is steeped in emotional sensibility and warm washes of goodness. The publishers of *Sweet Lavender* declared that 'it deals with no "problems", nor does it pretend to mirror the often sordid realities of life . . . a Victorian Fairy Tale of the Temple'. Clement Scott was loud in praise of *Sweet Lavender* for reasons central to his view of the whole purpose of drama: 'We all know how sad life *must* be as a rule; let us sometimes, even in a despised theatre, dream how happy and ideal and beautiful it *might* be. Rose-coloured spectacles are so much more soothing than the bare white glass, which only magnifies and seldom hides the defects of this ofttimes unlovely world.'[1]

The fact that Jones and Pinero were popular and successful dramatists of the 1890s shows that they appealed to more than a minority *avant-garde* audience that rejected rose-coloured spectacles. Their audience was the middle- and fashionable upper middle-class *cum* aristocratic audience of the St. James's, the Court, the Garrick, and the Criterion, theatres controlled by highly respectable and respected actor-managers: George Alexander, John Hare, and Charles Wyndham. This audience was prepared to accept more intellectual and serious comedy provided it did not offend social convention, and provided that its settings and characters were largely taken from the society with which it was comfortably familiar. Thus the comedy of Jones and Pinero employed social themes in settings which, like the settings of all late nineteenth-century middle-class drama,

---

[1] *The Drama of Yesterday and Today* (1899), ii. 189. See also Volume Two, p. 17.

were increasingly elaborate, realistic, and socially elevated; the social class of their *dramatis personae* was correspondingly raised. The growing sophistication of comedy and its tendency to stay in Mayfair meant a declining interest in rural settings and characters and the moral value of country simplicity and virtue. This kind of comedy was not an entirely new comedy, however, and, like Wilde and Shaw, Jones and Pinero assimilated subject-matter and techniques from their English predecessors.

Two significant characteristics of the comedy of the nineties are the improvement in plot construction and the more skilful intermingling of serious and comic elements; so-called comedies such as Jones's *The Crusaders* (1891) and Pinero's *The Benefit of the Doubt* (1895) are indistinguishable from dramas. Again this is nothing new, but dramatists had learned to blend comedy with pathos and potential tragedy rather than alternate them. Furthermore, comedies were written about marriage rather than courtship. Marital incompatibility and even sexual problems became thematically important and more prominent than before.

Henry Arthur Jones treated marital difficulties in *The Case of Rebellious Susan* (1894) and *The Liars* (1897) with an unqualified, burning moral conservatism and domestic idealism that condoned no departure from socially accepted *mores*. In the former play the *raisonneur* Sir Richard Kato persuades Lady Susan to return to her husband two years after she left him because of his infidelity. During that time she has fallen in love with Lucien Edensor, but Jones avoids allowing her a genuinely free choice by suddenly marrying off Edensor to another woman. In Jones's view Susan clearly does right to return to her worthless husband. The hero is obviously Kato himself, dispensing moral law with the authority of Jehovah. In a more overtly comic sub-plot, Jones condemns the New Woman in Elaine Pybus, a militant intellectual feminist who ruins the domestic life of her ineffective husband.[1] Kato lectures her fervently when she claims 'an immense future for Woman'. 'At her own fireside', he replies:

There is an immense future for women as wives and mothers, and a

---

[1] Very like Elaine, and given the same satirical treatment, is Miss Crane in Taylor's *Victims*. In 1857 Miss Crane is a repellent advocate of Female Emancipation.

very limited future for them in any other capacity. While you ladies without passions—or with disturbed and defeated passions—are raving and trumpeting all over the country, that wise, grim, old grandmother of us all, Dame Nature, is simply laughing up her sleeve and snapping her fingers at you and your new epochs and new movements. Go home! . . . Nature's darling woman is a stay-at-home woman who wants to be a good wife and a good mother, and cares very little for anything else. Go home!

While the marriages of all about him who disobey Jones's moral and social code are in pieces, it is fitting that the righteous man of principle, Kato, is the only one to receive a reward: the person and fortune of a wealthy young widow. Similarly, Sir Richard Deering of *The Liars*, another *raisonneur*-hero, wins the hand of another beautiful widow while forcing the gay and clever Lady Jessica Nepean to stay with her unpleasant and boorish husband Gilbert. What prevents her running off with Edward Falkner is a terrible fear of the consequences of social disgrace. This is a powerful weapon in Deering's hand; indeed, intense social awareness and social apprehension are distinguishing features of the Mayfair dramas and comedies of the nineties. Yet Deering has no better marital advice for the reluctantly reconciled couple than to tell Gilbert to take his wife to a good dinner at the Savoy. *The Liars* is ingeniously constructed, with an extremely clever penultimate act in which character after character becomes involved in a lie to save Lady Jessica's reputation. The view of Society taken here is much more trenchant and sardonic than in *The Case of Rebellious Susan*; thus the wit and intrigue are considerably more entertaining, although there is no questioning of Society's moral and social dictates. The weakest thing in the play is the incredible marriage of Lady Jessica and Gilbert: the whole plot depends upon their hopeless incompatibility, but it is difficult to believe that such a pair could have married in the first place.

The Manoeuvres of Jane (1898) is, for Jones, an unusually light comedy of young love bordering on the farcical, but two earlier plays, *The Crusaders* and *The Triumph of the Philistines* (1895) are sterner stuff. *The Crusaders*, a one-sided attack against puritanism, social philanthropy, and fashionable intellectualism, contains comic caricatures of a moral fanatic and a pessimist philosopher as well as the idealized figures of a social reformer and a saintly girl who adores him.[1] Jones was, in fact, a passionate idealist about men and women; several characters in his comedies and dramas partake of a spiritual and fanatic devotion to Duty and Goodness. In *The Triumph of the Philistines* a hypocritical puritan tries to drive Art and Gracious Living from Market Pewbury, but fails. Jones savagely condemns the hypocritical morality of the puritans but conveniently overlooks the narrow base of his own. Female evil is the sole province of an alluring French model and entirely remote from the kind of idealized Englishwoman (like the heroine) of whom the *raisonneur*-hero states, 'We know there are two kinds of women. And it's you, and not the others, that we will have at our firesides. It's you and not the others, that we will have for our mothers, and sisters, and wives.'

Having learnt more from French methods of construction, Pinero was a better craftsman than Jones, and, although by no means excusing his characters from meeting social standards and abiding by judgements dictated by social convention, did not possess Jones's penchant for tub-thumping social morality. Pinero did not develop a reputation or a distinctive style of his own until the Court Theatre farces of the 1880s. The last but one of these, *The Cabinet Minister* (1890), is less a farce than an ironic comedy showing the influence of *Engaged*, with bitter overtones foreshadowing *The Benefit of the Doubt*. The household of the cabinet minister, Sir Julian Twombley, sinks deep into debt through sumptuous living. The Moorish conservatory of the first act displays *'elaborate Algerian magnificence'*; the morning-room of the second, *'handsomely decorated and furnished'*, exhibits *'every evidence of luxury and refined taste'*. In order to avoid ruin, Lady Twombley is compelled against her will to introduce into Society the oilily unpleasant Jewish money-lender Joseph Lebanon and his socially ambitious sister, who are secretly supplying her with money and at the same time threatening exposure. The plot unfolds Lady Twombley's struggle with them and her efforts to marry her daughter to a fortune before the crash comes. Pinero's moral position is typically ambivalent. Lebanon, the vulgar lower-class black-

---

[1] Taylor's *Victims* not only satirizes Female Emancipation, but, anticipating *The Crusaders*, presents caricatures of an economist, a poet, a literary editor, and a metaphysician.

mailing bounder, part villain and part low comedian, receives appropriate retribution; much humour is obtained from his manners in a social set quite beyond and above him. But Lady Twombley, who is responsible for her family's financial predicament in the first place and who sells a cabinet secret to Lebanon in order to preserve herself, is given only the gentlest moral rebuke; the dénouement permits her to save the household and make a great deal of money at the same time. There is no disapproval of extravagance and fashionable living. And Lady Twombley's daughter accepts her true love—an explorer who had earlier appeared bearded and *'roughly dressed'* in his humble position of gamekeeper—only when he appears in the last act *'trimmed, shaven, and in immaculate evening dress'*.

The *nouveau-riche* of *The Times* (1891) is not a villain but a rich linen-draper, Bompas, who schemes to marry his daughter to the son of a peer as part of his plan to 'get on' in Society. The character type is a familiar one in Victorian comedy, but the tempestuous, drivingly ambitious, though basically simple and good-hearted Bompas is portrayed with some complexity and tragi-comic force. Largely because of his stupid son's untimely marriage with the coarse daughter of a low-class Irish widow, he learns that the past can never be hidden (there is an Ibsen influence here), fails in his marriage scheme, resigns from Parliament, and resolves to live a simple life abroad. In a genuinely affecting scene, Bompas and his wife, their hopes in ruins about them, talk quietly of how they lived in the old, unpretentious days; ironically, the sofa they sit on is part of *'a richly decorated and sumptuously furnished room . . . wealth and luxury are evident in all the appointments'*. Society cruelly rejects the Bompases, but its standards are never criticized. The moral might well be that linen-drapers should not 'get on' in Society; in fact Bompas himself says that 'there ought to be a law to stop men like me from "getting on" beyond a certain point'. In a sentimental compromise that weakens the end of the play the peer's son declares that he will marry Bompas's daughter anyway. Pinero's audiences were often able to have their cake and eat it too.

The Benefit of the Doubt (1895) is a much darker play, a drama rather than a comedy. The failure of two marriages is depicted with considerable emotional power, the more forceful for being tightly disciplined. What social comedy exists is bitterly ironic, and the play is comically enlivened by the presence of a foolish and pompous M.P., a character type whose long line of descent in nineteenth-century comedy culminates in the satirical excellence of this portrait. The weight of high society crushes Pinero's next comedy, *The Princess and the Butterfly* (1897), despite a serious theme of the fear of age and unattractiveness. Princess Pannonia and Sir George Lamorant, a fashionable pair approaching middle age, turn to each other for comfort but at the last moment follow the impulses of their hearts and marry much younger people. The plot is thin and spun out to great length, and its tedium is heightened by a superfluity of uninteresting characters from high life who indulge in a superfluity of banal dialogue. *Trelawney of the 'Wells'* (1898) is far better, a superior exercise in the nostalgic and sentimental recreation of the theatre of the sixties, the best nineteenth-century play written about the theatre. *The Gay Lord Quex* (1899) pits a reformed middle-aged profligate against a wily Bond Street manicurist in a struggle between his determination to behave impeccably during his engagement to an idealistic young woman and the manicurist's equal determination to sabotage the match. In spite of undoubted merits of characterization, dialogue, and situation, *The Gay Lord Quex* illustrates the dangers of a too careful attention to the plot requirements of a well-made play: the first two acts exist mainly to lead up to the excellent *scène à faire* in Act III, where Quex finally confronts his opponent in a bedroom at midnight, and the anti-climactic fourth act is there to resolve the questions arising from this scene.

Thus the comedy of the nineteenth century, in common with its tragedy and 'drama', ended in a decade emphasizing craftsmanship, social elegance, a considerable degree of economy and restraint, a great respect for social conventions, and an often elaborate verisimilitude of setting that formed the logical environment for a greater and more credible realism of characterization and dialogue. In 1900 comedy was even more solidly a middle-class and fashionable taste than it had been in 1800, and over the course of a century it gradually brought order and refinement out of the social and comic sprawl inherited from Colman and Reynolds and their successors. However, it preserved in its new decorum much of the theme material, moral viewpoint, and comic technique of those days and of the dramatic generation from the 1840s to the 1860s. No author of nineteenth-century comedies departed sharply from the practice and subject-matter of his immediate predecessors. Despite the great variety of work done and the apparent jumble of styles and materials, one can observe a remarkable continuity of development over a hundred years of comic writing.

JOHN BULL

OR THE ENGLISHMAN'S FIRESIDE

A COMEDY IN FIVE ACTS

BY

GEORGE COLMAN THE YOUNGER (1762–1836)

─────

*First performed at Covent Garden Theatre
5 March 1803*

─────

CAST

PEREGRINE	Mr. Cooke
SIR SIMON ROCHDALE	Mr. Blanchard
FRANK ROCHDALE	Mr. H. Johnston
LORD FITZ-BALAAM	Mr. Waddy
HONOURABLE TOM SHUFFLETON	Mr. Lewis
JOB THORNBERRY	Mr. Fawcett
JOHN BUR	Mr. Atkins
DENNIS BRULGRUDDERY	Mr. Johnstone
DAN	Mr. Emery
MR. PENNYMAN	Mr. Davenport
JOHN	Mr. Abbot
ROBERT	Mr. Truman
SIMON	Mr. Beverly
WILLIAMS	Mr. Klanert
LADY CAROLINE BRAYMORE	Mrs. H. Johnston
MRS. BRULGRUDDERY	Mrs. Davenport
MARY THORNBERRY	Mrs. Gibbs

─────

SCENE
Cornwall

PREFACE TO *JOHN BULL*

'NEVER, in my day, did play have such a run or create such a sensation. The jokes, the wit, the story, the Red Cow, Job Thornberry's immortal waistcoat, were in every body's mouth; and, night after night, week after week, month after month, did the intellectual part of England flock to laugh and cry with as excellent a company of actors as ever graced a theatre.'[1] William Robson, remembering the first production of *John Bull* long afterwards, was no more enthusiastic than many commentators in 1803, and the triumphant reception accorded the play confirmed Colman as the most popular comic dramatist of his day. Although opening late in the season *John Bull* was performed forty-eight times before Covent Garden closed on 23 June.[2] It was played regularly in the following season and entered the repertory of Drury Lane in 1808, with Bannister as Job Thornberry and Johnstone, who had left Covent Garden, as Dennis Brulgruddery. Estimates of Colman's income from the play vary between £850 and £1,200, including the copyright.[3]

By 1803 Colman had achieved a considerable reputation in several forms of drama: straight comedies such as *The Heir-at-Law* (1797) and *The Poor Gentleman* (1801); melodramas with songs and extensive comic relief, like *The Battle of Hexham* (1789), *The Mountaineers* (1793), and *The Iron Chest* (1796); a melodramatic spectacle, *Blue-Beard* (1798); and a kind of musical comedy of which *Inkle and Yarico* (1787) and *The Review* (1800) are good examples. Colman was also manager of the summer theatre in the Haymarket, which he took over from his father in 1794. In later life he became Examiner of Plays (his last dramatic piece was performed in 1822), succeeding John

---

[1] William Robson, *The Old Play-Goer* (1846), pp. 55–6. Munden, however, had declined the part written for him, Sir Simon Rochdale.

[2] The British Museum set of playbills for the Covent Garden season for 1802–3 records each night's receipts. *John Bull* took £20,495, nearly one-third of a season's total of £68,525, an average of £427 a night. These figures are even more remarkable when one sees that during the entire run only one benefit (for Lewis) and one royal command performance helped to swell receipts above those indicating the natural attraction of the play.

[3] Jeremy F. Bagster-Collins, *George Colman the Younger* (1946), p. 159.

Larpent in 1824 and attracting much criticism for allegedly
hypocritical moral severity and authoritarian conduct towards
playwrights.

Colman was not a popular Examiner of Plays, and even as an
author of successful comedies he received some abuse. Leigh
Hunt, though willing to admit that Colman, 'with all his
erroneous condescension to the faults of the present stage is able
perhaps to produce a more laughable farce than any English
humourist on record',[1] included him in his castigation of comic
authors in *The Feast of the Poets*. Apollo mistakes them for
waiters:

> There was Arnold, and Reynolds, and Dibdin, and Cherry,
> All grinning as who should say, 'Shan't we be merry?' . . .
> 'Twas lucky for Colman he wasn't there too,
> For his pranks would have certainly met with their due . . .
> The God fell a laughing to see his mistake,
> But stopp'd with a sigh for poor Comedy's sake.[2]

Hunt praised Colman for his superiority to his fellow dramatists,
but persisted in regarding him merely as the author of 'huge
farces', thus dismissing him, by implication, as a clever but
degraded buffoon. Certainly he did not inspire critical confidence by the management of his plots. *John Bull* is, to say the
least, loosely plotted, but neither Colman nor his colleagues
cared a whit for careful plotting, and they knew their audiences
did not care either. Commenting on the way he set about writing
his first play, *Two to One* (1784), Colman freely admitted that he
had no notion of plotting comedies, neither at that time nor since:

I had no materials for a plot, further than the commonplace foundation
of a marriage projected by parents, contrary to the secret views and
wishes of the parties to be united; and which, of course, is to be
obviated by the usual series of stratagems, accidents, and equivoques.
Alas! what those stratagems &.c. were to be, or how the second scene
was to be conducted, I had not any idea while I was writing the first:
but having finished the first, I hurried into the second with as little
forecast about the third—and so on, from scene to scene, spinning
stage business (as it is term'd) as I went along, and scribbling at
hap-hazard, 'as humours and conceits might govern', till I came to
the conclusion of Act One. One Act completed enabled me to proceed

---

[1] *Critical Essays on the Performers of the London Theatres*, p. 120.
[2] *The Feast of the Poets* (1814), p. 5.

somewhat less at random, in the two acts to come, by obliging me to
consider a little about the means of continuing and then unravelling
the perplexities I had already created; still I persevered, as to whole
Acts, in the same want of regular plan which had marked my progress
in respect to Scenes . . . In this improvident way I have written all
my dramas which are not founded either on some historical incident,
or on some story or anecdote which I have met with in print.[1]

Audiences wanted lively incident rather than careful structure,
and Colman was well able to satisfy this taste as well as supplying other popular ingredients of comedy. The very ease with
which he responded to audience demand annoyed critics in-
sisting on higher standards of writing and the preservation of
traditional comic values. Colman's comedies are interesting
examples of the skilful provision of everything an audience
might ask for, a variety of entertainment unsurprising in view
of his equal facility in comedy, melodrama, farce, spectacle,
dramatic satire, and song-writing. *John Bull* contains many of
the essentials of contemporary comic appeal: the mixture of
pathos, low comedy, and debased gentility; the distressed
heroine, the repentant seducer, and the middle-aged shrew;
hostility to the aristocracy and to town-bred morals; the
emotional intensity of a father–daughter relationship, the heavy
weight of sentiment and do-gooding morality; the uncompli-
cated jokes; the idealization of middle-class virtue. This last
point is worth a comment. Job Thornberry, the upright, good-
hearted tradesman, was universally regarded as the hero of the
play, as the sub-title *The Englishman's Fireside* might suggest.
Job is not only John Bull and therefore the true spirit of England,
not only a loving father and preserver of domestic happiness,
but also the apotheosis of middle-class rectitude. The preface to
The Dramatic Works of George Colman the Younger (1827) noted
that 'in the hero of the piece, honest Job Thornberry, we behold
an epitome of the best part and bulwark of the English character
—the middling class'. The perfect Englishness of it all appealed
strongly to a middle-class audience that enjoyed seeing their
own ideals dramatically depicted. The fundamental domesticity
of this appeal was also popular; the use of 'fireside' in the sub-
title was no accident, and indeed struck a holy note that was to
reverberate on stage through the whole of the nineteenth

[1] *Random Records* (1830), ii. 176–7.

century. This domesticity was also felt to be English; 'the ball-room, the card-table, the haunts of folly . . . are not comparable to those tranquil and endearing enjoyments that encircle the sanctuary of the Englishman's Fireside . . . The comedy is, in the truest sense, English; the sentiments are manly and pure, and the moral is calculated to render mankind better and happier.'[1]

The popularity of *John Bull* ensured repeated production for fifty years after its first performances. After 1850 its attraction began to wane, but Samuel Phelps, the most eminent Job Thornberry of his day, revived it at Sadler's Wells in 1859. It seems to have been last played in the West End at the Gaiety in 1872 and 1873.

There are basically two groups of texts for *John Bull*. The first comprises the pirated Dublin edition of 1803, the authorized London edition of 1805, the text in v. 21 of Inchbald's *British Theatre* (1808), and the text in v. 1 of *The Dramatic Works of George Colman the Younger*. With minor variants, these texts are the same. The second group consists of the acting editions: *Cumberland's British Theatre*, v. 36, *Duncombe's British Theatre*, v. 37, *Lacy's Acting Edition of Plays*, v. 42, and *Dicks' Standard Plays*, no. 21. The *Cumberland* and *Duncombe* are identical, as are the *Lacy* and *Dicks'*, the two former preserving the original five acts with some cuts, the two later versions being in three acts with further cuts and the omission of Lord Fitz-Balaam. All these texts have been consulted: the one printed here is a conflation of the 1805 edition with the *Cumberland* (the earliest acting edition) and two Drury Lane prompt-books of 1812 and 1818. The Lord Chamberlain's copy and the Inchbald text are useful in correcting occasional misprints in the 1805. As is usual, cuts were made in the licenser's copy for performance. An interesting aspect of this copy is the omission of almost all Colman's notorious oaths, which are, however, carefully inserted in the 1805 (perhaps through performance), and then largely omitted from the acting editions of a more decorous age.[2] The prologue was spoken by Brunton and Colman's epilogue sung by Johnstone.

---

[1] George Daniel, 'Remarks' on *John Bull* in *Cumberland's British Theatre*, v. 36.

[2] Embarrassed by the gulf between his stern morality as Examiner of Plays and his practice as a dramatist, a repentant Colman weakly defended himself on this matter before a parliamentary committee. (*Report from the Select Committee on Dramatic Literature* (1832), p. 60.)

PROLOGUE

Written by Mr. T. DIBDIN.

So you're all here, Box, Pit, and Gall'ry full
Of British Jurors, come to try John Bull.
'Who acts John Bull?' methinks I hear you say:
No Character's so named in all the Play.
'The title then's a trick!' We scorn the charge.
JOHN BULL is—British Character at large.
'Tis he, or he—where'er you mark a wight
Revering law, yet resolute for right;
Plain, blunt, his heart with feeling, justice full,
That is a Briton, that's (thank Heaven!) JOHN BULL.
And John, till now, we set it down for certain,
Has always ta'en his seat before the curtain.
And so he does; no matter where your places,
I see his gen'rous mind in all your faces.
Whether he sits by sweetheart, friend, or bride,
John Bull's as warm as at his own fireside.
Look up aloft, and you may safely swear
He's highly pleased, close to his lass—just there.
That hand which round her waist is kindly thrown,
Should any he mislest, wou'd knock him down.
For John is still (as tells the lyric page)
A lamb in love, a lion in his rage.

Where fashion's polish shews him more refin'd,
                                            [*To the boxes.*]
John still to social gaiety's inclin'd;
Freely, tho' aim'd at by satiric whim,
Laughs with the bards, who raise the laugh at him.
Or look below, and you may see him sit,
Gracing with critic state an English Pit;
To whom, thus midway placed, I say be kind,
JOHN BULL before—Oh spare JOHN BULL behind.
                                            [*Pointing off.*]

Shou'd you condemn sans mercy the poor elf,
'Twere suicide for JOHN to kill himself.
Nor blame the fear which makes the bard thus sue;
JOHN BULL ne'er trembles but in facing you.

PLATE 1

John Bull. Jack Johnstone as Dennis Brulgruddery

ACT I

SCENE I. *A Public-House on a Heath*, R. *Over the door the sign of the Red Cow, and the name of Dennis Brulgruddery; a finger-post*, R.

Enter DENNIS BRULGRUDDERY *and* DAN, *from the house—* DAN *opening the outward shutters of the house.*

DENNIS. A pretty blustratious night we have had, and the sun peeps through the fog this morning like the copper pot in my kitchen. Devil a traveller do I see coming to the Red Cow.

DAN. Na, measter, nowt do pass by here, I do think, but the carrion crows.

DENNIS. Dan, think you I will be ruined?

DAN. Ees, past all condemption. We be the undonestest family in all Cornwall. Your ale be as dead as my grandmother; mistress do set by the fire and sputter like an apple a-roasting; the pigs ha' gotten the measles; I be grown thinner nor an old sixpence; and thee hast drunk up all the spirity liquors.

DENNIS. By my soul, I believe my setting up the Red Cow a week ago was a bit of a bull—but that's no odds. Haven't I been married these three months—and who did I marry?

DAN. Why, a waddling woman wi' a mulberry feace.

DENNIS. Have done with your blarney, Mr. Dan. Think of the high blood in her veins, you bogtrotter!

DAN. Ees, I always do, when I do look at her nose.

DENNIS. Never you mind Mrs. Brulgruddery's nose. Wasn't she fat widow to Mr. Skinnygauge, the lean exciseman, of Lestwithiel? And didn't her uncle, who is fifteenth cousin to a Cornish baronet, say he'd leave her no money, if he ever happened to have any, becase she had disgraced her parentage by marrying herself to a taxman? Bathershan, man, and don't you think he'll help us out of the mud, now her second husband is an Irish jontleman, bred and born.

DAN. [*Laughing.*] He! he! Thee be'st a rum gentleman.

DENNIS. Troth, and myself, Mr. Dennis Brulgruddery, was brought up to the church.

DAN. Why, zure!

DENNIS. You may say that. I opened the pew doors in Belfast.

DAN. And what made 'em to turn thee out o' the treade?

DENNIS. I snored in sermon time. Dr. Snufflebags, the preacher, said I woke the rest of the congregation. [*Looking off.*] Arrah, Dan, don't I see a tall customer stretching out his arms in the fog?

DAN. Na, that be the road-post.

DENNIS. Faith, and so it is! Och! when I was turned out of my snug birth in Belfast, the tears ran down my eighteen-year old cheeks like buttermilk.

DAN. Pshaw, man, nonsense! Thee'dst never get another livelihood by crying.

DENNIS. Yes, I did; I cried oysters. Then I plucked up——[*Pointing.*] what's that—a customer?

DAN. [*Looking out.*] Na, a donkey.

DENNIS. Well, then I plucked up a parcel of my courage, and carried arms.

DAN. Waunds! What, a musket?

DENNIS. No, a reaping hook. I cut my way half through England, till a German larned me physic at a fair in Devonshire.

DAN. What, poticary's stuff?

DENNIS. I studied it in Doctor Von Quolchigronck's booth at Plympton. He cured the yellow glanders, and restored prolification to families who wanted an heir. I was of mighty use to him as an assistant.

DAN. Were you indeed?

DENNIS. But somehow the doctor and I had a quarrel; so I gave him something and parted.

DAN. And what didst thee give him pray?

DENNIS. I gave him a black eye, and set up for myself at Lestwithiel, where Mr. Skinnygauge, the exciseman, was in his honeymoon. Poor soul! he was my patient, and died one **day**;

but his widow had such a neat notion of my subscriptions that in three weeks she was Mrs. Brulgruddery.

DAN. [*Laughing.*] He! he! So you jumped into the old man's money?

DENNIS. Only a dirty hundred pounds. Then her brother-in-law, bad luck to him, kept the Red Cow upon Muckslush Heath, till his teeth chattered him out of the world, in an ague.

DAN. Why, that be this very house.

DENNIS. Ould Nick fly away with the roof of it! I took the remainder of the lease, per advice of my bride, Mrs. Brulgruddery; laid out her good-looking hundred pound for the furniture and the goodwill, bought three pigs that are going into a consumption, took a sarving-man that——

DAN. That's I. I be going into a consumption too, sin you hired me.

DENNIS. And devil a soul has darkened my doors for a pot of beer since I've been a publican.

DAN. [*Looking off.*] See! See, mun, see! Yon's a traveller, sure as eggs, and a-coming this road!

DENNIS. Och, hubbaboo! A customer at last! St. Patrick send he may be a pure dry one! Be alive, Dan, be alive! Run and tell him there's elegant refreshment at the Red Cow.

DAN. I wull. Oh, dang it, I doesn't mind a bit of a lie.

DENNIS. And hark ye—say there's an accomplished landlord.

DAN. Ees, and a genteel waiter; but he'll see that.

DENNIS. And Dan—sink that little bit of a thunder-storm that has soured all the beer, you know.

DAN. What, dost take me for an oaf? Dang me, if he ha'n't been used to drink vinegar, he'll find it out fast enow of himsel, I'se warrant un.   [*Exit.*

DENNIS. [*Calling.*] Wife! I must tell her the joyful news. Mrs. Brulgruddery! My dear! Devil choak my dear; she's as deaf as a trunkmaker! Mrs. Brulgruddery!

Enter MRS. BRULGRUDDERY, *from the house.*

MRS. BRULGRUDDERY. And what do you want now with Mrs. Brulgruddery? What's to become of us? Tell me that. How are we going on, I should like to know?

DENNIS. Mighty like a mile-stone, standing still at this present writing.

MRS. BRULGRUDDERY. A pretty situation we are in, truly!

DENNIS. Yes, upon Muckslush Heath, and be damned to it.

MRS. BRULGRUDDERY. And where is the fortune I brought you?

DENNIS. All swallowed up by the Red Cow.

MRS. BRULGRUDDERY. Ah, had you followed my advice, we should never have been in such a quandary.

DENNIS. Tunder and turf! Didn't yourself advise me to take this public-house?

MRS. BRULGRUDDERY. No matter for that. I had a relation who always kept it. But who advised you to drink out all the brandy?

DENNIS. No matter for that—I had a relation who always drank it.

MRS. BRULGRUDDERY. [*Crying.*] Ah! my poor dear Mr. Skinnygauge never brought tears into my eyes as you do.

DENNIS. I know that—I saw you at his funeral.

MRS. BRULGRUDDERY. You're a monster!

DENNIS. Am I? Keep it to yourself, then, my lambkin.

MRS. BRULGRUDDERY. You'll be the death of me—you know you will.

DENNIS. Look up, my sweet Mrs. Brulgruddery, while I give you a small morsel of consolation.

MRS. BRULGRUDDERY. Consolation, indeed!

DENNIS. Yes; there's a customer coming.

MRS. BRULGRUDDERY. [*Brightening.*] What!

DENNIS. A customer. Turn your neat jolly face over the heath yonder. Look at Dan, towing him along as snug as a cock-salmon into a fish basket.

MRS. BRULGRUDDERY. Jimminy, and so there is! Oh, my dear Dennis! But I knew how it would be if you had but a little patience. Remember, it was all by my advice you took the Red Cow.

DENNIS. Och, ho! it was, was it?

MRS. BRULGRUDDERY. I'll run and spruce myself up a bit. Aye, aye, I haven't prophesied a customer to-day for nothing.

[*Exit into the house.*

DENNIS. Troth, and it's prophesying on the sure side, to foretell a thing when it has happened.

Re-enter DAN, *conducting* PEREGRINE, *who carries a small trunk under his arm.*

PEREGRINE. I am indifferent about accommodations.

DAN. Our'n be a comfortable parlour, zur: you'll find it clean, for I washed un down mysen, wringing wet, five minutes ago.

PEREGRINE. You have told me so, twenty times.

DAN. This be the Red Cow, zur, as ye may see by the pictur; and here be measter—he'll treat ye in an hospital manner, zur, and show you a deal o' contention.

DENNIS. I'll be bound, sir, you'll get good entertainment, whether you are a man or a horse.

PEREGRINE. You may lodge me as either, friend. I can sleep as well in a stable as a bedchamber, for travel has seasoned me. [*Half aside, and pointing to the trunk under his arm.*] Since I have preserved this, I can lay my head upon it with tranquillity, and repose anywhere.

DENNIS. Faith, it seems a mighty decent hard bolster. What is it stuffed with, I wonder?

PEREGRINE. That which keeps the miser awake—money.

DAN. Waunds! All that money!

DENNIS. I'd be proud, sir, to know your upholsterer—he should make me a feather bed gratis of the same pretty materials. If this was all my own, I'd sleep like a pig, though I'm married to Mrs. Brulgruddery.

PEREGRINE. I shall sleep better because it is not my own.

DENNIS. Your own's in a snugger place, then? Safe from the sharks of this dirty world, and be hanged to 'em!

PEREGRINE. Except the purse in my pocket, 'tis now, I fancy, in a place most frequented by the sharks of this world.

DENNIS. London, I suppose?

PEREGRINE. The bottom of the sea.

DENNIS. By my soul, that's a watering place; and you'll find sharks there, sure enough, in all conscience.

Re-enter MRS. BRULGRUDDERY.

MRS. BRULGRUDDERY. [*To* PEREGRINE.] What would you choose to take, sir, after your walk this raw morning? We have any thing you desire.

DENNIS. Yes, sir, we have anything. [*Aside.*] Anything's nothing, they say.

MRS. BRULGRUDDERY. Dan, bustle about, and see the room ready and all tidy; do you hear?

DAN. I wull.

MRS. BRULGRUDDERY. What would you like to drink, sir?

PEREGRINE. Oh, mine is an accommodating palate, hostess. I have swallowed burgundy with the French, hollands with the Dutch, sherbet with the Turk, sloe juice with an Englishman, and water with a simple Gentoo.

DAN. [*Going.*] Dang me, but he's a rum customer! It's my opinion he'll take a fancy to our sour beer.   [*Exit.*

PEREGRINE. Is your house far from the sea-shore?

MRS. BRULGRUDDERY. About three miles, sir.

PEREGRINE. So! And I have wandered upon the heath four hours, before daybreak.

MRS. BRULGRUDDERY. Lack-a-day! Has anything happened to you, sir?

PEREGRINE. Shipwreck—that's all.

MRS. BRULGRUDDERY. Mercy on us! Cast away!

PEREGRINE. On your coast here.

DENNIS. Then, compliment apart, sir, you take a ducking as if you had been used to it.

PEREGRINE. Life's a lottery, friend, and man should make up his mind to the blanks. On what part of Cornwall am I thrown?

MRS. BRULGRUDDERY. We are two miles from Penzance, sir.

PEREGRINE. Ha! from Penzance! That's lucky!

MRS. BRULGRUDDERY. Lucky! [*Aside to* DENNIS.] Then he'll
go on, without drinking at our house.

DENNIS. Ahem! Sir, there has been a great big thunder-storm
at Penzance, and all the beer in the town's as thick as mustard.

PEREGRINE. I feel chilled—get me a glass of brandy.

DENNIS. [*Aside.*] Oh, the devil! [*Aloud to his wife.*] Bring the
brandy bottle for the jontleman, my jewel.

MRS. BRULGRUDDERY. [*Aside to* DENNIS.] Don't you know
you've emptied it, you sot you?

DENNIS. [*Aside.*] Draw a mug of beer—I'll palaver him..

MRS. BRULGRUDDERY. [*Aside.*] Ah, if you would but follow
my advice!   [*Exit.*

DENNIS. You see that woman that's gone, sir—she's my wife,
poor soul! She has got but one misfortune, and that's a
wapper.

PEREGRINE. What's that?

DENNIS. We had as neat a big bottle of brandy a week ago, and
damn the drop's left. But I say nothing—she's my wife, poor
creature, and she can tell who drank it. Wouldn't you like a
sup of sour—I mean, of our strong beer?

PEREGRINE. Psha! no matter what. Tell me, is a person of the
name of Thornberry still living in Penzance?

DENNIS. Is it one Mr. Thornberry you are asking after?

PEREGRINE. Yes. When I first saw him (indeed, it was the
first time and the last), he had just begun to adventure humbly
in trade. His stock was very slender, but his neighbours
accounted him a kindly man, and I know they spoke the truth.
Thirty years ago, after half an hour's intercourse, which
proved to me his benevolent nature, I squeezed his hand, and
parted.

DENNIS. Thirty years! Faith, after half an hour's dish of talk,
that's a reasonable long time to remember.

PEREGRINE. Not at all, for he did me a genuine service; and

gratitude writes her records in the heart that, till it ceases to beat, they may live in the memory.

Re-enter MRS. BRULGRUDDERY, *with a mug of beer.*

MRS. BRULGRUDDERY. [*Aside to* DENNIS.] What have you said about the brandy bottle?

DENNIS. [*Aside.*] I told him you broke it one day.

MRS. BRULGRUDDERY. [*Aside.*] Ah! I am always the shelter for your sins!

DENNIS. Hush! You know sir, I—hem! I mentioned to you poor Mrs. Brulgruddery's misfortune.

PEREGRINE. Ha! ha! You did indeed, friend.

MRS. BRULGRUDDERY. I am very sorry, sir, but——

DENNIS. Be asy, my lambkin, the jontleman excuses it. You are not the first that has cracked a bottle, you know. [*Taking the beer from his wife.*] My jewel, the jontleman was asking after one Mr. Thornberry.   [*Delaying to give the beer.*

MRS. BRULGRUDDERY. What, old Job Thornberry of Penzance, sir?

PEREGRINE. The very same. You know him, then?

MRS. BRULGRUDDERY. Very well, by hearsay, sir. He has lived there upwards of thirty years. [*To* DENNIS.] A very thriving man now, and well to do in the world, as others might be too, if they would but follow my advice.

PEREGRINE. I rejoice to hear it. Give me the beer, landlord; I'll drink his health in humble malt, then hasten to visit him.

DENNIS. [*Aside.*] By St. Patrick, then, you'll make wry faces on the road.
     [*Gives the mug to* PEREGRINE, *and, as he is about to drink, a shriek is heard at a small distance.*

PEREGRINE. Ha, the voice of a female in distress! Then 'tis a man's business to fly to her protection!
               [*Dashes the mug on the ground and exit.*

MRS. BRULGRUDDERY. Wheugh! What a whirligig! Why, Dennis, the man's mad!

DENNIS. I think that thing.

MRS. BRULGRUDDERY. He has thrown down all the beer before he tasted a drop.

DENNIS. That's it: if he had chucked it away afterwards, I shouldn't have wondered.

MRS. BRULGRUDDERY. Here he comes again, and, I declare, with a young woman leaning on his shoulder.

DENNIS. A young woman! Let me have a bit of a peep. Och, the crature! Och, the——

MRS. BRULGRUDDERY. Heyday! I shouldn't have thought of your peeping after a young woman, indeed!

DENNIS. Be asy, Mrs. Brulgruddery, it's a way we have in Ireland. There's a face!

MRS. BRULGRUDDERY. Well, and haven't I a face, pray?

DENNIS. That you have, my lambkin! You have had one these fifty years, I'll be bound for you.

MRS. BRULGRUDDERY. Fifty years! You are the greatest brute that ever dug potatoes.

Re-enter PEREGRINE, *supporting* MARY THORNBERRY.

PEREGRINE. This way; cheer your spirits! The ruffian with whom I saw you struggling has fled across the heath, but his speed prevented my saving your property. Was your money, too, in the parcel with your clothes?

MARY. All I possessed in the world, sir, and he has so frightened me! Indeed I thank you, sir; indeed I do!

PEREGRINE. Come, come; compose yourself. Whither are you going, pretty one?

MARY. I must not tell, sir.

PEREGRINE. Then whither do you come from?

MARY. Nobody must know, sir.

PEREGRINE. Umph! Then your proceedings, child, are a secret?

MARY. Yes, sir.

PEREGRINE. Yet you appear to need a friend to direct them. A heath is a rare place to find one. In the absence of a better, confide in me.

MARY. You forget that you are a stranger, sir.

PEREGRINE. I always do, when the defenceless want my assistance.

MARY. But perhaps you might betray me, sir.

PEREGRINE. Never, by the honour of a man!

MARY. Pray don't swear by that, sir, for then you'll betray me, I'm certain.

PEREGRINE. Have you ever suffered from treachery, then, poor innocence?

MARY. Yes, sir.

PEREGRINE. And may not one of your own sex have been treacherous to you?

MARY. No, sir; I'm very sure he was a man.

DENNIS. Oh, the blackguard!

MRS. BRULGRUDDERY. Hold your tongue, do!

PEREGRINE. Listen to me, child. I would proffer you friendship for your own sake—for the sake of benevolence. When ages, indeed, are nearly equal, nature is prone to breathe so warmly on the blossoms of a friendship between the sexes, that the fruit is desire; but Time, fair one, is scattering snow on my temples, while Hebe waves her freshest ringlets over yours. Rely, then, on one who has numbered years sufficient to correct his passions; who has encountered difficulties enough to teach him sympathy; and who would stretch forth his hand to a wandering female, and shelter her like a father.

MARY. [*Weeping.*] Oh, sir! I do want protection sadly indeed; I am very miserable!

PEREGRINE. Come, do not droop. The cause of your distress, perhaps, is trifling; but light gales of adversity will make women weep. A woman's tear falls like the dew that zephyrs shake from roses. Nay, confide in me.

MARY. I will, sir, [*Looking round.*] but——

PEREGRINE. [*To* DENNIS.] Leave us a little, honest friends.

DENNIS. Ahem! Come, Mrs. Brulgruddery; let you and I pair off, my lambkin.

MRS. BRULGRUDDERY. [*Going.*] Ah, she's no better than she should be, I'll warrant her.

DENNIS. By the powers, she's well enough, though, for all that!

[*Exeunt.*

PEREGRINE. Now, sweet one, your name?

MARY. Mary, sir.

PEREGRINE. What else?

MARY. Don't ask me that, sir; my poor father might be sorry it was mentioned now.

PEREGRINE. Have you quitted your father, then?

MARY. I left his house at daybreak this morning, sir.

PEREGRINE. What is he?

MARY. A tradesman in the neighbouring town, sir.

PEREGRINE. Is he aware of your departure?

MARY. No, sir.

PEREGRINE. And your mother?

MARY. I was very little when she died, sir.

PEREGRINE. Has your father, since her death, treated you with cruelty?

MARY. He! Oh, bless him, no! He is the kindest father that ever breathed, sir.

PEREGRINE. How must such a father be agonized by the loss of his child!

MARY. Pray, sir, don't talk of that!

PEREGRINE. Why did you fly from him?

MARY. Sir, I—I——but that's my story, sir.

PEREGRINE. Relate it, then.

MARY. Yes, sir. You must know, then, sir, that there was a young gentleman in this neighbourhood that——oh dear, sir, I'm quite ashamed!

PEREGRINE. Come, child, I will relieve you from the embarrassment of narration, and sum up your history in one word—love.

MARY. That's the beginning of it, sir, but a great deal happened afterwards.

PEREGRINE. And who is the hero of your story, my poor girl?

MARY. The hero of——oh, I understand. He is much above me in fortune, sir; to be sure, I should have thought of that before he got such power over my heart to make me so wretched, now he has deserted me.

PEREGRINE. He would have thought of that, had his own heart been generous.

MARY. He is reckoned very generous, sir; he can afford to be so. When the old gentleman dies, he will have all the great family estate. I am going to the house now, sir.

PEREGRINE. For what purpose?

MARY. To try if I can see him for the last time, sir; to tell him I shall always pray for his happiness when I am far away from a place which he has made it misery for me to abide in; and to beg him to give me a little supply of money, now I am penny-less and from home, to help me to London, where I may get into service, and nobody will know me.

PEREGRINE. And what are his reasons, child, for thus deserting you?

MARY. He sent me his reasons by letter yesterday, sir. He is to be married next week to a lady of high fortune; his father, he says, insists upon it. I know I am born below him, but after the oaths we plighted, heaven knows the news was a sad, sad shock to me! I did not close my eyes last night; my poor brain was burning; and as soon as day broke I left the house of my dear father, whom I should tremble to look at when he discovered my story, which I could not long conceal from him.

PEREGRINE. Poor, lovely, heart-bruised wanderer! O wealthy despoilers of humble innocence, splendid murderers of virtue, who make your vice your boast, and fancy female ruin a feather in your caps of vanity—single out a victim you have abandoned, and, in your hours of death, contemplate her: view her, care-worn, friendless, pennyless; hear her tale of sorrows, fraught with her remorse—her want—a hard world's scoffs—her parents' anguish; then, if ye dare, look inward upon your own bosoms, and, if they be not conscience-proof, what must be your compunctions! Who is his father, child?

MARY. Sir Simon Rochdale, sir, of the manor-house hard by.

PEREGRINE. [*Surprised.*] Indeed!

MARY. Perhaps you know him, sir.

PEREGRINE. I have heard of him, and on your account shall visit him.

MARY. Oh pray, sir, take care what you do! If you should bring his son into trouble by mentioning me, I should never, never forgive myself.

PEREGRINE. Trust to my caution. Promise only to remain at this house till I return from a business which calls me immediately two miles hence; I will hurry back to pursue measures for your welfare with more hope of success than your own weak means, poor simplicity, are likely to effect. What say you?

MARY. I hardly know what to say, sir; you seem good, and I am little able to help myself.

PEREGRINE. You consent, then?

MARY. Yes, sir.

PEREGRINE. [*Calling.*] Landlord!

Enter DENNIS, *followed by* MRS. BRULGRUDDERY.

DENNIS. Did you call, sir? Arrah now, Mrs. Brulgruddery, you are peeping after the young woman yourself.

MRS. BRULGRUDDERY. I choose it.

PEREGRINE. Prepare your room, good folks, and get the best accommodation you can for this young person.

DENNIS. That I will, with all my heart and soul, sir.

MRS. BRULGRUDDERY. [*Sulkily.*] I don't know that we have any room at all, for my part.

DENNIS. Whew! She's in her tantrums!

MRS. BRULGRUDDERY. People of repute can't let in young women (found upon a heath, forsooth!) without knowing who's who. I have learned the ways of the world, sir.

PEREGRINE. So it seems, which too often teach you to overrate the little good you can do in it, and to shut the door when the distressed entreat you to throw it open. But I have learnt the ways of the world, too. [*Taking out his purse.*] I shall return in a few hours. Provide all the comforts you can, and here are a couple of guineas to send for any refreshments you have not in the house.

DENNIS. Mighty pretty handsel for the Red Cow, my lambkin!

MRS. BRULGRUDDERY. A couple of guineas! Lord, sir, if I thought you had been such a gentleman! Pray, miss, walk in; your poor dear little feet must be quite wet with our nasty roads. I beg pardon, sir; but character's every thing in our business, and I never lose sight of my own credit.

DENNIS. That you don't, till you see other people's ready money.

PEREGRINE. Go in, child. I shall soon be with you again.

MARY. You will return, then, sir?

PEREGRINE. Speedily; rely on me.

MARY. I shall, sir; I am sure I may. Heaven bless you, sir!

MRS. BRULGRUDDERY. [*Courtesying.*] This way, miss—this way. [*Exeunt* MRS. BRULGRUDDERY *and* MARY.

DENNIS. Long life to your honour, for protecting the petticoats! Sweet cratures: I'd like to protect them myself, by bushels.

PEREGRINE. Can you get me a guide, friend, to conduct me to Penzance?

DENNIS. Get you a guide? There's Dan, my servant, shall skip before you over the bogs like a grasshopper. Oh, by the powers! my heart's full to see your generosity, and I owe you a favour in return: never you call for any of my beer till I get a fresh tap. [*Exit.*

PEREGRINE. Now for my friend Thornberry; then hither again to interest myself in the cause of this unfortunate, for which many would call me Quixotic—many would cant out 'Shame!' But I care not for the stoics, nor the puritans. Genuine nature and unsophisticated morality, that turn disgusted from the rooted adepts in vice, have ever a reclaiming tear to shed on the children of error. Then let the sterner virtues, that allow no plea for human frailty, stalk on to Paradise without me. The mild associate of my journey thither shall be charity; and my pilgrimage to the shrine of mercy will not, I trust, be worse performed for having aided the weak, on my way, who have stumbled in their progress.

Enter DAN.

DAN. I be ready, zur.

PEREGRINE. For what, friend?

DAN. Measter says you be a going to Penzance; if you be agreeable, I'll keep you company.

PEREGRINE. Oh, the guide! You belong to the house?

DAN. Ees, zur! I'se enow to do; I be head waiter and hostler, only we never have no horses, nor customers.

PEREGRINE. The path, I fancy, is difficult to find. Do you never deviate?

DAN. Na, zur; I always whistles.

PEREGRINE. Come on, friend. It seems a dreary route; but how cheerily the eye glances over a sterile tract when the habitation of a benefactor, whom we are approaching to requite, lies in the perspective!   [*Exeunt.*

ACT II

SCENE I. *A Library in the House of* SIR SIMON ROCHDALE—*books scattered on a writing table.*

Enter TOM SHUFFLETON.

SHUFFLETON. Nobody up yet? I thought so.

Enter JOHN.

Ah, John, is it you? How d'ye do, John?

JOHN. Thank your honour, I——

SHUFFLETON. Yes, you look so. Sir Simon Rochdale in bed? Mr. Rochdale not risen? Well, no matter: I have travelled all night, though, to be with them. How are they?

JOHN. Sir, they are both——

SHUFFLETON. I'm glad to hear it. Pay the postboy for me.

JOHN. Yes, sir. I beg pardon, sir, but when your honour last left us——

SHUFFLETON. Owed you three pound five. I remember; have you down in my memorandums. Honourable Tom Shuffleton, debtor to——what's your name?

JOHN. My christian name, sir, is——

SHUFFLETON. Muggins—I recollect. Pay the postboy, Muggins. And harkye, take particular care of the chaise; I borrowed it of my friend, Bobby Fungus, who sprang up a peer in the last bundle of barons: if a single knob is knocked out of his new coronets, he'll make me a sharper speech than ever he'll produce in Parliament. And John——

JOHN. Sir.

SHUFFLETON. What was I going to say?

JOHN. Indeed, sir, I can't tell.

SHUFFLETON. No more can I. 'Tis the fashion to be absent—that's the way I forgot your bill. There, run along. [*Exit* JOHN.] I've the whirl of Bobby's chaise in my head still. Cursed fatiguing, posting all night through Cornish roads to obey the summons of friendship. Convenient in some respects, for all that. If all loungers of slender revenues like mine could command a constant succession of invitations from men of estates in the country, how amazingly it would tend to the thinning of Bond Street! [*Throwing himself into a chair near the writing table.*] Let me see, what has Sir Simon been reading? 'Burn's Justice'—true, the old man's reckoned the ablest magistrate in the county: he hasn't cut open the leaves, I see. 'Chesterfield's Letters'—pooh! his system of education is extinct; Belcher and the Butcher have superseded it. 'Clarendon's History of——'

Enter SIR SIMON ROCHDALE.

SIR SIMON. Ah, my dear Tom Shuffleton!

SHUFFLETON. Baronet, how are you?

SIR SIMON. Such expedition is kind, now. You got my letter at Bath, and——

SHUFFLETON. Saw it was pressing—here I am. Cut all my engagements for you, and came off like a shot.

SIR SIMON. Thank you; thank you, heartily!

SHUFFLETON. Left every thing at sixes and sevens.

SIR SIMON. Gad, I'm sorry if——

SHUFFLETON. Don't apologise—nobody does now. Left all my bills in the place unpaid.

SIR SIMON. Bless me! I've made it monstrous inconvenient!

SHUFFLETON. Not a bit—I give you my honour I didn't find it inconvenient at all. How is Frank Rochdale?

SIR SIMON. Why, my son isn't up yet, and before he's stirring, do let me talk to you, my dear Tom Shuffleton. I have something near my heart, that——

SHUFFLETON. Don't talk about your heart, baronet—feeling's quite out of fashion.

SIR SIMON. Well then, I'm interested in——

SHUFFLETON. Aye, stick to that. We make a joke of the heart nowadays, but when a man mentions his interest, we know he's in earnest.

SIR SIMON. Zounds! I am in earnest. Let me speak, and call my
motives what you will.

SHUFFLETON. Speak, but don't be in a passion. We are always
cool at the clubs; the constant habit of ruining one another
teaches us temper. Explain.

SIR SIMON. Well, I will. You know, my dear Tom, how much
I admire your proficiency in the New School of breeding; you
are what I call one of the highest finished fellows of the
present day.

SHUFFLETON. Psha, baronet! You flatter.

SIR SIMON. No, I don't; only, in extolling the merits of the
newest fashioned manners and morals, I am sometimes
puzzled by the plain gentlemen who listen to me, here in the
country, most consumedly.

SHUFFLETON. I don't doubt it.

SIR SIMON. Why, 'twas but t'other morning I was haranguing
old Sir Noah Starchington in my library, and explaining to
him the shining qualities of a dasher of the year eighteen
hundred and three; and what do you think he did?

SHUFFLETON. Fell fast asleep.

SIR SIMON. No; he pulled down an English dictionary, where
(if you'll believe me) he found my definition of stylish living
under the word 'insolvency;' a fighting crop turned out a
'docked bull-dog;' and modern gallantry 'adultery and
seduction.'

SHUFFLETON. Noah Starchington is a damned old twaddler,
but the fact is, baronet, we improve. We have voted many
qualities to be virtues now that they never thought of calling
virtues formerly. The rising generation wants a new dictionary, damnably.

SIR SIMON. Deplorably, indeed! You can't think, my dear Tom,
what a scurvy figure you and the dashing fellows of your
kidney make in the old ones. But you have great influence
over my son Frank, and I want you to exert it. You are his
intimate—you come here and pass two or three months at a
time, you know.

SHUFFLETON. Yes, this is a pleasant house.

SIR SIMON. You ride his horses as if they were your own.

SHUFFLETON. Yes, he keeps a good stable.

SIR SIMON. You drink our claret with him till his head aches.

SHUFFLETON. Yours is famous claret, baronet.

SIR SIMON. You worm out his secrets; you win his money; you——in short, you are——

SHUFFLETON. His friend, according to the next new dictionary. That's what you mean, Sir Simon.

SIR SIMON. Exactly. But let me explain. Frank, if he doesn't play the fool and spoil all, is going to be married.

SHUFFLETON. To how much?

SIR SIMON. Damn it now, how like a modern man of the world that is! Formerly, they would have asked to who.

SHUFFLETON. We never do now; fortune's every thing. We say 'a good match' at the west end of the town, as they say 'a good man' in the city; the phrase refers merely to money. Is she rich?

SIR SIMON. Four thousand a year.

SHUFFLETON. What a devilish desirable woman! Frank's a happy dog!

SIR SIMON. He's a miserable puppy. He has no more notion, my dear Tom, of a modern 'good match' than Eve had of pin money.

SHUFFLETON. What are his objections to it?

SIR SIMON. I have smoked him, but he doesn't know that—a silly, sly amour, in another quarter.

SHUFFLETON. An amour! That's a very unfashionable reason for declining matrimony.

SIR SIMON. You know his romantic flights. The blockhead, I believe, is so attached, I shouldn't wonder if he flew off at a tangent and married the girl that has bewitched him.

SHUFFLETON. Who is she?

SIR SIMON. She—hem!—she lives with her father, in Penzance.

SHUFFLETON. And who is he?

SIR SIMON. He—upon my soul, I am ashamed to tell you.

SHUFFLETON. Don't be ashamed; we never blush at anything in the New School.

SIR SIMON. Damn me, my dear Tom, if he isn't a brazier.

SHUFFLETON. The devil!

SIR SIMON. A dealer in kitchen candlesticks, coal-skuttles, coppers, and cauldrons.

SHUFFLETON. And is the girl pretty?

SIR SIMON. So they tell me; a plump little devil, as round as a teakettle.

SHUFFLETON. I'll be after the brazier's daughter tomorrow.

SIR SIMON. But you have weight with him. Talk to him, my dear Tom—reason with him; try your power, Tom, do!

SHUFFLETON. I don't much like plotting with the father against the son—that's reversing the New School, baronet.

SIR SIMON. But it will serve Frank; it will serve me, who wish to serve you. And to prove that I do wish it, I have been keeping something in embryo for you, my dear Tom Shuffleton, against your arrival.

SHUFFLETON. For me?

SIR SIMON. When you were last leaving us, if you recollect, you mentioned, in a kind of a way, a—a sort of an intention of a loan of an odd five hundred pounds.

SHUFFLETON. Did I? I believe I might. When I intend to raise money, I always give my friends the preference.

SIR SIMON. I told you I was out of cash then, I remember.

SHUFFLETON. Yes; that's just what I told you, I remember.

SIR SIMON. I have the sum floating by me now, and much at your service. [*Presenting it.*

SHUFFLETON. [*Taking it.*] Why, as it's lying idle, baronet, I—I—don't much care if I employ it.

SIR SIMON. Use your interest with Frank, now.

SHUFFLETON. Rely on me. Shall I give you my note.

SIR SIMON. No, my dear Tom; that's an unnecessary trouble.

SHUFFLETON. Why, that's true, with one who knows me so well as you.

SIR SIMON. Your verbal promise to pay is quite as good.

SHUFFLETON. [*Going.*] I'll see if Frank's stirring.

SIR SIMON. [*Going.*] And I must talk to my steward.

SHUFFLETON. Baronet!

SIR SIMON. [*Returning.*] Eh?

SHUFFLETON. Pray, do you employ the phrase, 'verbal promise to pay,' according to the reading of old dictionaries, or as it's the fashion to use it at present?

SIR SIMON. Oh damn it, choose your own reading, and I'm content.   [*Exeunt severally.*

———

SCENE II. *A Dressing Room—a table and chairs,* C.; *a door,* R.

FRANK ROCHDALE *discovered sitting at the table writing,* WILLIAMS *attending.*

FRANK. [*Throwing down the pen.*] It don't signify—I cannot write. I blot and tear, and tear and blot, and——come here, Williams—do let me hear you once more. Why the devil don't you come here?

WILLIAMS. I am here, sir.

FRANK. Well, well, my good fellow, tell me. You found means to deliver her the letter yesterday?

WILLIAMS. Yes, sir.

FRANK. And she read it——and——did you say she——she was very much affected when she read it?

WILLIAMS. I told you last night, sir; she looked quite death-struck, as I may say.

FRANK. [*Much affected.*] Did——did she weep, Williams?

WILLIAMS. No, sir, but I did afterwards. I don't know what ailed me, but when I got out of the house into the street I'll be hanged if I didn't cry like a child.

FRANK. You are an honest fellow, Williams. [*A knock at the door.*] See who is at the door.   [WILLIAMS *opens the door.*

Enter JOHN.

WILLIAMS. Well, what's the matter?

JOHN. There's a man in the porter's lodge says he won't go away without speaking to Mr. Francis.

FRANK. See who it is, Williams. Send him to me, if necessary, but don't let me be teazed without occasion.

WILLIAMS. I'll take care, sir.   [*Exeunt* WILLIAMS *and* JOHN.

FRANK. Must I marry this woman whom my father has chosen for me, whom I expect here to-morrow? And must I, then, be told 'tis criminal to love my poor deserted Mary, because our hearts are illicitly attached? Illicit for the heart! Fine phraseology! Nature disowns the restriction. I cannot smother her dictates and fall in or out of love, as the law directs.

Enter DENNIS BRULGRUDDERY.

Well, friend, who do you come from?

DENNIS. I come from the Red Cow, sir.

FRANK. The Red Cow?

DENNIS. Yes, sir, upon Muckslush Heath—hard by your honour's father's house, here. I'd be proud of your custom, sir, and all the good-looking family's.

FRANK. [*Impatiently.*] Well, well, your business?

DENNIS. That's what the porter ax'd me. 'Tell me your business, honest man,' says he. 'I'll see you damn'd first, sir,' says I; 'I'll tell it your betters, and that's Mr. Francis Rochdale, Esquire.'

FRANK. Zounds! then why don't you tell it? I am Mr. Francis Rochdale. Who the devil sent you here?

DENNIS. Troth, sir, it was good-nature whispered me to come to your honour; but I believe I've disremembered her directions, for damn the bit do you seem acquainted with her.

FRANK. Well, my good friend, I don't mean to be violent; only be so good as to explain your business.

DENNIS. Oh, with all the pleasure in life. Give me good words, and I'm as asy as an ould glove; but bite my nose off with mustard, and have at you with pepper; that's my way. There's a little crature at my house—she's crying her eyes out—and she won't get such another pair at the Red Cow, for I've left nobody with her but Mrs. Brulgruddery.

FRANK. With her! With who? Who are you talking of?

DENNIS. I'd like to know her name myself, sir; but I have heard but half of it, and that's Mary.

FRANK. Mary! Can it be she? Wandering on a heath! Seeking refuge in a wretched hovel!

DENNIS. A hovel! Oh, fie for shame of yourself, to misbecall a genteel tavern! I'd have you to know my parlour is clean sanded once a week.

FRANK. Tell me directly—what brought her to your house?

DENNIS. By my soul, it was Adam's own carriage—a ten-toed machine the haymakers keep in Ireland.

FRANK. Damn it, fellow! Don't trifle, but tell your story, and, if you can, intelligibly.

DENNIS. Don't be bothering my brains, then, or you'll get it as clear as mud. Sure the young crature can't fly away from the Red Cow while I'm explaining to you the rights on't. Didn't she promise the gentleman to stay till he came back?

FRANK. Promised a gentleman! Who—who is the gentleman?

DENNIS. Arrah now, where did you larn manners? Would you ax a customer his birth, parentage, and education? 'Heaven bless you, sir, you'll come back again?' says she. 'That's what I will, before you can say parsnips, my darling,' says he.

FRANK. Damnation! what does this mean? Explain your errand clearly, you scoundrel, or——

DENNIS. Scoundrel! Don't be after affronting a housekeeper. Haven't I a sign at my door, three pigs, a wife, and a man-sarvant?

FRANK. Well, go on.

DENNIS. Damn the word more will I tell you.

FRANK. Why, you infernal——

DENNIS. Oh, be asy! See what you get, now, by affronting Mr. Dennis Brulgruddery! [*Searching his pockets.*] I'd have talked for an hour if you had kept a civil tongue in your head, but now you may read the letter.   [*Giving it.*

FRANK. A letter! Stupid booby, why didn't you give it to me at first? Yes, it is her hand!   [*Opens the letter.*

DENNIS. Stupid! If you're so fond of letters, you might larn to behave yourself to the postman.

FRANK. [*Reading, and agitated.*] 'Not going to upbraid you— couldn't rest at my father's—trifling assistance'—oh, heaven! does she then want assistance? 'The gentleman who has befriended me.' Damnation! The gentleman! 'Your unhappy Mary.' Scoundrel that I am! What is she suffering? But who, who is this gentleman? No matter—she is distressed, heart breaking, and I, who have been the cause—I, who———here— [*Running to the writing table, opening a drawer, and taking out a purse.*] Run! Fly! Despatch!

DENNIS. He's mad!

FRANK. Say I will be at your house myself—remember, positively come or send in the course of the day. In the meantime take this, and give it to the person who sent you.

DENNIS. A purse! Faith, and I'll take it. Do you know how much is in the inside?

FRANK. Psha, no! No matter.

DENNIS. Troth, now, if I'd trusted a great big purse to a stranger, they'd have called it a bit of a bull. [*Pouring the money on the table.*] But let you and I count it out between us, for damn him, say I, who would cheat a poor girl in distress of the value of a rap! [*Counting.*] One, two, three, &c.

FRANK. Worthy, honest fellow!

DENNIS. Eleven, twelve, thirteen———

FRANK. I'll be the making of your house, my good fellow.

DENNIS. Damn the Red Cow, sir; you put me out. Seventeen, eighteen, nineteen. Nineteen fat yellow boys and a seven shilling piece. Tell 'em yourself, sir; then chalk 'em up over the chimney-piece, or else you'll forget, you know.

FRANK. Oh friend, when honesty so palpably natural as yours keeps the account, I care not for my arithmetic. Fly, now!

Bid the servants give you any refreshment you choose; then hasten to execute your commission.

DENNIS. Thank your honour; good luck to you! I'll taste the beer; but by my soul, if the butler comes the Red Cow over me, I'll tell him I know sweet from sour.   [*Exit.*

FRANK. Let me read her letter once more. 'I am not going to upbraid you, but after I got your letter, I could not rest at my father's, where I once knew happiness and innocence. I wished to have taken a last leave of you, and to beg a trifling assistance, but the gentleman who has befriended me in my wanderings would not suffer me to do so; yet I could not help writing to tell you I am quitting this neighbourhood for ever. That you may never know a moment's sorrow will always be the prayer of your unhappy Mary.' My mind is hell to me! Love, sorrow, remorse, and—yes—and jealousy, all distract me, and no counsellor to advise with—no friend to whom I may——

Enter TOM SHUFFLETON.

FRANK. Tom Shuffleton! You never arrived more apropos in your life!

SHUFFLETON. That's what the women always say to me. I've rumbled on the road all night, Frank. My bones ache, my head's muzzy—and we'll drink two bottles of claret a piece after dinner, to enliven us.

FRANK. You seem in spirits, Tom, I think, now.

SHUFFLETON. Yes; I have had a windfall—five hundred pounds.

FRANK. A legacy?

SHUFFLETON. No. The patient survives who was sick of his money. 'Tis a loan from a friend.

FRANK. 'Twould be a pity, then, Tom, if the patient experienced improper treatment.

SHUFFLETON. Why, that's true; but his case is so rare, that it isn't well understood, I believe. Curse me, my dear Frank, if the disease of lending is epidemic.

FRANK. But the disease of trying to borrow, my dear Tom, I am afraid, is.

SHUFFLETON. Very prevalent indeed, at the west end of the town.

FRANK. And as dangerous, Tom, as the small-pox. They should inoculate for it.

SHUFFLETON. That wouldn't be a bad scheme, but I took it naturally. Psha! damn it, don't shake your head. Mine's but a mere *façon de parler*—just as we talk to one another about our coats. We never say, 'Who's your tailor?' We always ask, 'Who suffers?' Your father tells me you are going to be married; I give you joy.

FRANK. Joy! I have known nothing but torment and misery since this cursed marriage has been in agitation.

SHUFFLETON. Umph! Marriage was a weighty affair formerly; so was a family coach, but domestic duties now are like town chariots; they must be made light to be fashionable.

FRANK. Oh, do not trifle! By acceding to this match, in obedience to my father, I leave to all the pangs of remorse and disappointed love a helpless, humble girl, and rend the fibres of a generous, but too credulous heart, by cancelling, like a villain, the oaths with which I won it.

SHUFFLETON. I understand—a snug thing in the country. Your wife, they tell me, will have four thousand a year.

FRANK. What has that to do with sentiment?

SHUFFLETON. I don't know what you may think, but, if a man said to me, plump, 'Sir, I am very fond of four thousand a year,' I should say, 'Sir, I applaud your sentiment very highly.'

FRANK. But how does he act who offers his hand to one woman at the very moment his heart is engaged to another?

SHUFFLETON. He offers a great sacrifice.

FRANK. And where is the reparation to the unfortunate he has deserted?

SHUFFLETON. An annuity. A great many unfortunates sport a stylish carriage up and down St. James's Street, upon such a provision.

FRANK. An annuity flowing from the fortune, I suppose, of the woman I marry! Is that delicate?

SHUFFLETON. 'Tis convenient. We liquidate debts of play and usury from the same resources.

FRANK. And call a crowd of Jews and gentleman-gamesters together, to be settled with during the debtor's honeymoon.

SHUFFLETON. No, damn it, it wouldn't be fair to jumble the Jews into the same room with our gaming acquaintance.

FRANK. Why so?

SHUFFLETON. Because twenty to one the first half of the creditors would begin dunning the other.

FRANK. Nay, for once in your life be serious. Read this, which has wrung my heart, and repose it as a secret in your own.

[*Giving the letter.*

SHUFFLETON. [*Glancing over it.*] A pretty little crowquill kind of a hand. 'Happiness—innocence—trifling assistance—gentleman befriended me—unhappy Mary.' Yes, I see. [*Returning it.*] She wants money, but has got a new friend. The style's neat, but the subject isn't original.

FRANK. Will you serve me at this crisis?

SHUFFLETON. Certainly.

FRANK. I wish you to see my poor Mary in the course of the day. Will you talk to her?

SHUFFLETON. Oh yes, I'll talk to her. Where is she to be seen?

FRANK. She writes, you see, that she has abruptly left her father; and I learn by the messenger that she is now in a miserable retired house on the neighbouring heath. That musn't deter you from going.

SHUFFLETON. Me? Oh dear, no! I'm used to it. I don't care how retired the house is.

FRANK. Come down to my father, to breakfast. I will tell you afterwards all I wish you to execute. Oh, Tom! this business has unhinged me for society. Rigid morality, after all, is the best coat of mail for the conscience.

SHUFFLETON. Our ancesters, who wore mail, admired it amazingly; but to mix in the gay world with their rigid morality would be as singular as stalking into a drawing-room in their armour; for dissipation is now the fashionable habit with which, like a brown coat, a man goes into company to avoid being stared at.   [*Exeunt.*

SCENE III. *An Apartment in* JOB THORNBERRY'S *House.*

Enter JOB THORNBERRY *in a night gown, followed by*
JOHN BUR.

BUR. Don't take on so—don't you, now! Pray, listen to reason.

JOB. I won't!

BUR. Pray do!

JOB. I won't! Reason bid me love my child and help my friend:
what's the consequence? My friend has run one way and
broke up my trade; my daughter has run another and broke
my——no, she shall never have it to say she broke my heart.
If I hang myself for grief, she shan't know she made me.

BUR. Well, but master——

JOB. And reason told me to take you into my shop when the fat
churchwardens starved you at the workhouse—damn their
want of feeling for it!—and you were thumped about, a poor,
unoffending, ragged-rumped boy as you were—I wonder
you haven't run away from me too!

BUR. That's the first real unkind word you ever said to me. I've
sprinkled your shop two and twenty years, and never missed
a morning.

JOB. The bailiffs are below, clearing the goods; you won't have
the trouble any longer.

BUR. Trouble! Look ye, old Job Thornberry——

JOB. Well! What, are you going to be saucy to me now I'm
ruined?

BUR. Don't say one cutting thing after another. You have been
as noted, all round our town, for being a kind man, as being a
blunt one.

JOB. Blunt or sharp, I've been honest. Let them look at my
ledger—they'll find it right. I began upon a little; I made that
little great, by industry; I never cringed to a customer to get
him into my books, that I might hamper him with an over-
charged bill for long credit; I earned my fair profits; I paid my
fair way; I break by the treachery of a friend, and my first
dividend will be seventeen shillings in the pound. I wish every
tradesman in England may clap his hand on his heart and say
as much, when he asks a creditor to sign his certificate.

BUR. 'Twas I kept your ledger, all the time.

JOB. I know you did.

BUR. From the time you took me out of the workhouse.

JOB. Psha! Rot the workhouse!

BUR. You never mentioned it to me yourself till to-day.

JOB. I said it in a hurry.

BUR. And I've always remembered it at leisure. I don't want to brag, but I hope I've been faithful. It's rather hard to tell poor John Bur, the workhouse boy, after clothing, feeding, and making him your man of trust for two-and-twenty years, that you wonder he don't run away from you now you're in trouble.

JOB. [*Affected.*] John, I beg your pardon.
                                                 [*Stretching out his hand.*

BUR. [*Taking his hand.*] Don't say a word more about it!

JOB. I——

BUR. Pray now, master, don't say any more! Come, be a man; get on your things, and face the bailiffs that are rummaging the goods.

JOB. I can't, John—I can't. My heart's heavier than all the iron and brass in my shop.

BUR. Nay, consider—what confusion. Pluck up a courage—do, now!

JOB. Well, I'll try.

BUR. Aye, that's right; here's your clothes. [*Taking them from the back of a chair.*] They'll play the devil with all the pots and pans, if you aren't by. Why, I warrant you'll do. Bless you, what should ail you?

JOB. Ail me? Do you go and get a daughter, John Bur; then let her run away from you, and you'll know what ails me.

BUR. Come, here's your coat and waistcoat. [*Going to help him on with his clothes.*] This is the waistcoat young mistress worked with her own hands for your birth-day five years ago. Come, get into it as quick as you can.

JOB. [*Throwing it on the floor violently.*] I'd as lieve get into my coffin! She'll have me there soon. Psha, rot it! I'm going to snivel. Bur, go and get me another.

BUR. Are you sure you won't put it on?

JOB. No, I won't! [BUR *pauses.*] No, I tell you! [*Exit* BUR.] How
proud I was of that waistcoat five years ago! I little thought
what would happen now, when I sat in it at the top of my
table with all my neighbours to celebrate the day. There was
Collop on one side of me, and his wife on the other, and my
daughter Mary sat at the further end, smiling so sweetly—
like an artful, good-for-nothing——I shouldn't like to throw
away the waistcoat, neither—I may as well put it on. Yes, it
would be poor spite not to put it on. [*Putting his arms into it.*]
She's breaking my heart, but I'll wear it, I'll wear it! [*Button-
ing it as he speaks, and crying involuntarily.*] It's my child's—
she's undutiful, ungrateful, barbarous—but she's my child,
and she'll never work me another.

Re-enter JOHN BUR.

BUR. Here's another waistcoat, but it has laid by so long, I think
it's damp.

JOB. I was thinking so myself, Bur, and so——

BUR. Eh? what, you've got on the old one? Well now, I declare,
I'm glad of that! Here's your coat. [*Putting it on him.*] 'Sbobs!
this waistcoat feels a little damp about the top of the bosom.

JOB. [*Confused.*] Never mind, Bur, never mind. A little water has
dropped on it, but it won't give me cold, I believe.

[*A noise of voices in altercation, without.*

BUR. Heigh, they are playing up old Harry below! I'll run and
see what's the matter. Make haste after me—do, now.

[*Exit.*

JOB. I don't care for the bankruptcy now. I can face my creditors
like an honest man, and I can crawl to my grave afterwards
as poor as a church mouse. What does it signify? Job
Thornberry has no reason now to wish himself worth a groat;
the old ironmonger and brazier has nobody to hoard his
money for now! I was only saving for my daughter; and she
has run away from her doating, foolish father, and struck
down my heart—flat—flat!

Enter PEREGRINE.

Well—who are you?

PEREGRINE. A friend.

JOB. Then I'm sorry to see you. I have just been ruined by a friend, and never wish to have another friend again, as long as I live; no, nor any ungrateful, undutiful——poh! I don't recollect your face.

PEREGRINE. Climate and years have been at work on it. But do you remember no trace of me?

JOB. No, I tell you. If you have anything to say, say it. I have something to settle below with my daughter—I mean, with the people in the shop; they are impatient, and the morning has half run away before she knew I should be up—I mean, before I have had time to get on my coat and waistcoat she gave me—I mean—I mean, if you have any business, tell it at once.

PEREGRINE. I will tell it at once. You seem agitated. The harpies whom I passed in your shop informed me of your sudden misfortune, but do not despair yet.

JOB. Aye, I'm going to be a bankrupt—but that don't signify. Go on; it isn't that—they'll find all fair—but go on.

PEREGRINE. I will. 'Tis just thirty years since I left England.

JOB. That's a little after the time I set up in the hardware-business.

PEREGRINE. About that time a lad of fifteen years entered your shop; he had the appearance of a gentleman's son, and told you he had heard by accident, as he was wandering through the streets of Penzance, some of your neighbours speak of Job Thornberry's goodness to persons in distress.

JOB. I believe he told a lie there.

PEREGRINE. Not in that instance, though he did in another.

JOB. I remember him. He was a fine, bluff boy.

PEREGRINE. He had lost his parents, he said; and, destitute of friends, money, and food, was making his way to the next port to offer himself to any vessel that would take him on board, that he might work his way abroad and seek a livelihood.

JOB. Yes, yes, he did. I remember it.

PEREGRINE. You may remember, too, when the boy had finished his tale of distress, you put ten guineas in his hand. They were the first earnings of your trade, you told him, and could not be laid out to better advantage than in relieving a helpless orphan; and, giving him a letter of recommendation to a sea captain at Falmouth, you wished him good spirits and prosperity. He left you with a promise that, if fortune ever smiled upon him, you should one day hear news of Peregrine.

JOB. Ah, poor fellow, poor Peregrine! He was a pretty boy. I should like to hear news of him, I own.

PEREGRINE. I am that Peregrine.

JOB. Eh? What! You are—no! Let me look at you again. Are you the pretty boy that——bless us, how you are altered!

PEREGRINE. I have endured many hardships since I saw you—many turns of fortune, but I deceived you (it was the cunning of a truant lad) when I told you I had lost my parents. From a romantic folly, the growth of boyish brains, I had fixed my fancy on being a sailor, and had run away from my father.

JOB. [*With great emotion.*] Run away from your father! If I had known that, I'd have horse-whipped you within an inch of your life!

PEREGRINE. Had you known it, you had done right, perhaps.

JOB. Right! Ah, you don't know what it is for a child to run away from a father! Rot me if I wouldn't have sent you back to him, tied neck and heels, in the basket of the stage-coach.

PEREGRINE. I have had my compunctions—have expressed them by letter to my father, but I fear my penitence had no effect.

JOB. Served you right.

PEREGRINE. Having no answers from him, he died, I fear, without forgiving me.   [*Sighs.*

JOB. [*Starting.*] What! died without forgiving his child! Come, that's too much. I couldn't have done that, neither. But go on; I hope you've been prosperous. But you shouldn't—you shouldn't have quitted your father.

PEREGRINE. I acknowledge it; yet I have seen prosperity, though I traversed many countries, on my outset, in pain and poverty. Chance at length raised me a friend in India, by whose interest and my own industry I amassed considerable wealth in the factory at Calcutta.

JOB. And have just landed it, I suppose, in England?

PEREGRINE. I landed one hundred pounds last night in my purse, as I swam from the Indiaman, which was splitting on a rock, half a league from the neighbouring shore. As for the rest of my property—bills, bonds, cash, jewels—the whole amount of my toil and application, are, by this time I doubt not, gone to the bottom; and Peregrine is returned after thirty years to pay his debt to you, almost as poor as he left you.

JOB. I won't touch a penny of your hundred pounds—not a penny!

PEREGRINE. I do not desire you; I only desire you to take your own.

JOB. My own?

PEREGRINE. Yes; I plunged with this box, last night, into the waves. You see it has your name on it.

JOB. 'Job Thornberry,' sure enough. And what's in it?

PEREGRINE. The harvest of a kind man's charity, the produce of your bounty to one whom you thought an orphan. I have traded these twenty years on ten guineas (which from the first I had set apart as yours), till they have become ten thousand; take it—it could not, I find, come more opportunely. [*Giving him the box.*] Your honest heart gratified itself in administering to my need, and I experience that burst of pleasure a grateful man enjoys in relieving my reliever.

JOB. [*Squeezing* PEREGRINE's *hand, returning the box, and seeming almost unable to utter.*] Take it again.

PEREGRINE. Why do you reject it?

JOB. I'll tell you as soon as I'm able. T'other day I had a friend—— psha, rot it! I'm an old fool! [*Wiping his eyes.*] I lent a friend t'other day the whole profits of my trade, to save him from sinking. He walked off with them and made me a bankrupt. Don't you think he is a rascal?

PEREGRINE. Decidedly so.

JOB. And what should I be if I took all you have saved in the world and left you to shift for yourself?

PEREGRINE. But the case is different. This money is, in fact, your own. I am inured to hardships; better able to bear them, and am younger than you. Perhaps, too, I still have prospects of——

JOB. I won't take it. I'm as thankful to you as if I left you to starve, but I won't take it.

PEREGRINE. Remember, too, you have claims upon you which I have not. My guide, as I came hither, said you had married in my absence: 'tis true he told me you were now a widower, but it seems you have a daughter to provide for.

JOB. I have no daughter to provide for now.

PEREGRINE. Then he misinformed me.

JOB. No, he didn't. I had one last night, but she's gone.

PEREGRINE. Gone!

JOB. Yes; gone to sea, for what I know, as you did. Run away from a good father, as you did. This is a morning to remember: my daughter has run out, and the bailiffs have run in. I shan't soon forget the day of the month.

PEREGRINE. This morning, did you say?

JOB. Aye, before day-break; a hard-hearted, base——

PEREGRINE. And could she leave you, during the derangement of your affairs?

JOB. She didn't know what was going to happen, poor soul! I wish she had now. I don't think my Mary would have left her old father in the midst of his misfortunes.

PEREGRINE. [*Aside.*] Mary! It must be she! What is the amount of the demands upon you?

JOB. Six thousand. But I don't mind that; the goods can nearly cover it—let 'em take 'em—damn the gridirons and warming-pans! I could begin again, but now my Mary's gone I haven't the heart; but I shall hit upon something.

PEREGRINE. Let me make a proposal to you, my old friend. Permit me to settle with the officers and to clear all demands upon you. Make it a debt, if you please. I will have a hold, if it must be so, on your future profits in trade; but do this, and I promise to restore your daughter to you.

JOB. What? Bring back my child! Do you know where she is? Is she safe? Is she far off? Is——

PEREGRINE. Will you receive the money?

JOB. Yes, yes, on those terms—on those conditions—but where is Mary?

PEREGRINE. Patience—I must not tell you yet, but in four-and-twenty hours I pledge myself to bring her back to you.

JOB. What, here? To her father's house, and safe? Oh, 'sbud! when I see her safe, what a thundering passion I'll be in with her! But you are not deceiving me? You know the first time you came into my shop, what a bouncer you told me when you were a boy.

PEREGRINE. Believe me, I would not trifle with you now. Come, come down to your shop, that we may rid it of its present visitants.

JOB. I believe you dropped from the clouds, all on a sudden, to comfort an old, broken-hearted brazier.   [*Exeunt.*

ACT III

SCENE I. SIR SIMON ROCHDALE's *Library.*

SIR SIMON ROCHDALE *and* LORD FITZ-BALAAM *discovered sitting at a table,* C.

SIR SIMON. And now, since the marriage is concluded, as I may say, in the families, may I take the liberty to ask, my lord, what sort of a wife my son Frank may expect in Lady Caroline? Frank is rather of a grave, domestic turn; Lady Caroline, it seems, has passed the three last winters in London. Did her ladyship enter into all the spirit of the first circles?

LORD FITZ-BALAAM. She was as gay as a lark, Sir Simon.

SIR SIMON. Was she like the lark in her hours, my lord?

LORD FITZ-BALAAM. A great deal more like the owl, Sir Simon.

SIR SIMON. I thought so. Frank's mornings in London will begin where her ladyship's nights finish. But his case won't be very singular: many couples make the marriage bed a kind of cold matrimonial well, and the two family buckets dip into it alternately.

Enter LADY CAROLINE BRAYMORE.

LADY CAROLINE. Do I interrupt business?

SIR SIMON. Not in the least. Pray, Lady Caroline, come in; his lordship and I have just concluded.

LORD FITZ-BALAAM. And I must go and walk my three miles this morning.

SIR SIMON. Must you, my lord?

LORD FITZ-BALAAM. My physician prescribed it, when I told him I was apt to be dull after dinner.   [*Exit.*

SIR SIMON. I would attend your lordship, but since Lady Caroline favours me with——

LADY CAROLINE. No, no; don't mind me. I assure you, I had much rather you would go.

SIR SIMON. Had you? [*Aside.*] Hum! But the petticoats have
their New School of good breeding, too, they tell me. [*Aloud.*]
Well, we are gone. We have been glancing over the writings,
Lady Caroline, that form the basis of my son's happiness,
although his lordship isn't much inclined to read.

LADY CAROLINE. But I am. I came here to study very deeply
before dinner.

SIR SIMON. [*Showing the writings.*] What, would your ladyship
then wish to――――

LADY CAROLINE. To read that? My dear Sir Simon, all that
Hebrew, upon parchment as thick as a board! I came to see if
you had any of the last novels in your book-room.

SIR SIMON. The last novels! [*Aside.*] Most of the female New
School are ghost-bitten, they tell me! [*Aloud, pointing to the
table.*] There's Fielding's works, and you'll find Tom Jones,
you know.

LADY CAROLINE. Psha, that's such a hack!

SIR SIMON. A hack, Lady Caroline, that the knowing ones have
warranted sound.

LADY CAROLINE. But what do you think of those that have had
such a run lately?

SIR SIMON. Why, I think most of them have run too much, and
want firing.   [*Exit.*

LADY CAROLINE. I shall die of *ennui* in this moping manor-
house! Shall I read to-day? No, I'll walk; no, I'll――――yes, I'll
read first, and walk afterwards. [*Sitting at the table, taking up
a book, and ringing the bell.*] Pope. Come, as there are no
novels, this may be tolerable. This is the most *triste* house I
ever saw.

> 'In these deep solitudes, and awful cells,
>   Where heavenly-pensive――――'

Enter ROBERT.

ROBERT. Did you ring, my lady?

LADY CAROLINE. 'Contemplation dwells.' Sir? Oh, yes; I
should like to walk. Is it damp under foot, sir? 'And ever
musing――――

ROBERT. There has been a good deal of rain to-day, my lady.

LADY CAROLINE. 'Melancholy reigns.'

ROBERT. My lady?

LADY CAROLINE. Pray, sir, look out and bring me word if it is clean or dirty.

ROBERT. Yes, my lady.   [*Exit.*

LADY CAROLINE. This settling a marriage is a strange business. 'What means this tumult in a vestal's veins?'

SHUFFLETON. [*Without.*] Bid the groom lead the horse into the avenue, and I'll come to him.

LADY CAROLINE. Company in the house! Some Cornish squire, I suppose.   [*Resumes her reading.*

Enter TOM SHUFFLETON, *followed by* JOHN.

LADY CAROLINE. [*Still reading, and seated with her back to* SHUFFLETON.] 'Soon as thy letters, trembling, I unclose—'

JOHN. What horse will you have saddled, sir?

SHUFFLETON. Slyboots.   [*Exit* JOHN.

LADY CAROLINE. 'That well-known name awakens all my woes.'

SHUFFLETON. Lady Caroline Braymore!

LADY CAROLINE. Mr. Shuffleton! Lard! what can bring you into Cornwall?

SHUFFLETON. Sympathy, which has generally brought me near your ladyship, in London at least, for these three winters.

LADY CAROLINE. Psha! But seriously?

SHUFFLETON. I was summoned by friendship. I am consulted on all essential points in this family, and Frank Rochdale is going to be married.

LADY CAROLINE. Then you know to whom?

SHUFFLETON. No; not thinking that an essential point, I forgot to ask. He kneels at the pedestal of a rich shrine, and I didn't inquire about the statue. But dear Lady Caroline, what has brought you into Cornwall?

LADY CAROLINE. Me? I'm the statue.

SHUFFLETON. You?

LADY CAROLINE. Yes; I've walked off my pedestal, to be worshipped at the Land's End.

SHUFFLETON. You to be married to Frank Rochdale! Oh, Lady Caroline! What, then, is to become of me?

LADY CAROLINE. Oh, Mr. Shuffleton! Not thinking that an essential point, I forgot to ask.

SHUFFLETON. Psha, now you're laughing at me! But upon my soul I shall turn traitor, take advantage of the confidence reposed in me by my friend, and endeavour to supplant him.

LADY CAROLINE. What do you think the world would call such duplicity of conduct?

Re-enter ROBERT.

ROBERT. Very dirty, indeed, my lady.   [*Exit.*

SHUFFLETON. That infernal footman has been listening! I'll kick him round his master's park.

LADY CAROLINE. 'Tis lucky, then, you are booted; for you hear he says it is very dirty there.

SHUFFLETON. Was that the meaning of—pooh! But you see, the—the surprise—the—the agitation has made me ridiculous.

LADY CAROLINE. I see something has made you ridiculous, but you never told me what it was before.

SHUFFLETON. Lady Caroline, this is a crisis that—my attentions—that is, the——in short, the world, you know, my dear Lady Caroline, has given me to you.

LADY CAROLINE. Why, what a shabby world it is!

SHUFFLETON. How so?

LADY CAROLINE. To make me a present of something it sets no value on itself.

SHUFFLETON. I flattered myself I might not be altogether invaluable to your ladyship.

LADY CAROLINE. To me! Now I can't conceive any use I could make of you. No, positively, you are neither useful nor ornamental.

SHUFFLETON. Yet you were never at an opera without me at your elbow, never in Kensington Gardens that my horse wasn't constantly in leading at the gate. Haven't you danced with me at every ball? And haven't I, unkind, forgetful Lady Caroline, even cut the Newmarket meetings when you were in London?

LADY CAROLINE. Bless me! these charges are brought in like a bill. 'To attending your ladyship, at such a time; to dancing down twenty couple with your ladyship, at another;' and, pray, to what do they all amount?

SHUFFLETON. The fullest declaration.

LADY CAROLINE. Lard, Mr. Shuffleton! Why, it has, to be sure, looked a—a—a little foolish, but you—you never spoke anything to—that is—to justify such a——

SHUFFLETON. [*Aside.*] That's as much as to say, speak now. [*Aloud.*] To be plain, Lady Caroline, my friend does not know your value. He has an excellent heart—but that heart is— [*Coughing. Aside.*] damn the word, it's so out of fashion, it chokes me!—[*Aloud.*] is irrevocably given to another. But mine—by this sweet hand I swear——

[*Kneeling, and kissing her hand.*

Re-enter JOHN.

Well, sir?   [*Rising hastily.*

JOHN. Slyboots, sir, has been down on his knees, and the groom says he can't get out.

SHUFFLETON. Let him saddle another.

JOHN. What horse, sir, will you——

SHUFFLETON. Psha, any! What do you call Mr. Rochdale's favourite, now?

JOHN. Traitor, sir.

SHUFFLETON. When Traitor's in the avenue, I shall be there.
[*Exit* JOHN.

LADY CAROLINE. Answer me one question candidly, and perhaps I may entrust you with a secret. Is Mr. Rochdale seriously attached?

SHUFFLETON. Very seriously.

LADY CAROLINE. Then I won't marry him.

SHUFFLETON. That's spirited. Now, your secret.

LADY CAROLINE. Why—perhaps you may have heard that my father, Lord Fitz-Balaam, is somehow so much in debt that ——but no matter.

SHUFFLETON. Oh, not at all; the case is fashionable with both lords and commoners.

LADY CAROLINE. But an old maiden aunt, whom, rest her soul, I never saw, for family pride's sake bequeathed me an independence. To obviate his lordship's difficulty, I mean to—to marry into this humdrum Cornish family.

SHUFFLETON. I see—a sacrifice! Filial piety and all that—to disembarrass his lordship. But hadn't your ladyship better——

LADY CAROLINE. Marry to disembarrass you?

SHUFFLETON. By my honour, I'm disinterested.

LADY CAROLINE. By my honour, I am monstrously piqued, and so vexed that I can't read this morning, nor talk, nor— I'll walk.

SHUFFLETON. Shall I attend you?

LADY CAROLINE. No; don't fidget at my elbow as you do at the opera. But you shall tell me more of this by-and-by.

SHUFFLETON. [*Taking her hand.*] When? Where?

LADY CAROLINE. Don't torment me. This evening, or to-morrow, perhaps; in the park, or—psha, we shall meet at dinner! Do let me go now, for I shall be very bad company.

SHUFFLETON. [*Kissing her hand.*] Adieu, Lady Caroline!

LADY CAROLINE. Adieu!   [*Exit.*

SHUFFLETON. My friend Frank, here, I think, is very much obliged to me. I am putting matters pretty well *en train* to disencumber him of a wife; and now I'll canter over the heath, and see what I can do for him with the brazier's daughter.
                                                         [*Exit.*

SCENE II. *A Mean Parlour at the Red Cow. A window in flat,* c. *A cupboard in flat,* R. *A clock in flat,* L. *A door,* R.; *a fireplace,* L. *with plaister parrots on the mantle. Chairs, and table,* c.; *pen, ink, and paper on it.*

Enter MARY *and* MRS. BRULGRUDDERY.

MRS. BRULGRUDDERY. Aye, he might have been there and back, over and over again; but my husband's slow enough in his motions, as I tell him 'till I'm tired on't.

MARY. I hope he'll be here soon.

MRS. BRULGRUDDERY. Ods, my little heart! Miss, why so impatient? Haven't you as genteel a parlour as any lady in the land could wish to sit down in? The bed's turned up in a chest of drawers that's stained to look like mahogany; there's two poets, and a poll-parrot, the best images the Jew had on his head, over the mantelpiece; and, was I to leave you all alone by yourself, isn't there an eight-day clock in the corner that, when one's waiting lonesome-like for anybody, keeps going tick tack and is quite company?

MARY. Indeed, I did not mean to complain.

MRS. BRULGRUDDERY. Complain? No, I think not, indeed! When, besides having a handsome house over your head, the strange gentleman has left two guineas—though one seems light, and t'other looks a little brummish—to be laid out for you, as I see occasion. I don't say it for the lucre of anything I'm to make out of the money, but I'm sure you can't want to eat yet.

MARY. Not if it gives any trouble, but I was up before sunrise, and have tasted nothing to-day.

MRS. BRULGRUDDERY. Eh? Why, bless me, young woman! Aren't you well?

MARY. I feel very faint.

MRS. BRULGRUDDERY. Aye, this is a faintish time o'year; but I must give you a little something, I suppose. I'll open the window and give you a little air.

DENNIS. [*Passing the window and singing without.*]
>They handed the whiskey about,
>>'Till it smoked through the jaws of the piper;

The bride got a fine copper snout,
And the clergyman's pimples grew riper.
                    Whack doodlety bob,
                        Sing pip.

MARY. There's your husband.

MRS. BRULGRUDDERY. There's a hog; for he's as drunk as one, I know, by his beastly bawling.

Enter DENNIS BRULGRUDDERY.

DENNIS. [*Singing.*] Whack doodlety bob,
                    Sing pip.

MRS. BRULGRUDDERY. 'Sing pip,' indeed! Sing sot! And that's to your old tune.

MARY. Haven't you got an answer?

MRS. BRULGRUDDERY. Haven't you got drunk?

DENNIS. Be asy, and you'll see what I've got in a minute.
                    [*Pulls a bottle from his pocket.*

MRS. BRULGRUDDERY. What's that?

DENNIS. Good Madeira it was when the butler at the big house gave it me. It jolted so over the heath, that if I hadn't held it to my mouth, I'd have wasted half. [*Putting it on the table.*] There, miss, I brought it for you; and I'll get a glass from the cupboard, and a plate for this paper of sweet cakes that the gintlefolks eat after dinner in the desert.

MARY. But tell me if——

DENNIS. [*Running to the cupboard.*] Eat and drink, my jewel, and my discourse shall serve for the seasoning. [*Filling a glass.*] Drink now, my pretty one, for you have had nothing, I'll be bound. Och, by the powers! I know the ways of ould mother Brulgruddery.

MRS. BRULGRUDDERY. Old mother Brulgruddery!

DENNIS. Don't mind her; take your prog; she'd starve a saint.

MRS. BRULGRUDDERY. I starve a saint?

DENNIS. Let him stop at the Red Cow as plump as a porker, and you'd send him away in a week like a weasel. [*Offering the plate to* MARY.] Bite a maccaroony, my darling.

MARY. I thank you.

DENNIS. Faith, no merit of mine; 'twas the butler that stole it. Take some. [*Letting the plate fall.*] Slips, by St. Patrick!

MRS. BRULGRUDDERY. [*Screaming.*] Our best China plate broke all to shivers!

DENNIS. Delf, you deceiver, delf! The cat's dining dish, rivetted.

MARY. Pray, now, let me hear your news.

DENNIS. That I will. Mrs. Brulgruddery, I take the small liberty of begging you to get out, my lambkin.

MRS. BRULGRUDDERY. I shan't budge an inch. She needn't be ashamed of anything that's to be told, if she's what she should be.

MARY. I know what I should be if I were in your place.

MRS. BRULGRUDDERY. Marry come up! And what should you be, then?

MARY. More compassionate to one of my own sex, or to any one in misfortune. Had you come to me, almost broken-hearted, and not looking like one quite abandoned to wickedness, I should have thought on your misery and forgot that it might have been brought on by your faults.

DENNIS. At her, my little crature! By my soul, she'll bother the ould one! Faith, the Madeira has done her a deal of service.

MRS. BRULGRUDDERY. What's to be said is said before me, and that's flat.

MARY. [*To* DENNIS.] Do tell it, then; but for others' sakes don't mention names. I wish to hide nothing now on my own account; though the money that was put down for me, before you would afford me shelter, I thought might have given me a little more title to hear a private message.

MRS. BRULGRUDDERY. I've a character for virtue to lose, young woman.

DENNIS. When that's gone, you'll get another—that's of a damned impertinent landlady! Sure, she has a right to her parlour, and haven't I brought her cash enough to swallow the Red Cow's rent for these two years?

MRS. BRULGRUDDERY. Have you? Well, though the young lady misunderstands me, it's always my endeavour to be respectful to gentlefolks.

DENNIS. Och, botheration to the respect that's bought by knocking one shilling against another at an inn! Let the heart keep open house, I say; and if Charity isn't seated inside of it, like a beautiful barmaid, it's all a humbug to stick up the sign of the Christian.

MRS. BRULGRUDDERY. I'm sure miss shall have anything she likes, poor dear thing! There's one chicken——

DENNIS. A chicken! Fie on your double barbarity! Would you murder the tough dunghill cock to choke a customer? [*To* MARY.] A certain person that shall be nameless will come to you in the course of this day, either by himself, or by friend, or by handwriting.

MARY. And not one word—not one, by letter, now?

DENNIS. Be asy—won't he be here soon? In the meantime, here's nineteen guineas and a seven-shilling piece, as a bit of a postscript.

MRS. BRULGRUDDERY. Nineteen guineas and——

DENNIS. Hould your gab, woman! Count them, darling.
[*He puts the money on the table*—MARY *counts it.*

MRS. BRULGRUDDERY. [*Drawing* DENNIS *aside.*] What have you done with the rest?

DENNIS. The rest?

MRS. BRULGRUDDERY. Why, have you given her all?

DENNIS. I'll tell you what, Mrs. Brulgruddery; it's my notion, in summing up your last accounts, that when you begin to dot Ould Nick will carry one, and that's yourself, my lambkin!

SHUFFLETON. [*Without.*] Hollo! Red Cow!

DENNIS. You are called, Mrs. Brulgruddery.

MRS. BRULGRUDDERY. I, you Irish bear! Go and——[*Looking towards the window.*] Jimminy! A traveller on horseback, and the handsomest gentleman I ever saw in my life! [*Runs out.*

MARY. Oh then it must be he!

DENNIS. No, faith, it isn't the young squire.

MARY. [*Mournfully.*] No!

DENNIS. There—he's got off the outside of his horse: it's that flashy spark I saw crossing the court-yard, at the big house. Here he is.

Enter TOM SHUFFLETON.

SHUFFLETON. [*Aside, looking at* MARY.] Devilish good-looking girl, upon my soul! [*Seeing* DENNIS.] Who's that fellow?

DENNIS. Welcome to Muckslush Heath, sir.

SHUFFLETON. Pray, sir, have you any business here?

DENNIS. Very little this last week, your honour.

SHUFFLETON. Oh, the landlord. Leave the room!

DENNIS. [*Aside.*] Manners! But he's my customer. If he don't behave himself to the young crature, I'll bounce in and thump him blue. [*Exit.*

SHUFFLETON. [*Looking at* MARY.] Shy, but stylish—much elegance, and no brass: the most extraordinary article that ever belonged to a brazier. [*Addressing her.*] Don't be alarmed, my dear. Perhaps you didn't expect a stranger?

MARY. No, sir.

SHUFFLETON. But you expected somebody, I believe, didn't you?

MARY. Yes, sir.

SHUFFLETON. I come from him; here are my credentials. [*Giving her a letter.*] Read that, my dear little girl, and you shall see how far I am authorised.

MARY. [*Kissing the superscription.*] 'Tis his hand!

SHUFFLETON. [*As she is opening the letter.*] Fine blue eyes, faith, and very like my Fanny's. Yes, I see how it will end—she'll be the fifteenth Mrs. Shuffleton.

MARY. [*Reading.*] 'When the conflicts of my mind have subsided, and opportunity will permit, I will write to you fully. My friend is instructed from me to make every arrangement for your welfare. With heartfelt grief I add, family circumstances have torn me from you for ever.'

[*Drops the letter, and is falling.*

SHUFFLETON. [*Supporting her.*] Ha! damn it, this looks like earnest! They do it very differently in London.

MARY. [*Recovering.*] I beg pardon, sir; I expected this, [*Bursting into tears.*] but I—I——

SHUFFLETON. [*Aside.*] Oh, come, we are getting into the old train; after the shower, it will clear. My dear girl, don't flurry yourself; these are things of course, you know. To be sure, you must feel a little resentment at first, but——

MARY. Resentment! When I am never, never to see him again! Morning and night my voice will be raised to heaven, in anguish, for his prosperity! And tell him—pray, sir, tell him,— I think the many, many bitter tears I shall shed will atone for my faults; then you know, as it isn't himself but his station that sunders us, if news should reach him that I have died, it can't bring any trouble to his conscience.

SHUFFLETON. Mr. Rochdale, my love, you'll find will be very handsome.

MARY. I always found him so, sir.

SHUFFLETON. [*Giving her a note.*] He has sent you a hundred pound bank note till matters can be arranged, just to set you a going.

MARY. I was going sir, out of this country, for ever. Sure he couldn't think it necessary to send me this, for fear I should trouble him!

SHUFFLETON. Psha! my love, you mistake; the intention is to give you a settlement.

MARY. I intended to get one for myself, sir.

SHUFFLETON. Did you?

MARY. Yes, sir; in London. I shall take a place in the coach to-morrow morning; and I hope the people of the inn where it puts up at the end of the journey will have the charity to recommend me to an honest service.

SHUFFLETON. Service? Nonsense! You—you must think differently. I'll put you into a situation in town.

MARY. Will you be so humane, sir?

SHUFFLETON. Should you like Marybone parish, my love?

MARY. All the parishes are the same to me, now I must quit my own, sir.

SHUFFLETON. I'll write a line for you to a lady in that quarter, and——oh, here's pen and ink. [*Writing, and talking as he is writing.*] I shall be in London myself in about ten days, and then I'll visit you to see how you go on.

MARY. Oh, sir, you are indeed a friend!

SHUFFLETON. I mean to be your friend, my love. There. [*Giving her the letter.*] Mrs. Brown, Howland Street, an old acquaintance of mine, a very good-natured, discreet, elderly lady, I assure you.

MARY. You are very good, sir, but I shall be ashamed to look such a discreet person in the face if she hears my story.

SHUFFLETON. No, you needn't; she has a large stock of charity for the indiscretions of others, believe me.

MARY. I don't know how to thank you, sir. The unfortunate must look up to such a lady, sure, as a mother.

SHUFFLETON. She has acquired that appellation. You'll be very comfortable, and when I arrive in town I'll——

Enter PEREGRINE.

[*Aside.*] Who have we here? Oh! Ha, ha! This must be the gentleman she mentioned to Frank in her letter. Rather an ancient *ami*.

PEREGRINE. [*Aside.*] So! I suspected this might be the case. [*Aloud.*] You are Mr. Rochdale, I presume, sir?

SHUFFLETON. Yes, sir, you do presume, but I am not Mr. Rochdale.

PEREGRINE. I beg your pardon, sir, for mistaking you for so bad a person.

SHUFFLETON. Mr. Rochdale, sir, is my intimate friend. If you mean to recommend yourself in this quarter, [*Pointing to* MARY.] good breeding will suggest to you that it mustn't be done by abusing him before me.

PEREGRINE. I have not acquired that sort of good breeding, sir, which isn't founded on good sense; and when I call the betrayer of female innocence a bad character, the term, I think, is too true to be abusive.

SHUFFLETON. 'Tis a pity, then, you haven't been taught a little better what is due to polished society.

PEREGRINE. I am always willing to improve.

SHUFFLETON. I hope, sir, you won't urge me to become your instructor.

PEREGRINE. You are unequal to the task. If you quarrel with me in the cause of a seducer, you are unfit to teach me the duties of a citizen.

SHUFFLETON. You may make, sir, a very good citizen, but curse me if you'll do for the west end of the town.

PEREGRINE. I make no distinctions in the ends of towns, sir. The ends of integrity are always uniform; and 'tis only where those ends are most promoted that the inhabitants of a town, let them live east or west, most preponderate in rational estimation.

SHUFFLETON. Pray, sir, are you a Methodist preacher in want of a congregation?

PEREGRINE. Perhaps I'm a quack doctor in want of a Jack Pudding. Will you engage with me?

SHUFFLETON. Damn me if this is to be borne. Sir, the correction I must give you will——

PEREGRINE. [*With coolness.*] Desist, young man, in time, or you may repent your petulance.

MARY. [*Coming between them.*] Oh, gentlemen! Pray, pray don't! I am so frightened! [*To* PEREGRINE.] Indeed, sir, you mistake. [*Pointing to* SHUFFLETON.] This gentleman has been so good to me.

PEREGRINE. Prove it, child, and I shall honour him.

MARY. Indeed, indeed he has. Pray, pray don't quarrel! When two such generous people meet, it would be a sad pity. See, sir, he has recommended me to a place in London, an elderly lady in Marybone parish; and so kind, sir, everybody that knows her calls her mother.

PEREGRINE. [*Looking at the superscription.*] Infamous! Sit down and compose yourself, my love; the gentleman and I shall come to an understanding. [MARY *retires up, and sits.*] One word, sir. I have lived long in India, but the flies who gad

thither buzz in our ears till we learn what they have blown
upon in England. I have heard of the wretch in whose house
you meant to place that unfortunate.

SHUFFLETON. Well? And you meant to place her in snugger
lodgings, I suppose?

PEREGRINE. I mean to place her where——

SHUFFLETON. No, my dear fellow, you don't, unless you answer
it to me.

PEREGRINE. I understand you. In an hour, then, I shall be at
the manor-house, whence I suppose you come. Here we are
both unarmed, and there is one at the door who, perhaps,
might interrupt us.

SHUFFLETON. Who is he?

PEREGRINE. Her father—her agonised father, to whose en-
treaties I have yielded and brought him here prematurely. He
is a tradesman—beneath your notice, a vulgar brazier; but
he has some sort of feeling for his child whom, now your
friend has lured her to the precipice of despair, you would
hurry down the gulf of infamy. For your own convenience,
sir, I would advise you to avoid him.

SHUFFLETON. Your advice now begins to be a little sensible;
and if you turn out a gentleman, though I suspect you to be
one of the brazier's company, I shall talk to you at Sir
Simon's.   [*Exit.*

MARY. Is the gentleman gone, sir?

PEREGRINE. Let him go, child, and be thankful that you have
escaped from a villain.

MARY. A villain, sir?

PEREGRINE. The basest, for nothing can be baser than manly
strength, in the specious form of protection, injuring an unhappy woman. When we should be props to the lily in the
storm, 'tis damnable to spring up like vigorous weeds and
twine about the drooping flower till we destroy it.

MARY. Then where are friends to be found, sir? He seemed
honest—so do you, but perhaps you may be as bad.

PEREGRINE. Do not trust me. I have brought you a friend,
child, in whom Nature tells us we ever should confide.

MARY. What, here, sir?

PEREGRINE. Yes. When he hurts you, he must wound himself; and so suspicious is the human heart become, from the treachery of society, that it wants that security. I will send him to you.   [*Exit.*

MARY. Who can he mean? I know nobody but Mr. Rochdale that, I think, would come to me; for my poor dear father, when he knows all my crime, will abandon me as I deserve.

Enter JOB THORNBERRY, *hastily.*

JOB. Mary! [*She shrieks, and falls into her father's arms.*] My dear Mary! Speak to me!

MARY. [*Recovering.*] Don't look kindly on me, my dear father! Leave me! I left you, but I was almost mad.

JOB. I'll never leave you till I drop down dead by your side! How could you run away from me, Mary? [*She shudders.*] Come, come, kiss me, and we'll talk of that another time.

MARY. You haven't heard half the story, or I'm sure you'd never forgive me.

JOB. Never mind the story now, Mary; 'tis a true story that you're my child, and that's enough for the present. I hear you have met with a rascal; I haven't been told who yet. Some folks don't always forgive; braziers do. Kiss me again, and we'll talk on't bye-and-bye. But why would you run away, Mary?

MARY. I couldn't stay and be deceitful, and it has often cut me to the heart to see you show me that affection which I knew I didn't deserve.

JOB. Ah, you jade! I ought to be angry, but I can't. Look here—don't you remember this waistcoat? You worked it for me, you know.

MARY. [*Kissing him.*] I know I did.

JOB. I had a hard struggle to put it on this morning, but I squeezed myself into it, a few hours after you ran away. If I could do that, you might have told me the worst, without much fear of my anger. How have they behaved to you, Mary?

MARY. The landlord is very humane, but the landlady——

JOB. Cruel to you? I'll blow her up like gunpowder in a copper!
We must stay here to-night; for there's Peregrine, that king
of good fellows—we must stay here till he comes back from
a little way off, he says.

MARY. He that brought you here?

JOB. Aye, he. I don't know what he intends, but I trust all to
him, and when he returns we'll have such a merry-making!
[*Calling.*] Hollo! House! Oh, damn it, I'll be good to the
landlord, but I'll play hell with his wife! Come with me, and
let us call about us a bit. Hollo, house! Come, Mary. Odsbobs!
I'm so happy to have you again! House! Come, Mary.

[*Exeunt.*

PLATE 2

I be Dan the Head Waiter,
Sure you all know me now.

John Bull. John Emery as Dan. The Harvard Theatre Collection

ACT IV

SCENE I. *The Outside of the Red Cow.*

Enter DENNIS BRULGRUDDERY, *from the house.*

DENNIS. I've stretched my neck half a yard longer, looking out
after that rapscallion, Dan. Och! and is it yourself I see at
last? There he comes, in a snail's trot, with a basket behind
him, like a stage-coach.

Enter DAN, *with a basket at his back.*

Dan, you divil! Aren't you a beast of a waiter?

DAN. What for?

DENNIS. To stay out so, the first day of company.

DAN. Come, that be a good un! I ha' waited for the company a
week, and I defy you to say I ever left the house till they
comed.

DENNIS. Well, and that's true. Pacify me with a good reason,
and you'll find me a dutiful master. Arrah, Dan, what's that
hump grown out at your back, on the road?

DAN. Plenty o' meat and drink. [*Putting the basket on the
ground.*] I han't had such a hump o' late at my stomach.

DENNIS. And who harnessed you, Dan, with all that kitchen
stuff?

DAN. He as ware racked and took I wi' un to Penzance for a
companion. He ordered I, as I said things ware a little
famished-like here, to buy this for the young woman and the
old man he ha' brought back wi' un.

DENNIS. Then you have been gabbling your ill-looking stories
about my larder, you stone-eater!

DAN. Larder! I told un you had three live pigs as ware dying.

DENNIS. Oh, fie! Think you, won't any master discharge a
mansarvant that shames him? Thank your luck, I can't blush.
But is the old fellow our customer has brought his intimate
friend he never saw but once, thirty years ago?

DAN. Ees, that be old Job Thornberry, the brazier; and as sure as you stand there, when we got to his shop they ware a going to make him a banker.

DENNIS. A banker! I never saw one made; how do they do it?

DAN. Why, the bum-baileys do come into his house and claw away all his goods and furniture.

DENNIS. By the powers, but that's one way of setting a man going in business!

DAN. When we got into the shop, there they ware, as grum as thunder. You ha' seen a bum-bailey?

DENNIS. I'm not curious that way. I might have seen one, once or twice; but I was walking mighty fast, and had no time to look behind me.

DAN. My companion—our customer—he went up stairs, and I bided below, and then they began a knocking about the goods and chapels. That ware no business o' mine.

DENNIS. Sure it was not.

DAN. Na, for sartin; so I ax'd 'em what they ware a doing; and they told I, wi' a broad grin, taking an invention of the misfortunate man's defects.

DENNIS. Choke their grinning!

DAN. They comed down stair—our customer and the brazier; and the head bailey he began a bullocking at the old man, in my mind, just as one Christian shouldn't do to another. I had nothing to do wi' that.

DENNIS. Damn the bit!

DAN. Na, nothing at all, and so my blood began to rise. He made the poor old man almost fit to cry.

DENNIS. That wasn't your concern, you know.

DAN. Bless you, mun! 'twould ha' looked busy-like in me to say a word; so I took up a warming-pan, and I banged bumbailey wi' the broad end on't, till he fell o' the floor, as flat as twopence.

DENNIS. Oh, hubbaboo! lodge in my heart, and I'll never ax you for rent. You're a friend in need. Remember, I've a warming-pan—you know where it hangs, and that's enough.

DAN. They had like to ha' warmed I finely, I know. I ware nigh being hauled to prison 'cause, as well as I could make out their cant, it do seem I had rescued myself and broke a statue.

DENNIS. Och, the Philistines!

DAN. But our traveller—I do think he be the devil—he settled all in a jiffy; for he paid the old man's debts, and the bailey's broken head ware chucked into the bargain.

DENNIS. And what did he pay?

DAN. Guess, now.

DENNIS. A hundred pounds.

DAN. Six thousand, by gum!

DENNIS. What! On the nail?

DAN. Na, on the counter.

DENNIS. Whew! six thousand pou——oh, by the powers, this man must be the philosopher's stone! Dan——

DAN. Hush, here he be!

Enter PEREGRINE, *from the house.*

PEREGRINE. So, friend, you have brought provision, I perceive.

DAN. Ees, sir; three boiled fowls, three roast, two chicken pies, and a capon.

PEREGRINE. You have considered abundance more than variety. And the wine?

DAN. A dozen o' capital red port, sir; I axed for the newest they had i' the cellar.

DENNIS. [*Abstractedly.*] Six thousand pounds upon a counter!

PEREGRINE. [*To* DAN.] Carry the hamper in doors; then return to me instantly. You must accompany me in another excursion.

DAN. What, now?

PEREGRINE. Yes; to Sir Simon Rochdale's. You are not tired, my honest fellow?

DAN. Na, not a walking wi' you; but, dang me, when you die, if all the shoemakers shouldn't go into mourning.

[*He takes the hamper into the house.*

DENNIS. [*Ruminating.*] Six thousand pounds! By St. Patrick, it's a sum!

PEREGRINE. How many miles from here to the manor-house?

DENNIS. Six thousand!

PEREGRINE. Six thousand! Yards you mean, I suppose, friend.

DENNIS. Sir! Eh? Yes, sir, I—I mean yards—all upon a counter!

PEREGRINE. Six thousand yards upon a counter! Mine host here seems a little bewildered; but he has been anxious, I find, for poor Mary, and 'tis national in him to blend eccentricity with kindness. John Bull exhibits a plain, undecorated dish of solid benevolence, but Pat has a gay garnish of whim around his good nature; and if now and then 'tis sprinkled in a little confusion, they must have vitiated stomachs who are not pleased with the embellishment.

Re-enter DAN, *booted.*

DAN. Now, sir, you and I'll stump it.

PEREGRINE. Is the way we are to go now so much worse, that you have cased yourself in those boots?

DAN. Quite clean; that's why I put 'em on. I should ha' dirtied 'em in t'other job.

PEREGRINE. Set forward, then.

DAN. Na, sir, axing your pardon; I be but the guide, and 'tisn't for I to go first.

PEREGRINE. Ha, ha! Then we must march abreast, boy, like lusty soldiers, and I shall be side by side with honesty; 'tis the best way of travelling through life's journey, and why not over a heath? Come, my lad.

DAN. Cheek by jowl, by gum! [*Exeunt* PEREGRINE *and* DAN.

DENNIS. That walking philosopher—perhaps he'll give me a big bag of money. Then, to be sure, I won't lay out some of it to make me easy for life; for I'll settle a separate maintenance upon ould mother Brulgruddery.

JOB THORNBERRY *peeps out at the door of the public-house.*

JOB. Landlord!

DENNIS. Coming, your honour!

JOB. [*Coming forward.*] Hush, don't bawl! Mary has fallen asleep. You have behaved like an emperor to her, she says. Give me your hand, landlord.

DENNIS. Behaved! [*Refusing his hand.*] Arrah now, get away with your blarney.

JOB. Well, let it alone. I'm an old fool, perhaps; but as you comforted my poor girl in her trouble, I thought a squeeze from her father's hand—as much as to say, 'thank you for my child'—might not have come amiss to you.

DENNIS. And is it yourself who are that crature's father?

JOB. Her mother said so, and I always believed her. You have heard some'at of what has happened, I suppose? It's all over our town, I take it, by this time. Scandal is an ugly, trumpeting devil. Let 'em talk; a man loses little by parting with a herd of neighbours who are busiest in publishing his family misfortunes, for they are just the sort of cattle who would never stir over the threshhold to prevent 'em.

DENNIS. Troth, and that's true; and some will only sarve you becase you're convenient to 'em for the time present, just as my customers come to the Red Cow.

JOB. I'll come to the Red Cow, hail, rain, or shine, to help the house, as long as you are landlord, though I must say that your wife——

DENNIS. [*Putting his hand before* JOB's *mouth.*] Decency! Remember your own honour and my feelings. I mustn't hear any thing bad, you know, of Mrs. Brulgruddery, and you'll say nothing good of her without telling damned lies; so be asy!

JOB. Well, I've done, but we mustn't be speaking ill of all the world, neither; there are always some sound hearts to be found among the hollow ones. Now he that has just gone over the heath——

DENNIS. What, the walking philosopher?

JOB. I don't know anything of his philosophy, but if I live these thousand years I shall never forget his goodness. Then there's another: I was thinking, just now, if I had tried him I might have found a friend in my need, this morning.

DENNIS. Who is he?

JOB. A monstrous good young man, and as modest and affable as if he had been bred up a 'prentice instead of a gentleman.

DENNIS. And what's his name?

JOB. Oh, everybody knows him in this neighbourhood; he lives hard by—Mr. Francis Rochdale, the young squire at the manor-house.

DENNIS. Mr. Francis Rochdale!

JOB. Yes; he's condescending, and took quite a friendship for me and mine. He told me t'other day he'd recommend me in trade to all the great families twenty miles round; and said he'd do I don't know what all for my Mary.

DENNIS. He did! Well, faith, you mayn't know what, but by my soul he has kept his word.

JOB. Kept his word! What do you mean?

DENNIS. Harkye: if Scandal is blowing about your little fireside accident, 'twas Mr. Francis Rochdale recommended him to your shop to buy his trumpet.

JOB. Eh! What? No! Yes—I see it at once! Young Rochdale's a rascal! [*Bawling.*] Mary!

DENNIS. Hush! you'll wake her, you know.

JOB. I intend it; I'll——a glossy, oily, smooth rascal! Warming me in his favour like an unwholesome February sun! Shining upon my poor cottage and drawing forth my child—my tender blossom—to suffer blight and mildew! Mary! I'll go directly to the manor-house; his father's in the commission. I mayn't find justice, but I shall find a justice of peace.

DENNIS. Fie now! and can't you listen to reason?

JOB. Reason! Tell me a reason why a father shouldn't be almost mad, when his patron has ruined his child? Damn his protection! Tell me a reason why a man of birth's seducing my daughter doesn't almost double the rascality? Yes, double it—for my fine gentleman, at the very time he is laying his plans to make her infamous, would think himself disgraced in making her the honest reparation she might find from one of her equals!

DENNIS. Arrah, be asy now, Mr. Thornberry.

JOB. And this spark, forsooth, is now canvassing the county, but if I don't give him his own at the hustings! How dare a man set himself up for a guardian of his neighbour's rights, who has robbed his neighbour of his dearest comforts? How dare a seducer come into freeholders' houses and have the impudence to say, send me up to London as your representative? Mary!

Enter MARY, *from the house.*

MARY. Did you call, my dear father?

JOB. [*Passionately.*] Yes, I did call.

DENNIS. Don't you frighten that poor young crature!

MARY. Oh, dear, what has happened? You are angry, very angry. I hope it isn't with me. If it is, I have no reason to complain.

JOB. [*Softened, and folding her in his arms.*] My poor, dear child! I forgive you twenty times more now than I did before.

MARY. Do you, my dear father?

JOB. Yes, for there's twenty times more excuse for you when rank and education have helped a scoundrel to dazzle you. [*Taking her hand.*] Come.

MARY. Come! Where?

JOB. [*Impatiently.*] To the manor-house with me, directly.

MARY. To the manor-house! Oh, my dear father, think of what you are doing—think of me!

JOB. Of you? I think of nothing else. I'll see you righted. Don't be terrified, child—damn it, you know I doat on you; but we are all equals in the eye of the law, and rot me if I won't make a baronet's son shake in his shoes for betraying a brazier's daughter. Come, love, come!   [*Exeunt* JOB *and* MARY.

DENNIS. There'll be a big botheration at the manor-house. My customers are all gone that I was to entertain; nobody's left but my lambkin, who don't entertain me. Sir Simon's butler gives good Madeira; so I'm off after the rest, and the Red Cow and Mother Brulgruddery may take care of one another.

                                        [*Exit.*

SCENE II. *A Hall at* SIR SIMON ROCHDALE'S.

Enter SIR SIMON ROCHDALE *and* FRANK ROCHDALE,
severally.

SIR SIMON. Why, Frank, I thought you were walking with
Lady Caroline?

FRANK. No, sir.

SIR SIMON. Ha! I wish you would learn some of the gallantries
of the present day from your friend, Tom Shuffleton, but
from being careless of coming up to the fashion, damn it, you
go beyond it; for you neglect a woman three days before
marriage as much as half the Tom Shuffletons three months
after it.

FRANK. As by entering into this marriage, sir, I shall perform
the duties of a son, I hope you will do me the justice to
suppose I shall not be basely negligent as a husband.

SIR SIMON. Frank, you're a fool, and———

Enter a SERVANT.

Well, sir?

SERVANT. A person, Sir Simon, says he wishes to see you on
very urgent business.

SIR SIMON. And I have very urgent business just now with my
steward. Who is the person? How did he come?

SERVANT. On foot, Sir Simon.

SIR SIMON. Oh, let him wait. [*Exit* SERVANT.] At all events,
I can't see this person for these two hours; I wish you would
see him for me.

FRANK. Certainly, sir. [*Aside, going.*] Anything is refuge to me
now from the subject of matrimony.

SIR SIMON. But a word before you go. Damn it, my dear lad,
why can't you perceive I am labouring this marriage for your
good? We shall ennoble the Rochdales; for though my
father, your grandfather, did some service in elections (that
made him a baronet), amassed property, and bought lands
and so on, yet your great-grandfather—come here—[*Half
whispering.*] your great-grandfather was a miller.

FRANK. [*Smiling.*] I shall not respect his memory less, sir, for knowing his occupation.

SIR SIMON. But the world will, you blockhead, and for your sake—for the sake of our posterity, I would cross the cart breed as much as possible by blood; so no more of the miller.

[*Exeunt severally.*

Enter LADY CAROLINE BRAYMORE, *followed by* TOM SHUFFLETON.

SHUFFLETON. 'The time is come for Iphigene to find
          The miracle she wrought upon my mind—'

LADY CAROLINE. Don't talk to me.

SHUFFLETON. 'For now, by love, by force, she shall be mine,
          Or death, if force should fail, shall finish my design.'

LADY CAROLINE. I wish you would finish your nonsense.

SHUFFLETON. Nonsense! 'Tis poetry; somebody told me 'twas written by Dryden.

LADY CAROLINE. Perhaps so; but all poetry is nonsense.

SHUFFLETON. Hear me, then, in prose.

LADY CAROLINE. Psha! that's worse.

SHUFFLETON. Then I must express my meaning in pantomime. Shall I ogle you?

LADY CAROLINE. You are a teazing wretch! I have subjected myself, I find, to very ill treatment in this petty family, and begin to perceive I am a very weak woman.

SHUFFLETON. [*Aside.*] Pretty well for that matter!

LADY CAROLINE. To find myself absolutely avoided by the gentleman I meant to honour with my hand, so pointedly neglected!

SHUFFLETON. I must confess it looks a little like a complete cut.

LADY CAROLINE. And what you told me of the low attachment that——

SHUFFLETON. Nay, my dear Lady Caroline, don't say that I told you more than——

LADY CAROLINE. I won't have it denied, and I'm sure 'tis all true. See here—here's an odious parchment Lord Fitz-Balaam put into my hand in the park. A marriage license, I think he calls it, but if I don't scatter it in a thousand pieces——

SHUFFLETON. [*Preventing her.*] Softly, my dear Lady Caroline! That's a license of marriage, you know; the names are inserted of course. Some of them may be rubbed a little in the carriage, but they may be filled up at pleasure, you know. Frank's my friend; and if he has been negligent I say nothing, but the parson of the parish is as blind as a beetle.

LADY CAROLINE. Now don't you think, Mr. Shuffleton, I am a very ill-used person?

SHUFFLETON. I feel inwardly for you, Lady Caroline, but my friend makes the subject delicate. Let us change it. Did you observe the steeple upon the hill, at the end of the park pales?

LADY CAROLINE. Psha! No.

SHUFFLETON. It belongs to one of the prettiest little village churches you ever saw in your life. Let me show you the inside of the church, Lady Caroline.

LADY CAROLINE. I am almost afraid; for if I should make a rash vow there, what is to become of my Lord Fitz-Balaam?

SHUFFLETON. Oh, that's true—I had forgot his lordship; but as the exigencies of the times demand it, let us hurry the question through the Commons, and when it has passed, with such strong independent interest on our side, it will hardly be thrown out by the peerage.　　　　　　　　　　[*Exeunt.*

ACT V

SCENE I. *A Hall in the Manor-House—voices are heard wrangling without.*

JOB. [*Without.*] I will see Sir Simon!

SIMON. [*Without.*] You can't see Sir Simon!

Enter JOB THORNBERRY, MARY, *and* SIMON.

JOB. Don't tell me! I come upon justice business!

SIMON. Sir Simon be a gentleman justice.

JOB. If the justice allows all his servants to be as saucy as you, I can't say much for the gentleman.

SIMON. But these ben't his hours.

JOB. Hours for justice! I thought one of the blessings of an Englishman was to find justice at any time.

MARY. Pray don't be so——

JOB. Hold your tongue, child! What are his hours?

SIMON. Why, from twelve to two.

JOB. Two hours out of four-and-twenty! I hope all that belong to law are a little quicker than his worship; if not, when a case wants immediate remedy, it's just eleven to one against us. Don't you know me?

SIMON. Na.

JOB. I'm sure I have seen you in Penzance.

SIMON. My wife ha' got a chandler's shop there.

JOB. Haven't you heard we've a fire engine in the church?

SIMON. What o' that?

JOB. Suppose your wife's shop was in flames, and all her bacon and farthing candles frying?

SIMON. And what then?

JOB. Why then, while the house was burning, you'd run to the church for the engine. Shouldn't you think it plaguy hard if the sexton said, 'Call for it to-morrow, between twelve and two?'

SIMON. That be neither here nor there.

JOB. Isn't it? [*Menacing.*] Then do you see this stick?

SIMON. Psha, you be a foolish old fellow!

JOB. Why, that's true. Every now and then a jack-in-office like you provokes a man to forget his years. The cudgel is a stout one, and some'at like your master's justice—'tis a good weapon in weak hands, and that's the way many a rogue escapes a good dressing. What! You are laughing at it?

SIMON. Ees.

JOB. Ees! You Cornish baboon in a laced livery! Here's something to make you grin more. [*Holding up a half-crown between his finger and thumb.*] Here's half-a-crown.

SIMON. [*Laughing.*] He! he!

JOB. He! he! Damn your Land's End chops! 'Tis to get me to your master; but before you have it, though he keeps a gentleman-justice-shop, I shall make free to ring it on his counter. [*Throwing it on the floor.*] There, pick it up! [SIMON *picks up the money.*] I am afraid you are not the first underling that has stooped to pocket a bribe before he'd do his duty. Now, tell the gentleman-justice I want to see him.

SIMON. I'll try what I can do for you.   [*Exit.*

JOB. What makes you tremble so, Mary?

MARY. I can't help it; I wish I could persuade you to go back again.

JOB. I'll stay till the roof falls, but I'll see some of 'em.

MARY. Indeed, you don't know how you terrify me. But if you go to Sir Simon, you'll leave me here in the hall; you won't make me go with you, father?

JOB. Not take you with me? I'll go with my wrongs in my hand, and make him blush for his son.

MARY. I hope you'll think better of it.

JOB. Why?

MARY. Because, when you came to talk, I should sink with shame if he said anything to you that might—that——

JOB. Might what?

MARY. [*Sighing, and hanging down her head.*] Make you blush for your daughter.

JOB. I won't have you waiting like a petitioner in this hall, when you come to be righted—no, no!

MARY. You wouldn't have refused me anything once, but I know I have lost your esteem now.

JOB. Lost! Forgive is forgive, all the world over. You know, Mary, I have forgiven you; and making it up by halves is making myself a brass tea-kettle, warm one minute, cold the next, smooth without and hollow within.

MARY. Then pray don't deny me! I'm sure you wouldn't if you knew half I am suffering.

JOB. Do as you like, Mary, only never tell me again you have lost my esteem; it looks like suspicion o' both sides. Never say that, and I can deny you nothing in reason, or perhaps a little beyond it.

Re-enter SIMON.

Well, will the justice do a man the favour to do his duty? Will he see me?

SIMON. Come into the room next his libery. A stranger who's with young master ha' been waiting for un longer nor you, but I'll get you in first.

JOB. I don't know that that's quite fair to the other.

SIMON. Ees it be, for t'other didn't gi' I half-a-crown.

JOB. Then stay till I come back, Mary. I see, my man, when you take a bribe, you are scrupulous enough to do your work for it; for which, I hope, somebody may duck you with one hand and rub you dry with the other.   [*Exeunt* JOB *and* SIMON.

MARY. I wished to come to this house in the morning, and now I would give the world to be out of it. Hark, here's somebody! Oh, mercy on me, 'tis he himself! What will become of me?
                                              [*Retires up.*

Enter FRANK ROCHDALE.

FRANK. My father, then, shall see this visitor, whatever be the event. I will prepare him for the interview, and—[*Seeing* MARY.] Good heaven! Why—why are you here?

MARY. [*Advancing to him eagerly.*] I don't come willingly to trouble you; I don't, indeed!

FRANK. What motive, Mary, has brought you to this house, and who is the stranger under whose protection you have placed yourself, at the house on the heath? Surely you cannot love him!

MARY. I hope I do.

FRANK. You hope you do!

MARY. Yes; for I think he saved my life this morning, when I was struggling with the robber who threatened to kill me.

FRANK. And had you taken no guide with you, Mary, no protector?

MARY. I was thinking too much of one who promised to be my protector always, to think of any other.

FRANK. Mary, I—I—'twas I then, it seems, who brought your life into such hazard.

MARY. I hope I haven't said anything to make you unhappy.

FRANK. Nothing, my dearest Mary, nothing! I know it is not in your nature even to whisper a reproof. Yet I sent a friend, with full power from me, to give you the amplest protection.

MARY. I know you did, and he gave me a letter that I might be protected when I got to London.

FRANK. Why then commit yourself to the care of a stranger?

MARY. Because the stranger read the direction of the letter—here it is—[*Taking it from her pocket.*] and said your friend was treacherous.

FRANK. [*Looking at the letter.*] Villain!

MARY. Did he intend to lead me into a snare, then?

FRANK. Let me keep this letter. I may have been deceived in the person I sent to you, but—[*Aside.*] damn his rascality! But could you think me base enough to leave you unsheltered? I had torn you from your home—with anguish I confess it—but I would have provided you another home, which want should not have assailed. Would this stranger bring you better comfort?

MARY. Oh, yes, he has; he has brought me my father.

FRANK. Your father! From whom I made you fly!

MARY. Yes; he has brought a father to his child that she might kiss off the tears her disobedience had forced down his aged cheeks, and restored me to the only home which could give me any comfort now. And my father is here.

FRANK. Here!

MARY. Indeed, I couldn't help his coming, and he made me come with him.

FRANK. I—I am almost glad, Mary, that it has happened.

MARY. Are you?

FRANK. Yes: when a weight of concealment is on the mind, remorse is relieved by the very discovery which it has dreaded. But you must not be waiting here, Mary. There is one in the house to whose care I will entrust you.

MARY. I hope it isn't the person you sent to me to-day.

FRANK. He! I would sooner cradle infancy with serpents! Yet this is my friend! I will now confide in a stranger—the stranger, Mary, who saved your life.

MARY. Is he here?

FRANK. He is. Oh, Mary, how painful if, performing the duty of a son, I must abandon at last the expiation of a penitent! But so dependent on each other are the delicate combinations of probity, that one broken link perplexes the whole chain, and an abstracted virtue becomes a relative iniquity.   [*Exeunt.*

SCENE II. *The Library in the Manor-House—table and chairs,* C.

SIR SIMON ROCHDALE *and* MR. PENNYMAN, *his steward, discovered at the table.* JOB THORNBERRY *standing at a little distance from them.*

SIR SIMON. Remember, the money must be ready tomorrow, Mr. Pennyman.

MR. PENNYMAN. [*Going.*] It shall, Sir Simon.

SIR SIMON. [*To* JOB.] So, friend, your business, you say, is——

and Mr. Pennyman, give Robin Ruddy notice to quit his cottage directly.

MR. PENNYMAN. I am afraid, Sir Simon, if he's turned out it will be his ruin.

SIR SIMON. He should have recollected that before he ruined his neighbour's daughter.

JOB. [*Starting.*] Eh!

SIR SIMON. What's the matter with the man? [*To* PENNYMAN.] His offence is attended with great aggravation. Why doesn't he marry her?

JOB. [*Emphatically.*] Aye!

SIR SIMON. Pray, friend, be quiet.

MR. PENNYMAN. He says it would make her more unfortunate still; he's too necessitous to provide even for the living consequence of his indiscretion.

SIR SIMON. That doubles his crime to the girl. He must quit. I'm a magistrate, you know, Mr. Pennyman, and 'tis my duty to discourage all such immorality.

MR. PENNYMAN. Your orders must be obeyed, Sir Simon.
[*Exit.*

SIR SIMON. Now, yours is justice-business, you say. You come at an irregular time, and I have somebody else waiting for me; so be quick. What brings you here?

JOB. My daughter's seduction, Sir Simon, and it has done my heart good to hear your worship say 'tis your duty to discourage all such immorality.

SIR SIMON. To be sure it is, but men like you shouldn't be too apt to lay hold of every sentiment justice drops, lest you mis-apply it. 'Tis like an officious footman snatching up his mistress's perriwig and clapping it on again, hind part before. What are you?

JOB. A tradesman, Sir Simon. I have been a freeholder in this district for many a year.

SIR SIMON. A freeholder! [*Aside.*] Zounds! One of Frank's voters, perhaps, and of consequence at his election. [*Aloud.*] Won't you, my good friend, take a chair?

JOB. Thank you, Sir Simon; I know my proper place. I didn't come here to sit down with Sir Simon Rochdale because I am a freeholder; I came to demand my right because you are a justice.

SIR SIMON. A man of respectability, a tradesman, and a freeholder, in such a case as yours, had better have recourse to a court of law.

JOB. I am not rich now, Sir Simon, whatever I may have been.

SIR SIMON. A magistrate, honest friend, can't give you damages; you must fee counsel.

JOB. I can't afford an expensive law-suit, Sir Simon; and, begging your pardon, I think the law never intended that an injured man, in middling circumstances, should either go without redress or starve himself to obtain it.

SIR SIMON. Whatever advice I can give you you shall have it for nothing, but I can't jump over justice's hedges and ditches. Courts of law are broad high roads, made for national convenience; if your way lie through them 'tis but fair you should pay the turnpikes. Who is the offender?

JOB. He lives upon your estate, Sir Simon.

SIR SIMON. Oho, a tenant! Then I may carry you through your journey by a short cut. Let him marry your daughter, my honest friend.

JOB. He won't.

SIR SIMON. Why not?

JOB. He's going to marry another.

SIR SIMON. Then he turns out; the rascal shan't disgrace my estate four-and-twenty hours longer! Injure a reputable tradesman, my neighbour—a freeholder! and refuse to—— did you say he was poor?

JOB. No, Sir Simon; and, bye and bye, if you don't stand in his way, he may be very rich.

SIR SIMON. Rich, eh? Why, zounds! is he a gentleman?

JOB. I have answered that question already, Sir Simon.

SIR SIMON. Not that I remember.

JOB. I thought I had been telling you his behaviour.

SIR SIMON. Umph!

JOB. I reckon many of my neighbours honest men, though I can't call them gentlemen, but I reckon no man a gentleman that I can't call honest.

SIR SIMON. Harkye, neighbour: if he's a gentleman (and I have several giddy young tenants with more money than thought), let him give you a good round sum, and there's an end.

JOB. A good round sum! [*Aside.*] Damn me, I shall choke! [*Aloud.*] A ruffian with a crape puts a pistol to my breast and robs me of forty shillings; a scoundrel with a smiling face creeps to my fireside and robs my daughter of her innocence. The judge can't allow restitution to spare the highwayman. Then pray, Sir Simon—I wish to speak humbly—pray don't insult the father by calling money a reparation from the seducer!

SIR SIMON. [*Aside.*] This fellow must be dealt with quietly, I see. [*Aloud.*] Justice, my honest friend, is—is justice. As a magistrate, I make no distinction of persons. Seduction is a heinous offence, and whatever is in my power I——

JOB. The offender is in your power, Sir Simon.

SIR SIMON. Well, well, don't be hasty, and I'll take cognizance of him. We must do things in form, but you mustn't be passionate. [*Going to the table and taking up a pen.*] Come, give me his christian and surname, and I'll see what's to be done for you. Now, what name must I write?

JOB. [*Emphatically.*] Francis Rochdale!

SIR SIMON. [*Dropping the pen, looking at* JOB, *and starting up.*] Damn me, if it isn't the brazier!

JOB. Justice is justice, Sir Simon. I am a respectable tradesman, your neighbour, and a freeholder. Seduction is a heinous offence; a magistrate knows no distinction of persons; and a rascal mustn't disgrace your estate four-and-twenty hours longer.

SIR SIMON. [*Sheepishly.*] I believe your name is Thornberry.

JOB. It is, Sir Simon. I never blushed at my name till your son made me blush for yours.

SIR SIMON. Mr. Thornberry, I—I heard something of my son's—a—little indiscretion some mornings ago.

JOB. Did you, Sir Simon? You never sent to me about it; so I suppose the news reached you at one of the hours you don't set apart for justice.

SIR SIMON. This is a—a very awkward business, Mr. Thornberry, something like a hump back—we can never set it quite straight; so we must bolster it.

JOB. How do you mean, Sir Simon?

SIR SIMON. Why, 'tis a disagreeable affair, and—we—we must hush it up.

JOB. Hush it up! A justice compound with a father to wink at his child's injuries! If you and I hush it up so, Sir Simon, how shall we hush it up here? [*Striking his breast.*] In one word, will your son marry my daughter?

SIR SIMON. What! My son marry the daughter of a brazier?

JOB. He has ruined the daughter of a brazier. If the best lord in the land degrades himself by a crime, you can't call his atonement for it a condescension.

SIR SIMON. Honest friend, I don't know in what quantities you may sell brass at your shop, but when you come abroad, and ask a baronet to marry his son to your daughter, damn me if you aren't a wholesale dealer!

JOB. And I can't tell, Sir Simon, how you may please to retail justice, but when a customer comes to deal largely with you, damn me if you don't shut up the shop-windows!

SIR SIMON. You are growing saucy. Leave the room, or I shall commit you!

JOB. Commit me! You will please to observe, Sir Simon, I remembered my duty till you forgot yours. You asked me at first to sit down in your presence—I knew better than to do so before a baronet and a justice of the peace. But I lose my respect for my superior in rank when he's so much below my equals in fair dealing; and, since the magistrate has left the chair, [*Slamming the chair into the middle of the room.*] I'll sit down on it. [*Sitting down.*] There! 'Tis fit it should be filled by somebody, and damn me if I leave the house till you redress my daughter, or I shame you all over the county!

SIR SIMON. Why, you impudent mechanic! I shouldn't wonder

if the scoundrel called for my clerk and signed my mittimus. [*Ringing the bell.*] Fellow, get out of that chair!

JOB. I shan't stir. If you want to sit down, take another. This is the chair of justice: it's the most uneasy for you of any in the room.

Enter SIMON.

SIR SIMON. Tell Mr. Rochdale to come to me directly.

SIMON. Ees, Sir Simon. [*Seeing* JOB.] He! he!

SIR SIMON. Don't stand grinning, you booby, but go.

SIMON. Ees, Sir Simon. He! he! [*Exit, laughing.*

JOB. [*Reaching a book from the table.*] 'Burn's Justice!'

SIR SIMON. And how dare you take it up?

JOB. Because you have laid it down. Read it a little better, and then I may respect you more. [*Throwing it on the floor.*] There it is!

Enter FRANK ROCHDALE, *followed by* PEREGRINE.

SIR SIMON. So, sir, prettily I am insulted on your account!

FRANK. Good heaven, sir! What is the matter?

SIR SIMON. The matter! [*Pointing to* JOB.] Lug that old bundle of brass out of my chair directly.
[FRANK *casts his eyes on* JOB, *then on the ground, and stands abashed.*

JOB. He dare as soon jump into one of your tin mines. Brass! There is no baser metal than hypocrisy. He came with that false coin to my shop, and it passed, but see how conscience nails him to the spot now!

FRANK. [*To* SIR SIMON.] Sir, I came to explain all.

SIR SIMON. Sir, you must be aware that all is explained already. You provoke a brazier almost to knock me down, and bring me news of it when he is fixed as tight in my study as a copper in my kitchen.

FRANK. [*Advancing to* JOB.] Mr. Thornberry, I——

JOB. Keep your distance! I'm an old fellow; but if my daughter's seducer comes near me, I'll beat him as flat as a stew-pan!

FRANK. [*Still advancing.*] Suffer me to speak, and——

JOB. [*Rising from his chair, and holding up his cane.*] Come an inch nearer, and I'll be as good as my word!

PEREGRINE. [*Advancing.*] Hold!

JOB. Eh? you here! Then I have some chance, perhaps, of getting righted at last.

PEREGRINE. Do not permit passion to weaken that chance.

JOB. Oh, plague! You don't know—I wasn't violent till——

PEREGRINE. Nay, nay; cease to grasp that cane. While we are so conspicuously blessed with laws to chastise a culprit, the mace of justice is the only proper weapon for the injured. Let me talk with you.   [PEREGRINE *and* JOB *retire up.*

SIR SIMON. [*To* FRANK.] Well, sir, who may this last person be, whom you have thought proper should visit me?

FRANK. A stranger in this country, sir, and——

SIR SIMON. And a friend, I perceive, of that old ruffian.

FRANK. I have reason to think, sir, he is a friend to Mr. Thornberry.

SIR SIMON. Sir, I am very much obliged to you. You send a brazier to challenge me, and now I suppose you have brought a travelling tinker for his second. Where does he come from?

FRANK. India, sir. He leaped from the vessel that was foundering on the rocks this morning, and swam to shore.

SIR SIMON. Did he? I wish he had taken the jump with the brazier tied to his neck!

          [PEREGRINE *and* JOB *come forward.*

PEREGRINE. [*Aside to* JOB.] I can discuss it better in your absence. Be near with Mary: should the issue be favourable, I will call you.

JOB. [*Aside to* PEREGRINE.] Well, well, I will; you have a better head at it than I. Justice! Oh, if I was Lord Chancellor, I'd knock all the family down with the mace in a minute!
          [*Exit.*

PEREGRINE. Suffer me to say a few words, Sir Simon Rochdale, in behalf of that unhappy man.   [*Points off.*

SIR SIMON. And pray, sir, what privilege have you to interfere in my domestic concerns?

PEREGRINE. None, as it appears abstractedly. Old Thornberry has just deputed me to accommodate his domestic concerns with you; I would willingly not touch upon yours.

SIR SIMON. Pooh, pooh! You can't touch upon one without being impertinent about the other.

PEREGRINE. Have the candour to suppose, Sir Simon, that I mean no disrespect to your house. Although I may stickle lustily with you in the cause of an aggrieved man, believe me, early habits have taught me to be anxious for the prosperity of the Rochdales.

SIR SIMON. Early habits!

PEREGRINE. I happened to be born on your estate, Sir Simon, and have obligations to some part of your family.

SIR SIMON. Then, upon my soul, you have chosen a pretty way to repay them!

PEREGRINE. I know no better way of repaying them than by consulting your family honour. In my boyhood, it seemed as if nature had dropped me a kind of infant subject on your father's Cornish territory and the whole pedigree of your house is familiar to me.

SIR SIMON. Is it? [*Aside.*] Confound him, he has heard of the miller! [*Aloud.*] Sir, you may talk this tolerably well, but 'tis my hope—my opinion, I mean—you can't tell who was my grandfather.

PEREGRINE. Whisper the secret to yourself, Sir Simon; and let reason also whisper to you that when honest industry raises a family to opulence and honours, its very original lowness sheds lustre on its elevation; but all its glory fades when it has given a wound and denies a balsam to a man as humble, and as honest, as your own ancestor!

SIR SIMON. But I haven't given the wound! [*To* FRANK.] And why, good sir, won't you be pleased to speak your sentiments?

FRANK. [*Advancing.*] The first are obedience to my father, sir; and if I must proceed, I own that nothing in my mind but the amplest atonement can extinguish true remorse for a cruelty.

SIR SIMON. Ha! In other words, you can't clap an extinguisher upon your feelings without a father-in-law who can sell you one. But Lady Caroline Braymore is your wife, or I am no longer your father.

Enter TOM SHUFFLETON *and* LADY CAROLINE BRAYMORE.

SHUFFLETON. How d'ye do, good folks? How d'ye do?

SIR SIMON. Ha, Lady Caroline! Tom, I have had a little business. The last dinner-bell has rung, Lady Caroline, but I'll attend you directly.

SHUFFLETON. Baronet, I'm afraid we shan't be able to dine with you to-day.

SIR SIMON. Not dine with me!

LADY CAROLINE. No; we are just married.

SIR SIMON. Hell and the devil! Married!

SHUFFLETON. Yes; we are married, and can't stay.

PEREGRINE. [*Aside.*] Then 'tis time to speak to old Thornberry.   [*Exit.*

SIR SIMON. Lady Caroline!

LADY CAROLINE. I lost my appetite in your family this morning, Sir Simon, and have no relish for anything you can have the goodness to offer me.

SHUFFLETON. Don't press us, baronet; that's quite out in the New School.

SIR SIMON. Oh, damn the New School! Who will explain all this mystery?

FRANK. Mr. Shuffleton shall explain it, sir, and other mysteries too.

Enter LORD FITZ-BALAAM.

SIR SIMON. My lord, it is painful to be referred to you, when so much is to be said. What is it all?

LORD FITZ-BALAAM. You are disappointed, Sir Simon, and I am ruined!

SIR SIMON. But my lord——

[SIR SIMON *and* LORD FITZ-BALAAM *retire up.* LADY CAROLINE *throws herself carelessly into a chair.*

SHUFFLETON. [*Advancing to* FRANK.] My dear Frank, I—I have had a devilish deal of trouble in getting this business off your hands; but you see I have done my best for you.

FRANK. For yourself, you mean.

SHUFFLETON. Come, damn it, my good fellow, don't be ungrateful to a friend.

FRANK. Take back this letter of recommendation you wrote for Mary, as a friend. When you assume that name with me, Mr. Shuffleton, for myself I laugh; for you I blush; but for sacred friendship's profanation I grieve!   [*Turns from him.*

SHUFFLETON. That all happens from living so much out of town.

Enter PEREGRINE, JOB THORNBERRY, *and* MARY.

PEREGRINE. Now, Sir Simon, as accident seems to have thwarted a design which probity could never applaud, you may perhaps be inclined to do justice here.

JOB. Justice is all I come for; damn their favours. Cheer up, Mary!

SIR SIMON. [*To* PEREGRINE.] I was in hopes I had got rid of you. You are an orator from the sea-shore, but you must put more pebbles in your mouth before you harangue me into a tea-kettle connexion.

SHUFFLETON. That's my new friend at the Red Cow. He is the new-old *cher ami* to honest tea-kettle's daughter.

FRANK. Your insinuation is false, sir!

SHUFFLETON. [*Advancing towards* FRANK.] False!

LADY CAROLINE. [*Rising, and coming between them.*] Hush, don't quarrel: we are only married to-day.

SHUFFLETON. That's true. I won't do anything to make you unhappy for these three weeks. So, adieu, Sir Simon!
          [*Exeunt* SHUFFLETON *and* LADY CAROLINE.

PEREGRINE. Sir Simon Rochdale, if my oratory fail, and which, indeed, is weak, may interest prevail with you?

SIR SIMON. No: rather than consent, I'd give up every acre of my estate.

PEREGRINE. Your conduct proves you unworthy of your estate; and, unluckily for you, you have roused the indignation of an elder brother, who now stands before you and claims it!

SIR SIMON. Eh? Zounds! Peregrine!

PEREGRINE. I can make my title too good in an instant for you to dispute it. My agent in London has long had documents on the secret he has kept, and several old inhabitants here, I know, are prepared to identify me.

SIR SIMON. I had a run-away brother—a boy that everybody thought dead. How came he not to claim till now?

PEREGRINE. Because, knowing he had given deep cause of offence, he never would have asserted his abandoned right had he not found a brother neglecting what no Englishman should neglect—justice and humanity to his inferiors.

Enter DENNIS BRULGRUDDERY.

DENNIS. Stand asy, all of you, for I've big news for my half-drowned customer. [*Seeing* PEREGRINE.] Och, bless your mug! and is it there you are?

SIR SIMON. What's the matter now?

DENNIS. Hould your tongue, you little man! There's a great post just come to your manor-house, and the Indiaman's worked into port.

JOB. [*To* PEREGRINE.] What, the vessel with all your property?

DENNIS. By all that's amazing, they say you have a hundred thousand pounds in that ship!

PEREGRINE. My losses might have been somewhat more without this recovery. [*To* JOB.] I have entered into a sort of partnership with you, my friend, this morning: how can we dissolve it?

JOB. You are an honest man—so am I; so settle that account as you like.

PEREGRINE. [*Handing* MARY *forward.*] Come forth, then, injured simplicity! Of your own cause you shall be now the arb tress.

MARY. Do not make me speak, sir! I am so humbled—so abashed——

JOB. Nonsense! We are sticking up for right!

PEREGRINE. Will you then speak, Mr. Rochdale?

FRANK. My father is bereft of a fortune, sir; but I must hesitate till his fiat is obtained, as much as if he possessed it.

SIR SIMON. Nay, nay; follow your own inclinations now.

FRANK. May I, sir? Oh, then, let the libertine now make reparation, and claim a wife!

[*Running to* MARY, *and embracing her.*

DENNIS. His wife! Och, what a big dinner we'll have at the Red Cow!

PEREGRINE. [*To* SIR SIMON.] What am I to say, sir?

SIR SIMON. Oh, you are to say what you please.

PEREGRINE. [*To* FRANK *and* MARY.] Then bless you both! And though I have passed so much of my life abroad, English equity, brother, is dear to my heart. Respect the rights of honest John Bull, and our family concerns may be easily arranged.

JOB. That's upright. [*To* FRANK.] I forgive you, young man, for what has passed; but no one deserves forgiveness who refuses to make amends when he has disturbed the happiness of an Englishman's fireside!

EPILOGUE

Since Epilogue-speaking to me is quite new,
Pray, allow me the help of a fiddle or two;
I'm as strange to this job as the Man in the Moon,
But I think if I sing I shall speak to some tune.
                                        Fal de ral.

Now, touching this Comedy, Criticks may say
'Tis a trumpery, Bartlemy-fair kind of play;
It smells, faith, of Smithfield, we all must allow,
For it's all about Bull, and the Scene's the Red Cow.
                                        Fal de ral.

Yet not without moral the Author indites,
For he points to the blessings of Englishmen's rights;
Let a Duke wrong a Brazier—the Barristers all
Know that brass can do wonders in Westminster-hall.
                                        Fal de ral.

But was ever a tale so improbably told,
As Peregrine swimming with large lumps of gold!
Should a man who sinks cash with his cash try to swim,
For a pound to a shilling his cash will sink him.
                                        Fal de ral.

Let us find some excuse for this strange oversight,
Let's suppose that his guineas were most of 'em light;
Nay, the guineas for grappling the Shore he might thank,
'Tis amazing of late how they stick in the Bank.
                                        Fal de ral.

One circumstance keeps probability's law,
A beautiful female commits a *faux-pas*;
That's nature; but Criticks, who don't praise in haste,
Will certainly not call the incident chaste.
                                        Fal de ral.

Now in Art, if not Nature, Tom Shuffleton's found,
He's one of those puppies who better were drown'd;
Of the worst Bond-street litter—such whelps none admire;
Chuck 'em all in the Thames; they won't set it on fire.

Fal de ral.

Mr. Dennis Brulgruddery lives with his dear;
They're in stile, and agree just like thunder and beer;
An Irishman's blunders are pretty well hack't,
But how charmingly, sure, Mr. Johnstone did act!

Fal de ral.

Now I've touch'd on the principal parts of the play:
Shall it run a few nights, or to-night run away?
Your votes, Friends and Criticks, we now rest upon;
They ayes have it, I think—though it mayn't be *nem. con.*

Fal de ral.

Then success to JOHN BULL! Let this toast be his pride,
Bless the King of JOHN BULL, and JOHN BULL's fireside;
At JOHN BULL's fireside, shou'd a foe dare to frown,
May JOHN ne'er want a poker to knock the foe down.

Fal de ral.

APPENDIX

THE ACTING OF EARLY
NINETEENTH-CENTURY COMEDY

CONTEMPORARY critics tended to dislike what seemed to them a
trivial and degraded comedy, but they nearly all recognized the exceptional merit of the actors to whom this comedy was entrusted. The
production of new comedies in the 1790s and the following decade
was dominated by the Covent Garden company; thus most of the
comedies written by Morton, Reynolds, Colman, and their colleagues
were performed at Covent Garden. One of the chief accusations against
them was that they devised characters solely to suit the talents and
idiosyncrasies of individual performers rather than drawing from human
nature; that they fitted parts to actors and not actors to parts. Given
the traditional nature of stock company organization and its division
into lines of business, each one belonging by right to a particular
actor, something of the sort was inevitable. So vigorously, however,
did critics press charges of this kind that obviously they believed
dramatists had gone much further in this direction than theatrical
custom warranted, and had tarnished the drama and the dignity of
authorship by making playwrights mere handservants to the players.
Leigh Hunt complained that 'if any man, not very fond of music, will
reflect a little between the acts of one of the modern comedies, he will
find that his chief entertainment has arisen from the actors totally
abstracted from the author. The phrases, the sentiments, the fancies,
will appear to his reason very monotonous and inefficient when
separated from the grins of MUNDEN and the chatterings of FAWCETT.'
The author went about the business of creating character in a particular way:

His principal design in forming a character is to adapt it to that peculiar
style of the actor, which the huge farces have rendered necessary to their
existence. If there is a countryman, it must be adapted to EMERY; if an
Irishman, to JOHNSTONE; if a gabbling humourist, it must be copied from
nothing but the manner of FAWCETT . . . The loss of LEWIS, for instance,
whose gaiety of limb is of so much benefit to modern comedy, would be
a perfect rheumatism to MR. REYNOLDS; and the loss of MUNDEN, who
gives it such an agreeable variety of grin, would affect him little less than
a lock-jaw.[1]

[1] *Critical Essays on the Performers of the London Theatres*, pp. vi–viii.

An anonymous poem upon the actors of the day made the same point:

> Bards study actors, and not actors them.
> To suit the play'r the drama is design'd,
> And Reynolds copies Munden, not mankind.
> The modern Muse, neglecting ancient grace,
> Adapts her art to medley and grimace.

To this is added a note:

Messrs. Colman and Reynolds, &.c. never consider whether their characters are adapted to the audience; they are satisfied with adapting them to the actor. Hence we seldom see any natural delineation of manners or of habits in our late pieces. Mr. Johnstone, for instance, acts an Irishman only. Mr. Johnstone must also be employed. Hence almost every new comedy has an Irishman in it. If, when Bannister's finger was almost blown off by the explosion of a pistol, his arm had been blown off instead, I will venture to say, that every subsequent comedy wou'd have contained a weather-beaten, one-armed sailor.[1]

What the critics then argued was that because the dramatists provided actors with poor and 'unnatural' material, the latter were forced into 'unnatural' acting in order to make the plays pleasurable for audiences. Almost to a man, they also complained about the size and problems of seeing and hearing in the new and much larger patent houses (Covent Garden was greatly enlarged in 1792 and rebuilt in 1809) and their allegedly deleterious effect upon acting: delicacy, grace, and refinement seemed of little use in theatres where strongly marked and broad styles were most effective. In some respects, then, the content of comedy at this time was probably influenced by the size of theatres. If the first charge were true, it meant of course that acting style perfectly suited dramatic content, but that would not have satisfied hostile critics.

> The play'r, whose fame upon our mirth must lean,
> Unable to extract it from the scene,
> With gestic humour must divert our mind,
> And make the merriment he fails to find;
> Deform his features, shrug, and strut, and strain;
> Because his empty author lacks a brain.
> If plays want pathos, nature, humour, wit,
> What but grimace remains to charm the Pit?[2]

Leigh Hunt, whose main targets in this area were the writing of Reynolds and the acting of Munden, was concerned about the extension of this acting style into better drama than the comedies of Reynolds to which it should properly be confined:

---

[1] *The Thespiad* (1809), p. 10.   [2] Ibid., p. 41.

If the principal characters of REYNOLDS and DIBDIN are always out of nature, their representation . . . must be unnatural also; and as our comic actors are perpetually employed upon these punchinellos, as they are always labouring to grimace and grin them into applause, they become habituated and even partial to their antics, and can never afterwards separate the effect from the means; the applause from the unnatural style of acting. The extravagance therefore of look and gesture, so necessary to the caricatures of our farci-comic writers, they cannot help carrying into the characters of our best dramatists, to which it is every way injurious.[1]

Whatever the merits of the case against the authors and actors of comedy, there is little doubt that not only did dramatists like Reynolds and Colman construct their plays around an experienced and brilliant ensemble of comedians—with no one star to dominate the others and require a disproportionately large part for himself—but also that this method of construction was necessary for the success of the plays. To give the pathetic and potentially tragic portions dramatic power was important; the fact that the serious characters were played by actors with little or no talent for comedy was not at all stylistically inharmonious, since the dramatic element of this kind of comedy was usually quite separate from the comic. Several actresses played the stock loving daughter and distraught heroine; Charles Kemble or Henry Johnston was perfectly suited to romantic, manly young heroes; gloomy, proud, bitter, and passionate gentlemen with mysterious and dreadful pasts were specially designed for John Philip Kemble or George Frederick Cooke. The necessary comic balance was provided, in play after play, by Joseph Munden as the blustery and elderly eccentric; by John Emery (and later John Liston) as the low-comedy provincial, farmer, or servant from the country; by William Lewis as the feverishly active and erratic fop; by Jack Johnstone as the rough and shrewd Irishman with a heart of gold (with virtually all characters possessing hearts of gold, this is scarcely a distinguishing characteristic); by Isabella Mattocks or Mary Ann Davenport as the shrewish and affected widow or spinster with a sharp tongue and mildly villainous tendencies. This list is by no means complete for a company at the height of its comic powers for twenty years; additionally, smaller parts were competently filled by minor players. Unless our imaginations are extraordinarily recreative, we have in the reading of these plays little sense of the wonderful mastery of an individual comic style that each leading performer brought to his or her part, or of the total effect of ensemble. That the results were superb was admitted even by the enemies of both the playwrights and the alleged excesses of style. Even Leigh Hunt, diligently fulfilling his

[1] *Critical Essays on the Performers of the London Theatres*, p. 81.

self-appointed role as castigator of 'the barbarities of modern comedy', admitted reluctantly that examples of the best acting could be drawn from the worst plays, and when he considered individual performers was frequently lavish with his praise. Admiration for the acting and condemnation of the comedy was standard critical posture.

To give an impression of this acting, and to place a comedy like *John Bull* in some sort of stage context, it may be helpful to refer to contemporary observations of actors who played in it (by common consent, *John Bull* was 'gloriously acted'),[1] such as Lewis and Emery, comedians whose domination of their own lines of business was unchallenged in their day. After Lewis retired from the stage in 1809 Reynolds wrote no more comedies, possibly because there was no one like Lewis to play the rattling fops and impetuous eccentrics who were such an important aspect of Reynolds's comic appeal. The first Covent Garden cast of *John Bull* was considered a superb ensemble; the only substitutes as good as or better than their originals were Tyrone Power in Dennis Brulgruddery and John Bannister, whose Job Thornberry Leigh Hunt much admired:

There is a vulgarity about the man, but it renders his grief more natural; his thoughts, unrestrained by refinement, suggest no concealment of emotion, and therefore he is loud and bitter in his sorrow. This abandonment to his feelings, acting upon manners naturally coarse, produces now and then a kind of awkward pathetic, at which we cannot but smile: the actor's skill, therefore, should prevent the pathetic from degenerating into a mere laughable eccentricity; it should interest our feeling while it provokes our risibility; in short it should depress while it enlivens and enliven while it depresses. This union of opposite effects requires some portion of tragic as well as comic powers, and BANNISTER's *Job Thornberry* is respected with all its bluntness, and pitied with all its oddity; the tears and the smiles of his audience break out together, and sorrow and mirth are united. When the spectators are inclined to be merry, he recalls their sympathy with some look or gesture of manly sorrow; when they are fixed on his grief, he strikes out their smiles by some rapid touch of peevish impatience or some whimpering turn of voice.[2]

Hunt considered Bannister superior in this role to Fawcett, its creator:

MR. FAWCETT makes vulgarity predominate over feeling and is unintentionally ludicrous when he should be entirely pathetic: when BANNISTER undertook the part he exhibited a new alternation of the humourous and pathetic; MR. FAWCETT's grief is ludicrous in itself, MR. BANNISTER's in its alteration to peevishness or obstinacy. MR. FAWCETT blubbers when he should weep, since it does not follow, that when a brazier weeps we should discover his profession by his mode of weeping, for sorrow can

---

[1] James Boaden, *Memoirs of John Philip Kemble* (1825), iii. 342.
[2] *Critical Essays on the Performers of the London Theatres*, pp. 71–2.

sometimes throw an air of refinement even on vulgarity: MR. BANNISTER knows this, and gains the respect of his audience by a manly sorrow. MR. FAWCETT in short is pathetic where his author has distributed touches of feeling that the rudest hand cannot efface. MR. BANNISTER gives his author additional feeling as well as additional humour; he holds the sympathy of the audience in the nicest balance, and with a word or a sigh can influence the scale as he pleases.[1]

Leigh Hunt's discriminative powers, detailed perception, and deep interest in the comic as well as the tragic stage, make him an invaluable source for material on the acting of comedy. An extended description of the countrymen of Emery is relevant here, not only because Emery played Dan in *John Bull*, but also because Hunt comments on two characterizations in plays discussed in the Introduction, Morton's *Speed the Plough* and *The School of Reform*. The description vividly emphasizes what is evident from a perusal of the plays themselves, that the stage rustic could serve pathetic, moral, and sentimental purposes as well as those of low comedy, and thus could be a more complex character than might be initially assumed. It required an actor of Emery's quality to serve all these purposes well:

EMERY's class of rustics may be divided into three parts, the serious, the comic, and the tragi-comic . . . Of that expression which diverts with its manner while it raises a serious impression with its sentiments, and which is therefore so difficult in its complication, MR. EMERY exhibits a powerful instance in the character of *Farmer Ashfield* in *Speed the Plough*. Inferior actors indulge their want of discrimination in representing every countryman as a lounging vulgar boor, for, as they catch externals only, they are obliged to exaggerate them in order to supply the deficiency of a more thorough imitation. MR. EMERY understands all the gradations of rusticity: his *Farmer Ashfield*, though it occasionally raises our mirth by its familiarity and its want of town manners, is manly and attractive of respect: like the master of a family, he always appears attentive to the concerns of those about him, and never breaks out of his natural cares and employments to amuse the audience at the expense of forgetting his character. In an actor who excels chiefly in gross rusticity, this species of refinement might well have set bounds both to his own expectation of variety and to that of the audience; but the play called the *School of Reform* gave new light to his genius, and in the character of the rustic villain *Tyke* he astonished the town by a display of feeling and passion almost amounting to the most thrilling tragedy. His performance in this play I must call tragi-comic, not because he displayed that amalgamation of the humourous and the serious which the word tragi-comedy in our age implies, but because, as its ancient meaning signified, he excelled in alternate scenes of comedy and tragedy. . . . Every tragic effect . . . short as it may be, which is possible to be produced from a vulgar character, MR. EMERY

[1] Ibid., pp. 91–2.

certainly produces from this. *Tyke* is a villainous rustic, who has not sufficient strength of mind to shake off his depraved habits, though he is occasionally agonised by the tortures of conscience. It is in the scene where he describes the agony of his old father, as he stood upon the beach to witness his son's transportation, that he surprised us with this tragic originality. His description of their last adieu, of his parent kneeling to bless him just as the vessel was moving, of his own despair, the blood that seemed to burst from his eyes, and his fall of senselessness to the ground, was given with so unexpected an elevation of manner, so wild an air of wretchedness, and with actions of such pitiable self-abhorrence, that in spite of his country dialect, which he still very naturally preserved, and the utter vulgarity of his personal appearance, the audience on the first night were electrified for the moment with the truest terror and pity. His haggard demeanour and the outcry of his despair live before me at this instant.[1]

Emery's great rival in the part of stage rustics was Liston. When Emery died in 1822, Liston still had fifteen years of acting ahead of him, but their careers in London had overlapped since 1805. Leigh Hunt's comparison of Liston and Emery is instructive, not only in giving further information about the latter, but also in banishing for ever (if the previous description had not) the notion that acting the stage rustic was a stupid, loutish, straw-chewing sort of business:

If our two stage-rustics, EMERY and LISTON, are compared, it will be found that the former is more skilled in the habits and cunning of rusticity, and the latter in its simplicity and ignorance. EMERY has appropriated to himself the dialects and the personal peculiarities of countrymen; LISTON is the rustic merely because nothing so ignorant and so gaping is ever discovered in town. EMERY excels in vain insolence, in the fatigue of comprehending another, and in the meditation of a cunning answer; LISTON in the apparent inability to object, in a hopelessness of perception, and in the fatuity of mere astonishment. Their expression of vanity is in proportion to their expression of ignorance: what is the affectation of superiority in EMERY, becomes an important self-conviction in LISTON. EMERY, full of whim and artifice, is the countryman who has associated with the geniuses of inns, and has preserved his rusticity and his ignorance after acquiring a contempt for both; LISTON is the confirmed, inexperienced, and stupid bumpkin, with all the prejudices of unvaried locality, and with not even sufficient intelligence to imbibe the manner and eccentricities of his neighbours. Upon the whole, LISTON is more dry in his humour, more effective with a little exertion and upon inefficient subjects, and altogether more unaffected; but the greater genius must certainly be allowed to EMERY, who exhibits a more discriminative minuteness and variety of expression, and who excels at once in the habits and the passions of the country.[2]

[1] *Critical Essays on the Performers of the London Theatres*, pp. 106–10.
[2] Ibid., pp. 112–13.

A few years later Hunt was even more convinced that Emery was the better actor:

We used formerly to contrast Mr. Liston and Mr. Emery, chiefly where they came in contact in rustic characters; but there is no real ground for such a comparison. Mr. Emery is an excellent actor, of an entirely different cast; he is not of so genial and comic a nature, and identifies himself in a most remarkable manner with his respective characters, though they are of a confined class, and he ought never to step out of a certain rusticity . . . the countryman at all periods of life, and in all sorts of humours, comic or serious, sullen or good-tempered, placid or full of passion, is exclusively and entirely his. His robust look, his thick, round features, his I-tell-you-what sort of manner, and something altogether between a cunning and clod-hopping air, admirably fit him for his favourite Yorkshire characters; and like several other of our best comedians (which, by the way, is a favourable thing to say of the general sensibility of their countrymen) he unites a considerable feeling of the serious and pathetic with his drollery.[1]

An actor specializing in quite different roles was Lewis, whose Tom Shuffleton in *John Bull* was in his usual line of bustling fops but did not comprehend the careless good-heartedness of other roles. Hunt, though objecting to Lewis's extreme vivacity even in dull speeches and unimportant moments, his extravagance of dress, and his flippancy in serious dialogue with, and gentlemanly address to, the ladies, nevertheless described him as 'without doubt the most complete fop on the stage: he inimitably affects all the laborious carelessness of action, the important indifference of voice, and the natural vacuity of look, that are the only social distinctions of those ineffable animals called loungers.'[2] Hazlitt also had a high opinion of 'the gay, fluttering, hair-brained Lewis':

All life, and fashion, and volubility, and whim; the greatest comic *mannerist* that perhaps ever lived; whose head seemed to be in his heels, and his wit at his fingers' ends; who never let the stage stand still, and made your heart light and your head giddy with his infinite vivacity, and bustle, and hey-dey animal spirits. We wonder how Death ever caught him in his mad, whirling career, or ever fixed his volatile spirit in a dull *caput mortuum* of dust and ashes? Nobody could break open a door, or jump over a table, or scale a ladder, or twirl a cocked hat, or dangle a cane, or play a jockey-nobleman, or a nobleman's jockey, like him.[3]

J. W. Cole, Charles Kean's biographer, remembered Lewis clearly:

Lewis had a natural animation, an overflowing exuberance of spirits, which never tired, and of which modern audiences and actors have not the

[1] *The Examiner*, 29 January 1815.
[2] *Critical Essays on the Performers of the London Theatres*, p. 78.
[3] *The London Magazine*, i (January 1820), 66.

most remote conception. Were he suddenly to be produced now, he would be pronounced insufferably extravagant, and set down as a lunatic escaped from Hanwell or Bedlam. We have seen *light comedians . . .* take more time with a sentence than he usually allowed to a scene. The very sound of his voice at the wing, before he entered, was the signal for mirth and increased pulsation, which flagged no more until the curtain fell. He was never quiet for an instant. His speed anticipated the express train and the electric telegraph. He was here, there, and everywhere, in a twinkling, always doing something, and although it must be admitted that he not unfrequently 'o'erstepped the modesty of nature', yet there was a grace and charm in his extravagance, and an epidemic infection in his hilarity, which belonged to himself alone. Long before the audience had time to think whether he was right or wrong, or whether they ought to laugh or appear shocked, he was off to something else, which carried them along with him in spite of themselves, and drowned criticism in a tempestuous whirlwind of applause.[1]

James Boaden, too, praised Lewis but expressed reservations about the contemporary interpretation of the fop. Commenting upon the elegant fop of James William Dodd in the 1780s, Boaden compared him favourably with the modern stage fop (who must have been strongly influenced by Lewis), 'a creature of a different kind—he is pert and volatile, incessantly in action, and becoming risible by awkward gestures and mere grimaces. He has no dignity to keep up; you may laugh, not only at him but in his face. Besides he is usually taken from low life, and is a caricature rather than a character.'[2]

Leigh Hunt, indeed, did not think Lewis entitled to his sobriquet of 'Gentleman', for 'it does not follow that he who never acts vulgarly should always act with refinement.'[3] In Hazlitt's opinion comic acting no longer possessed the same 'gentility' and 'correctness' it had enjoyed before, and it was increasingly difficult for modern actors to present the refinement of the older comedy. Reviewing *The School for Scandal* at Covent Garden in 1815, Hazlitt declared that 'genteel comedy cannot be acted at present', and that he 'never saw a play more completely vulgarized in the acting than this'.[4] Lewis, Hazlitt and Hunt agreed, was without vulgarity, but in this respect he was regarded as exceptional. Many critics complained of the disappearance of fine manners on the stage. For Boaden the portrayal of the fine gentleman of an earlier generation required a skill and polish in formal social technique that had vanished from both daily life and the stage:

The fine gentleman in comedy was then very different from what it has since become—it was regulated by higher manners, and seemed indeed

---

[1] *The Life and Theatrical Times of Charles Kean* (1859), i. 7–8.
[2] *Memoirs of the Life of John Philip Kemble*, i. 55–6.
[3] *Critical Essays on the Performers of the London Theatres*, p. 75.
[4] *The Examiner*, 15 October 1815.

born in polished life and educated in drawing rooms. The dress kept the performer up to the character. It was necessary to wear the sword and to manage it gracefully. As the hair was dressed and powdered, the hat was supported under the arm. The mode of approaching the lady was more respectful; and it required the most delicate address to lead and seat her upon the stage. It will be recollected that ladies wore the hoop, and in all the brilliancy of court dress, appeared very formidable beings. The flippancy of the modern style makes a bow look like a mockery; it does not seem naturally to belong to a man in pantaloons and a plain blue coat, with a white or a black waistcoat. I cannot doubt that what is called genteel comedy, among us, suffers greatly from the comparative undress of our times.[1]

Praising William Smith, the original Charles Surface, Boaden distinguished between the 'manly gaiety' of Smith and the 'frivolity' of modern actors; the Charles Surface of a past age was dead, although 'the moderns give us, very beautifully I admit, a Charles of the *present day*.' For the change from manly gaiety to frivolity, Boaden blamed, in part, 'the alteration of our dress' and 'the consequent familiarity of our manners'.[2]

The acting of early nineteenth-century comedy of course reflected the changes in society that had produced a *John Bull* rather than another *School for Scandal*. The new comedy, increasingly bourgeois in its attitudes and characters, had no significant place for the fine gentleman of a previous age; it was anything but genteel. Neither was the acting, nor could it be. Bustling, extravagant, noisy, emotional, and cut of a coarser cloth than its predecessor, this comedy found superb actors who could perfectly express its style and content. The fact that the quality of the material upon which their talents were exercised was lower than before is no reflection upon them: a new age needed a new comedy, and the actors, in representing the world their dramatists depicted, were only doing their job. In judging that comedy it is impossible to avoid consideration of the performers for whom it was expressly written; the printed word cannot be divorced from the stage that gave it comic meaning, and the seemingly gross defects of the author are transformed by the magic of the theatre into the triumphs and glories of the actor.

[1] *Memoirs of the Life of John Philip Kemble*, i. 51–2.   [2] Ibid., i. 388.

MONEY

A COMEDY IN FIVE ACTS

BY

EDWARD BULWER-LYTTON (1803–1873)

———

First performed at the Haymarket Theatre
8 December 1840

———

CAST

LORD GLOSSMORE	Mr. F. Vining
SIR JOHN VESEY, BART., Knight of the Guelph, F.R.S., F.S.A.	Mr. Strickland
SIR FREDERICK BLOUNT	Mr. W. Lacy
STOUT	Mr. D. Rees
GRAVES	Mr. Webster
EVELYN	Mr. Macready
CAPTAIN DUDLEY SMOOTH	Mr. Wrench
SHARP, the lawyer	Mr. Waldron
TOKE, the butler	Mr. Oxberry
OLD MEMBER	Mr. Willmott
FLAT	Mr. Worrell
GREEN	Mr. F. F. Mathews
FRANTZ, tailor	Mr. O. Smith
TABOURET, upholsterer	Mr. Howe
MACFINCH, jeweller and silversmith	Mr. Gough
MACSTUCCO, architect	Mr. Morgue
KITE, horse-dealer	Mr. Santer
CRIMSON, portrait-painter	Mr. Gallot
GRUB, publisher	Mr. Caulfield
PATENT, coach-builder	Mr. Clark
PAGE, to Sir John	Miss Grove
FOOTMEN	Messrs. Bishop, Green, Ennis &c.

LADY FRANKLIN, half-sister to Sir John   Mrs. Glover
GEORGINA, daughter to Sir John   Miss P. Horton
CLARA DOUGLAS, companion to
    Lady Franklin, cousin to Evelyn   Miss H. Faucit
       Members of the *** Club, Waiters, &c.

SCENE

London, 1840

PREFACE TO *MONEY*

As in his previous plays, *The Duchess de la Vallière* (1837), *The Lady of Lyons* (1838), *Richelieu* (1839) and *The Sea-Captain* (1839), of which the first and last were failures and the other two resounding successes, Bulwer-Lytton collaborated closely with Macready on *Money* (its original title was *Appearances*), and the result was almost as much Macready's work as his own.[1] There is no doubt, however, that in the short time he had been writing plays Bulwer-Lytton had considerably improved his construction and stagecraft; from this point of view *Money* is his most satisfying play. He deliberately set out to make what he believed to be an important contribution to comedy. In letters to Forster he declared his intention to 'restore to the Haymarket . . . its old realm of genteel comedy'[2] and to write a play in a 'new genre' that 'certainly admits stronger and more real grave passions than the comedy of the last century'.[3]

Bulwer-Lytton did not seem to realize that his 'new genre' with strong and grave passions had been the predominant kind of comedy for the first two decades of the century, but this does not detract from the significance of his contribution and its place in the development of nineteenth-century comedy. In *Money* he carried into comedy the themes of class bitterness and the conflict between love and pride that proved so popular when dramatized in *The Lady of Lyons*. Alfred Evelyn, with his powerful sense of humble origins, his antagonism towards a class he deems his oppressors, his desire for revenge, and his rhetorical eloquence on all these subjects, is a reworking in a much more specifically observed social context of Claude Melnotte of *The Lady of Lyons*; the fact that his cup runneth over with the very same abundance of material rewards of wealth, property, and position which are the distinguishing comforts of

---

[1] The extensive and interesting correspondence concerning the plays that passed between Macready and his author, and John Forster also, is fully recorded in Charles H. Shattuck, *Bulwer and Macready* (1958). See Volume One, pp. 237–40 for further comment on Bulwer-Lytton.

[2] *Bulwer and Macready*, p. 165.

[3] Ibid., p. 155.

his class enemies places Evelyn in the same category of success
as Melnotte, morally ambiguous to us perhaps, but not in the
least disturbing to Victorian audiences. Like Melnotte and many
a hero in the Victorian theatre, Evelyn is maritally and socially
acceptable only when he has achieved position and fortune.
Despite the play's satirical treatment of a society that judges
a man by the possession of these things, Evelyn must have
them, surely with the full approval of his creator. Like Melnotte
also, who is supposed to be a peasant but actually gives himself
the education of a Renaissance aristocrat (fencing, dancing,
painting, singing, etc.), Evelyn has a perfectly respectable
social background (his poverty apart) and has gone to university.
Both men are really Victorian gentlemen. Their rapid rise to
wealth and fame did not therefore transgress inviolable class
boundaries, and their achievement was both progressive and
exciting enough to win the approval of middle-class audiences
without being sufficiently revolutionary to frighten them. Both
characters are placed comfortingly within the ambience of
middle-class social ambitions and illusions.[1] The haughty and
class-proud Deschappelles of *The Lady of Lyons* are paralleled
by the much more credible and dramatically alive Veseys; like
M. Deschappelles, Sir John Vesey is quite willing to sell his
daughter to the highest bidder for financial advantage.

Money is significant not only because it combined so well
many of the distinguishing features of earlier comedy—the
mixture of comic, pathetic, and dramatic components in a
framework of rhetorical prose, the presence of eccentric,
'humours' characters, the glowingly idealized heroine, the firm
basis of moral platitude and sentimental indulgence—but also
because of its influence upon subsequent comedy. Its impact was
soon apparent. Boucicault attempted to imitate *Money*'s social
gentility and controlled extravagance of characterization in
London Assurance in 1841, and appropriated the themes of
money and class for *The School for Scheming* in 1847. Later
dramatists, such as Taylor and Robertson, further developed
Money's concerns with class antagonisms and adjustments to
class differences that sometimes had to be made in the interests

---

[1] Thomas Purnell said that Bulwer-Lytton's success was 'due to his ability in
making common-place sentiment agreeable to the common-place mind'. (*Dramatists
of the Present Day* (1871), p. 29.)

of love and social harmony; a comedy like Robertson's *Society* is particularly indebted to *Money* in more respects than these. Indeed, the main themes of *Money*—wealth, class, social ambition, and social pride—became the general subject-matter of so much Victorian comedy that the tracing of influences upon individual plays would be repetitious and pointless. *Money* simultaneously looks back to the old comedy and forward to the new; thus as a transitional play and as an influential one it is probably the most important comedy of the nineteenth century. Although the scenes between Evelyn and Clara, essential to Bulwer-Lytton and at the emotional centre of the play, may weigh heavily upon modern sensibilities, *Money*'s combination of genuine humour, satirical characterization, cutting if unsubtle irony, and comic set-pieces—the reading of the will and the scene in Crockford's club—also makes it one of the best.

Despite his opinion of the worth of the play and its great success, Macready came to dislike the role of Evelyn, considering it an 'ineffective, inferior part'[1] quite subordinate on stage to that of Clara Douglas, in whom Helen Faucit made a considerable impression, especially in the final duet with Evelyn. Under Macready's careful direction *Money* was undoubtedly well performed, with high standards of ensemble, and even minor actors contributed much to its success, an unusual occurrence in a period dominated by stars. With a variety of excellent acting roles, both major and minor, a relatively well-managed plot, and containing many of the vital ingredients of nineteenth-century comic appeal, it is not surprising that *Money* attracted actors and audiences until the end of the century. For the original production and two years' London rights the author received £600 from Webster, the Haymarket manager; the play was performed eighty times in its first season and revived in London by a long succession of stars: Phelps and Mrs. Warner at Sadler's Wells in 1846, the Keans at the Haymarket in 1848, Barry Sullivan and Mrs. Stirling at the same theatre in 1852, George Vandenhoff, Charles Dillon, and Hermann Vezin in the 1850s, Henry Neville and Kate Terry at the Olympic in 1866. The Bancrofts played it three times, at the Prince of Wales's in 1872 and 1875, and at the Haymarket in 1880. It was performed at the Gaiety in 1875,

[1] *The Diaries of William Charles Macready*, ed. William Toynbee (1912), ii. 110.

the Olympic in 1878, the Haymarket in 1879, the Vaudeville in 1882 and 1891, the last major revival being Hare's at the Garrick in 1894, where it achieved 107 performances. Its last appearance in the West End seems to have been at a royal command performance at Drury Lane in 1911, with an all-star cast headed by George Alexander as Evelyn and Irene Vanbrugh as Clara. In the provinces, like any other nineteenth-century hit, *Money* enjoyed an even more extensive life.

From an editorial point of view *Money* is textually complicated, especially in the absence of Macready's promptbook. As with his other plays, the text that Bulwer-Lytton saw through the press was longer than the acting version initially performed. *Money* was first acted on 8 December 1840; as had been his practice with *Richelieu*, its author continued to tinker with the play. On 19 December Macready noted that Bulwer-Lytton had made 'some short cuts';[1] on 23 December 'principal alterations' were submitted, including additions for Glossmore and Stout and two new speeches for Evelyn at the end of Act IV;[2] these were put into effect. On 31 December Bulwer-Lytton hinted that minor changes would be made to 'make the present Plot as clear & tangible as possible'.[3] None of the early editions of *Money* or the play as printed in the *Dramatic Works* (1841) shows these revisions, but the acting editions, all different, undoubtedly incorporate many of them. The text printed here is a conflation of the first edition of 1840; the British Museum copy of the fourth edition of 1840 with manuscript alterations and notes in the author's hand and cuts made by the Haymarket copyist; a copy of the text in the *Dramatic Works*, preserved in the Forster Collection at the Victoria and Albert Museum, containing a considerable number of alterations for the last three acts in Forster's hand, and three acting editions: *French's Acting Edition*, v. 119, *Routledge* (1874), and *Dicks' Standard Plays*, no. 318. Only the first three acts of *Money* are in manuscript in the Lord Chamberlain's collection. Internal evidence suggests that the *Routledge* is the most authentic of the acting editions; that is, closest to the performance text of *Money* as it emerged after much cutting and altering during its first long run at the

[1] Ibid., ii. 111.
[2] *Bulwer and Macready*, p. 186.
[3] Ibid., p. 187.

Haymarket. All the acting editions, however, reflect the increasing tendency to shorten the play still further and eliminate the characters of the tradesmen, whose numbers would put too much of a strain on the resources of a minor provincial or touring company.

ACT I

A drawing-room in SIR JOHN VESEY'S *house; folding-doors* C., *which open on another drawing-room. To the right a table, with newspapers, books, &c.;* L., *a sofa writing-table.*

SIR JOHN, GEORGINA.

SIR JOHN. [*Reading a letter edged with black.*] Yes, he says at two precisely. 'Dear Sir John, as since the death of my sainted Maria'—hum!—that's his wife; she made him a martyr, and now he makes her a saint.

GEORGINA. Well, as since her death—

SIR JOHN. [*Reading.*] 'I have been living in chambers, where I cannot so well invite ladies, you will allow me to bring Mr. Sharp, the lawyer, to read the will of the late Mr. Mordaunt (to which I am appointed executor) at your house—your daughter being the nearest relation. I shall be with you at two precisely. Henry Graves.'

GEORGINA. And you really think I shall be uncle Mordaunt's heiress? And you really think the fortune he made in India is half a million?

SIR JOHN. Ay, I have no doubt you will be the richest heiress in England. But sit down, my dear Georgy. Upon this happy— I mean melancholy occasion, I feel that I may trust you with a secret. You see this fine house—our fine servants—our fine plate—our fine dinners: every one thinks Sir John Vesey a rich man.

GEORGINA. And are you not, papa?

SIR JOHN. Not a bit of it—all humbug, child—all humbug, upon my soul! There are two rules in life—First, men are not valued for what they are, but what they seem to be. Secondly, if you have no merit or money of your own, you must trade on the merits and money of other people. My father got the title by services in the army, and died penniless. On the strength of his services I got a pension of £400 a year; on the strength of £400 a year I took credit for £800; on the strength of £800 a year I married your mother with £10,000; on the strength of £10,000 I took credit for £40,000, and paid Dicky Gossip three guineas a week to go about everywhere calling me 'Stingy Jack!'

GEORGINA. Ha, ha! A disagreeable nickname.

SIR JOHN. But a valuable reputation. When a man is called stingy, it is as much as calling him rich; and when a man's called rich, why, he's a man universally respected. On the strength of my respectability I wheedled a constituency, changed my politics, resigned my seat to a minister, who, to a man of such stake in the country, could offer nothing less in return than a patent office of £2,000 a year. That's the way to succeed in life. Humbug, my dear! All humbug, upon my soul.

GEORGINA. I must say that you——

SIR JOHN. Know the world, to be sure. Now, for your fortune: as I spend more than my income, I can have nothing to leave you; yet even without counting your uncle you have always passed for an heiress on the credit of your expectations from the savings of 'Stingy Jack.' Apropos of a husband: you know we thought of Sir Frederick Blount.

GEORGINA. Ah, papa, he is charming.

SIR JOHN. He was so, my dear, before we knew your poor uncle was dead; but an heiress such as you will be should look out for a duke. Where the deuce is Evelyn this morning?

GEORGINA. I've not seen him, papa. What a strange character he is—so sarcastic; and yet he can be agreeable.

SIR JOHN. A humourist—a cynic! One never knows how to take him. My private secretary, a poor cousin, has not got a shilling, and yet, hang me, if he does not keep us all at a sort of a distance.

GEORGINA. But why do you take him to live with us, papa, since there's no good to be got by it?

SIR JOHN. There you are wrong; he has a great deal of talent: prepares my speeches, writes my pamphlets, looks up my calculations. Besides, he is our cousin—he has no salary;

kindness to a poor relation always tells well in the world, and benevolence is a useful virtue—particularly when you can have it for nothing. With our other cousin, Clara, it was different: her father thought fit to leave me her guardian, though she had not a penny—a mere useless encumbrance. So, you see, I got my half-sister, Lady Franklin, to take her off my hands.

GEORGINA. How much longer is Lady Franklin's visit to be?

SIR JOHN. I don't know, my dear; the longer the better, for her husband left her a good deal of money at her own disposal. Ah, here she comes!

Enter LADY FRANKLIN *and* CLARA.

SIR JOHN. My dear sister, we were just loud in your praises. But how's this? Not in mourning?

LADY FRANKLIN. Why should I go into mourning for a man I never saw?

SIR JOHN. Still, there may be a legacy.

LADY FRANKLIN. Then there'll be less cause for affliction. Ha, ha! My dear Sir John, I'm one of those who think feelings a kind of property, and never take credit for them upon false pretences.

SIR JOHN. [*Aside.*] Very silly woman! But Clara, I see you are more attentive to the proper decorum: yet you are very, very, very distantly connected with the deceased—a third cousin, I think?

CLARA. Mr. Mordaunt once assisted my father, and these poor robes are all the gratitude I can show him.

SIR JOHN. Gratitude! Humph! I am afraid the minx has got expectations.

LADY FRANKLIN. So Mr. Graves is the executor—the will is addressed to him? The same Mr. Graves who is always in black, always lamenting his ill-fortune and his sainted Maria, who led him the life of a dog?

SIR JOHN. The very same. His liveries are black—his carriage is black—he always rides a black galloway—and faith, if he ever marry again, I think he will show his respect to the sainted Maria by marrying a black woman.

LADY FRANKLIN. Ha, ha! We shall see. [*Aside.*] Poor Graves, I always liked him; he made an excellent husband.

Enter EVELYN; *seats himself at table and takes up a book unobserved.*

SIR JOHN. What a crowd of relations this will brings to light! Mr. Stout, the political economist, Lord Glossmore——

LADY FRANKLIN. Whose grandfather kept a pawnbroker's shop, and who accordingly entertains the profoundest contempt for everything popular, parvenu, and plebeian.

SIR JOHN. Sir Frederick Blount——

LADY FRANKLIN. Sir Fwedewick Blount, who objects to the letter R as being too *w*ough, and therefore d*w*ops its acquaintance: one of the new class of prudent young gentlemen, who, not having spirits and constitution for the hearty excesses of their predecessors, entrench themselves in the dignity of a lady-like langour. A man of fashion in the last century was riotous and thoughtless—in this he is tranquil and egotistical. He never does anything that is silly, or says anything that is wise. I beg your pardon, my dear; I believe Sir Frederick is an admirer of yours, provided, on reflection, he does not see 'what harm it could do him' to fall in love with your beauty and expectations. Then, too, our poor cousin the scholar—[CLARA *touches* LADY FRANKLIN *and points to* EVELYN. *All turn and look at him.*] Oh, Mr. Evelyn, there you are!

SIR JOHN. Evelyn—the very person I wanted: where have you been all day? Have you seen to those papers? Have you written my epitaph on poor Mordaunt? Latin, you know. Have you reported my speech at Exeter Hall? Have you looked out the debates on the Customs? And, oh, have you mended up all the old pens in the study?

GEORGINA. And have you brought me the black floss silk? Have you been to Storr's for my ring—and, as we cannot go out on this melancholy occasion, did you call at Hookham's for the last H.B. and the Comic Annual?

LADY FRANKLIN. And did you see what was really the matter with my bay horse? Did you get me the Opera-box? Did you buy my little Charley his peg-top?

EVELYN. [*Always reading.*] Certainly, Paley is right upon that point; for, put the syllogism thus——[*Looking up.*] ma'am—sir—Miss Vesey—you want something of me? Paley observes, that to assist even the undeserving tends to the better regulation of our charitable feelings. No apologies—I am quite at your service.

SIR JOHN. Now he's in one of his humours!

LADY FRANKLIN. You allow him strange liberties, Sir John.

EVELYN. You will be the less surprised at that, madam, when I inform you that Sir John allows me nothing else. I am now about to draw on his benevolence.

LADY FRANKLIN. I beg your pardon, sir, and like your spirit. Sir John, I'm in the way, I see; for I know your benevolence is so delicate that you never allow any one to detect it! [*Exit.*

EVELYN. I could not do your commissions to-day—I have been to visit a poor woman who was my nurse and my mother's last friend. She is very poor, very—sick—dying—and she owes six months' rent.

SIR JOHN. You know I should be most happy to do anything for yourself. But the nurse—[*Aside.*] Some people's nurses are always ill—there are so many impostors about! We'll talk of it to-morrow. This most mournful occasion takes up all my attention. [*Looking at his watch.*] Bless me, so late! I've letters to write, and—none of the pens are mended!   [*Exit.*

GEORGINA. [*Taking out her purse.*] I think I will give it to him—and yet if I don't get the fortune after all! Papa allows me so little! Then I must have those earrings. [*Puts up the purse.*] Mr. Evelyn, what is the address of your nurse?

EVELYN. [*Writes and gives it.*] She has a good heart with all her foibles! Ah, Miss Vesey, if that poor woman had not closed the eyes of my lost mother, Alfred Evelyn would not have been this beggar to your father.

GEORGINA. [*Reading.*] 'Mrs. Stanton, 14, Amos Street, Pentonville.'

> [CLARA *writes down the address as she hears* GEORGINA *read it.*

I will certainly attend to it—[*Aside.*] if I get the fortune.

SIR JOHN. [*Calling without.*] Georgy, I say!

GEORGINA. Yes, papa.   [*Exit.*
   [EVELYN *has seated himself again at the table and leans his*
   face on his hands.

CLARA. His noble spirit bowed to this! Ah, at least here I may
   give him comfort. [*Sits down to write.*] But he will recognize
   my hand.

                     Enter LADY FRANKLIN.

LADY FRANKLIN. [*Looking over her shoulder.*] What bill are
   you paying, Clara? Putting up a bank-note?

CLARA. Hush! O Lady Franklin, you are the kindest of human
   beings. This is for a poor person—I would not have her
   know whence it came, or she would refuse it. Would you?
   No, he knows her handwriting also!

LADY FRANKLIN. Will I—what?—give the money myself?
   With pleasure! Poor Clara—why, this covers all your
   savings—and I am so rich!

CLARA. Nay, I would wish to do all myself. It is a pride—a
   duty; it is a joy, and I have so few joys! But hush! this way.
   [*They retire into the inner room and converse in dumb show.*

EVELYN. And thus must I grind out my life for ever! I am
   ambitious, and Poverty drags me down; I have learning, and
   Poverty makes me the drudge of fools! I love, and Poverty
   stands like a spectre before the altar! But no, no—if, as I
   believe, I am but loved again, I will—will—what?—turn
   opium eater, and dream of the Eden I may never enter.

                     [LADY FRANKLIN *and* CLARA *advance.*

CLARA. But you must be sure that Evelyn never knows that I
   sent this money to his nurse.

LADY FRANKLIN. Never fear, I will get my maid to copy and
   direct this—she writes well, and her hand will never be discovered. I will have it done and sent instantly.   [*Exit.*

                Enter SIR FREDERICK BLOUNT.

BLOUNT. No one in the woom! Oh, Miss Douglas! Pway don't
   let me disturb you. Where is Miss Vesey—Georgina?
                     [*Taking* CLARA's *chair as she rises.*

EVELYN. [*Looking up, gives* CLARA *a chair and re-seats himself.*
   Aside.] Insolent puppy!

CLARA. Shall I tell her you are here, Sir Frederick?

BLOUNT. Not for the world. Vewy pwetty girl, this companion!

CLARA. What did you think of the Panorama the other day, cousin Evelyn?

EVELYN. [*Reading.*]
   'I cannot talk with civet in the room,
    A fine puss gentleman that's all perfume!'
Rather good lines, these.

BLOUNT. Sir!

EVELYN. [*Offering the book.*] Don't you think so? Cowper.

BLOUNT. [*Declining the book.*] Cowper!

EVELYN. Cowper.

BLOUNT. [*Shrugging his shoulders, to* CLARA.] Stwange person, Mr. Evelyn! Quite a chawacter! Indeed the Panowama gives you no idea of Naples—a delightful place. I make it a wule to go there evewy second year—I am vewy fond of twavelling. You'd like Wome—bad inns, but vewy fine wuins; gives you quite a taste for that sort of thing!

EVELYN. [*Reading.*]
   'How much a dunce that has been sent to roam
   Excels a dunce that has been kept at home!'

BLOUNT. Sir!

EVELYN. Cowper.

BLOUNT. [*Aside.*] That fellow Cowper says vewy odd things! Humph! It is beneath me to quawwell. [*Aloud.*] It will not take long to wead the will, I suppose. Poor old Mordaunt—I am his nearest male welation. He was vewy eccentwic. [*Draws his chair nearer.*] By the way, Miss Douglas, did you wemark my cuwicle? It is bwinging cuwicles into fashion. I should be most happy if you will allow me to dwive you out. Nay—nay —I should, upon my word.   [*Trying to take her hand.*]

EVELYN. [*Starting up.*] A wasp, a wasp! Just going to settle. Take care of the wasp, Miss Douglas!

BLOUNT. A wasp! Where? Don't bwing it this way. Some people don't mind them; I've a particular dislike to wasps; they sting damnably!

EVELYN. I beg pardon—it's only a gadfly.

Enter PAGE.

PAGE. Sir John will be happy to see you in his study, Sir Frederick. [*Exit.*

BLOUNT. Vewy well. Upon my word, there is something vewy nice about this girl. To be sure, I love Georgina—but if this one would take a fancy to me. [*Thoughtfully.*] Well, I don't see what harm it could do me! *Au plaisir*! [*Exit.*

EVELYN. Clara!

CLARA. Cousin!

EVELYN. And you too are a dependant!

CLARA. But on Lady Franklin, who seeks to make me forget it.

EVELYN. Ay, but can the world forget it? This insolent condescension—this coxcombry of admiration—more galling than the arrogance of contempt! Look you now: robe Beauty in silk and cashmere—hand Virtue into her chariot—lackey their caprices—wrap them from the winds—fence them round with a golden circle—and Virtue and Beauty are as goddesses both to peasant and to prince. Strip them of the adjuncts—see Beauty and Virtue poor—dependant—solitary—walking the world defenceless! Oh, then the devotion changes its character —the same crowd gather eagerly around—fools—fops— libertines—not to worship at the shrine, but to sacrifice the victim!

CLARA. My cousin, you are cruel! I can smile at the pointless insolence.

EVELYN. Smile—and he took your hand! Oh, Clara, you know not the tortures that I suffer hourly! When others approach you—young—fair—rich—the sleek darlings of the world— I accuse you of your very beauty—I writhe beneath every smile that you bestow. No—speak not! My heart has broken its silence, and you shall hear the rest. For you I have endured the weary bondage of this house—the fool's gibe—the hireling's sneer—the bread purchased by toils that should have led me to loftier ends: yes, to see you—hear you— breathe the same air—be ever at hand—that if others slighted, from one at least you might receive the luxury of respect.

For this—for this I have lingered, suffered, and forborne. Oh, Clara! We are orphans both—friendless both; you are all in the world to me. Turn not away—my very soul speaks in these words—I love you!   [*Kneels.*

CLARA. No—Evelyn—Alfred—no! Say it not; think it not! It were madness.

EVELYN. Madness! Nay, hear me yet. I am poor, penniless— a beggar for bread to a dying servant. True! But I have a heart of iron. I have knowledge—patience—health, and my love for you gives me at last ambition. I have trifled with my own energies till now, for I despised all things till I loved you. With you to toil for—your step to support—your path to smooth—and I—I, poor Alfred Evelyn—promise at last to win for you even fame and fortune! Do not withdraw your hand—this hand—shall it not be mine?

CLARA. Ah, Evelyn! Never—never!

EVELYN. Never!   [*Rises.*

CLARA. Forget this folly; our union is impossible, and to talk of love were to deceive both!

EVELYN. [*Bitterly.*] Because I am poor!

CLARA. And I too! A marriage of privation—of penury—of days that dread the morrow! I have seen such a lot. Never return to this again.

EVELYN. Enough—you are obeyed. I deceived myself—ha, ha! I fancied that I too was loved. I, whose youth is already half gone with care and toil, whose mind is soured—whom nobody can love—who ought to have loved no one!

CLARA. [*Aside.*] And if it were only I to suffer, or perhaps to starve? Oh, what shall I say? [*Aloud.*] Evelyn—cousin.

EVELYN. Madam.

CLARA. Alfred—I—I——

EVELYN. Reject me!

CLARA. Yes! It is past!   [*Exit.*

EVELYN. Let me think. It was yesterday her hand trembled when mine touched it. And the rose I gave her—yes, she pressed her lips to it once when she seemed as if she saw me not. But it was a trap—a trick—for I was as poor then as now. This will be a jest for them all! Well, courage! It is but a poor heart that a coquet's contempt can break!

Enter LORD GLOSSMORE, *preceded by* PAGE.

PAGE. I will tell Sir John, my lord.

[*Exit.* EVELYN *takes up the newspaper.*

GLOSSMORE. The secretary—hum! Fine day, sir; any news from the east?

EVELYN. Yes, all the wise men have gone back there.

SERVANT *announces* STOUT.

GLOSSMORE. Ha, ha! Not all, for here comes Mr. Stout, the great political economist.

Enter STOUT.

STOUT. Good morning, Glossmore.

GLOSSMORE. Glossmore! The parvenu!

STOUT. Afraid I might be late—been detained at the vestry— astonishing how ignorant the English poor are! Took me an hour and a half to beat it into the head of a stupid old widow with nine children that to allow her three shillings a week was against all the rules of public morality!

EVELYN. Excellent—admirable—your hand, sir!

GLOSSMORE. What! you approve such doctrines, Mr. Evelyn? Are old women only fit to be starved?

EVELYN. Starved! Popular delusion! Observe, my lord, to squander money upon those who starve is only to afford encouragement to starvation!

STOUT. A very superior person, that.

GLOSSMORE. Atrocious principles! Give me the good old times when it was the duty of the rich to succour the distressed.

EVELYN. On second thoughts, you are right, my lord. I, too, know a poor woman—ill—dying—in want. Shall she too perish?

GLOSSMORE. Perish! Horrible—in a Christian country! Perish! Heaven forbid!

EVELYN. [*Holding out his hand.*] What then will you give her?

GLOSSMORE. Ehem! Sir—the parish ought to give.

STOUT. By no means!

GLOSSMORE. By all means!

STOUT. No, no, no! Certainly not!

GLOSSMORE. No, no? But I say yes, yes! And if the parish refuse to maintain the poor, the only way left to a man of firmness and resolution, holding the principles that I do, and adhering to the constitution of our fathers, is to force the poor on the parish by never giving them a farthing oneself.

STOUT. No, no, no!

GLOSSMORE. Yes, yes, yes!

EVELYN. Gentlemen, perhaps Sir John will decide.

Enter SIR JOHN, LADY FRANKLIN, GEORGINA, *and* BLOUNT.

SIR JOHN. How d'ye do? Ah, how d'ye do, gentlemen? This is a most melancholy meeting. The poor deceased! What a man he was!

BLOUNT. I was chwistened Fwedewick after him. He was my first cousin.

SIR JOHN. And Georgina his own niece—next of kin. An excellent man, though odd—a kind heart, but no liver. I sent him twice a year thirty dozen of the Cheltenham waters. It's a comfort to reflect on these little attentions at such a time.

STOUT. And I, too, sent him the Parliamentary Debates regularly, bound in calf. He was my second cousin—sensible man—and a follower of Malthus: never married to increase the surplus population and fritter away his money on his own children. And now——

EVELYN. He reaps the benefit of celibacy in the prospective gratitude of every cousin he had in the world!

LADY FRANKLIN. Ha, ha, ha!

SIR JOHN. Hush, hush! Decency, Lady Franklin, decency!

Enter PAGE.

PAGE. Mr. Graves—Mr. Sharp.

SIR JOHN. Oh, here's Mr. Graves; that's Sharp the lawyer, who brought the will from Calcutta.

Enter GRAVES *and* SHARP, *who goes immediately to table and prepares his papers.*

SIR JOHN, GLOSSMORE, BLOUNT, STOUT. [*In chorus.*] Ah, sir —ah, Mr. Graves!

        [GEORGINA *holds her handkerchief to her eyes.*

SIR JOHN. A sad occasion!

GRAVES. But everything in life is sad. Be comforted, Miss Vesey. True, you have lost an uncle; but I—I have lost a wife —such a wife!—the first of her sex—and the second cousin of the defunct. Excuse me, Sir John; at the sight of your mourning my wounds bleed afresh.

Enter SERVANTS, *who hand round wine and sandwiches.*

SIR JOHN. Take some refreshment—a glass of wine.

GRAVES. Thank you. Very fine sherry! Ah, my poor sainted Maria! Sherry was her wine; everything reminds me of Maria! Ah, Lady Franklin; you knew her. Nothing in life can charm me now. [*Aside.*] A monstrous fine woman, that!

SIR JOHN. And now to business. Evelyn, you may retire.

        [*All sit. Exit* SERVANTS; EVELYN *is going.*

SHARP. [*Looking at his notes.*] Evelyn—any relation to Alfred Evelyn?

EVELYN. The same.

SHARP. Cousin to the deceased, seven times removed. Be seated, sir; there may be some legacy, though trifling: all the relations, however distant, should be present.

LADY FRANKLIN. Then Clara is related—I will go for her.

        [*Exit.*

GEORGINA. Ah, Mr. Evelyn; I hope you will come in for something—a few hundreds, or even more.

SIR JOHN. Silence! Hush! Wugh! Ugh! Attention!

Enter LADY FRANKLIN *and* CLARA, *while the lawyer opens the will.*

SHARP. The will is very short—being all personal property. He was a man that always came to the point.

SIR JOHN. I wish there were more like him!

        [*Groans and shakes his head.* CHORUS *groan and shake their heads.*

SHARP. [*Reading.*] 'I, Frederick James Mordaunt, of Calcutta, being at the present date of sound mind, though infirm body, do hereby give, will and bequeath—imprimis, to my second cousin, Benjamin Stout, Esq., of Pall Mall, London—— [STOUT *puts a large silk handkerchief to his eyes.* CHORUS *exhibit lively emotion.*] being the value of the Parliamentary Debates with which he has been pleased to trouble me for some time past—deducting the carriage thereof, which he always forgot to pay—the sum of £14 2s. 4d.'

[STOUT *removes the handkerchief;* CHORUS *breathe more freely.*

STOUT. Eh, what! £14? Oh, hang the old miser!

SIR JOHN. Decency—decency! Proceed, sir. Go on, sir, go on.

SHARP. 'Item. To Sir Frederick Blount, Baronet, my nearest male relative——'   [CHORUS *exhibit lively emotion.*

BLOUNT. Poor old boy!

[GEORGINA *puts her arm over* BLOUNT'*s chair.*

SHARP. 'Being, as I am informed, the best-dressed young gentleman in London, and in testimony to the only merit I ever heard he possessed, the sum of £500 to buy a dressing-case.'

[CHORUS *breathe more freely;* GEORGINA *catches her father's eye, and removes her arm.*

BLOUNT. [*Laughing confusedly.*] Ha, ha, ha! Vewy poor wit—low!—vewy, vewy low!

SIR JOHN. Silence, now, will you?

SHARP. 'Item. To Charles, Lord Glossmore—who asserts that he is my relation—my collection of dried butterflies, and the pedigree of the Mordaunts from the reign of King John.'

[CHORUS *as before.*

GLOSSMORE. Butterflies! Pedigree! I disown the plebeian!

SIR JOHN. [*Angrily.*] Upon my word, this is too revolting! Decency! Go on.

SHARP. 'Item. To Sir John Vesey, Baronet, Knight of the Guelph, F.R.S., F.S.A., &c.——'   [CHORUS *as before.*

SIR JOHN. Hush! Now it is really interesting!

SHARP. 'Who married my sister and who sends me every year the Cheltenham waters, which nearly gave me my death, I bequeath—the empty bottles.'

SIR JOHN. Why, the ungrateful, rascally, old——

LADY FRANKLIN. Decency, Sir John—decency.

CHORUS. Decency, Sir John—decency.

SHARP. 'Item. To Henry Graves, Esq., of the Albany——'

[CHORUS *as before.*

GRAVES. Pooh, gentlemen—my usual luck, not even a ring, I dare swear.

SHARP. 'The sum of £5,000 in the Three per Cents.'

LADY FRANKLIN. I wish you joy!

GRAVES. Joy—pooh! Three per Cents! Funds sure to go! Had it been land, now—though only an acre! Just like my luck.

SHARP. 'Item. To my niece Georgina Vesey——'

[CHORUS *as before.*

SIR JOHN. Ah, now it comes!

SHARP. 'The sum of £10,000 India stock, being, with her father's reputed savings, as much as a single woman ought to possess.'

SIR JOHN. And what the devil, then, does the old fool do with all his money?

LADY FRANKLIN *and* CHORUS. Really, Sir John, this is too revolting. Decency! Hush!

SHARP. 'And, with the aforesaid legacies and exceptions, I do will and bequeath the whole of my fortune, in India stock, Bonds, Exchequer bills, Three per Cents, Consols, and in the Bank of Calcutta (constituting him hereby sole residuary legatee and joint executor with the aforesaid Henry Graves, Esq.), to Alfred Evelyn, now or formerly of Trinity College, Cambridge—

[*All turn to* EVELYN; *universal excitement.* EVELYN *starts up, closes his book, and casts it upon the table.*

Being, I am told, an oddity like myself—the only one of my

relations who never fawned on me; and who, having known privation, may the better employ wealth.'

> [*All rise.* EVELYN *advances, as if in a dream.*

And now, sir, I have only to wish you joy, and give you this letter from the deceased—I believe it is important.

> [*Gives letter to* EVELYN.

EVELYN. Ah, Clara, if you had but loved me!

CLARA. [*Turning away.*] And his wealth, even more than poverty, separates us for ever!

> [*All crowd round to congratulate* EVELYN.

SIR JOHN. [*To* GEORGINA.] Go, child, put a good face on it—he's an immense match! My dear fellow, I wish you joy; you are a great man now—a very great man! I wish you joy.

EVELYN. [*Aside.*] And her voice alone is silent!

GLOSSMORE. If I can be of any use to you——

STOUT. Or I, sir——

BLOUNT. Or I? Shall I put you up at the clubs?

SHARP. You will want a man of business. I transacted all Mr. Mordaunt's affairs.

SIR JOHN. Tush, tush! Mr. Evelyn is at home here—always looked upon him as a son! Nothing in the world we would not do for him! Nothing!

EVELYN. Lend me £10 for my old nurse!

> [CHORUS *put their hands into their pockets.*

ACT II

SCENE I. *An anteroom in* EVELYN's *new house; at one corner, behind a large screen,* SHARP *writing at a desk,* L., *books and parchments before him.* CRIMSON, *the portrait-painter;* GRUB, *the publisher;* MACSTUCCO, *the architect;* TABOURET, *the upholsterer;* MACFINCH, *the silversmith;* PATENT, *the coachmaker;* KITE, *the horse-dealer; and* FRANTZ, *the tailor.* SERVANTS *in livery cross the stage.*

PATENT. [*To* FRANTZ, *showing a drawing.*] Yes, sir; this is the Evelyn vis-à-vis. No one more the fashion than Mr. Evelyn. Money makes the man, sir.

FRANTZ. But de tailor, de schneider, make de gentleman! It is Mr. Frantz of St. James's who take his measure and his cloth, and who make de fine handsome noblemen and gentry, where de faders and de mutters make only de ugly little naked boys!

MACSTUCCO. He's a mon o' teeste, Mr. Evelyn. He taulks o' buying a veela just to pool down and build oop again. Ah, Mr. Macfinch! A design for a piece of pleete, eh?

MACFINCH. [*Showing the drawing.*] Yees, sir; the shield o' Alexander the Great, to hold ices and lemonade! It will coost two thousand poon'!

Enter EVELYN.

EVELYN. A levee, as usual. Good day. Ah, Tabouret, [TABOURET *presents a drawing.*] your designs for the draperies; very well. [*Exit* TABOURET.] And what do you want, Mr. Crimson?

CRIMSON. Sir, if you'd let me take your portrait, it would make my fortune. Every one says you're the finest judge of paintings.

EVELYN. Of paintings! Paintings! Are you sure I'm a judge of paintings?

CRIMSON. Oh, sir, didn't you buy the great Correggio for £4,000.

EVELYN. True—I see. So £4,000 makes me an excellent judge of paintings. I'll call on you, Mr. Crimson,—good day. [*Exit* CRIMSON.] Mr. Grub—oh, you're the publisher who once refused me £5 for my poem? You are right, it was sad doggrel.

GRUB. Doggrel! Mr. Evelyn, it was sublime! But times were bad then.

EVELYN. Very bad times with me.

GRUB. But now, sir, if you will give me the preference, I'll push it, sir—I'll push it! I only publish for poets in high life, sir; and a gentleman of your station ought to be pushed! £500 for the poem, sir!

EVELYN. £500 when I don't want it, where £5 once would have seemed a fortune.
'Now I am rich, what value in the lines!
How the wit brightens—how the sense refines!'

KITE. Thirty young horses from Yorkshire, sir!

PATENT. [*Showing drawing.*] The Evelyn vis-à-vis!

MACFINCH. [*Showing drawing.*] The Evelyn salver!

FRANTZ. [*Opening his bundle, and with dignity.*] Sare, I have brought de coat—de great Evelyn coat.

EVELYN. Oh, go to—that is, go home! Make me as celebrated for vis-à-vis, salvers, furniture, and coats, as I already am for painting, and shortly shall be for poetry. I resign myself to you—go! [*Exeunt* MACFINCH, PATENT, *&c.*

Enter STOUT.

EVELYN. Stout, you look heated!

STOUT. I hear that you have just bought the great Groginhole property.

EVELYN. It is true. Sharp says it's a bargain.

STOUT. Well, my dear friend Hopkins, member for Groginhole, can't live another month—but the interests of mankind forbid regret for individuals. The patriot Popkins intends to start for the borough the instant Hopkins is dead; your interest will secure his election. Now is your time; put yourself forward in the march of enlightenment! By all that is bigoted, here comes Glossmore!

Enter GLOSSMORE; SHARP *still at his desk.*

GLOSSMORE. So lucky to find you at home! Hopkins of Groginhole is not long for this world. Popkins, the brewer, is already canvassing underhand (so very ungentlemanlike!). Keep your interest for young Lord Cipher—a most valuable candidate. This is an awful moment—the constitution depends on his return. Vote for Cipher!

STOUT. Popkins is your man!

EVELYN. [*Musingly*]. Cipher and Popkins—Popkins and Cipher. Enlightenment and Popkins—Cipher and the Constitution. I am puzzled! Stout, I am not known at Groginhole.

STOUT. Your property's known there!

EVELYN. But purity of election—independence of votes——

STOUT. To be sure: Cipher bribes abominably. Frustrate his schemes—preserve the liberties of the borough—turn every man out of his house who votes against enlightenment and Popkins!

EVELYN. Right! Down with those who take the liberty to admire any liberty except our liberty! That is liberty!

GLOSSMORE. Cipher has a stake in the country—will have £50,000 a year. Cipher will never give a vote without considering beforehand how people of £50,000 a year will be affected by the motion.

EVELYN. Right: for as without law there would be no property, so to be the law for property is the only proper property of law. That is law!

STOUT. Popkins is all for economy. There's a sad waste of the public money; they give the Speaker £5,000 a year when I've a brother-in-law who takes the chair at the vestry, and who assures me confidentially he'd consent to be Speaker for half the money!

GLOSSMORE. Enough, Mr. Stout. Mr. Evelyn has too much at stake for a leveller.

STOUT. And too much sense for a bigot.

GLOSSMORE. Bigot, sir?

STOUT. Yes, sir, a bigot!

EVELYN. Mr. Evelyn has no politics at all. Did you ever play at battledore?

STOUT *and* GLOSSMORE. Battledore!

EVELYN. Battledore—that is a contest between two parties; both parties knock about something with singular skill— something is kept up—high—low—here—there—every- where—nowhere! How grave are the players, how anxious the bystanders, how noisy the battledores! But when this something falls to the ground, only fancy—it's nothing but cork and feather! Go, and play by yourselves—I'm no hand at it!

STOUT. [*Aside.*] Sad ignorance! Aristocrat!

GLOSSMORE. Heartless principles! Parvenu!

STOUT. Then you don't go against us? I'll bring Popkins to- morrow.

GLOSSMORE. Keep yourself free till I present Cipher to you.

STOUT. I must go to inquire after Hopkins. The return of Popkins will be an era in history.   [*Exit.*

GLOSSMORE. I must be off to the club—the eyes of the country are upon Groginhole. If Cipher fail, the constitution is gone!
                                                       [*Exit.*

EVELYN. Both sides alike! Money versus Man! Sharp, come here—let me look at you. You are my agent, my lawyer, my man of business. I believe you honest, but what is honesty? Where does it exist—in what part of us?

SHARP. In the heart, I suppose, sir.

EVELYN. Mr. Sharp, it exists in the breeches-pocket! Observe: I lay this piece of yellow earth on the table—I contemplate you both; the man there—the gold here. Now, there is many a man in those streets honest as you are, who moves, thinks, feels and reasons as well as we do; excellent in form— imperishable in soul, who, if his pockets were three days empty, would sell thought, reason, body, and soul too, for that little coin! Is that the fault of the man? No, it is the fault of mankind! God made man; behold what mankind have made a god! When I was poor I hated the world; now I am rich I despise it! Fools—knaves—hypocrites! By the bye, Sharp, send £100 to the poor bricklayer whose house was burned down yesterday——

Enter GRAVES.

Ah, Graves, my dear friend, what a world this is!

GRAVES. It is an atrocious world! But astronomers say that there is a travelling comet which must set it on fire one day, and that's some comfort!

EVELYN. Every hour brings its gloomy lesson—the temper sours—the affections wither—the heart hardens into stone. Zounds, Sharp! what do you stand gaping there for; have you no bowels? Why don't you go and see to the bricklayer?

[*Exit* SHARP.

EVELYN. Graves, of all my new friends—and their name is Legion—you are the only one I esteem; there is sympathy between us—we take the same views of life. I am cordially glad to see you.

GRAVES. [*Groaning.*] Ah, why should you be glad to see a man so miserable?

EVELYN. [*Sighs.*] Because I am miserable myself.

GRAVES. You! Pshaw, you have not been condemned to lose a wife!

EVELYN. But plague on it, man, I may be condemned to take one! Sit down, and listen. I want a confidant. Left fatherless, when yet a boy, my poor mother grudged herself food to give me education. Some one had told her that learning was better than house and land—that's a lie, Graves.

GRAVES. A scandalous lie, Evelyn!

EVELYN. On the strength of that lie I was put to school—sent to college, a sizar. Do you know what a sizar is? In pride he is a gentleman—in knowledge he is a scholar—and he crawls about, amidst gentleman and scholars, with the livery of a pauper on his back. I carried off the great prizes—I became distinguished—I looked to a high degree, leading to a fellowship; that is, an independence for myself—a home for my mother. One day a young lord insulted me—I retorted— he struck me—refused apology—refused redress. I was a sizar, a Pariah, a thing to be struck! Sir, I was at least a man, and I horsewhipped him in the hall before the eyes of the whole College! A few days, and the lord's chastisement was forgotten. The next day the sizar was expelled—the career of a life blasted! That is the difference between rich and poor: it takes a whirlwind to move the one—a breath may uproot the other! I came to London. As long as my mother lived, I had one to toil for; and I did toil—did hope—did struggle to be something yet. She died, and then somehow my spirit broke—I resigned myself to my fate; the Alps above me seemed too high to ascend—I ceased to care what became of me. At last I submitted to be the poor relation—the hanger- on and gentleman-lackey of Sir John Vesey. But I had an object in that—there was one in that house whom I had loved at the first sight.

GRAVES. And were you loved again?

EVELYN. I fancied it, and was deceived. Not an hour before I inherited this mighty wealth I confessed my love and was rejected because I was poor. Now, mark: you remember the letter which Sharp gave me when the will was read?

GRAVES. Perfectly; what were the contents?

EVELYN. After hints, cautions, and admonitions—half in irony, half in earnest—ah, poor Mordaunt had known the world!— it proceeded—but I'll read it to you: 'Having selected you as my heir, because I think money a trust to be placed where it seems likely to be best employed, I now—not impose a condition, but ask a favour. If you have formed no other and insuperable attachment, I could wish to suggest your choice: my two nearest female relations are my niece Georgina and my third cousin, Clara Douglas, the daughter of a once dear friend. If you could see in either of these one whom you could make your wife, such would be a marriage that, if I live long enough to return to England, I would seek to bring about before I die.' My friend, this is not a legal condition—the fortune does not rest on it; yet need I say that my gratitude considers it a moral obligation? Several months have elapsed since thus called upon—I ought now to decide; you hear the names. Clara Douglas is the woman who rejected me!

GRAVES. But now she would accept you.

EVELYN. And do you think I am so base a slave to passion, that I would owe to my gold what was denied to my affection?

GRAVES. But you must choose one, in common gratitude; you ought to do so. Yes, there you are right.

EVELYN. Of the two, then, I would rather marry where I should exact the least. A marriage to which each can bring sober esteem and calm regard may not be happiness, but it may be content. But to marry one whom you could adore, and whose heart is closed to you—to yearn for the treasure, and only to claim the casket—to worship the statue that you never may warm to life—oh! such a marriage would be a hell, the more terrible because Paradise was in sight.

GRAVES. Georgina is pretty, but vain and frivolous. [*Aside.*] But he has no right to be fastidious—he has never known Maria. [*Aloud.*] Yes, my dear friend, now I think on it, you will be as wretched as myself. When you are married we will mingle our groans together!

EVELYN. You may misjudge Georgina: she may have a nobler nature than appears on the surface. On the day, but before the hour in which the will was read, a letter, in a strange or disguised hand, signed 'From an unknown friend to Alfred Evelyn,' and enclosing what to a girl would have been a considerable sum, was sent to a poor woman for whom I had implored charity, and whose address I had only given to Georgina.

GRAVES. Why not assure yourself?

EVELYN. Because I have not dared. For sometimes, even against my reason, I have hoped that it might be Clara! [*Taking a letter from his bosom and looking at it.*] No, I can't recognize the hand. Graves, I detest that girl.

GRAVES. Who? Georgina?

EVELYN. No, Clara! But I've already, thank Heaven, taken some revenge upon her. Come nearer. [*Whispers.*] I've bribed

Sharp to say that Mordaunt's letter to me contained a codicil leaving Clara Douglas £20,000.

GRAVES. And didn't it?

EVELYN. Not a farthing. But I'm glad of it—I've paid the money—she's no more a dependant. No one can insult her now—she owes it all to me, and does not guess it, man—does not guess it! Owes it to me—me, whom she rejected, me, the poor scholar! Ha, ha! There's some spite in that, eh?

GRAVES. You're a fine fellow, Evelyn, and we understand each other. Perhaps Clara may have seen the address and dictated this letter after all.

EVELYN. Do you think so? I'll go to the house this instant!

GRAVES. Eh? Humph! Then I'll go with you. That Lady Franklin is a fine woman! If she were not so gay, I think—I could——

EVELYN. No, no, don't think any such thing; women are even worse than men.

GRAVES. True; to love is a boy's madness!

EVELYN. To feel is to suffer.

GRAVES. To hope is to be deceived.

EVELYN. I have done with romance!

GRAVES. Mine is buried with Maria!

EVELYN. If Clara did but write this——

GRAVES. Make haste, or Lady Franklin will be out! [EVELYN *catches his eye; he changes his tone.*] A vale of tears, a vale of tears!

EVELYN. A vale of tears, indeed!   [*Exeunt.*

Re-enter GRAVES *for his hat.*

GRAVES. And I left my hat behind me! Just like my luck! If I had been bred a hatter, little boys would have come into the world without heads.   [*Exit.*

SCENE II. *Drawing-rooms at* SIR JOHN VESEY'S, *as in Act I.*

LADY FRANKLIN, CLARA.

LADY FRANKLIN. Ha, ha, ha! Talking of marriage, I've certainly made a conquest of Mr. Graves.

CLARA. Mr. Graves! I thought he was inconsolable.

LADY FRANKLIN. For his sainted Maria! Poor man! Not contented with plaguing him while she lived, she must needs haunt him now she is dead.

CLARA. But why does he regret her?

LADY FRANKLIN. Why? Because he has everything to make him happy—easy fortune, good health, respectable character. And since it is his delight to be miserable, he takes the only excuse the world will allow him. For the rest—it's the way with widowers; that is, whenever they mean to marry again. But my dear Clara, you seem absent—pale—unhappy—tears, too?

CLARA. No, no—not tears. No!

LADY FRANKLIN. Ever since Mr. Mordaunt left you £20,000 every one admires you. Sir Frederick is desperately smitten.

CLARA. [*With disdain.*] Sir Frederick!

LADY FRANKLIN. Ah! Clara, be comforted. I know your secret. I am certain that Evelyn loves you.

CLARA. If he did, it is past now. He misconceived me when he was poor; and now he is rich, it is not for me to explain.

Enter SIR JOHN *and turns over the books, &c., on the table, as if to look for the newspaper.*

LADY FRANKLIN. Let me only tell him that you dictated that letter—that you sent that money to his old nurse. Poor Clara, it was your little all. He will then know, at least, if avarice be your sin.

CLARA. He would have guessed it had his love have been like mine.

LADY FRANKLIN. Guessed it—nonsense! The hand-writing unknown to him—every reason to think it came from Georgina.

SIR JOHN. [*Aside.*] Hum! Came from Georgina!

LADY FRANKLIN. Come, let me tell him this. I know the effect it would have upon his choice.

CLARA. Choice! Oh, that humiliating word! No, Lady Franklin, no! Promise me!

LADY FRANKLIN. But——

CLARA. No! Promise—faithfully—sacredly.

LADY FRANKLIN. Well, I promise.

CLARA. Thanks. I—I—forgive me—I am not well. [*Exit.*

LADY FRANKLIN. What fools these girls are! They take as much pains to lose a husband as a poor widow does to get one!

SIR JOHN. Have you seen the Times newspaper? Where the deuce is the newspaper? I can't find the Times newspaper.

LADY FRANKLIN. I think it is in my room. Shall I fetch it?

SIR JOHN. My dear sister—you're the best creature. Do.
                        [*Exit* LADY FRANKLIN.
Ugh! You unnatural conspirator against your own family! What can this letter be? Ah! I recollect something.

Enter GEORGINA.

GEORGINA. Papa, I want——

SIR JOHN. Yes, I know what you want well enough! Tell me, were you aware that Clara had sent money to that old nurse Evelyn bored us about the day of the will?

GEORGINA. No. He gave me the address, and I promised, if——

SIR JOHN. Gave you the address? That's lucky. Hush!

Enter PAGE.

PAGE. Mr. Graves—Mr. Evelyn.   [*Exit.*

Enter GRAVES, EVELYN, *and* LADY FRANKLIN.

LADY FRANKLIN. Here is the newspaper.

GRAVES. Ay—read the newspapers; they'll tell you what this world is made of. Daily calendars of roguery and woe! Here, advertisements from quacks, money-lenders, cheap warehouses, and spotted boys with two heads. So much for dupes and impostors! Turn to the other column—police reports, bankruptcies, swindling, forgery, and a biographical sketch of the snub-nosed man who murdered his own three little cherubs at Pentonville. Do you fancy these but exceptions to the general virtue and health of the nation? Turn to the leading article, and your hair will stand on end at the horrible wickedness or melancholy idiotism of that half the population who think differently from yourself. In my day I have seen already eighteen crises, six annihilations of Agriculture and Commerce, four overthrows of the Church, and three last, final, awful, and irremediable destructions of the entire Constitution. And that's a newspaper!

LADY FRANKLIN. Ha, ha! Your usual vein; always so amusing and good-humoured!

GRAVES. [*Frowning and very angry.*] Ma'am—good-humoured!

LADY FRANKLIN. Ah, you should always wear that agreeable smile; you look so much younger, so much handsomer— when you smile!

GRAVES. [*Softened.*] Ma'am. [*Aside.*] A charming creature, upon my word!

LADY FRANKLIN. You have not seen the last H.B.? It is excellent. I think it might make you laugh. But by the bye, I don't think you can laugh.

GRAVES. Ma'am—I have not laughed since the death of my sainted Ma——

LADY FRANKLIN. Ah! and that spiteful Sir Frederick says you never laugh because——but you'll be angry?

GRAVES. Angry! Pooh! I despise Sir Frederick too much to let anything he says have the smallest influence over me. He says I don't laugh because——

LADY FRANKLIN. You have lost your front teeth.

GRAVES. Lost my front teeth! Upon my word! Ha, ha, ha! That's too good—capital! Ha, ha, ha!   [*Laughing from ear to ear.*

LADY FRANKLIN. Ha, ha, ha!
          [*They retire to the table in the inner drawing-room.*

EVELYN. [*Aside.*] Of course Clara will not appear—avoids me as usual! But what do I care—what is she to me? Nothing!

SIR JOHN. [*To* GEORGINA.] Yes—yes—leave me to manage:
you took his portrait, as I told you?

GEORGINA. Yes—but I could not catch the expression. I got
Clara to touch it up.

SIR JOHN. That girl's always in the way!

PAGE *announces* CAPTAIN DUDLEY SMOOTH.

Enter CAPTAIN DUDLEY SMOOTH.

SMOOTH. Good morning, dear John. Ah, Miss Vesey, you have
no idea of the conquests you made at Almack's last night!

EVELYN. [*Examining him curiously while* SMOOTH *is talking to*
GEORGINA.] And that's the celebrated Dudley Smooth!

SIR JOHN. More commonly called Deadly Smooth! The finest
player at whist, écarté, billiards, chess, and piquet, between
this and the Pyramids. The sweetest manners; always calls
you by your Christian name. But take care how you play at
cards with him.

EVELYN. He does not cheat, I suppose?

SIR JOHN. Hist! No, but he always wins! He's an uncommonly
clever fellow!

EVELYN. Clever? Yes! When a man steals a loaf we cry down
the knavery—when a man diverts his neighbour's mill-
stream to grind his own corn, we cry up the cleverness. And
every one courts Captain Dudley Smooth!

SIR JOHN. Why, who could offend him? The best-bred,
civilest creature—and a dead shot! There is not a cleverer
man in the three kingdoms.

EVELYN. A study, a study; let me examine him! Such men are
living satires on the world.

SMOOTH. [*Passing his arm caressingly over* SIR JOHN's *shoulder.*]
My dear John, how well you are looking! A new lease of
life! Introduce me to Mr. Evelyn.

EVELYN. Sir, it's an honour I've long ardently desired.
[*They bow and shake hands.* PAGE *announces* SIR FREDERICK
BLOUNT.

Enter SIR FREDERICK BLOUNT.

BLOUNT. How d'ye do, Sir John? Ah, Evelyn—I wished so
much to see you.

EVELYN. 'Tis my misfortune to be visible!

BLOUNT. A little this way. You know, perhaps, that I once paid my addwesses to Miss Vesey; but since that vewy eccentwic will Sir John has shuffled me off, and hints at a pwior attachment—[*Aside.*] which I know to be false.

Enter CLARA.

EVELYN. A prior attachment! Ha, Clara! Well, another time, my dear Blount.

BLOUNT. Stay a moment. Why are you in such a howwid hurry? I want you to do me a favour with regard to Miss Douglas.

EVELYN. Miss Douglas!

BLOUNT. It is whispered about that you mean to pwopose to Georgina. Nay, Sir John more than hinted that was her pwior attachment.

EVELYN. Indeed!

BLOUNT. Yes. Now, as you are all in all with the family, if you could say a word for me to Miss Douglas, I don't see what harm it could do me.

EVELYN. 'Sdeath, man, speak for yourself! You are just the sort of man for young ladies to like—they understand you— you're of their own level. Pshaw, you're too modest—you want no mediator!

BLOUNT. My dear fellow, you flatter me. I'm well enough in my way. But you, you know, would cawwy evewything before you—you're so confoundedly wich!

EVELYN. Miss Douglas, what do you think of Sir Frederick Blount? Observe him. He is well dressed—young—tolerably handsome—[BLOUNT *bows*.] bows with an air—has plenty of small talk—every thing to captivate. Yet he thinks that, if he and I were suitors to the same lady, I should be more successful because I am richer. What say you? Is love an auction, and do women's hearts go to the highest bidder?

CLARA. Their hearts? No.

EVELYN. But their hands—yes! You turn away. Ah, you dare not answer that question!

BLOUNT. I wish you would take my opewa-box next Saturday—
'tis the best in the house. I'm not wich, but I spend what
I have on myself. I make it a wule to have everything of
the best in a quiet way. Best opewa-box—best dogs—best
horses—best house of its kind. I want nothing to complete my
establishment but the best wife.

CLARA. [*Abstractedly.*] That will come in good time, Sir
Frederick.

GEORGINA. [*Aside.*] Sir Frederick flirting with Clara? I'll
punish him for his perfidy. You are the last person to talk so,
Mr. Evelyn! You, whose wealth is your smallest attraction;
you, whom every one admires—so witty, such taste, such
talent! Ah, I'm very foolish!

SIR JOHN. [*Clapping him on the shoulder.*] You must not turn
my little girl's head. Oh, you're a sad fellow! Apropos, I must
show you Georgina's last drawings. She has wonderfully
improved since you gave her lessons in perspective.

GEORGINA. No, papa! No, pray no! Nay, don't!

SIR JOHN. Nonsense, child! It's very odd, but she's more afraid
of you than of any one!

SMOOTH. [*To* BLOUNT, *taking snuff.*] He's an excellent father,
our dear John, and supplies the place of a mother to her.
[*Lounges off.*

CLARA. So, so—he loves her then! Misery, misery! But he
shall not perceive it! No, no—I can be proud too. Ha, ha, Sir
Frederick—excellent, excellent! You are so entertaining.

[SIR JOHN *brings a portfolio and places it on the table.*
EVELYN *and* GEORGINA *look over the drawings;* SIR
JOHN *leans over them.* BLOUNT *converses with* CLARA,
EVELYN *watching them.*

EVELYN. Beautiful! A view from Tivoli. (Death! She looks down
while he speaks to her!) Is there a little fault in that colouring?
(She positively blushes!) But this Jupiter is superb. (What a
d——d coxcomb it is!) [*Rising.*] Oh, she certainly loves him.
I too can be loved elsewhere. I too can see smiles and blushes
on the face of another.

GEORGINA. Are you not well?

EVELYN. I beg pardon. Yes, you are indeed improved. Ah, who so accomplished as Miss Vesey? [*Taking up a portrait.*] Why, what is this? My own——

GEORGINA. You must not look at that—you must not, indeed. I did not know it was there.

SIR JOHN. Your own portrait, Evelyn! Why, child, I was not aware you took likenesses; that's something new. Upon my word it's a strong resemblance.

GEORGINA. Oh, no—it does not do him justice. Give it to me. I will tear it. [*Aside.*] That odious Sir Frederick!

EVELYN. Nay, you shall not.
　　　　[CLARA *looks at him reproachfully, and walks aside with* SIR
　　FREDERICK.
But where is the new guitar you meant to buy, Miss Vesey— the one inlaid with tortoise shell? It is nearly a year since you set your heart on it, and I don't see it yet.

SIR JOHN. [*Taking him aside confidentially.*] The guitar—oh, to tell you a secret—she applied the money I gave her for it to a case of charity several months ago—the very day the will was read. I saw the letter lying on the table, with the money in it. Mind, not a word to her—she'd never forgive me!

EVELYN. Letter! Money! What was the name of the person she relieved! Not Stanton?

SIR JOHN. I don't remember, indeed.

EVELYN. [*Taking out letter.*] This is not her hand.

SIR JOHN. No. I observed at the time it was not her hand, but I got out from her that she did not wish the thing to be known, and had employed some one else to copy it. May I see the letter? Yes, I think this is the wording. Still, how did she know Mrs. Stanton's address? You never gave it to me.

EVELYN. I gave it to her, Sir John.

CLARA. [*To* BLOUNT.] Yes, I'll go to the opera if Lady Franklin will. On Saturday, then, Sir Frederick.
　　　　　　　　[BLOUNT *bows to* CLARA *and exit.*

EVELYN. Sir John, to a man like me this simple act of un-ostentatious generosity is worth all the accomplishments in the world. A good heart—a tender disposition—a charity that

shuns the day—a modesty that blushes at its own excellence—
an impulse towards something more divine than Mammon;
such are the true accomplishments which preserve beauty for
ever young. Such I have sought in the partner I would take
for life; such have I found—alas, not where I had dreamed!
Miss Vesey, I will be honest. [GEORGINA *advances.*] I say
then, frankly—[*Raising his voice, as* CLARA *approaches, and
looking fixedly at her.*] I have loved another—deeply—truly—
bitterly—vainly! I cannot offer to you, as I did to her, the fair
first love of the human heart—rich with all its blossoms and
its verdure. But if esteem—if gratitude—if an earnest resolve
to conquer every recollection that would wander from your
image; if these can tempt you to accept my hand and fortune,
my life shall be a study to deserve your confidence.

> [CLARA *stands motionless, clasping her hands and then slowly
> seats herself.*

SIR JOHN. The happiest day of my life!

> [CLARA *falls back in her chair.*

EVELYN. [*Darting forward. Aside.*] She is pale; she faints!
What have I done? Oh, heaven! Clara!

CLARA. [*Rising with a smile.*] Be happy, my cousin—be happy!
Yes, with my whole heart I say it—be happy, Alfred Evelyn!

> [*She sinks again into the chair, overcome by emotion; the rest
> form a picture of consternation and selfish joy.*

ACT III

SCENE I. *The drawing-rooms in* SIR JOHN VESEY'S *house, as before.*

SIR JOHN, GEORGINA.

SIR JOHN. And he has not pressed you to fix the wedding-day?

GEORGINA. No, and since he proposed he comes here so seldom, and seems so gloomy. Heigho! Poor Sir Frederick was twenty times more amusing.

SIR JOHN. But Evelyn is fifty times as rich.

GEORGINA. But do you not fear lest he discover that Clara wrote the letter?

SIR JOHN. No, and I shall get Clara out of the house. But there is something else that makes me very uneasy. You know that no sooner did Evelyn come into possession of his fortune than he launched out in the style of a prince. His house in London is a palace, and he has bought a great estate in the country. Look how he lives! Balls—banquets—fine arts—fiddlers—charities—and the devil to pay!

GEORGINA. But if he can afford it——

SIR JOHN. Oh, so long as he stopped there I had no apprehension, but since he proposed for you he is more extravagant than ever. They say he has taken to gambling and he is always with Captain Smooth. No fortune can stand Deadly Smooth! If he gets into a scrape he may fall off from the settlements. We must press the marriage at once.

GEORGINA. Heigho! Poor Frederick! You don't think he is really attached to Clara?

SIR JOHN. Upon my word I can't say. Put on your bonnet, and come to Storr and Mortimer's to choose the jewels.

GEORGINA. The jewels; yes, the drive will do me good.

SIR JOHN. Tell Clara to come to me.   [*Exit* GEORGINA.

Yes, I must press on this marriage. Georgina has not wit enough to manage him—at least till he's her husband, and then all women find it smooth sailing. This match will make me a man of prodigious importance! I suspect he'll give me up her ten thousand pounds. I can't think of his taking to gambling, for I love him as a son—and I look on his money as my own.

Enter CLARA.

SIR JOHN. Clara, my love!

CLARA. Sir——

SIR JOHN. My dear, what I am going to say may appear a little rude and unkind, but you know my character is frankness. To the point, then: my poor child, I am aware of your attachment to Mr. Evelyn——

CLARA. Sir! My attachment?

SIR JOHN. It is generally remarked. Lady Kind says you are falling away. My poor girl, I pity you—I do, indeed! [CLARA *weeps.*] My dear Clara, don't cry; I would not have said this for the world, if I was not a little anxious about my own girl. Georgina is so unhappy at what every one says of your attachment——

CLARA. Every one? Oh, torture!

SIR JOHN. That it preys on her spirits—it even irritates her temper. In a word, I fear these little jealousies and suspicions will tend to embitter their future union. I'm a father—forgive me.

CLARA. Embitter their union! Oh, never! What would you have me do, sir?

SIR JOHN. Why, you're now independent. Lady Franklin seems resolved to stay in town. You are your own mistress. Mrs. Carlton, aunt to my late wife, is going abroad for a short time, and would be delighted if you would accompany her.

CLARA. It is the very favour I would have asked of you. [*Aside.*] I shall escape at least the struggle and the shame. When does she go?

SIR JOHN. In five days—next Monday. You forgive me?

CLARA. Sir, I thank you.

SIR JOHN. Suppose, then, you write a line to her yourself, and
settle it at once?   [*Takes* CLARA *to table.*

Enter PAGE.

PAGE. The carriage, Sir John; Miss Vesey is quite ready.

SIR JOHN. James, if Mr. Serious, the clergyman, calls, say I'm
gone to the great meeting at Exeter Hall; if Lord Spruce
calls, say you believe I'm gone to the rehearsal of Cinderella.
Oh, and if MacFinch should come—MacFinch, who duns me
three times a week—say I've hurried off to Garraway's to bid
for the great Bulstrode estate. Just put the Duke of Lofty's
card carelessly on the hall table. [*Exit* PAGE.] One must
have a little management in this world. All humbug! All
humbug, upon my soul!   [*Exit.*

CLARA. [*Folding the letter.*] There, it is decided! A few days,
and we are parted for ever—a few weeks, and another will
bear his name—his wife! Oh, happy fate! She will have the
right to say to him—though the whole world should hear
her—'I am thine!' And I embitter their lot—I am the cloud
upon their joyous sunshine! And yet, O Alfred, if she loves
thee—if she knows thee—if she values thee—and, when
thou wrong'st her, if she can forgive, as I do—I can bless her
when far away and join her name in my prayer for thee!

EVELYN. [*Without.*] Miss Vesey just gone? Well, I will write a
line.

Enter EVELYN *preceded by* PAGE, *who exits immediately.*

EVELYN. [*Aside.*] So—Clara! Do not let me disturb you, Miss
Douglas.

CLARA. [*Going.*] Nay, I have done.

EVELYN. I see that my presence is always odious to you; it is a
reason why I come so seldom. But be cheered, madam: I am
here but to fix the day of my marriage, and I shall then go
into the country—till—till—in short, this is the last time my
visit will banish you from the room I enter.

CLARA. [*Aside.*] The last time—and we shall then meet no
more! And to part thus for ever—in scorn—in anger—I
cannot bear it! [*Approaching him.*] Alfred, my cousin, it is

true this may be the last time we shall meet—I have made my arrangements to quit England.

EVELYN. To quit England?

CLARA. But before I go let me thank you for many a past kindness, which it is not for an orphan easily to forget.

EVELYN. [*Mechanically.*] To quit England!

CLARA. Evelyn, now that you are betrothed to another—now, without recurring to the past, something of our old friendship may at least return to us. And if, too, I dared, I have that on my mind which only a friend—a sister—might presume to say to you.

EVELYN. [*Moved.*] Miss Douglas—Clara—if there is aught that I could do—if, while hundreds—strangers, beggars—tell me that I have the power, by opening or shutting this worthless hand, to bid sorrow rejoice, or poverty despair; if—if my life, my heart's blood—could render to you one such service as my gold can give to others—why, speak!—and the past you allude to—yes, even that bitter past—I will cancel and forget.

CLARA. [*Holding out her hand.*] We are friends, then! [EVELYN *takes her hand.*] You are again my cousin, my brother!

EVELYN. [*Dropping her hand.*] Brother! Ah, say on!

CLARA. I speak, then, as a sister—herself weak, inexperienced— might speak to a brother, in whose career she felt the ambition of a man. Oh, Evelyn, when you inherited this vast wealth I pleased myself with imagining how you would wield the power delegated to your hands. I knew your benevolence—your intellect—your genius! I saw before me the noble and bright career open to you at last, and I often thought that in after years, when far away—as I soon shall be—I should hear your name identified, not with what fortune can give the base, but with deeds and ends to which, for the great, fortune is but the instrument. I often thought that I should say to my own heart—weeping proud and delicious tears—'And once this man loved me!'

EVELYN. No more, Clara! Oh, heavens, no more!

CLARA. But has it been so, have you been true to your own self? Pomp—parade—luxuries—pleasures—follies; all these might distinguish others—they do but belie the ambition and the soul of Alfred Evelyn! Oh, pardon me—I am too bold—I pain—I offend you. Ah, I should not have dared thus much had I not thought at times that—that——

EVELYN. That these follies—these vanities—this dalliance with a loftier fate were your own work! You thought that, and you were right. But you—did not you reject me because I was poor? Despise me if you please! My revenge might be unworthy; I wished to show you the luxuries, the gaud, the splendour I thought you prized—to surround with the attributes your sex seems most to value the station that, had you loved me, it would have been yours to command. But vain—vain alike my poverty and my wealth! You loved me not in either, and my fate is sealed!

CLARA. A happy fate, Evelyn! You love!

EVELYN. And at last I am beloved. [*After a pause, and turning to her abruptly.*] Do you doubt it?

CLARA. No, I believe it firmly. And now that there is nothing unkind between us—not even regret—and surely [*with a smile*] not revenge, my cousin, you will rise to your nobler self—and so, farewell! [*Going.*

EVELYN. No; stay—one moment—you still feel interest in my fate! Have I been deceived? Oh, why—why did you spurn the heart whose offerings were lavished at your feet? Could you still—still——? Distraction—I know not what I say: my honour pledged to another—my vows accepted and returned! Go, Clara, it is best so! Yet you will miss some one, perhaps, more than me—some one to whose follies you have been more indulgent—some one to whom you would permit a yet tenderer name than that of brother!

CLARA. [*Aside.*] It will make him, perhaps, happier to think it. Think so, if you will, but part friends.

EVELYN. Friends—and that is all! Look you, this is life! The eyes that charmed away every sorrow—the hand whose lightest touch thrilled to the very core—the presence that, like moonlight, shed its own hallowing beauty over the meanest things: a little while—a year, a month, a day, and we smile that we could dream so idly. All—all—the sweet enchantment, known but once, never to return again, vanished from the world! And the one who forgets the soonest—the one who robs your earth for ever of its summer—comes to you with a careless lip and says, 'Let us part friends!' Go, Clara, go, and be happy if you can!

CLARA. [*Weeps.*] Cruel—cruel—to the last! Heaven forgive you, Alfred!   [*Exit.*

EVELYN. Soft! Let me recall her words, her tones, her looks. Does she love me? There is a voice at my heart which tells me I have been the rash slave of a jealous anger. But I have made my choice—I must abide the issue.

Enter GRAVES, *preceded by* PAGE.

PAGE. Lady Franklin is dressing, sir.

GRAVES. Well, I'll wait. [*Exit* PAGE.] She was worthy to have known the lost Maria! So considerate to ask me hither—not to console me, that is impossible, but to indulge the luxury of woe. It will be a mournful scene. [*Seeing* EVELYN.] Is that you, Evelyn? I have just heard that the borough of Groginhole is vacant at last. Why not stand yourself? With your property you might come in without even a personal canvass.

EVELYN. I, who despise these contests for the colour of a straw? [*Aside.*] And yet Clara spoke of ambition. She would regret me if I could be distinguished——[*Aloud.*] To be sure, after all, Graves, you are right. An Englishman owes something to his country.

GRAVES. He does, indeed! [*Counting on his fingers.*] East winds, fogs, rheumatism, pulmonary complaints, and taxes. Oh, you are a pretty fellow! One morning you tell me you love Clara, or at least detest her, which is the same thing (poor Maria often said she detested me), and that very afternoon you propose to Georgina!

EVELYN. Clara will easily console herself—thanks to Sir Frederick.

GRAVES. Nevertheless, Clara has had the bad taste to refuse an offer from Sir Frederick. I have it from Lady Franklin.

EVELYN. My dear friend—is it possible?

GRAVES. But what then? You must marry Georgina, who, to
believe Lady Franklin, is sincerely attached to—your fortune.
Go and hang yourself, Evelyn; you have been duped by them.

EVELYN. By them—bah! If deceived, I have been my own dupe.
Is it not a strange thing that in matters of reason—of the
arithmetic and logic of life—we are sensible, shrewd, prudent
men? But touch our hearts—move our passions—take us for
an instant from the hard safety of worldly calculation—and
the philosopher is duller than the fool! Duped—if I thought it
—but Georgina?

GRAVES. Plays affection to you in the afternoon, after practising
first with Sir Frederick in the morning.

EVELYN. On your life, sir, be serious: what do you mean?

GRAVES. That in passing this way I see her very often walking
in the square with Sir Frederick.

EVELYN. Ha! say you so?

GRAVES. What then? Man is born to be deceived. You look
nervous—your hand trembles; that comes of gaming. They
say at the clubs that you play deeply.

EVELYN. Ha, ha! Do they say that? A few hundreds lost or won
—a cheap opiate—anything that can lay the memory to
sleep. The poor man drinks and the rich man gambles—the
same motive to both! But you are right—it is a base resource;
I will play no more.

GRAVES. I am delighted to hear it, for your friend Captain
Smooth has ruined half the young heirs in London. Even Sir
John is alarmed. I met him just now in Pall Mall. By the bye,
I forgot—do you bank with Flash, Brisk, Credit, and Co.?

EVELYN. So, Sir John is alarmed. [Aside.] Gulled by this
cogging charlatan? Aha, I may beat him yet at his own
weapons! Humph! Bank with Flash! Why do you ask me?

GRAVES. Because Sir John has just heard that they are in a very
bad way, and begs you to withdraw anything you have in
their hands.

EVELYN. I'll see to it. So Sir John is alarmed at my gambling?

GRAVES. Terribly! He even told me he should go himself to the
club this evening, to watch you.

PLATE 3

Money. Macready as Alfred Evelyn. The Harvard Theatre Collection

EVELYN. To watch me! Good; I will be there.

GRAVES. But you will promise not to play.

EVELYN. Yes—to play. I feel it is impossible to give it up!

GRAVES. No, no! 'Sdeath, man, be as wretched as you please: break your heart, that's nothing, but damme, take care of your pockets!

EVELYN. Hark ye, Graves, if you are right, I will extricate myself yet. The duper shall be duped. In the next twenty-four hours I may win back the happiness of a life. Oh, if this scheme do but succeed!

GRAVES. Scheme! What scheme?

EVELYN. I will be there—I will play with Captain Smooth— I will lose as much as I please—thousands—millions— billions; and if he presume to spy on my losses, hang me if I don't lose Sir John himself into the bargain! [*Going out and returning.*] I am so absent! What was the bank you mentioned? Flash, Brisk, and Credit? Bless me, how unlucky! And it's too late to draw out today. Tell Sir John I'm very much obliged to him, and he'll find me at the club any time before daybreak, hard at work with my friend Smooth!   [*Exit.*

GRAVES. He's certainly crazy, but I don't wonder at it. What the approach of the dog-days is to the canine species, the approach of the honeymoon is to the human race.

Enter SERVANT.

SERVANT. Lady Franklin's compliments—she will see you in the *boudoir*, sir.

GRAVES. In the *boudoir*! Go, go—I'll come directly.
                                        [*Exit* SERVANT.
My heart beats—it must be for grief. Poor Maria! [*Searching his pockets for his handkerchief.*] Not a white one—just like my luck: I call on a lady to talk of the dear departed, and I've nothing about me but a cursed gaudy, flaunting, red, yellow, and blue abomination from India, which it's even indecent for a disconsolate widower to exhibit. Ah! Fortune never ceases to torment the susceptible. The *boudoir*! Ha, ha, the *boudoir*!   [*Exit.*

SCENE II. *A Boudoir in the same house.*

Enter LADY FRANKLIN.

LADY FRANKLIN. I take so much compassion on this poor man, who is determined to make himself wretched, that I am equally determined to make him happy. Well, if my scheme does but succeed, he shall laugh, he shall sing, he shall— mum! here he comes.

Enter GRAVES.

GRAVES. [*Sighing.*] Ah, Lady Franklin!

LADY FRANKLIN. [*Sighing.*] Ah, Mr. Graves! [*They seat themselves.*] Pray excuse me for having kept you so long. Is it not a charming day?

GRAVES. An east wind, ma'am, but nothing comes amiss to you —'tis a happy disposition! Poor Maria! She too was naturally gay.

LADY FRANKLIN. Yes, she was gay. So much life, and a great deal of spirit.

GRAVES. Spirit? Yes! Nothing could master it. She would have her own way! Ah, there was nobody like her!

LADY FRANKLIN. And then, when her spirit was up, she looked so handsome! Her eyes grew so brilliant!

GRAVES. Did not they? Ah, ah! Ha, ha, ha! And do you remember her pretty trick of stamping her foot? The tiniest little foot—I think I see her now. Ah, this conversation is very soothing!

LADY FRANKLIN. How well she acted in your private theatricals!

GRAVES. You remember her Mrs. Oakley, in 'The Jealous Wife?' Ha, ha, how good it was!

LADY FRANKLIN. Ha, ha! Yes, in the very first scene, when she came out with [*Mimicking.*] 'Your unkindness and barbarity will be the death of me!'

GRAVES. No, no, that's not it! More energy. [*Mimicking.*] 'Your unkindness and barbarity will be the DEATH of me.' Ha, ha! I ought to know how she said it, for she used to practise it on me twice a day. Ah, poor dear lamb!   [*Wipes his eyes.*

LADY FRANKLIN. And then she sang so well, was such a composer! What was that little French air she was so fond of?

GRAVES. Ha, ha! Sprightly, was it not? Let me see—let me see.

LADY FRANKLIN. [*Humming.*] Tum ti—ti tum—ti—ti—ti. No, that's not it.

GRAVES. [*Humming.*] Tum ti—ti—tum ti—ti—tum—tum—tum.

LADY FRANKLIN *and* GRAVES. Tum ti—ti—tum ti—ti—tum —tum—tum. Ha, ha!

GRAVES. [*Throwing himself back in his chair.*] Ah, what recollections it revives! It is too affecting.

LADY FRANKLIN. It is affecting, but we are all mortal. [*Sighs.*] And at your Christmas party at Cyprus Lodge, do you remember her dancing the Scotch reel with Captain Macnaughten?

GRAVES. Ha, ha, ha! To be sure—to be sure.

LADY FRANKLIN. Can you think of the step? Somehow thus, was it not?   [*Dancing.*

GRAVES. No—no—quite wrong! Just stand there. Now then. [*Humming the tune.*] La—la-la-la. La-la, &c. [*They dance.*] That's it—excellent—admirable!

LADY FRANKLIN. [*Aside.*] Now it's coming.

Enter SIR JOHN, BLOUNT, *and* GEORGINA; *they stand amazed.*
LADY FRANKLIN *continues to dance.*

GRAVES. Bewitching—irresistible! It's Maria herself that I see before me! Thus—thus—let me clasp——oh, the devil! Just like my luck!
     [*Stopping opposite* SIR JOHN. LADY FRANKLIN *runs off.*

SIR JOHN. Upon my word, Mr. Graves!

GEORGINA *and* BLOUNT. Encore—encore! Bravo—bravo!

GRAVES. It's all a mistake! I—I—Sir John. Lady Franklin, you see—that is to say—I——Sainted Maria! You are spared, at least, this affliction!
          [*Runs off, followed by the others, laughing.*

SCENE III. *The interior of * * * *'s Club, night. Lights, &c.*
Small sofa tables with books, papers, tea, coffee, &c. Several
MEMBERS *grouped by the fireplace: one* MEMBER *with his legs over*
the back of his chair, another with his legs over his table, a third
with his legs on the chimney-piece. L. *and down* C. *an* OLD MEMBER
reading the newspaper, seated by a small round table; R. *a card-*
table, before which CAPTAIN DUDLEY SMOOTH *is seated and*
sipping lemonade. At the bottom of the stage, R., *another card-table.*
              GLOSSMORE *and* STOUT, C.

GLOSSMORE. You don't often come to the club, Stout?

STOUT. No; time is money. An hour spent at a club is un-
    productive capital.

OLD MEMBER. [*Reading the newspaper.*] Waiter! the snuff-box.
                                        [WAITER *brings it.*

GLOSSMORE. So Evelyn has taken to play? I see Deadly
    Smooth, 'hushed in grim repose, awaits his evening prey.'
    Deep work to-night, I suspect, for Smooth is drinking
    lemonade—keeps his head clear—monstrous clever dog!

Enter EVELYN; *salutes and shakes hands with different* MEMBERS.

EVELYN. How d'ye do, Glossmore? How are you, Stout?
    You don't play, I think? Political Economy never plays at
    cards, eh? Never has time for anything more frivolous than
    rents and profits, wages and labour, high prices, and low—
    Corn-Laws, Poor-Laws, tithes, currency—dot-and-go-one—
    rates, puzzles, taxes, riddles, and botheration! Smooth is the
    man. Aha, Smooth. Piquet, eh? You owe me my revenge!
    [MEMBERS *touch each other significantly.* STOUT *walks away*
    with the snuff-box; OLD MEMBER *looks at him savagely.*

SMOOTH. My dear Alfred, anything to oblige.
                        [*They seat themselves.* SMOOTH *deals.*

OLD MEMBER. Waiter! the snuff-box.
    [WAITER *takes it from* STOUT *and brings it back to* OLD
    MEMBER.

                    Enter BLOUNT.

BLOUNT. So! Evelyn at it again—eh, Glossmore?

GLOSSMORE. Yes, Smooth sticks to him like a leech. Clever
    fellow, that Smooth!

SMOOTH. Your point?

EVELYN. Five!

SMOOTH. Not good. Six—sequence—five!

EVELYN. Good!

SMOOTH. Three aces!

EVELYN. Good! [*They continue playing;* EVELYN *deals.*

BLOUNT. Will you make up a wubber?

GLOSSMORE. Have you got two others?

BLOUNT. Yes, Flat and Green.

GLOSSMORE. Bad players.

BLOUNT. I make it a wule to play with bad players; it is five per
cent. in one's favour. I hate gambling. But a quiet wubber, if
one is the best player out of four, can't do any harm.

GLOSSMORE. Clever fellow, that Blount!
  [BLOUNT *takes up the snuff-box and walks off with it;* OLD
  MEMBER *looks at him savagely.* BLOUNT, GLOSSMORE,
  FLAT, *and* GREEN *make up a table at the bottom of the stage.*

SMOOTH. A thousand pardons, my dear Alfred. Ninety repique
—ten cards—game!

EVELYN. [*Passing a note to him.*] Game! Before we go on, one
question. This is Thursday—how much do you calculate to
win of me before Tuesday next?

SMOOTH. *Ce cher Alfred!* He is so droll!

EVELYN. [*Writing in his pocket-book.*] Forty games a night—
four nights, minus Sunday—our usual stakes; that would be
right, I think.

SMOOTH. [*Glancing over the account.*] Quite—if I win all,
which is next to impossible.

EVELYN. It shall be possible to win twice as much, on one
condition. Can you keep a secret?

SMOOTH. My dear Alfred, I have kept myself. I never inherited
a farthing—I never spent less than £4,000 a year—and I
never told a soul how I managed it.

EVELYN. Hark ye, then—it is a matter to me of vast importance
—a word with you. [*They whisper.*

OLD MEMBER. Waiter! the snuff-box.

> [WAITER *takes it from* BLOUNT, *&c.*

Enter SIR JOHN.

EVELYN. You understand?

SMOOTH. Perfectly; anything to oblige.

EVELYN. [*Cutting.*] It is for you to deal.   [*They go on playing.*

SIR JOHN. There's my precious son-in-law, that is to be, spending my consequence, and making a fool of himself.

> [*Takes up snuff-box;* OLD MEMBER *looks at him savagely.*

SMOOTH. [*Playing.*] Six to the point.

EVELYN. Good! Three queens.

SMOOTH. Not good.

BLOUNT. [*Rising from the table; another* MEMBER *takes his place.*] I'm out. Flat, a pony on the odd twick. [*Takes the money.*] That's wight. [*Comes up, counting his money.*] Well, Sir John, you don't play?

SIR JOHN. Play? No! [*Looking over* EVELYN's *hand.*] Confound him—lost again!

EVELYN. Hang the cards! Double the stakes!

SMOOTH. Anything to oblige—done.

SIR JOHN. Done, indeed!

OLD MEMBER. Waiter! the snuff-box.

> [WAITER *takes it from* SIR JOHN.

BLOUNT. I've won eight points and the bets—I never lose—I never play in the Deadly Smooth set.

> [*Takes up the snuff-box;* OLD MEMBER *as before.*

SIR JOHN. [*Looking over* SMOOTH's *hand, and, fidgeting backwards and forwards, walks all around the table.*] Lord have mercy on us! Smooth has seven for his point! What's the stakes?

EVELYN. Don't disturb us—I only throw out four. Stakes, Sir John? Immense! Was ever such luck? Not a card for my point. Do stand back, Sir John—I'm getting irritable.

> [*All gather round* EVELYN's *table.*

BLOUNT. One hundred pounds on the next game, Evelyn?

SIR JOHN. Nonsense—nonsense—don't disturb him! All the fishes come to the bait! Sharks and minnows all nibbling away at my son-in-law!

EVELYN. One hundred pounds, Blount? Ah, the finest gentleman is never too fine a gentleman to pick up a guinea. Done! Treble the stakes, Smooth!

SIR JOHN. I'm on the rack! Be cool, Evelyn! Take care, my dear boy! Be cool—be cool. Now, don't ye—now don't!

[SMOOTH *shows his cards.*

EVELYN. What—what? You have four queens! Five to the king. Confound the cards! A fresh pack.

[*Throws the cards behind him over* SIR JOHN. WAITER *brings a new pack of cards to* EVELYN.]

OLD MEMBER. Waiter! the snuff-box.

[*Different* MEMBERS *gather round, and all the* WAITERS *on.*

FIRST MEMBER. I never before saw Evelyn out of temper. He must be losing immensely.

SECOND MEMBER. Yes, this is interesting.

SIR JOHN. Interesting! There's a wretch!

BLOUNT. Poor fellow! He'll be ruined in a month!

SIR JOHN. I'm in a cold sweat.

SECOND MEMBER. Smooth is the very devil.

SIR JOHN. The devil's a joke to him!

GLOSSMORE. [*Slapping* SIR JOHN *on the back.*] A clever fellow that Smooth, Sir John, eh? [*Takes up the snuff-box;* OLD MEMBER *as before.*] £100 on the game, Evelyn?

EVELYN. You! Well done the Constitution! Yes, £100!

OLD MEMBER. Waiter! the snuff-box.

STOUT. I think I'll venture. £200 on this game, Evelyn?

EVELYN. Ha, ha, ha! Enlightenment and the Constitution on the same side of the question at last! Oh Stout, Stout! Greatest happiness of the greatest number—greatest number, number one! Done, Stout! £200! Ha, ha, ha! Deal, Smooth. Well done, Political Economy. Ha, ha, ha!

SIR JOHN. Quite hysterical—drivelling! Aren't you ashamed of yourselves? His own cousins—all in a conspiracy—a perfect gang of them.   [MEMBERS *indignant.*

STOUT. [*To* MEMBERS.] Hush! He's to marry Sir John's daughter.

FIRST MEMBER. What, Stingy Jack's? Oh!

MEMBERS. Oh! oh!

SIR JOHN. Oh, dear—oh, dear!

EVELYN. By Heaven, there never was such luck! It's enough to drive a man wild! This is mere child's play, Smooth. Double or quits on the whole amount!

SMOOTH. Anything to oblige. [*Great excitement.*

EVELYN. [*Throwing down his cards, and rising in great agitation.*] No more, no more—I've done! Quite enough. Glossmore, Stout, Blount—I'll pay you tomorrow. I—I—death, this is ruinous!
 [*Seizes the snuff-box;* OLD MEMBER *as before.*

SIR JOHN. Ruinous? I dare say it is! What has he lost? What has he lost, Smooth? Not much? Eh, eh?
 [MEMBERS *look at* EVELYN; *others gather round* SMOOTH.

SMOOTH. Oh, a trifle, dear John! Excuse me. We never tell our winnings. [*To* BLOUNT.] How d'ye do, Fred? [*To* GLOSSMORE.] By the bye, Charles, don't you want to sell your house in Grosvenor Square? £12,000, eh?

GLOSSMORE. Yes, and the furniture at valuation. About £3,000 more.

SMOOTH. [*Looking over his pocket-book.*] Um! Well, we'll talk of it.

SIR JOHN. Twelve and three—£15,000. What a cold-blooded rascal it is! £15,000, Smooth?

SMOOTH. Oh, the house itself is a trifle; but the establishment—I'm considering whether I have enough to keep it up, my dear John.

OLD MEMBER. Waiter! the snuff-box. [*Scraping it round, and with a wry face.*] And it's all gone!
 [*Gives it to the* WAITER *to fill.*

SIR JOHN. [*Turning round.*] And it's all gone!

EVELYN. [*Starting up and laughing hysterically.*] Ha, ha, all gone? Not a bit of it. Smooth, this club is so noisy. Sir John, you are always in the way. Come to my house, come! Champagne and a broiled bone. Nothing venture, nothing have! The luck must turn, and by Jupiter we'll make a night of it!   [*Going;* SIR JOHN *stops him.*

SIR JOHN. A night of it! For heaven's sake, Evelyn! Evelyn! Think what you are about! Think of Georgina's feelings! Think of your poor lost mother! Think of the babes unborn! Think of——

EVELYN. I'll think of nothing! Zounds! you don't know what I have lost, man; it's all your fault, distracting my attention. Pshaw—pshaw! Out of the way, do! [*Throws* SIR JOHN *off.*] Come, Smooth. Ha, ha! A night of it, my boy—a night of it!
    [*Exeunt* SMOOTH *and* EVELYN.

SIR JOHN. [*Following.*] You must not, you shall not! Evelyn, my dear Evelyn! He's drunk—he's mad! Will no one send for the police?   [*Exit.*

MEMBERS. Ha, ha, ha! Poor old Stingy Jack!

OLD MEMBER. [*Rising for the first time, and in a great rage.*] Waiter! the snuff-box.

ACT IV

SCENE I. *The Anteroom in* EVELYN's *house.* TABOURET, MAC-
FINCH, FRANTZ, *and other* TRADESMEN *discovered.*

TABOURET. [*Half whispers.*] So, I hear that Mr. Evelyn is
turned gamester! There are strange reports about to-day—
I don't know what to make of it! We must look sharp, Mr.
Macfinch, we poor tradesmen, and make hay while the sun
shines.

MACFINCH. I wuish those geeming-houses were aw at the
deevil! [*All shake their heads approvingly.*

Enter SMOOTH *with a pocketbook and pencil in his hand.*

SMOOTH. [*Looking round.*] Hum! ha! Fine pictures!
[*Feeling the curtains.*
The new-fashioned velvet, hem! Good-proportioned rooms!
Yes, this house is better than Glossmore's. Oh, Mr. Ta-
bouret, the upholsterer; you furnished these rooms. All of
the best, eh?

TABOURET. Oh, the very best! Mr. Evelyn is not a man to
grudge expense, sir.

SMOOTH. He is not indeed. You've been paid, I suppose,
Tabouret?

TABOURET. No, sir, no—I never send in my bills when a
customer is rich. [*Aside.*] Bills are like trees, and grow by
standing.

SMOOTH. Humph! Not paid? Humph! [*All gather round.*

MACFINCH. I dinna like that hoomph; there's something vara
suspeecious abun' it.

TABOURET. [*To the* TRADESMEN.] It's the great card-player,
Captain Smooth—finest player in Europe—cleaned out the
Duke of Silly Val. Uncommonly clever man!

SMOOTH. [*Pacing about the room.*] Thirty-six feet by twenty-eight—um! I think a bow-window there would be an improvement: could it be done easily, Tabouret?

MACFINCH. If Mr. Evelyn wuishes to pool about his house, there's no mon like my friend Mr. Macstucco.

SMOOTH. Evelyn? I was speaking of myself. Mr. Macstucco? Humph!

TABOURET. Yourself? Have you bought the house, sir?

SMOOTH. Bought it? Hum! Ha! It depends. So you've not been paid yet? Um! Nor you—nor you—nor you? Hum? Ah!

TABOURET. No, sir; what then? No fear of Mr. Evelyn! Ha, ha!

ALL. [*Anxiously.*] Ha, ha! What then?

MACFINCH. Ah, sir, what then? I'm a puir mon with a family. Captain, Captain—a leetle this way. You've a leetle account in the buiks; an' we'll e'en wipe it out altogether gin you'll say what you mean by that Hoom ha!

SMOOTH. Macfinch, my dear fellow, don't oblige me to cane you; I would not have Mr. Evelyn distressed for the world. Poor fellow! he holds very bad cards. So you've not been paid yet? Don't send in your bills on any account, mind! Yes, I don't dislike the house with some alteration. Good day to you—hum! ha!

[*Exit, looking about him, examining the chairs, tables, &c.*

TABOURET. Plain as a pikestaff! Staked his very house on an odd trick!

Enter SHARP, *agitated and in a hurry.*

SHARP. O Lord! O Lord! Who'd have thought it? Cards are the devil's book! John! Thomas! Harris!   [*Ringing the bell.*

Enter SERVANTS.

Tom, take this letter to Sir John Vesey's. If not at home, find him—he will give you a cheque. Go to his banker's and get it cashed instantly. Quick—quick; off with you!

TABOURET. [*Seizing* SERVANT.] What's the matter? What's the matter? How's Mr. Evelyn?

SERVANT. Bad—very bad! Sat up all night with Captain Smooth!   [*Runs off.*

SHARP. [*To the other* SERVANT.] Yes, Harris, your poor master! Oh, dear! Oh, dear! You will take this note to the Belgian minister, Portland-place. Passport for Ostend! Have the travelling carriage ready at a moment's notice!

MACFINCH. [*Stopping* SERVANT.] Passport! Harkye, my mon; is he gaun to pit the saut seas between us and the siller?

SERVANT. Don't stop me—something wrong in the chest— change of air—late hours—and Captain Smooth! [*Exit.*

SHARP. [*Walking about.*] And if the bank should break! If the bank is broke, and he can't draw out! Bound to Smooth!

TABOURET. Bank! What bank?

SHARP. Flash's bank! Flash, brother-in-law to Captain Smooth. What have you heard—eh? Eh?

TABOURET. That there's an awful run on it!

SHARP. I must be off. Go—go—you can't see Mr. Evelyn today.

TABOURET. My account, sir!

MACFINCH. I've a muckle bairns and a sma' bill!

FRANTZ. O sare, de great gentlemen always tink first of de tailor!

SHARP. Call again—call again at Christmas. The bank, the cards—the cards, the bank! Oh, dear! Oh, dear! [*Exit.*

TABOURET. The bank!

MACFINCH. The passport!

FRANTZ. And all dat vill be seen of de great Evelyn coat is de back of it. *Donner und Hagel!* I vil arrest him—I vil put de salt on de tail of it!

TABOURET. [*Aside.*] I'll slip down to the City and see how the bank goes!

MACFINCH. [*Aside.*] I'll e'en gang to my coosin the la'yer. Nothing but peetience for us, Mr. Tabouret.

TABOURET. Ay, ay—stick by each other—share and share alike—that's my way, sir.

ALL. Share and share alike. [*Exeunt.*

Enter TOKE, GLOSSMORE, *and* BLOUNT.

TOKE. My master is not very well, my lord, but I'll let him know.   [*Exit.*

GLOSSMORE. I am very curious to learn the result of his gambling tête-à-tête. There are strange reports abroad, and the tradesmen have taken the alarm.

BLOUNT. Oh, he's so howwidly wich, he can afford even a tête-à-tête with Deadly Smooth.

GLOSSMORE. Poor old Stingy Jack! Why, Georgina was your intended.

BLOUNT. Yes, and I really liked the girl, though out of pique I pwoposed to her cousin. But what can a man do against money?

Enter EVELYN.

If we could start fair, you'd see whom Georgina would pwefer, but she's sacwificed by her father. She as much as told me so.

EVELYN. [*Aside.*] I'll work still further upon Sir John through these excellent friends of mine. So, so, good morning, gentlemen, we've a little account to settle—one hundred each.

GLOSSMORE *and* BLOUNT. Don't talk of it.

EVELYN. [*Putting up his pocketbook.*] Well, I won't! [*Taking* BLOUNT *aside.*] Ha, ha! you'd hardly believe it—but I'd rather not pay you just at present; my money is locked up, and I must wait, you know, for the Groginhole rents. So, instead of owing you one hundred pounds, suppose I owe you five? You can give me a cheque for the other four. And harkye! not a word to Glossmore.

BLOUNT. Glossmore! The gweatest gossip in London! I shall be delighted! [*Aside.*] It never does harm to lend to a wich man; one gets it back somehow. By the way, Evelyn, if you want my gwey cab-horse, you may have him for two hundwed pounds, and that will make seven.

EVELYN. [*Aside.*] That's the fashionable usury: your friend does not take interest—he sells you a horse. [*Aloud.*] Blount, it's a bargain.

BLOUNT. [*Writing a cheque, and musingly.*] No, I don't see what harm it can do me; that off leg must end in a spavin.

EVELYN. [*To* GLOSSMORE.] That hundred pounds I owe you is rather inconvenient at present; I've a large sum to make up for the Groginhole property—perhaps you would lend me five or six hundred more—just to go on with?

GLOSSMORE. Certainly! Hopkins is dead; your interest for Cipher would——

EVELYN. Why, I can't promise that at this moment. But as a slight mark of friendship and gratitude, I shall be very much flattered if you'll accept a splendid grey cab-horse I bought to-day—cost two hundred pounds.

GLOSSMORE. Bought to-day! Then I'm safe. My dear fellow, you're always so princely!

EVELYN. Nonsense! Just write the cheque; and harkye, not a syllable to Blount.

GLOSSMORE. Blount? He's the town-crier!

BLOUNT. [*Giving* EVELYN *the cheque.*] Wansom's, Pall-mall East.

EVELYN. Thank you. So you proposed to Miss Douglas?

BLOUNT. Hang it! yes; I could have sworn that she fancied me. Her manner, for instance, that vewy day you pwoposed for Miss Vesey.

GLOSSMORE. [*Giving the cheque.*] Ransom's, Pall-mall East. Tell me, did you win or lose last night?

EVELYN. Win! Lose! Oh! No more of that, if you love me. I must send off at once to the banker's.

[*Looking at the two cheques.*

GLOSSMORE. [*Aside.*] Why, he's borrowed from Blount, too!

BLOUNT. [*Aside.*] That's a cheque from Lord Glossmore!

EVELYN. Excuse me, I must dress; I have not a moment to lose. You remember you dine with me to-day—seven o'clock. You'll meet Smooth. [*With tears in his eyes.*] It may be the last time I shall ever welcome you here! My——what am I saying? Oh, merely a joke! Good bye—good bye.

[*Shaking them heartily by the hand. Exit.* GLOSSMORE *and* BLOUNT *stare at each other in astonishment.*

BLOUNT. Glossmore!

GLOSSMORE. Blount!

BLOUNT. I am afwaid all's not wight.

GLOSSMORE. I incline to your opinion.

BLOUNT. But I've sold my gwey cab-horse.

GLOSSMORE. Grey cab-horse! You! What is he really worth now?

BLOUNT. Since he is sold, I will tell you. Not a sixpence!

GLOSSMORE. Not a sixpence? He gave it to me!

BLOUNT. That was devilish unhandsome! Do you know, I feel nervous.

GLOSSMORE. Nervous! Let us run and stop payment of our cheques.

Enter TOKE; *he runs across the stage.*

BLOUNT. Hollo, John! Where so fast?

TOKE. [*In great haste.*] Beg pardon, Sir Frederick, to Pall-mall East—Messrs. Ransom.   [*Exit.*

BLOUNT. [*Solemnly.*] Glossmore, we are fwoored!

GLOSSMORE. Sir, the whole town shall know of it.   [*Exeunt.*

SCENE II. *A splendid saloon in* EVELYN's *house. Handsome furniture; every article as costly as possible. Settee, c., with the Three Graces. Pictures, small tables at sides, with roses, statues, handsome writing materials, &c. Doors c., leading to the dining-room.*

EVELYN *and* GRAVES *discovered seated.*

GRAVES. Why, you don't mean to say you've borrowed money of Sir John Vesey?

EVELYN. Yes, £500. Observe how I'll thank him for it; observe how delighted he will be to find that five hundred was really of service to me.

GRAVES. You are grown so mysterious that I know no more what you would be at than if you were a French minister.

But, by the way, you've withdrawn your money from Flash and Brisk?

EVELYN. No.

GRAVES. No! Then——

Enter SIR JOHN, LADY FRANKLIN, GEORGINA, *and* STOUT.

SIR JOHN. You got the cheque for £500 safely? Too happy to——

EVELYN. My best thanks! My warmest gratitude! So kind in you, so seasonable! That £500—you don't know the value of that £500. I shall never forget your nobleness of conduct.

SIR JOHN. Gratitude! Nobleness! [*Aside.*] I can't have been taken in?

EVELYN. And in a moment of such distress.

SIR JOHN. [*Aside.*] Such distress! He picks out the ugliest words in the whole dictionary!

EVELYN. I've done with Smooth. But I'm still a little crippled, and you must do me another favour. I've only as yet paid the deposit of ten per cent. for the great Groginhole property. I am to pay the rest this week—nay, I fear to-morrow. I've already sold out of the Funds. The money lies at the bankers, and of course I can't touch it; for if I don't pay by a certain day I forfeit the estate and the deposit.

SIR JOHN. What's coming now, I wonder?

EVELYN. Georgina's fortune is £10,000. I always meant, my dear Sir John, to present you with that little sum.

SIR JOHN. Oh, Evelyn! Your generosity is positively touching!
[*Wipes his eyes.*

EVELYN. But the news of my losses has frightened my tradesmen. I have so many heavy debts at this moment that—that—that——. But I see Georgina is listening, and I'll say what I have to say to her.

SIR JOHN. No, no—no, no. Girls don't understand business!

EVELYN. The very reason I speak to her. This is an affair not of business, but of feeling. Stout, show Sir John my Correggio.

SIR JOHN. [*Aside.*] Devil take his Correggio! The man is born to torment me!

EVELYN. My dear Georgina, whatever you may hear said of me, I flatter myself that you feel confidence in my honour.

GEORGINA. Can you doubt it?

EVELYN. I confess that I am embarrassed at this moment; I have been weak enough to lose money at play. I promise you never to gamble again as long as I live. My affairs can be retrieved, but for the first few years of our marriage it may be necessary to retrench.

GEORGINA. Retrench!

EVELYN. To live, perhaps, altogether in the country.

GEORGINA. Altogether in the country!

EVELYN. To confine ourselves to a modest competence.

GEORGINA. Modest competence! I knew something horrid was coming!

Enter BLOUNT.

EVELYN. And now, Georgina, you may have it in your power at this moment to save me from much anxiety and humiliation. My money is locked up—my debts of honour must be settled— you are of age—your £10,000 in your own hands——

SIR JOHN. I'm standing on hot iron!

EVELYN. If you could lend it to me for a few weeks——.You hesitate! Can you give me this proof of your confidence? Remember, without confidence, what is wedlock?

SIR JOHN. [*Aside to her.*] No! [*Aloud, pointing his glass at the Correggio.*] Yes, the painting may be fine.

STOUT. But you don't like the subject?

GEORGINA. [*Aside.*] He may be only trying me! Best leave it to papa.

EVELYN. Well——

GEORGINA. You—you shall hear from me to-morrow. [*Aside.*] Ah, there's that dear Sir Frederick!   [*Goes up to* BLOUNT.

Enter GLOSSMORE *and* SMOOTH. EVELYN *salutes them, paying* SMOOTH *servile respect.*

LADY FRANKLIN. [*To* GRAVES.] Ha, ha! To be so disturbed yesterday—was it not droll?

GRAVES. Never recur to that humiliating topic.

GLOSSMORE. [*To* STOUT.] See how Evelyn fawns upon Smooth!

STOUT. How mean in him! Smooth—a professional gambler—
a fellow who lives by his wits. I would not know such a man
on any account!

SMOOTH. [*To* GLOSSMORE.] So Hopkins is dead—you want
Cipher to come in for Groginhole, eh?

GLOSSMORE. What! Could you manage it? [*Aside.*] Why, he
must have won his whole fortune.

SMOOTH. *Ce cher Charles*, anything to oblige!

GLOSSMORE. It is not possible he can have lost Groginhole!

STOUT. Groginhole! What can he have to do with Groginhole?
Glossmore, present me to Smooth.

GLOSSMORE. What, the gambler—the fellow who lives by his
wits?

STOUT. Why, his wits seem to be an uncommonly productive
capital. I'll introduce myself. How d'ye do, Captain Smooth?
We have met at the club, I think—I am charmed to make your
acquaintance in private. I say, sir, what do you think of the
affairs of the nation? Bad, very bad! No enlightenment—
great fall off in the revenue—no knowledge of finance!
There's only one man who can save the country——and
that's Popkins!

SMOOTH. Is he in Parliament, Mr. Stout? What's your Christian
name, by the bye?

STOUT. Benjamin. No, constituencies are so ignorant they don't
understand his value. He's no orator: in fact he stammers a
little—that is, a great deal—but devilish profound. Could not
we ensure him for Groginhole?

SMOOTH. My dear Benjamin, it is a thing to be thought on.

EVELYN. [*Advancing.*] My friends, pray be seated. [*They sit.*]
I wish to consult you. This day twelve months I succeeded to
an immense income, and as, by a happy coincidence, on the
same day I secured your esteem, so now I wish to ask you if
you think I could have spent that income in a way more
worthy your good opinion.

GLOSSMORE. Impossible! Excellent taste—beautiful house!

BLOUNT. Vewy good horses—[*Aside to* GLOSSMORE.] especially the gwey cab!

LADY FRANKLIN. Splendid pictures!

GRAVES. And a magnificent cook, ma'am!

SMOOTH. [*Thrusting his hands in his pockets.*] It's my opinion, Alfred—and I'm a judge—that you could not have spent your money better.

ALL. [*Except* SIR JOHN.] Very true!

GEORGINA. Certainly. [*Coaxingly.*] Don't retrench, my dear Alfred!

GLOSSMORE. Retrench! Nothing so plebeian!

STOUT. Plebeian, sir! Worse than plebeian! It is against all the rules of public morality. Every one knows now-a-days that extravagance is a benefit to the population—encourages art—employs labour—and multiplies spinning-jennies.

EVELYN. You reassure me. I own I did think that a man worthy of friends so sincere might have done something better than feast—dress—drink—play——

GLOSSMORE. Nonsense! We like you the better for it. [*Aside.*] I wish I had my £600 back, though.

EVELYN. And you are as much my friends now as when you offered me £10 for my old nurse?

SIR JOHN. A thousand times more so, my dear boy!

                                         [*All approve.*

Enter SHARP.

SMOOTH. But who's our new friend?

EVELYN. Who? The very man who first announced to me the wealth which you allow I have spent so well. But what's the matter, Sharp?   [SHARP *whispers to him.*

EVELYN. [*Aloud.*] The bank's broke!   [*All start up.*

SIR JOHN. Bank broke! What bank?

EVELYN. Flash, Brisk, and Co.

SIR JOHN. But I warned you—you withdrew?

EVELYN. Alas, no!

SIR JOHN. Oh! Not much in their hands?

EVELYN. Why, I told you the purchase-money for Groginhole was at my bankers'——but no, no, don't look so frightened! It was not placed with Flash—it is at Hoare's—it is, indeed. Nay, I assure you it is. A mere trifle at Flash's, upon my word, now! To-morrow, Sharp, we'll talk of this. One day more—one day, at least, for enjoyment. [*Walks to and fro.*

SIR JOHN. Oh, a pretty enjoyment!

BLOUNT. And he borrowed £700 of me!

GLOSSMORE. And £600 of me!

SIR JOHN. And £500 of me!

STOUT. Oh, a regular Jeremy Diddler! [*To* SIR JOHN.] I say, you have placed your daughter in a very unsafe investment. Transfer the stock.

SIR JOHN. [*Going to* GEORGINA.] Ha! I'm afraid we've been very rude to Sir Frederick. A monstrous fine young man!

Enter TOKE, *with a letter.*

TOKE. [*To* EVELYN.] Sir, I beg your pardon, but Mr. Macfinch insists on my giving you this letter instantly.

EVELYN. [*Reading.*] How! Sir John, this fellow Macfinch has heard of my misfortunes and insists on being paid; a lawyer's letter—quite insolent. Now read that letter—you'll be quite amused with it.

TOKE. And sir, Mr. Tabouret is below, and declares he will not stir till he's paid.   [*Exit.*

EVELYN. Won't stir till he's paid! What's to be done, Sir John? Smooth, what is to be done?

SMOOTH. If he'll not stir till he's paid, make him up a bed, and I'll take him in the inventory, as one of the fixtures, Alfred.

EVELYN. It is very well for you to joke, Mr. Smooth. But——

Enter SHERIFF'S OFFICER *giving a paper to* EVELYN, *and whispering.*

EVELYN. What's this? Frantz, the tailor. Why, the impudent scoundrel! Faith, this is more than I bargained for—Sir John, the bailiffs are in the house!

STOUT. The bailiffs in the house, [*Slapping* SIR JOHN *on the back with glee.*] old gentleman! But I didn't lend him a farthing.

EVELYN. And for a mere song—£150! Sir John, pay this fellow, will you, or see that my people kick out the bailiffs, or do it yourself, or something—while we go to dinner.

SIR JOHN. Pay—kick—I'll be d——d if I do! Oh, my £500, my £500! Mr. Alfred Evelyn, I want my £500!

GRAVES. I'm going to do a very silly thing. I shall lose both my friend and my money—just like my luck! Evelyn, go to dinner—I'll settle this for you.

LADY FRANKLIN. I love you for that!

GRAVES. Do you? Then I am the happiest—— ah, ma'am, I don't know what I am saying!   [*Exeunt* GRAVES *and* OFFICER.

EVELYN. [*To* GEORGINA.] Don't go by these appearances! I repeat, £10,000 will more than cover all my embarrassments. I shall hear from you to-morrow?

GEORGINA. Yes—yes!

EVELYN. But you're not going? You, too, Glossmore? You, Blount? You, Stout?

GLOSSMORE. Oh, this might have been expected from a man of such ambiguous political opinions!

STOUT. Don't stop me, sir. No man of common enlightenment would have squandered his substance in this way. Pictures and statues—baugh!

EVELYN. Why, you all said I could not spend my money better! Ha, ha, ha! The absurdest mistake! You don't fancy I'm going to prison? Ha, ha! Why don't you laugh, Sir John? Ha, ha, ha!

SIR JOHN. Sir, this horrible levity! Take Sir Frederick's arm, my poor, injured, innocent child.

SMOOTH. But, my dear John, it is for us at least to put an execution on the dinner.

Enter TOKE.

TOKE. Dinner is served.

GLOSSMORE. [*Pausing.*] Dinner!

STOUT. Dinner! It's a very good smell.

EVELYN. [*To* SIR JOHN.] Turtle and venison too.

> [*They stop irresolute.*

EVELYN. That's right—come along—come along—but I say, Blount—Stout—Glossmore—Sir John—one word first: will you lend me £10 for my old nurse? Ah! you fall back. Behold a lesson for all who build friendship upon their fortune and not their virtues! You lent me hundreds this morning to squander upon pleasure—you would refuse me £10 now to bestow upon benevolence. Go—we have done with each other—go!

> [*Exeunt, indignantly, all but* EVELYN *and* SMOOTH.

Re-enter GRAVES.

GRAVES. Heyday! What's all this?

EVELYN. Ha, ha! The scheme prospers—the duper is duped! Come, my friends—come: when the standard of money goes down in the great battle between man and fate—why, a bumper to the brave hearts that refuse to desert us!

> [*Exeunt.*

ACT V

SCENE I. * * * *'s *Club. Chandeliers not alight; no lamps or candles.* SMOOTH, GLOSSMORE, *and other* MEMBERS *discovered.*

GLOSSMORE. Will his horses be sold, think you?

SMOOTH. Very possibly, Charles. A fine stud—hum! ha! Waiter, a glass of sherry!

Enter WAITER, *with sherry.*

GLOSSMORE. They say he must go abroad.

SMOOTH. Well, it's the best time of year for travelling, Charles.

GLOSSMORE. We are all to be paid to-day, and that looks suspicious.

SMOOTH. Very suspicious, Charles. Hum—ah!

GLOSSMORE. My dear fellow, you must know the rights of the matter: I wish you'd speak out. What have you really won? Is the house itself gone?

SMOOTH. The house itself is certainly not gone, Charles, for I saw it exactly in the same place this morning at half-past ten —it has not moved an inch.

[WAITER *gives a letter to* GLOSSMORE.

GLOSSMORE. [*Reading.*] From Groginhole—an express! What's this? I'm amazed! [*Reading.*] 'They've actually, at the eleventh hour, started Mr. Evelyn, and nobody knows what his politics are. We shall be beat; the Constitution is gone! Cipher!' Oh, this is infamous in Evelyn! Gets into Parliament just to keep himself out of the Bench.

SMOOTH. He's capable of it.

GLOSSMORE. Not a doubt of it, sir. Not a doubt of it! The man saves himself at the expense of his country. If Groginhole is lost, there's an end of the Constitution. [*Exit.*

Enter SIR JOHN *and* BLOUNT, *talking.*

SIR JOHN. My dear boy, I'm not flint! I am but a man! If Georgina really loves you—and I am sure that she does—I will never think of sacrificing her happiness to ambition. She is yours; I told her so this very morning.

BLOUNT. [*Aside.*] The old humbug!

SIR JOHN. She's the best of daughters, the most obedient, artless creature. Oh, she's been properly brought up: a good daughter makes a good wife. Dine with me at seven, and we'll talk of the settlements.

BLOUNT. Yes, I don't care for fortune, but——

SIR JOHN. Her £10,000 will be settled on herself—that of course.

BLOUNT. All of it, sir? Weally, I——

SIR JOHN. What then, my dear boy? I shall leave you both all I've laid by. Ah, you know I'm a close fellow! 'Stingy Jack,' eh? After all, worth makes the man!

SMOOTH. And the more a man's worth, John, the worthier man he must be.   [*Exeunt* MEMBERS *and* SMOOTH.

BLOUNT. [*Aside.*] Yes, he has no other child! She must have all his savings; I don't see what harm it could do me. Still, that £10,000—I want that £10,000: if she would but wun off now, one could get wid of the settlements.

Enter STOUT, *wiping his forehead, and takes* SIR JOHN *aside.*

STOUT. Sir John, we've been played upon! My secretary is brother to Flash's head clerk; Evelyn had not £300 in the bank!

SIR JOHN. Bless us and save us; you take away my breath! But then—Deadly Smooth—the execution—the——oh, he must be done up!

STOUT. As to Smooth, he'd 'do anything to oblige.' All a trick, depend upon it! Smooth has already deceived me, for before the day's over Evelyn will be member for Groginhole. I've had an express from Popkins; he's in despair, not for himself but for the country, Sir John—what's to become of the country?

SIR JOHN. But what could be Evelyn's object?

STOUT. Object? Do you look for an object in a whimsical creature like that, a man who has not even any political opinions? Object! Perhaps to break off his match with your daughter. Take care, Sir John, or the borough will be lost to your family.

SIR JOHN. Aha! I begin to smell a rat. But it's not too late yet.

STOUT. My interest in Popkins made me run to Lord Spendquick, the late proprietor of Groginhole. I told him that Evelyn could not pay the rest of the money, and he told me that——

SIR JOHN. What?

STOUT. Mr. Sharp had just paid it him; there's no hope for Popkins! England will rue this day.

[*Goes up and looks at papers.*

SIR JOHN. [*Aside.*] Georgina shall lend him the money! I'll lend him—every man in my house shall lend him—I feel again what it is to be a father-in-law! Sir Frederick, excuse me—you can't dine with me to-day. And on second thoughts I see that it would be very unhandsome to desert poor Evelyn now he's down in the world. Can't think of it, my dear boy— can't think of it! Very much honoured, and happy to see you as a friend. Waiter, my carriage! Um! What, humbug Stingy Jack, will they? Ah, a good joke indeed! [*Exit.*

BLOUNT. Mr. Stout, what have you been saying to Sir John? Something against my chawacter. I know you have; don't deny it. Sir, I shall expect satisfaction!

STOUT. Satisfaction, Sir Frederick? Pooh, as if a man of enlightenment had any satisfaction in fighting! Did not mention your name; we were talking of Evelyn. Only think; he's no more ruined than you are.

BLOUNT. Not wuined? Aha, now I understand! So, so! Stay, let me see—she's to meet me in the square.

[*Pulls out his watch; a very small one.*

STOUT. [*Pulling out his own; a very large one.*] I must be off to the vestry. [*Exit.*

BLOUNT. Just in time! Ten thousand pounds! Gad, my blood's up, and I won't be tweated in this way if he were fifty times Stingy Jack! [*Exit.*

SCENE II. *The drawing-rooms in* SIR JOHN VESEY'S *house.*

LADY FRANKLIN, GRAVES.

GRAVES. Well, well, I am certain that poor Evelyn loves Clara still, but you can't persuade me that she cares for him.

LADY FRANKLIN. She has been breaking her heart ever since she heard of his distress. Nay, I am sure she would give all she has, could it save him from the consequences of his own folly.

GRAVES. [*Half aside.*] She would only give him his own money, if she did. I should just like to sound her.

LADY FRANKLIN. [*Ringing the bell.*] And you shall. I take so much interest in her that I forgive your friend everything but his offer to Georgina.

Enter PAGE.

Where are the young ladies?

PAGE. Miss Vesey is, I believe, still in the square; Miss Douglas is just come in, my lady.

LADY FRANKLIN. What, did not she go out with Miss Vesey?

PAGE. No, my lady; I attended her to Drummond's, the banker.   [*Exit.*

LADY FRANKLIN. Drummond's!

Enter CLARA.

Why, child, what on earth could take you to Drummond's at this hour of the day?

CLARA. [*Confused.*] Oh, I—that is—I——ah, Mr. Graves! How is Mr. Evelyn? How does he bear up against so sudden a reverse?

GRAVES. With an awful calm. I fear all is not right here! [*Touching his head.*] The report in the town is that he must go abroad instantly—perhaps to-day.

CLARA. Abroad! To-day!

GRAVES. But all his creditors will be paid, and he only seems anxious to know if Miss Vesey remains true in his misfortunes.

CLARA. Ah, he loves her so much, then!

GRAVES. Um! That's more than I can say.

CLARA. She told me last night that he said £10,000 would free him from all his liabilities; that was the sum, was it not?

GRAVES. Yes, he persists in the same assertion. Will Miss Vesey lend it?

LADY FRANKLIN. [*Aside.*] If she does, I shall not think so well of her poor dear mother; for I am sure she'd be no child of Sir John's!

GRAVES. I should like to convince myself that my poor friend has nothing to hope from a woman's generosity.

LADY FRANKLIN. Civil! And are men, then, less covetous?

GRAVES. I know one man at least, who, rejected in his poverty by one as poor as himself, no sooner came into a sudden fortune than he made his lawyer invent a codicil which the testator never dreamt of, bequeathing independence to the woman who had scorned him.

LADY FRANKLIN. And never told her?

GRAVES. Never! There's no such document at Doctors' Commons, depend on it! You seem incredulous, Miss Clara. Good day!

CLARA. [*Following him.*] One word, for mercy's sake! Do I understand you right? Ah, how could I be so blind? Generous Evelyn!

GRAVES. You appreciate, and Georgina will desert him. Miss Douglas, he loves you still. If that's not just like me! Meddling with other people's affairs, as if they were worth it—hang them!   [*Exit.*

CLARA. Georgina will desert him? Do you think so?

LADY FRANKLIN. She told me last night that she would never see him again. To do her justice, she's less interested than her father, and as much attached as she can be to another. Even while engaged to Evelyn, she has met Sir Frederick every day in the square.

CLARA. And he is alone—sad—forsaken—ruined. And I, whom he enriched—I, the creature of his bounty—I, once the woman of his love—I stand idly here to content myself with tears and prayers! Oh, Lady Franklin, have pity on me—on him! We are both of kin to him—as relations we have both a right to comfort. Let us go to him—come!

LADY FRANKLIN. No! it would scarcely be right—remember the world—I cannot!

CLARA. All abandon him—then I will go alone!

LADY FRANKLIN. Alone—what will he think? What but——

CLARA. What but—that, if he love me still, I may have enough for both, and I am by his side! But that is too bright a dream. He told me I might call him brother! Where, now, should a sister be? But—but—I—I—I—tremble! If, after all—if—if——. In one word, am I too bold? The world—my conscience can answer that—but do you think that he could despise me?

LADY FRANKLIN. No, Clara, no! Your fair soul is too transparent for even libertines to misconstrue. Something tells me that this meeting may make the happiness of both! You cannot go alone. My presence justifies all. Give me your hand—we will go together!   [*Exeunt.*

———

SCENE III. *A room in* EVELYN's *house as in Act IV, Scene II.*

EVELYN *discovered seated.*

EVELYN. Yes; as yet all surpasses my expectations. I am sure of Smooth—I have managed even Sharp; my election will seem but an escape from a prison. Ha, ha! True, it cannot last long; but a few hours more are all I require, and for that time at least I shall hope to be thoroughly ruined.

Enter GRAVES.

Well, Graves, and what do people say of me?

GRAVES. Everything that's bad!

EVELYN. Three days ago I was universally respected. I awake this morning to find myself singularly infamous. Yet I'm the same man.

GRAVES. Humph! Why, gambling——

EVELYN. Cant! It was not criminal to gamble—it was criminal to lose. Tut! Will you deny that if I had ruined Smooth instead of myself, every hand would have grasped mine yet more cordially, and every lip would have smiled congratulation on my success? Man, man! I've not been rich and poor for nothing! The Vices and the Virtues are written in a language the world cannot construe; it reads them in a vile translation, and the translators are—Failure and Success! You alone are unchanged.

GRAVES. There's no merit in that. I am always ready to mingle my tears with any man. [*Aside.*] I know I'm a fool, but I can't help it. Hark ye, Evelyn! I like you—I'm rich; and anything I can do to get you out of your hobble will give me an excuse to grumble for the rest of my life. There, now it's out.

EVELYN. [*Touched.*] There's something good in human nature after all! My dear friend, I will now confide in you: I am not the spendthrift you think me—my losses have been trifling— not a month's income of my fortune. [GRAVES *shakes him heartily by the hand.*] No, it has been but a stratagem to prove if the love on which was to rest the happiness of a whole life were given to the money or the man. Now you guess why I have asked from Georgina this one proof of confidence and affection. Think you she will give it?

GRAVES. Would you break your heart if she did not?

EVELYN. It is in vain to deny that I still love Clara; our last conversation renewed feelings which would task all the energies of my soul to conquer. No! The heart was given to the soul as its ally, not as its traitor.

GRAVES. What do you tend to?

EVELYN. This: if Georgina prove by her generosity that she loves me for myself, I will shut Clara for ever from my thoughts. I am pledged to Georgina, and I will carry to the altar a soul resolute to deserve her affection and fulfil its vows.

GRAVES. And if she reject you?

EVELYN. [*Joyfully.*] If she do, I am free once more! And then— then I will dare to ask, for I can ask without dishonour, if Clara can explain the past and bless the future!

Enter TOKE, *with a letter on a salver;* EVELYN *takes it. Exit*
TOKE.

EVELYN. [*After reading it.*] The die is cast—the dream is over!
Generous girl! Oh, Georgina! I will deserve you yet.

GRAVES. Georgina! Is it possible?

EVELYN. And the delicacy, the womanhood, the exquisite grace
of this! How we misjudge the depth of the human heart! How,
seeing the straws on the surface, we forget that the pearls
may lie hid below! I imagined her incapable of this devotion.

GRAVES. And I too.

EVELYN. It were base in me to continue this trial a moment
longer; I will write at once to undeceive that generous heart.
[*Goes to table and writes.*

GRAVES. I would have given £1,000 if that little jade Clara
had been beforehand. But just like my luck; if I want a man to
marry one woman, he's sure to marry another on purpose to
vex me.

EVELYN. Graves, will you ring the bell?   [GRAVES *rings bell.*

Enter TOKE.

EVELYN. Take this instantly to Miss Vesey; say I will call in an
hour. [*Exit* TOKE.] And now Clara is resigned for ever! Why
does my heart sink within me? Why, why, looking to the fate
to come, do I see only the memory of what has been?

GRAVES. You are re-engaged then to Georgina?

EVELYN. Irrevocably.

Enter TOKE, *announcing* LADY FRANKLIN *and* CLARA.

LADY FRANKLIN. My dear Evelyn, you may think it strange
to receive such visitors at this moment, but indeed it is no
time for ceremony. We are your relations—it is reported you
are about to leave the country—we come to ask frankly what
we can do to serve you?

EVELYN. Madam—I——

LADY FRANKLIN. Come, come—do not hesitate to confide in
us; Clara is less a stranger to you than I am; your friend here

will perhaps let me consult with him. [*Aside to* G R A V E S.] Let us leave them to themselves.

G R A V E S. You're an angel of a widow, but you come too late, as whatever is good for anything generally does.

[*They retire into the inner room.*

E V E L Y N. Miss Douglas, I may well want words to thank you; this goodness—this sympathy——

C L A R A. [*Abandoning herself to her emotion.*] Evelyn, Evelyn! Do not talk thus! Goodness! Sympathy! I have learned all— all! It is for me to speak of gratitude! What! even when I had so wounded you—when you believed me mercenary and cold —when you thought that I was blind and base enough not to know you for what you are; even at that time you thought but of my happiness—my fortunes—my fate! And to you—you— I owe all that has raised the poor orphan from servitude and dependence! While your words were so bitter, your deeds so gentle! Oh, noble Evelyn, this then was your revenge!

E V E L Y N. You owe me no thanks—that revenge was sweet! Think you it was nothing to feel that my presence haunted you, though you knew it not? That in things the pettiest as the greatest, which that gold could buy—the very jewels you wore—the very robe in which, to other eyes, you might seem more fair—in all in which you took the woman's young and innocent delight, I had a part, a share? That even if separated for ever—even if another's—even in distant years—perhaps in a happy home, listening to sweet voices that might call you 'mother'; even then, should the uses of that dross bring to your lips one smile, that smile was mine—due to me—due as a sacred debt to the hand that you rejected—to the love that you despised!

C L A R A. Despised! See the proof that I despised you! See: in this hour, when they say you are again as poor as before, I forget the world—my pride—perhaps too much my sex. I remember but your sorrows—I am here!

E V E L Y N. And is this the same voice that, when I knelt at your feet—when I asked but one day the hope to call you mine— spoke only of poverty, and answered 'Never'?

C L A R A. Because I had been unworthy of your love if I had ensured your misery. Evelyn, hear me! My father, like you, was poor, generous; gifted, like you, with genius, ambition; sensitive, like you, to the least breath of insult. He married as you would have done—married one whose only dower was penury and care. Alfred, I saw that genius the curse to itself! I saw that ambition wither to despair! I saw the struggle—the humiliation—the proud man's agony—the bitter life—the early death, and heard over his breathless clay my mother's groan of self-reproach! Alfred Evelyn, now speak! Was the woman you loved so nobly to repay you with such a doom?

EVELYN. Clara, we should have shared it!

CLARA. Shared? Never let the woman who really loves comfort her selfishness with such delusion! In marriages like this the wife cannot share the burden; it is he—the husband—to provide, to scheme, to work, to endure—to grind out his strong heart at the miserable wheel! The wife, alas, cannot share the struggle—she can but witness the despair. And therefore, Alfred, I rejected you.

EVELYN. Yet you believe me as poor now as I was then.

CLARA. But I am not poor: we are not so poor. Of this fortune, which is all your own—if, as I hear, one half would free you from your debts, why, we have the other half still left, Evelyn. It is humble—but it is not penury. No, Alfred, even yet you do not know me.

EVELYN. Know you! Fair angel, too excellent for man's harder nature to understand, at least it is permitted me to revere. Why were such blessed words not vouchsafed to me before; why, why come they now? Too late! Oh, Heaven—too late!

CLARA. Too late! What, then, have I said?

EVELYN. Wealth! What is it without you? With you, I recognise its power: to forestall your every wish—to smooth your every path—to make all that life borrows from grace and beauty your ministrant and handmaid; and then, looking to those eyes, to read there the treasures of a heart that excelled all that kings could lavish—why, that were to make gold indeed a god! But vain—vain—vain! Bound by every tie of faith, gratitude, loyalty, and honour, to another!

CLARA. Another! Is she then true to your reverses? I did not know this—indeed I did not! And I have thus betrayed myself! O shame! he must despise me now!

Enter SIR JOHN; *at the same time* GRAVES *and* LADY FRANKLIN *advance from the inner room.*

SIR JOHN. [*With dignity and frankness.*] Evelyn, I was hasty yesterday. You must own it natural that I should be so. But Georgina has been so urgent in your defence, that——that I cannot resist her. What's money without happiness? So give me your security, for she insists on lending you the £10,000.

EVELYN. I know, and have already received it.

SIR JOHN. Already received it! Is he joking? Faith, for the last two days I believe I have been living amongst the Mysteries of Udolpho! Sister, have you seen Georgina?

LADY FRANKLIN. Not since she went out to walk in the square.

SIR JOHN. [*Aside.*] She's not in the square, nor the house— where the deuce can the girl be?

EVELYN. I have written to Miss Vesey—I have asked her to fix the day for our wedding.

SIR JOHN. [*Joyfully.*] Have you? Go, Lady Franklin, find her instantly—she must be back by this time. Take my carriage; it is but a step—you won't be two minutes gone. [*Aside.*] I'd go myself, but I'm afraid of leaving him a moment while he's in such excellent dispositions.

LADY FRANKLIN. [*Repulsing* CLARA.] No, no; stay till I return.   [*Exit.*

SIR JOHN. And don't be down-hearted, my dear fellow; if the worst come to the worst, you will have everything I can leave you. Meantime, if I can in any way help you——

EVELYN. Ha, you! You too? Sir John, you have seen my letter to Miss Vesey? [*Aside.*] Or could she have learned the truth before she ventured to be generous?

SIR JOHN. No, on my honour. I only just called at the door on my way from Lord Spend——that is, from the City. Georgina was out; was ever anything so unlucky?

VOICES. [*Without.*] Hurrah, hurrah! Blue for ever!

SIR JOHN. What's that?

Enter SHARP.

SHARP. Sir, a deputation from Groginhole—poll closed in an hour—you are returned! Holloa, sir—holloa!

EVELYN. And it was to please Clara!

SIR JOHN. Mr. Sharp, Mr. Sharp—I say, how much has Mr. Evelyn lost by Messrs. Flash and Co.?

SHARP. Oh, a great deal, sir—a great deal!

SIR JOHN. [*Alarmed.*] How! A great deal!

EVELYN. Speak the truth, Sharp—concealment is all over.

SHARP. £223 6s. 3d.—a great sum to throw away!

SIR JOHN. Eh! What, my dear boy,—what? Ha, ha! All humbug, was it? All humbug, upon my soul! So, Mr. Sharp, isn't he ruined after all, not the least, wee, rascally little bit in the world ruined?

SHARP. Sir, he has never even lived up to his income.

SIR JOHN. Worthy man! I could jump up to the ceiling! I am the happiest father-in-law in the three kingdoms. [*Knocking.*] And that's my sister's knock, too.

CLARA. Since I was mistaken, cousin, since now you do not need me—forget what has passed; my business here is over. Farewell!

EVELYN. Could you but see my heart at this moment—with what love, what veneration, what anguish it is filled—you would know how little, in the great calamities of life, fortune is really worth. And must we part now—now, when—when I——

Enter LADY FRANKLIN *and* GEORGINA, *followed by* BLOUNT, *who looks shy and embarrassed.*

GRAVES. Georgina herself—then there's no hope.

SIR JOHN. What the deuce brings that fellow Blount here? Georgy, my dear Georgy, I want to——

EVELYN. Stand back, Sir John!

SIR JOHN. But I must speak a word to her—I want to——

EVELYN. Stand back, I say—not a whisper—not a sign. If your daughter is to be my wife, to her heart only will I look for a reply to mine. Georgina, it is true, then, that you trust me with your confidence—your fortune. Is it also true that when you did so you believed me ruined? Oh, pardon the doubt! Answer as if your father stood not there—answer me from that truth the world cannot yet have plucked from your soul—answer as the woman's heart, yet virgin and unpolluted, should answer to one who has trusted to it his all!

GEORGINA. What can he mean?

SIR JOHN. [*Making signs.*] She won't look this way, she won't, hang her! Hem!

EVELYN. You falter. I implore—I adjure you—answer!

LADY FRANKLIN. Speak!

GEORGINA. Mr. Evelyn, your fortune might well dazzle me, as it dazzled others. Believe me, I sincerely pity your reverses.

SIR JOHN. Good girl! You hear her, Evelyn?

GEORGINA. What's money without happiness?

SIR JOHN. Clever creature! My own sentiments.

GEORGINA. And so, as our engagement is now annulled—papa told me so this very morning—I have promised my hand where I have given my heart, to Sir Frederick Blount.

SIR JOHN. I told you—I? No such thing—no such thing; you frighten her out of her wits—she don't know what she's saying.

EVELYN. Am I awake? But this letter—this letter, received to-day——

LADY FRANKLIN. [*Looking over the letter.*] Drummond's—from a banker!

EVELYN. Read—read.

LADY FRANKLIN. 'Ten thousand pounds just placed to your account—from the same unknown friend to Alfred Evelyn.' Oh, Clara, I know now why you went to Drummond's this morning.

EVELYN. Clara! What! And the former note with the same signature, on the faith of which I pledged my hand and sacrificed my heart——

LADY FRANKLIN. Was written under my eyes, and the secret kept that——

EVELYN. How could I be so blind! I am free! I am released! Clara, you forgive me? You love me? You are mine! We are rich—rich! I can give you fortune, power—I can devote to you my whole life, thought, heart, soul—I am all yours, Clara—my own—my wife! [*Embraces her.*

SIR JOHN. [*To* GEORGINA.] A pretty mess you've made of it, to bubble your own father! And you too, Lady Franklin— I am to thank you for this!

LADY FRANKLIN. You've to thank me that she's not now on the road to Scotland with Sir Frederick. I chanced on them by the Park just in time to dissuade and save her. But to do her justice, a hint of your displeasure was sufficient.

GEORGINA. [*Half sobbing.*] And you know, papa, you said this very morning that poor Frederick had been very ill used, and you would settle it all at the club.

BLOUNT. Come, Sir John, you can only blame yourself and Evelyn's cunning device. After all, I'm no such vewy bad match; and as for the £10,000——

EVELYN. I'll double it. Ah, Sir John, what's money without happiness!

SIR JOHN. Pshaw—nonsense—stuff!

LADY FRANKLIN. But if you don't consent, she'll have no husband at all.

SIR JOHN. Hum! there's something in that. [*Aside to* EVELYN.] Double it, will you? Then settle it all tightly on her. Well— well—my foible is not avarice. Blount, make her happy. Child, I forgive you. [*Pinching her arm.*] Ugh, you fool!

GRAVES. [*To* LADY FRANKLIN.] I'm afraid it's catching. What say you? I feel the symptoms of matrimony creeping all over me. Shall we, eh? Frankly, now, frankly——

LADY FRANKLIN. Frankly, now, there's my hand.

GRAVES. Accepted. Is it possible? Sainted Maria—
[*She checks him before he can finish.*

Enter SMOOTH.

SMOOTH. How d'ye do, Alfred? I intrude, I fear! Quite a family party.

BLOUNT. Wish us joy, Smooth. Georgina's mine, and——

SMOOTH. And our four friends there apparently have made up another rubber. John, my dear boy, you look as if you had something at stake on the odd trick.

SIR JOHN. Sir, your very——confound the fellow! And he's a dead shot, too!

Enter STOUT *and* GLOSSMORE *hastily, talking with each other.*

STOUT. I'm sure he's of our side; we've all the intelligence.

GLOSSMORE. I'm sure he's of ours if his future is safe, for we've all the property.

STOUT. Just heard of your return, Evelyn. Congratulate you. The great motion of the session is fixed for Friday. We count on your vote. Progress with the times!

GLOSSMORE. Preserve the Constitution!

STOUT. Your money will do wonders for the party! Advance!

GLOSSMORE. The party respects men of your property! Stick fast!

EVELYN. I have the greatest respect, I assure you, for the worthy and intelligent flies upon both sides the wheel; but whether we go too fast or too slow does not, I fancy, depend so much on the flies as on the Stout Gentleman who sits inside and pays the post-boys. Now, all my politics as yet is to consider what's best for the Stout Gentleman.

SMOOTH. Meaning John Bull. *Ce cher* old John!

EVELYN. Smooth, we have yet to settle our first piquet account, and our last! And I sincerely thank you for the service you have rendered to me, and the lesson you have given these gentlemen. Ah, Clara, you—you have succeeded where wealth had failed! You have reconciled me to the world and to mankind. My friends—we must confess it—amidst the humours and the follies, the vanities, deceits, and vices that play their parts in the great Comedy of Life—it is our own fault if we do not find such natures, though rare and few, as redeem the rest, brightening the shadows that are flung from the form and body of the time with glimpses of the everlasting holiness of truth and love.

GRAVES. But for the truth and the love, when found, to make us tolerably happy, we should not be without——

LADY FRANKLIN. Good health.

GRAVES. Good spirits.

CLARA. A good heart.

SMOOTH. An innocent rubber.

GEORGINA. Congenial tempers.

BLOUNT. A pwoper degwee of pwudence.

STOUT. Enlightened opinions.

GLOSSMORE. Constitutional principles.

SIR JOHN. Knowledge of the world.

EVELYN. And——plenty of Money!

NEW MEN AND OLD ACRES

AN ORIGINAL COMEDY IN THREE ACTS

BY

TOM TAYLOR (1817–1880) and
AUGUSTUS WILLIAM DUBOURG (1830–1910)

―――

First performed at the Theatre Royal, Manchester
20 August 1869
and at the Haymarket Theatre
25 October 1869

―――

CAST

MARMADUKE VAVASOUR, ESQ., of Cleve Abbey	Mr. Chippendale
SAMUEL BROWN, a Liverpool merchant	Mr. Howe
BERTIE FITZ-URSE	Mr. Buckstone, Jun.
MR. BUNTER, a self-made man	Mr. Buckstone
BERTHOLD BLASENBALG, a mining agent and financier	Mr. Rogers
SECKER	Mr. Braid
GANTRY, butler at Cleve Abbey	Mr. Weathersby
TURBIT, Clerk of the Works	Mr. James
MONTMORENCY, servant to Bunter	Mr. Crouch
SERVANT, to Vavasour	Mr. Webster
TELEGRAPH MESSENGER	Master Fielder
LADY MATILDA VAVASOUR	Mrs. Chippendale
LILIAN VAVASOUR	Miss M. Robertson
MRS. BUNTER	Mrs. E. Fitzwilliam
FANNY BUNTER	Miss C. Hill
MRS. BRILL, housekeeper at Cleve Abbey	Miss Harrison

―――

TIME
Present Day

PREFACE TO *NEW MEN AND OLD ACRES*

TOM TAYLOR has always been regarded as the principal author of *New Men and Old Acres*, and the part played by Dubourg is unknown. Dubourg himself was a minor literary figure. He published a novel, *Four Studies of Love*, in 1877, and *Four Original Plays* (one of which was acted) in 1883. He collaborated with Taylor on a drama, *A Sister's Penance* (1866), his first recorded work for the theatre, and with Edmund Yates on another drama, *Without Love* (1872). Eight other plays— comedies, dramas, and an interlude—are attributed to him, and all his theatrical work was done between 1866 and 1892. Dubourg also held the position of Chief Clerk of the Judicial Office at the House of Lords.

New Men and Old Acres was originally submitted to the Wigans at the Queen's Theatre, and then to the Bancrofts in 1868. They were unable to produce it owing to existing commitments, and Taylor withdrew the manuscript and sent it to Buckstone at the Haymarket.[1] There it ran for ninety-five performances, and was revived for eleven more before the end of the season. In Manchester it had been given once only as part of the Haymarket company's touring repertory. It was presented at Wallack's Theatre in New York in 1870. Hare's revival at the Court in 1876 with Ellen Terry as Lilian Vavasour was a much greater success than the original production and was performed 196 times. The play was revived again at the Court in 1884.

New Men and Old Acres was Taylor's last comedy; henceforth he largely confined himself to historical dramas.[2] Beginning with *Victims* and *An Unequal Match* in 1857, Taylor wrote nine comedies in twelve years for the company at the Haymarket, which during those years was one of the best comedy companies in England: actors like Buckstone, Howe, the Chippendales, and

---

[1] *Mr. and Mrs. Bancroft On and Off the Stage*, i. 263–4. Dubourg's name is not mentioned in this account of the play's passage from theatre to theatre. Ellen Terry refers to Taylor but not to Dubourg when she discusses *New Men and Old Acres* in *The Story of My Life*.

[2] For further comment on Taylor, see Volume Two, pp. 79–81.

Compton had been playing together for years and had developed their own style of comic ensemble to perfection. Apart from *Victims* and *An Unequal Match*, which have been mentioned in the Introduction, Taylor's most interesting contributions to Haymarket comedy were *The Contested Election* (1859), *The Overland Route* (1860), and *Our American Cousin* (1861). The first of these is a farcical and satirical treatment of an election in a country town in which the electors, fearing that the absence of a contest between the two candidates (one of whom has secretly agreed to stand down at the last moment) will mean the absence of the usual bribes and lavish spending on food and drink, put up a third candidate—a retiring middle-aged gentleman who does not want to run at all—to ensure that a free-spending contest does indeed take place. Nobody is interested in obtaining a good member for the borough. The best scene is that in which rival political deputations interview the bewildered new candidate, who is hopelessly out of his depth, and are completely satisfied with absolutely contradictory answers given on his behalf by his fast-talking agent. *The Overland Route* is a good example of a crowded, plot-crammed pre-Robertsonian comedy, missing Robertson's economy and simplicity but bursting with an excess of the energy, bustle, and comic incident lacking in his comedies. The first two acts are laid on the P. & O. sailing ship 'Simoon' out of Calcutta. The plot has many strands: Mrs. Sebright pretends to be a widow and coquettes with pompous Sir Solomon Fraser and Colepepper, who both propose to her; the low-comedy Lovibond is taken for a criminal and arrested by the detective Moleskin; unknown to Lovibond his wife, whom he left ten years before, is also on board and receives the jealous attentions of fiery Major McTurk; Dexter, a doctor, tends the sick and moves like a guardian angel among the other passengers. At the end of Act II the 'Simoon' is shipwrecked, and Act III is set on a coral reef in the Red Sea. Dexter continues his role as melodramatic hero (in Act I he leaps overboard to save a drowning man), organizing supplies and medicines and diving through ten fathoms of water to rescue from the wreck a box containing vouchers that will clear Colepepper of charges hanging over him. The other characters suffer a Gilbertian transformation: Colepepper pitches in with the chores and ceases to be an idle bore, realizing the folly of his past conduct towards Mrs. Sebright; the ponderously talkative Sir Solomon is forced to remain silent because he has lost his false teeth; McTurk becomes a coward; Moleskin loses his boots, and helpless without them on the sharp coral is unable to act as Lovibond's captor; in fact their roles are reversed; and Lovibond masterfully asserts his authority over his now doting wife. Colepepper's daughter perceives the worthlessness of her formerly favoured suitor Clavering and accepts Dexter. The real criminal is discovered, exonerating Lovibond; a steamer arrives captained by the husband of the now contrite Mrs. Sebright, and a rescue is effected. A mixture of melodrama, eccentric humour, low comedy, domestic idealism, and great extravagance of plot and characterization, *The Overland Route*, with all its faults, is typical of the best work done in comedy before the arrival of Robertson as an established playwright, and deserves study for that reason as well as for being a perfect specimen of a play suited specifically to the strengths of the pre-eminent comedy company of the day. *Our American Cousin*, first performed in New York in 1858, is an excellent example of another kind of actor–author relationship—or rather the absence of it. Faced with a small eccentric comedy part in a weak melodramatic plot concerned with an unscrupulous steward blackmailing his master by demanding the hand of his daughter in return for not exposing him to ruin (the intervention of a good-hearted Yankee brings mortgage documents to light which save the day), E. A. Sothern expanded his role of Lord Dundreary to the extent that it dominated the play, and achieved stardom because of it. In fact he rewrote his part entirely, independent of Taylor, before the Haymarket production. The brilliant and original performance that resulted and so influenced dramatists and actors for the next twenty years owed little to the author and almost everything to the creative invention of the actor.

New Men and Old Acres is a departure from Taylor's comic practice of the previous decade in that it clearly demonstrates the influence of Robertson. The briefest comparison with, for instance, *The Overland Route*, shows that Taylor had learned something from Robertson about restraint, dialogue, and the writing of love scenes. Thematically, *New Men and Old Acres* is indebted, not only to the general subject-matter of Victorian comedy, but particularly to *Society* and *Caste* and their inter-class marriages, dominating aristocratic mothers, and class hostilities. However, it is my opinion that with the exception of *Caste*, *New Men and Old Acres* is superior to any Robertson comedy: there is nothing of Robertson's often effete senti-mentalism, languorous delicacy, thematic timidity, and in-credible plotting. Taylor combined aspects of Robertsonian technique with the exposition of general social themes of con-siderable interest and his own powers of forceful, vitally human characterization and vigorous if broad humour. The result has more significance and life than anything Robertson could manage outside his best work.

The only English text of *New Men and Old Acres* appears to be *Lacy's Acting Edition of Plays*, v. 90; this has been used here and collated with the Lord Chamberlain's copy, which is entitled *Love and Money*. The American acting edition, *De Witt's Acting Plays*, no. 115, differs considerably from the *Lacy* in dialogue and even in the names of characters; it largely eliminates the English speech characteristics of the original. The *De Witt* text may have been printed from a promptbook of the New York production of 1870.

ACT I

SCENE. *The Library of Cleve Abbey, opening by French window,* R.C., *to garden and shrubbery. In the distance, a finely-timbered park; beyond the lawn picturesque Abbey ruin. Doors,* R. *and* L., *and door up* L., *facing audience. The room is handsomely furnished in an old-fashioned style, with buhl and marqueterie cabinets, old oak panelling, &c.; rich draperies to window; the furniture shows marks of age and long use.*

GANTRY *discovered arranging the contents of letter-bag on table,* C.

Enter MRS. BRILL.

MRS. BRILL. Mr. Gantry, can I say a word to you, please?

GANTRY. If you can't, Mrs. Brill, who can? What is it?

MRS. BRILL. Mr. Secker's card for a friend of his to see over the ruins. [*Gives card.*

GANTRY. Mr. Secker's card—eh? [*Looks at card, and returns it.*] Then, I should say, Mrs. Brill, attend to it.

MRS. BRILL. But Thursday's the show-day, and what's Mr. Secker, I'd like to know? Only an attorney.

GANTRY. Only an attorney! Only the party as has his fingers in every pie in the county, and the licking of 'em afterwards. Take my word, Mrs. Brill, if you don't feel at home in 'ot water, always keep out of law and in with the lawyer.

Enter SECKER.

Talk of the old gentleman—here he comes.

SECKER. Let Mr. Vavasour know I'm here, Mr. Gantry. Oh, Mrs. Brill, did you get my card?

MRS. BRILL. And attended to it; you may be sure of that, Mr. Secker.
[*Curtseys.* GANTRY *obsequiously relieves* SECKER *of his hat, gloves, and papers.*

SECKER. That's right. Now, my minutes are six-and-eight-pences. Look sharp, Gantry!
[*Arranging his papers. Exit* GANTRY, *with letter-bag.*

MRS. BRILL. [*Aside.*] Drat them papers of his! There's mischief in 'em—I know there is! [*Exit.*

SECKER. [*Looking over papers.*] Yes, the crash must come. If clients won't look ruin in the face till it's more than a match for them, so much the worse for clients.

Enter VAVASOUR.

Good morning, sir.

VAVASOUR. Ah, Secker, good morning. Glad to see you.

SECKER. [*Shrugging his shoulders.*] Ah.

VAVASOUR. Bright, cheery weather—eh?

SECKER. We shall want it—I'm afraid, sir—for the business I've come upon.

VAVASOUR. The old story—eh? More bother about money matters? I wish I saw my way out of it.

SECKER. I'm afraid I see my way out of it at last, Mr. Vavasour.

VAVASOUR. *Afraid* you see your way out of it, Secker?

SECKER. Heavy arrears of interest—no means of raising it; mortgagee insists on his money, and has served the usual six months' notice. [*Points to paper.*

VAVASOUR. Confound it, Secker! I thought he was to give us time. He has given us time for two years——

SECKER. And he's tired of it at last, sir. He announces his determination to force a sale——

VAVASOUR. [*In consternation.*] Sell Cleve Abbey? This will be terrible news for Lady Matilda. Is there no way to stave off ruin a little longer?

SECKER. Only by making it more complete when it does come. A sale now will leave you with a few thousands margin; another year would swallow them up, and leave you with nothing.

VAVASOUR. It's not for myself I care, but for Lady Matilda and the children. There's the money to be lodged for Stanhope's commission and Lilian's outfit for the season—her first season, you know, Secker, on which her mother counts so much. Who's to break this to my lady?

SECKER. You promised to prepare Lady Matilda for the worst last audit day.

VAVASOUR. Yes, yes, but have you no feeling? Don't you see that sort of thing isn't to be done on the spur of the moment, sir?

SECKER. Further concealment is impossible. My advice is—tell Lady Vavasour the worst at once.

VAVASOUR. But do have a little consideration for my position, Secker, as the head of an ancient family—a family, sir, that has held Cleve Manor since the Conquest, and returned county members in the reign of Henry IV. [*His voice trembles.*] And now, to leave the old place, where one's heart has grown to every stone, every tree—where the old name seems to have taken root like the old timber—to be shouldered out by some mushroom money-maker. Confess, Secker, it is hard to bear!

SECKER. Families are like crops, Mr. Vavasour; they will exhaust the soil if you keep always taking out and never putting in, and then there's nothing for it but new soiling.

VAVASOUR. I never expected to hear such revolutionary sentiments from you, Secker.

SECKER. We lawyers must look facts in the face, Mr. Vavasour, revolutionary or otherwise. After all, the world moves, sir, and it will only give us the lie if we say it stands still. I'd better leave you to break the unpleasant news to Lady Matilda.

VAVASOUR. Stay, stay, my good friend! It would come so much better from you; Lady Matilda is quite a woman of business. *I* can't put it to her in a business point of view; *you* can, you know.

SECKER. I make it a rule never to interfere between husband and wife. You must face the facts.

VAVASOUR. Confound it, sir! I am quite ready to face the facts, but how am I to face Lady Vavasour?

Enter LADY MATILDA VAVASOUR.

Good gracious! here she is.
    [*Both rise;* SECKER, *gathering up his papers, bows to* LADY MATILDA *and is going off.*

LADY MATILDA. Don't run away, Mr. Secker; I've some commissions for you. My love, I've a letter from my sister announcing that poor Reginald Fitz-Urse is laid up with the measles. Only think, Mr. Secker, of his catching the measles two years after marriage! And in her P.S. my sister most kindly offers to take charge of dear Lilian for the season.

VAVASOUR. That's lucky!

LADY MATILDA. Lucky?

VAVASOUR. I mean, my dear, it'll save our taking a house for ourselves.

LADY MATILDA. [*Compassionately.*] It is well he has you and me to look after him, Mr. Secker.

VAVASOUR. Why, it seems to me a very sisterly offer.

LADY MATILDA. Sisterly—eh?

VAVASOUR. Well, motherly—if you like it better.

LADY MATILDA. Yes, I like motherly better. Jane has four daughters of her own, on hand; you don't suppose dear Lilian would be allowed a chance of anything eligible till they are provided for? So, my dear Mr. Secker, I want you to write at once and engage a good house for the season. I think I should prefer Mayfair to Belgravia; and on the whole I think we'd better not take our own horses, so you'll be good enough to arrange with Anderson; and—let me see— what else? [*Looking at her tablets.*

VAVASOUR. [*Aside to* SECKER.] Tell her it can't be done, Secker.

SECKER. [*Aside to* VAVASOUR.] Tell her yourself, Mr. Vavasour.

LADY MATILDA. Whispering? Why, my dear Marmaduke, what a remarkably long face! And yours is almost as long, Mr. Secker.

VAVASOUR. The fact is, my dear, Secker has some rather unpleasant news to break to you.

SECKER. I beg your pardon; Mr. Vavasour wishes your ladyship to understand——

VAVASOUR. And so—I leave Secker to explain——

SECKER. That if arrangements are to be made for a season in town, your ladyship must find the means as well as give the orders.

LADY MATILDA. Pardon me; that's your affair. As Chancellor of the Exchequer, you settle the Budget—I only vote the Appropriation Bill.

VAVASOUR. But how if the ways and means are not forthcoming, my dear?

LADY MATILDA. [*Gaily.*] Oh, then we must take a vote on account till the Budget's brought in. It won't be the first time, you know—we did it last year.

VAVASOUR. In fact we've done it so often that we can't do it again.

LADY MATILDA. I don't understand you.

VAVASOUR. Tell her, Secker—I haven't the heart.

SECKER. In plain English, my lady, we've come to the end of the tether—you in the way of spending, and I in the way of raising money. Cleve Abbey's mortgaged up to the hilt— and, short of a miracle, I don't see how we can stave off a sale of the property before the year's out.

LADY MATILDA. [*After a pause, and in an altered voice.*] Marmaduke, is this true?

VAVASOUR. Well, really, I understand it is; that is—I don't understand exactly, but I'm afraid it is, my dear.

LADY MATILDA. And I have been kept in the dark while the avalanche was gathering, to be told of it just as it is ready to crush us. Have I deserved this?

VAVASOUR. Has either of us deserved it? I'm sure I did my best to pull up. I've done everything that courage could do.

LADY MATILDA. Except the one thing it was your duty to do above all others—trust *me*. When the captain abandons the ship, it is time for his mate to take the helm! [*To* SECKER.] This sale must be prevented, at all costs and at all hazards.

SECKER. *Must* be prevented, my lady? With all my heart, but I don't see how.

LADY MATILDA. [*To* SECKER.] Those mortgages! There are

heavy arrears of interest, you say? The man cannot have been very pressing?

VAVASOUR. [*Lugubriously.*] Hasn't he, though? If you knew how I've begged and prayed to him for time—only to look round; why, I've as good as gone on my knees to the fellow—by letter, of course.

LADY MATILDA. I must try what I can do, without going on my knees. We must have no secrets from you now, Mr. Secker. It is not our fortunes that are at stake here, but our children's prospects. This is to be Lilian's first season in London. What would be her chances of marrying as a daughter of a ruined man? I tell you this sale must be prevented—at least for this season. Is the mortgagee an acquaintance of yours?

SECKER. An old acquaintance. But for that he would hardly have been so forbearing.

LADY MATILDA. Is he a man of fortune?

SECKER. Leading partner in one of the oldest and wealthiest firms in Liverpool.

LADY MATILDA. In trade? Persons of that class are always open to social influences. We must invite him down here at once.

SECKER. He's been in the neighbourhood this week past. I sent him over with my card to see the ruins this morning. He should be somewhere about now.

VAVASOUR. [*Bitterly.*] 'Taking stock,' I suppose he would call it, of Cleve Abbey. Confounded shopkeeper!

LADY MATILDA. And you never offered to do the honours of the old place. [*To* VAVASOUR.] Go at once and say Lady Matilda Vavasour particularly desires the pleasure of his acquaintance.

VAVASOUR. Eh? Say—that—ah—egad! I begin to smell a rat! A capital idea of my lady's, eh—Secker? I'm glad I had the pluck to tell her the worst. Let us take this fellow my lady's invitation.   [*Exeunt* VAVASOUR *and* SECKER *by window.*

LADY MATILDA. Anything to gain time. A year's respite—six months, even—may be our salvation! Lilian's happiness shall not be wrecked if a mother's wit and will can save it.

Enter LILIAN, *speaking off.*

LILIAN. At your peril, Bertie, if you stir till I tell you. Good morning, mamma! [*Kisses her, then joining her hands in mock contrition.*] Please, beg pardon for playing truant at breakfast, but I was so floored with the ball!

LADY MATILDA. 'Floored,' my love? I suppose you mean fatigued. Do drop that detestable slang.

LILIAN. Oh, but Stannie and Bertie say I'm such fun!

LADY MATILDA. Take my opinion before theirs, dear. Men may think slang girls 'such fun,' but they seldom see any fun in fast wives. But this is all that wretched Bertie's doing. He shan't stay in the house another week.

LILIAN. Oh, but just think, mamma, where he'll go to in the Civil Service examination if you tear him away from his coach!

LADY MATILDA. His coach?

LILIAN. Me, mamma! I'm grinding him up in his history and things. Stewing down hard facts into portable historical soup, suited to Bertie's limited digestion; Liebig's extract of beef is a trifle to my essence of history. Why, I've actually packed the two first lines of French kings into a neat four-in-hand of my own, to the tune of 'Sing, old Rose, and burn the bellows!'

LADY MATILDA. You are as great a tom-boy as he is a tom-fool! And now tell me seriously, darling—what sort of a ball had you?

LILIAN. Oh, awfully nice; I mean very jolly—that is, no end of a crowd. I didn't sit out one dance.

LADY MATILDA. You danced only in your own set, I hope?

LILIAN. Oh, of course, mamma—except twice.

LADY MATILDA. And that was——

LILIAN. With a friend of the Bunters.

LADY MATILDA. [*In horror.*] Danced twice with a friend of the Bunters, Lilian! Those odious parvenus—who seem to think society's a show, to be entered by paying at the door. If I hate anyone—I hope I don't—but if I do, it's the Bunters, and the upstart class they belong to. And you actually had the recklessness to dance with one of their set!

LILIAN. Oh, but I assure you, mamma, he was not in their style. Not the least loud in his dress, and I should think he's thirty at least, quite what Bertie calls 'an old fogy.'

LADY MATILDA. Lilian!

LILIAN. And then I wasn't at all nice to him of course. Oh, I snubbed and chaffed him frightfully——

LADY MATILDA. Really, Lilian!

LILIAN. And Lady Weston's carriage couldn't get up—I suppose her John had some of the Fleece beer—they don't get too much at Weston Hanger, you know—

LADY MATILDA. My dear, don't gossip.

LILIAN. Mamma, you never will let me talk—and the Bunters offered to set me down——

LADY MATILDA. You declined the honour?

LILIAN. [*Apologetically.*] No, I didn't, mamma. Well, you see, I thought I should rather like it—Mrs. Bunter is such fun with her old point and her new diamonds, and not an 'H' to her back, mamma! And then Fanny Bunter—in spite of her Ruskinism-run-mad—isn't half a bad sort; and then, of course, dear ma, I didn't dance more than was necessary, and I——

LADY MATILDA. Lilian, I must talk very seriously to you, and I hardly know where to begin. Every other word you utter is of the vilest slang. You've danced with some low person of the Bunters' set—you've accepted a seat in the Bunters' carriage——

LILIAN. Oh, but I did that partly for the fun of making Mr. Brown ride outside.

LADY MATILDA. Mr. Brown? And pray who is Mr. Brown? I'm not aware that we have the honour of knowing a Mr. Brown.

LILIAN. He was the partner I told you of.

LADY MATILDA. Lilian, this heedlessness of yours at once alarms and distresses me. You never had so much need as now of a proper sense of what you owe to society, to your family, to yourself. Who knows, my dear child, but that this first season may land you in a brilliant success, or a horrible

fiasco! I have never, like too many mothers, given you a
sentimental view of life. I have tried to prepare you for the
world as you will find it. Let me see you reward my maternal
care!   [*Kisses her.*

LILIAN. Yes, I know, you've told me all this before, mamma.

LADY MATILDA. I have never deceived you, my darling. Your
papa is not rich.

LILIAN. Oh, if I could fill his dear old pockets!

LADY MATILDA. It is indispensable that in marrying you
should look to a good establishment. Fortunately, you have
always had a mother to guide you. Ah, if I had had that
invaluable blessing at your age!

LILIAN. I suppose you would not have married papa?

LADY MATILDA. I did not say anything to warrant that,
Lilian. But I have lived to see more and more clearly that
in our station fortune is the main, nay, the indispensable
requisite for happiness; without that, nothing can make life
pleasant. With that, most things that make life unpleasant
can be got over. Never forget that, darling.
                              [*Patting her under the chin.*

LILIAN. I won't, mamma, depend upon it.   [*Kisses her.*

LADY MATILDA. And do oblige me by dropping slang—keeping people like the Bunters and this Mr. Brown at a proper
distance, and not being quite so free and easy with young
men. Your cousin Bertie, for instance.

LILIAN. Oh, mamma, I'm sure there's no danger there.

LADY MATILDA. To you, perhaps. How do you know what
there may be to him?

LILIAN. Oh, nobody ever fell in love with his coach.

LADY MATILDA. [*Looking annoyed.*] His 'coach?'

LILIAN. That isn't slang—really it isn't, mamma; it's the
regular thing. I mean it's the correct card. But seriously, if
Bertie ever does talk any nonsense of that kind, I'll be down
on him like a hammer.

LADY MATILDA. My dear!

LILIAN. Mamma, you don't seem to understand me.

LADY MATILDA. I own I do not, my child.

LILIAN. Well, I mean, I'll shut him up. Put the extinguisher on him.

LADY MATILDA. Worse and worse!

FITZ-URSE. [*Outside.*] I say, Lily!

Enter FITZ-URSE.

Beg pardon, aunty. I say, Lily, how do you divide one million one hundred and eighty one thousand six hundred pounds five shillings and two pence, by six shillings and eight pence? Sixes into five you can't, you know, and eights into two I'll be hanged if you can.

LILIAN. Oh, you stupid! Reduce them both to a common denomination.

FITZ-URSE. A common what?

LILIAN. Here, I'll show you. Only a minute, mamma. You see, compound division is rather hard for him. They didn't do arithmetic at Eton. Now, you old muff—
[*They go up, talking till quite off.*

LADY MATILDA. Dear girl! If she were a little less heedless. Ah! [*Turns as* SECKER *appears with* BROWN *at window.*

SECKER. Mr. Vavasour has been detained by his woodman. Will you allow me to present Mr. Brown to Lady Matilda Vavasour?

LADY MATILDA. [*Startled, but immediately suppressing it.*] Mr. Brown! Singular coincidence. I and my daughter were just talking of you.

BROWN. Indeed! My morning has been full of surprises.

LADY MATILDA. Lilian was telling me how she enjoyed last night's ball. Thanks, not a little, to her agreeable new partner.

BROWN. I should never have guessed from her manner last night that I was the sort of partner she thought it worth while to be pleasant to.

LADY MATILDA. Lilian is a little brusque sometimes.

BROWN. So it struck me last night.

LADY MATILDA. You know what girls are nowadays, Mr. Brown.

BROWN. Well, not much; but Miss Vavasour seemed very much amused, and I am very glad if I amused her.

LADY MATILDA. [*Laughing.*] That shows how little you men know of a woman's real impression of you. Come, I suppose Mr. Vavasour has shown you the homestead and the stables. You must let me do the honours of my own poor little flower garden. Women have so few resources in the country—our flowers become our companions—almost our friends.

BROWN. They have one invaluable quality for friendship; they have no tongues to say more than they mean.

LADY MATILDA. And they never belie their looks—as men and women do—only too often.

[*Exeunt* LADY MATILDA *and* BROWN, *at window.*

SECKER. [*Looking after them.*] Look out for your pockets, Sam Brown. Why can't the law let a woman like that stand in her husband's shoes, as well as wear his small clothes?

Enter LILIAN *with books, and* FITZ-URSE *with papers.*

LILIAN. Now let me see that you've got the question down right. [*Reads from book;* FITZ-URSE *writes it down.*] 'If twelve men can dig a trench fifteen yards long and four broad in three days of twelve hours each, in how many days of nine hours can eight men dig a trench twenty yards long and eight broad?'

FITZ-URSE. [*Who has followed the question, looks up from paper.*] How is a fellow to find that out unless he knows how strong the other fellows are?

LILIAN. Bertie, you are a duffer! In these questions the strength is always presumed to be equal.

FITZ-URSE. I like that. As if one fellow ever was just as strong as another fellow. You might just as well ask: if it takes you ten minutes to get up the names, weights, and colours of the Derby Card, how long will it take me to floor the births, deaths, and marriages of the kings of England?

LILIAN. Well, suppose we tried. Here's your manual. Will you say your 'Principal Treaties' or your 'Decisive Battles?'

FITZ-URSE. I know one decisive battle between Bertie Fitz-Urse and his coach. By Jove! I wonder you've got the patience sometimes.

LILIAN. I want you to get through, sir, and I mean to pull you through.

FITZ-URSE. Ah, but suppose they put the examination off as they've done once already—I shall have to be crammed over again.

LILIAN. Ah, one must be careful how one puts in the new charge before firing off the old one—it might burst the gun.

FITZ-URSE. Sometimes I feel I'd better cut the Civil Service altogether, and try Australia. Fellows say the kangaroos give one a capital run sometimes; or there's Natal—one might go in for an elephant, you know.

LILIAN. Oh, yes; and come back a lion, with a mane of tawny beard and a tale—in two volumes—to the bosom of your family, and the embraces of the Geographical Society.

FITZ-URSE. Oh, I say—you do chaff a fellow so. You see, one don't mind chaff from a girl one don't care for. But I do care for you, Lily—I do, honour bright.

LILIAN. [*Slily.*] I don't believe you.

FITZ-URSE. You're an awfully jolly girl, and I only wish you would let me ask you——

LILIAN. Anything you like about the history of England.

FITZ-URSE. Hang that! I mean whether you think you could ever care a bit about me—I don't mean as a coach, you know, but in the way of a—lov—a——   [*Pause.*

LILIAN. [*Laughs aside.*] Now Bertie, be a good boy, and don't talk nonsense.

FITZ-URSE. Nonsense! One don't like going on one's knees, you know, but if that's the correct thing——
                [*Takes out handkerchief and about to kneel.*

LILIAN. Anything but the correct thing. Forbidden by the table of prohibited degrees. A man mustn't go on his knees to his coach.   [*Laughing.*
                [LADY MATILDA *appears at window.*

FITZ-URSE. Hang it all! If you don't care for a fellow, don't poke fun at him.

LILIAN. [*Gravely.*] Listen to me, Bertie. You and I can't afford to fall in love with each other. [*Walking arm-in-arm.*] Two noughts are nothing; you know arithmetic enough for that. You must look out for a wife who wants connection, and has plenty of money to buy it with. And I—well—I know what I must look out for.

FITZ-URSE. But I don't care a rap about money.

LILIAN. [*In* LADY MATILDA's *manner.*] Hush, Bertie! Naughty boy! Remember that in our class fortune is the main—nay, the indispensable condition of happiness; without that, nothing can make life pleasant; with that, most things that make life unpleasant can be got over. Never forget that, darling.   [*Chucking him under the chin.*

LADY MATILDA. [*At window, aside.*] Excellent girl! My lesson, to the letter!

FITZ-URSE. Lilian, I didn't think you were one of that sort. I always thought you were the style of girl to value a fellow's love—a good fellow's, I mean—though he hadn't a brown.

LILIAN. Can't afford it, I tell you! Ain't to be done at the price! I'll tell you what—if you're a very good boy I'll coach you into matrimony, as well as multiplication. I should recommend you strongly to make up to Fanny Bunter. She's a very pretty girl—a girl of the period—and she'll have no end of money.

FITZ-URSE. Take care—you might drive a fellow to do something desperate! I don't believe you'd half like it if I did make up to Fanny Bunter.

LILIAN. Just you try. Now go and have another good grind at the Plantagenet kings. Be off, sir! Am I your coach, or am I not?   [*Points to door.*

FITZ-URSE. I tell you what it is: the next time I see Fanny Bunter, if I don't make desperate running with her, just to spite you, and see how you like that!   [*Exit.*

LILIAN. You can do just as you like. I don't care a bit.
                        [*Turns, and sees* LADY MATILDA.

LADY MATILDA. Nothing could have been better, my dear.

LILIAN. [*Surprised.*] Were you there, mamma?

LADY MATILDA. Yes, nearly all the time, and delighted to hear you talk so sensibly to that silly boy. [LILIAN *laughs aside.*] And delighted to hear you've laid my lesson to heart. You may laugh, but you'll be thankful one day, too. And now come into the garden. We've a visitor—a visitor who has been inquiring after you. Look!   [*Points outside window.*

LILIAN. [*Astonished.*] Mr. Brown! I assure you, mamma, I didn't ask him.

LADY MATILDA. I am perfectly aware of that. I now wish you to make yourself particularly agreeable to him.

LILIAN. Agreeable to that Mr. Brown, mamma—a friend of the Bunters!

LADY MATILDA. Oh, quite a mistake, that. He's in business, it's true, but he's evidently a superior person.

LILIAN. Mamma!

LADY MATILDA. There are reasons why we should pay him every attention. You know, when I say there are reasons——

Enter VAVASOUR, *with a telegram.*

VAVASOUR. A telegram just arrived, my dear! Reginald Fitz-Urse has died of the measles.

LADY MATILDA. Is it possible? What a very sad thing for his wife.

VAVASOUR. Although we weren't on terms, still—one can't help feeling.

LADY MATILDA. It is most distressing! This will make a great difference in Bertie's prospects.

VAVASOUR. I should think it would! Why, he stands next in the title, failing issue of poor Reginald.

LADY MATILDA. Lilian, I think you had better break it to your cousin Bertie. See that he writes a proper letter, poor fellow, and be kind to him; I'm afraid you treated him a little too harshly just now.

LILIAN. I thought you wished it, mamma!

LADY MATILDA. Yes, but there is a way of doing these things. Go, my love.

LILIAN. All right, ma. I'll make him write a stunning letter.

[*Exit.*

LADY MATILDA. This is terrible news!

VAVASOUR. Well, my dear, these things will happen; but considering we haven't spoken to them for five years, we can hardly be expected to break our hearts over poor Reginald.

LADY MATILDA. [*Sharply.*] Reginald! This will prevent Lilian's coming out, and destroy all her chances for the season! We might have staved off ruin, or kept it quiet for this year, but by the next the worst must be known. Lilian's prospects will be hopelessly blighted.

VAVASOUR. Just like Reginald—always doing things at the wrong time. Why couldn't he have his measles after the season.

LADY MATILDA. Yes, it is the only resource! Mr. Vavasour, are you willing to clear yourself from embarrassments, to preserve our position in the county, to keep Cleve Abbey in the family?

VAVASOUR. Willing! Only tell me how it is to be done.

LADY MATILDA. By marrying Lilian to this Mr. Brown.

VAVASOUR. Matilda!

LADY MATILDA. The man holds the mortgage on the property. It rests with him to force a sale or prevent one. By this means, and this only, I see a way to redeem the family fortunes.

VAVASOUR. What! Marry Lilian to one of these money-grubbers? It's enough to make all the Vavasours rise from the family vault to forbid the banns.

LADY MATILDA. It is our duty to sink our own feelings in the interests of our children. Stanhope must marry a fortune to keep up the old name—Lilian must sacrifice the old name to marry a fortune. What does it matter, after all, whether Cleve Abbey descends in the male or female line?

VAVASOUR. It will be a bitter pill, but I suppose it's a law of nature that these money-grubs should eat up the good old family trees. But how are you to bring this unnatural match about? Lilian's her father's girl all over; she hates a snob.

LADY MATILDA. Mr. Brown is not a snob, Marmaduke. He is one of England's merchant princes—one of the class which has made of this tiny island an empire on which the sun never sets!

Enter LILIAN.

VAVASOUR. Good gracious, Matilda! Have you been to the Manchester school too?

LILIAN. Bertie's writing his letter, mamma. But I've been thinking of such a difficulty: one can't be presented in mourning.

LADY MATILDA. No, Lilian; we must give up the season in town altogether.

LILIAN. [*Ruefully.*] Give up the season, and all the delights I've been dreaming of so long—operas and balls, picnic parties, Rotten Row, and the Zoo on Sundays? Oh, I could cry with disappointment.

LADY MATILDA. I sympathise with you, my poor child—but proper feeling must be shown on these occasions.

LILIAN. But you know we didn't care a bit about cousin Reginald in his life-time, [LADY MATILDA *holds up her finger;* LILIAN *turns to* VAVASOUR.] and I call it downright hypocrisy to shut up ourselves in black now he's gone!

VAVASOUR. Very true, Lily—very true, but one mustn't say so.

LADY MATILDA. You must remember, Lilian, family mourning is one of the usages of good society. My dear Marmaduke, we are neglecting our visitor.

VAVASOUR. [*Aside.*] What a woman that is! Got a reason for everything.   [*Exit.*

LADY MATILDA. Lilian, this unfortunate affair not only destroys the pleasure of your season—it is likely to seal the ruin of your family. I feel I may trust you. Your father is deeply, nay, desperately involved. I had counted on arranging a brilliant marriage for you before this was discovered. It can't be kept back another year.

LILIAN. I know what you wished, mamma, and I wished it too, so much, that I might keep up the old place, and help Stannie with his steps—and get papa out of these weary money troubles. Girls are so useless generally, and I felt so proud of going out to set everything right.

LADY MATILDA. My brave affectionate girl, your chance may be damaged, but it is not desperate—only be guided by me.

Enter VAVASOUR, *with* BROWN.

VAVASOUR. I must hand you over to the ladies, Mr. Brown, while I write my letter of condolence. [BROWN *bows.*] Poor Lily!   [*Sighs and exit.*

LADY MATILDA. Here's a young lady been making humble confession—and begging me to ask absolution for her sauciness last night.

BROWN. Plenary absolution, if Miss Vavasour will accept it at my hand.   [*Offers his hand.*

LILIAN. I'm afraid I was very rude.

BROWN. It seemed to amuse you, and it didn't hurt me.

LADY MATILDA. Well, I must leave Lily to prove her penitence, as it is close on post-time. You have heard of our sad family bereavement—our first cousin—Lord Bearholm's only son——

BROWN. I understand from Mr. Vavasour that you had not been on terms for some years.

LADY MATILDA. Yes. How any shadow of past unkindness deepens the melancholy of such a moment!
                                    [*Wipes her eyes, and exit.*

LILIAN. [*Playing piano.*] I wish I could feel as mamma does, but I never saw cousin Reginald—and one can't pretend to care much about a man one never saw, can one?

BROWN. I hope not.

LILIAN. I confess I do feel dreadfully sorry for the loss of the London season——

BROWN. Regret London—with such a beautiful place as this? Why, I think Cleve Abbey would reconcile me even to the loss of Liverpool!

LILIAN. Oh, please don't compare London to Liverpool! Why, London means pleasure, gaiety, society, triumphs!

BROWN. And Liverpool means business. I dare say you think it odd a man should miss ledgers and dock warrants, noisy wharves and dingy offices, but these have been my life, you know.

LILIAN. How awfully dull you must have found it.

BROWN. Not half so dull as what you call amusement. I'm afraid I'm spoilt for an idle man. Why, even if I lived in the country, I fancy I should settle down into something like a gentleman farmer.

LILIAN. Oh, but a gentleman farmer's life is perfection. Sit down. [*They sit.*] Pottering about the fields on a hundred guinea cob, baiting one's bailiffs, coaxing the crops, and grumbling at the weather; and then think of the darling little lambs, and the lovely calves that poke their dear little wet noses into one's hands.

BROWN. Ahem! I'm afraid that's young lady farming. I think I should go in for pigs—short-haired, black Berkshires.

LILIAN. Oh, I'm very fond of pigs, too. I do think a fat round small-eared quite lovely! Then there's hunting, and shooting, and riding into the justice meetings, and looking after the schools and the old women——

BROWN. I don't know so much about the old women.

LILIAN. And feeling oneself welcome in every hall, farm-house, and labourer's cottage for ten miles round. Oh, if I were only a gentleman farmer!

BROWN. I'm afraid that's out of the question, but you might help to transform me into one.

LILIAN. You?

BROWN. Yes; I've been thinking of buying an estate.

LILIAN. In this county?

BROWN. Yes; in this immediate neighbourhood.

LILIAN. But there's no place in the market hereabouts.

BROWN. There may be one shortly.

LILIAN. I'm so glad.

BROWN. Thank you.

LILIAN. Oh, no—it's thank you. In the country one's always thankful for a new neighbour.

BROWN. My acquaintances, the Bunters, don't seem to have felt themselves particularly welcome.

LILIAN. Oh, they seemed so satisfied that their money was to open all the doors in the county—no wonder people took a pleasure in shutting them in their faces. You must own that poor Mr. Bunter is an unmistakeable cad. (BROWN *raises his eyebrows.*] And his wife—well, she's a caution for snakes! [BROWN *opens his eyes still wider. After a slight pause.*] That's what Bertie calls them—Bertie, my cousin. He's here, reading for the Civil Service examination. I'm coaching him in his English history.

BROWN. And he's giving you lessons in the English language.

LILIAN. [*Reading his look.*] Have I said anything very dreadful?

BROWN. Well, 'cad' and 'a caution for snakes' are rather strong expressions for a lady.

LILIAN. I like words there's no mistake about.

BROWN. I should have thought there might be some mistake about words of that sort in a lady's mouth.

LILIAN. [*Rather hurriedly and hotly.*] Naturally, we old families don't choose to be walked atop of by these pushing parvenus. They seem to forget there are things money can't buy.

BROWN. Will you tell me what they are?

LILIAN. [*Proudly.*] The dignity of an old name, the associations of long descent, the recollections of a stately past! What should people who can't identify their great-grandfathers know of these?

BROWN. I admit the past is yours, Miss Vavasour, but how about the future?

LILIAN. The future can't belong to people like the Bunters, or it wouldn't be a future.

BROWN. I rather think it belongs more to those whose brains and hands shape the world about them, than to those who stand on the dignity of old names.

LILIAN. You cannot be expected to feel as I do on such points.

BROWN. No. I can't identify my great-grandfather; he is lost in the large family of Browns. It's a comfort, though, to think one must have had a great-grandfather.

Enter LADY MATILDA.

LADY MATILDA. Now, Mr. Brown, I'm quite at your service for the fernery. I hope Lilian has made her peace with you.

BROWN. I wasn't aware there had ever been a war.

LADY MATILDA. Even if there had been, I don't think Lily would have been a very implacable enemy. [*Aside to him.*] The sweetest temper, Mr. Brown! Ah, you can make allowances for a mother's weakness.

[*Exeunt* LADY MATILDA *and* BROWN.

LILIAN. [*Playing piano.*] I don't like him a bit! What right had he to find fault with my language and to sneer at ancestors? Why is mamma so civil to him, I wonder? I'm sure I hope we shan't have him for a neighbour.

Enter GANTRY, *with cards on salver.*

GANTRY. Mr., Mrs., and Miss Bunter, Miss, and Mr. Blasenbalg.

LILIAN. I'm sure mamma's not at home to them. Say everybody's out, Gantry.

Enter, on GANTRY's *heels,* MR., MRS., *and* FANNY BUNTER, *and* BLASENBALG. *Exit* GANTRY.

MRS. BUNTER. It's only us, Miss Vavasour. We've brought back the fan you left last night in the carriage.

BUNTER. Country neighbours and no ceremony, you know. [*Rubbing his hands.*] Mrs. B. was all for pasteboard, but my rule is—where I call, I come in.

LILIAN. How d'ye do, Miss Bunter? I'm glad to see you're not looking a bit the worse for the ball.

BUNTER. Let's see; you don't know Mr. Berthold Blasenbalg. [BLASENBALG *bows profoundly.*] My Chancellor of the Exchequer, First Commissioner of Works, and Head of the Science and Art Department, rolled into one.

BLASENBALG. Go along with you! Perhaps you didn't know Bunter was such a wag, Miss Vavasour. Humour is his strong point.

BUNTER. Don't blush, B. Though you mightn't think it to look at him, I don't know a man who knows more than my friend B. B. I ain't given to exaggeration; when Benjamin Bunter says a thing, he means it.

BLASENBALG. [*Aside to* BUNTER.] Now's my time. I'll take a squint round, and reconnoitre the ground a bit.

BUNTER. [*Aside to him.*] Go and squint! [*Exit* BLASENBALG.

LILIAN. Mamma will be sorry not to see you, but a death in the family prevents her receiving you to-day.

MRS. BUNTER. A death in the family? Might I ask which branch—the Shortlands or the Bearholms?

LILIAN. My cousin, Reginald Fitz-Urse, has died suddenly.

MRS. BUNTER. The Honorable Reginald Fitz-Urse dead, and only two years married—and no children yet, if I remember! Pray tell her ladyship how much we feel for her.

BUNTER. Ah, we are cut down as a flower!

LILIAN. Mamma will be so sorry not to see you.

BUNTER. Assure her, Miss Vavasour, the regret is mutual. [*Glibly.*] It's true, we're not members of the same order. You belong to the old landed gentry; I'm a self-made man. Not that I blush for it! Maria there will tell you Benjamin Bunter don't care who knows he came into the City of London a ragged boy, without a shoe to his foot, and the sum of THREE PENCE [*Emphasizing each word.*] IN COPPER in his pocket. But I had had good parents, and I hope I honour 'em. They taught me to read, write, and to cypher. I 'ad henergy—though I say it—and hindustry; and I rose, ma'am, by little and little, to the proud position of the 'umble individual who now stands before you.

MRS. BUNTER. Really, Mr. B., I don't see what call you've got to go back like that.

BUNTER. Because I've come forrard like this, Maria, and we are told it is good not to be puffed up.

MRS. BUNTER. What a beautiful place you have here, Miss Vavasour—only if I were you, I would get rid of them nasty shabby ruins.

FANNY. Oh, mamma! How can you suggest such a thing? I adore ruins; they speak to me with the voices of the past! [*To* LILIAN.] I am sure you hear them—even now. Hark!

[*Sentimentally looking off*.

LILIAN. It's only the wind in the chimneys. Yes, I like ruins.

MRS. BUNTER. So I see, by the furnitur'. I like things that look like the money you've put into them.

BUNTER. [*Sententiously*.] Everything has its place, Mrs. B. Old families and old furnitur', like theirs—modern hopulence with modern elegance, like ours.

LILIAN. [*Aside*.] Oh, I shall die of these people! Why don't they go?

MRS. BUNTER. But one thing I should like to see while we are here—that's the gardens and the glass. B. is all for glass——

BUNTER. And iron, Maria. Glass and iron are, I often say, the right and left 'ands of 'orticulture. Thanks to them and 'ot-water pipes, we can conquer climate and annilliate the helements! I've three acres under glass at Beaumanor Park, three-quarters of a mile of fernery; and our forcing 'ouses are considered equal to Chatsworth—at least, so my gardeners tell me. I don't pretend to know—still less boast. What is man, that he should set up his 'orn? A poor worm! You're 'ere to-day, and gone you are to-morrow!

LILIAN. I'll send one of the men to show you the gardens. [*Aside*.] For what I have escaped may my stars make me truly thankful!   [*Exit*.

FANNY. [*Looking at cabinet*.] Oh, mamma—papa, do come and look at this lovely buhl!

BUNTER. A bull, my dear? Not in the flower garden, surely?

FANNY. [*Deprecatingly*.] Oh, papa!

BUNTER. I'll be bound it's only one of them little Breton cows, tethered on the lawn.

FANNY. [*Contemptuously*.] Who mentioned cows? I said buhl, papa—B, U, H, L—buhl!

BUNTER. No, Fanny, fashion may change some things, but B, U, double L still spells 'bull,' all the world over.

FANNY. Oh, it's no use talking to papa! Do look, mamma, at this lovely bit of marqueterie.

BUNTER. Ah, a bit of marketry. That's something like! 'Tain't often you take an interest in anything like house-keeping.

FANNY. Oh, this is too barbarous!

[*She and* MRS. BUNTER *look at furniture together.*

Enter BLASENBALG; *he takes* BUNTER *aside.*

BLASENBALG. De eisen is all right, sure enough, in de mountain limestone. Such beautiful kidneys! Pot-holes full of dem! All von mit de Saxon and Furness hematites. De iron is dere —a mine of velth under our feet!

[MRS. BUNTER *takes out her 'Pocket Peerage' and thumbs it.*

BUNTER. Under our feet—eh? We must manage to get the kidneys into our pockets. I say, Brown's been poking his nose about the place. Suppose he was up to snuff, as well as you and I?

BLASENBALG. Snuff? Snuff of a candle. Brown knows nothing. I've sounded him.

MRS. BUNTER. Yes, I'm sure it's him. [*Appealing to* BUNTER.] My dear, you know that Mr. Bertie Fitz-Urse, that was so attentive to Fanny last night——

FANNY. And waltzed so beautifully, mamma?

MRS. BUNTER. That very elegant young man, you know——

BUNTER. Elegant—eh? Keeps an account at the Bank of Elegance, I should say, and nowhere else. What about this elegant party?

FANNY. Party!

MRS. BUNTER. Now Lord Bearholm's only son is dead, he's next for the title, after the Honourable Mrs. Reginald's baby —supposing she has one.

FANNY. There was something very distinguished about him.

BUNTER. And if he *is* next to the title, Maria, what's that to us? We ain't members of a bloated aristocracy. I hope me and mine reckon such distinctions at their proper value.

'The rank is but the guinea stamp.
The man's the man, for a' that.'

BLASENBALG. A noble sentiment, that!

BUNTER. The sort of thing that comes home to a man's business and his bosom—that does.

'The man's the man, for a' that.'

MRS. BUNTER. All the same—it's a pleasure to know who's who.

FANNY. And where do we find so much elegance and refinement as among the aristocracy?

Enter FITZ-URSE, *with a letter in his hand.*

FITZ-URSE. I say, Lily, how d'ye spell 'sympathy'—'i' or 'y?' [*Seeing the* BUNTERS.] I beg your pardon! None the worse for the ball, Miss Bunter? [*Shakes hands—bows to* BUNTER.] I'd no notion there was anybody here.

MRS. BUNTER. Miss Vavasour will be back directly. She's kindly offered to show us the gardens.

FITZ-URSE. Oh, I say, Mrs. Bunter, let me show you.

MRS. BUNTER. Oh, we couldn't think of presuming——

FITZ-URSE. Delighted—honour bright! I've nothing to do.

Enter LILIAN.

LILIAN. Nothing to do, sir? How dare you say that?

FITZ-URSE. Nothing I like doing, I mean.

BUNTER. While you ladies are among the flowers—your native element, as I may call it—me and my friend here will take a turn round the Home Park. What is there like the works of natur'—especially under steam cultivation, 'abroad in the meadows'—eh, B.?

BLASENBALG. To view de young lodes—eh, B.?

[*Exeunt* BUNTER *and* BLASENBALG.

FITZ-URSE. Like flowers, Miss Bunter?

[LILIAN *shows* MRS. BUNTER *the furniture.*

FANNY. I adore them! As Ruskin says, they are a revelation. Don't you feel they are a revelation? What sweet society—even in the hedgerow weed!

FITZ-URSE. Yes, one never feels lonely with a weed.

FANNY. And to think there are people who cannot appreciate their fragrance!

FITZ-URSE. Can't stand 'em, even in the open air.

FANNY. As Wordsworth says—

> 'A primrose on the river's brim
> A yellow primrose was to him,
> And it was nothing more!'

FITZ-URSE. [*Repeating mechanically.*] 'Nothing more!' [*Aside.*] I wonder what the deuce it should have been.
[*They stroll into the garden. During this conversation,* MRS. BUNTER *has been in animated conversation with* LILIAN *over the 'Pocket Peerage.'*]

MRS. BUNTER. I declare, Mr. Fitz-Urse and Fanny have walked off tatur-tatur!

LILIAN. There's a gardener at your orders.

MRS. BUNTER. [*Looks into garden.*] And if yonder ain't your ma and Mr. Brown, of all people! I must say, I think Brown would have shown better taste to have kept away. But some people has no delicacy.

LILIAN. I don't understand why Mr. Brown should feel any delicacy. Do you mean after the snubbing I gave him last night?

MRS. BUNTER. I mean considering the money he has lent your papa on mortgage, and that your papa hasn't found it convenient to pay him. In course, money will be tight; as Bunter says—'it is it's nature to!'

LILIAN. Papa owe Mr. Brown money?

MRS. BUNTER. You see, Bunter makes it his business to know these things. No saying he mightn't bid for the property himself when it's for sale.

LILIAN. For sale?

MRS. BUNTER. But perhaps Brown mayn't be so pressing as some people. I shouldn't wonder if your ma talked him over. It's wonderful how women can talk men over, when they give their minds to it. The cheques I've swindled Bunter out of—often and often—and you'd think, to look at him——

LILIAN. I think your daughter is beckoning to you.

MRS. BUNTER. [*Going towards window.*] I do hope for your sake, my dear, that your pa won't have to sell the property. Perhaps I'd better not go to your ma, as she's got Brown on hand. Two's company, you know—three's none.　　[*Exit.*

LILIAN. Can this be the truth? Now I understand mamma's reason for treating him so civilly. Sell Cleve Abbey! Leave the dear old place! It will kill poor papa!

Enter BROWN.

BROWN. Lady Vavasour insists on our exchanging good-byes. She will have it there's a cloud between us, though I told her you were ready to give me a lesson in gentleman-farming. Eh! Miss Vavasour, if you look so grave I shall begin to think your mamma was right.

LILIAN. I know now what you meant when you spoke of buying an estate here. It was Cleve Abbey! Oh, tell me—do you think papa will be forced to sell it?

BROWN. I beg your pardon; I don't think that's a subject for you and me to enter on.

LILIAN. I see; you think me a silly girl, like all the rest of them.

BROWN. No, indeed!

LILIAN. Then prove it, by answering my question. Do tell me—do!

BROWN. I'm afraid your father is too much encumbered to clear himself without——　　　　　　　　　　　　[*Pausing.*

LILIAN. I understand. He will have to sell the Abbey—and you mean to buy it?

BROWN. Of course you will hate me for that?

LILIAN. Somebody must buy it.

BROWN. I wish there was anything I could do to expiate my offence. If you would only tell me—anything you wished seen to——

LILIAN. [*After an effort, and collecting herself.*] I hope you'll keep up the old garden, and the maze, and the old sun-dial with the broken nose, and the fish-pond—it's full of duckweed and there are no fish in it, but please don't have it filled up.

BROWN. Certainly not. I'll have the duckweed kept in and the fish kept out—religiously. I'll change nothing you wish left as it is.

LILIAN. Thank you so much! And there's the schools—you'll look particularly after them?

BROWN. Oh, that'll be a job after my own heart. I'll have a thoroughly efficient master and mistress——

LILIAN. Oh, but you must keep the old ones!

BROWN. Are they up to the mark?

LILIAN. I don't know, but they've been there ever since I can remember. And there's the old women in the Vavasour Almshouses. How they'll miss me on Wednesdays!

BROWN. I'm afraid I can't make up for that disappointment.

LILIAN. Well, I think tobacco would go a long way, or tea.

BROWN. I'll try both. Anything else?

LILIAN. The old thoroughbred brood mare and Nep, my black retriever—they are past moving. And then there's the old lame peacock, with one eye. I shouldn't mind leaving them, if you'd promise to take great care of them all.

BROWN. I'll be as good as a father to them. I promise you that.

LILIAN. I think what you promise you mean.

BROWN. You may rely on that. Anything more?
                                        [*Takes her hand.*

LILIAN. Nothing—thank you. [*Pause.*] Good morning.

BROWN. [*After pause.*] Good morning, Miss Vavasour.
                                [*Goes slowly up to window.*

LILIAN. [*Breaks down in a fit of sobbing.*] Oh, I can't bear it!
                                        [*Falls on chair.*

BROWN. [*Turning back hastily.*] Miss Vavasour, why have you exposed yourself and me to this? Compose yourself! I feel for you—all—very deeply!   [*Takes her hand soothingly.*
                        [LADY MATILDA *appears at window.*

LADY MATILDA. What's the meaning of this? [*Seeing the state of the case, she turns rapidly to the* BUNTERS, *who are approaching.*] To the right, if you please, Mrs. Bunter. That is the magnolia I particularly wish you to admire!

ACT II

SCENE. *Croquet lawn in the ruins of Cleve Abbey. The lawn, with its clumps of bright flowers and close-shaven turf, fills the interior of the ruin. At either side are the transept arches, giving glimpses here and there of the park, and serving for entrance and exit; the trees grow over among them. At the back the great west window arch, with a few broken mullions hung with ivy, and on the R. and L. lancet windows; through all these the country is seen. The great window is practicable, being broken away below.*

LILIAN, FITZ-URSE, *and* FANNY *discovered with their mallets.* LILIAN *is about to croquet* FITZ-URSE's *ball.*

LILIAN. [*Croquetting.*] One for his heels! [*Sends her own ball through the last hoop.*] There, I'm a rover. [*Sings.*] I'm at post, I'm at post, and the rover is free!

FANNY. Oh, we've no chance! I give up the game. Mr. Fitz-Urse won't help me a bit.

FITZ-URSE. Come, I say, haven't I stuck to you like a brick, going up and coming down? But Lilian's too many for us. Let her coach you till Brown comes back, and I'll sit out. [*Sits on garden seat,* R., *and takes out cigar case.*] You don't mind a cigarette? [*Lighting one.*] By Jove! After that awful Civil Service examination, one wants a sedative. [*Lying back on seat.*] Now play away, ladies!

LILIAN. Poor dear thing! Do you know, Fanny, I'm sometimes afraid he's suffering from cram upon the brain. It's a very serious complaint if it strikes in.

FITZ-URSE. Very. I hope I may get over it—with the help of fresh air, nourishing diet, and cheerful society.

LILIAN. And time. A man can't be expected to get over a rush of facts to the head all at once. Now, Fanny.

FANNY. Oh, I shall be so thankful for a lesson, Miss Vavasour.

LILIAN. If you call me Miss Vavasour again, I'll croquet you beyond redemption. My name's Lilian—just as much as yours is Fanny.

Enter BROWN.

Here comes Mr. Brown. I can give you a lesson both at once.

BROWN. I haven't mastered the grammar yet.

LILIAN. You are an awful muff! [BROWN *looks warningly at her.*] I beg your pardon—you are very awkward. But Bertie there will tell you what a patient master I am—I didn't say 'coach,' did I?—if he was not so very busy telling Fanny something far more interesting to both of them.

FANNY. Those dear wood-anemonies! Oh, do let me show you where they grow!

[FITZ-URSE *and* FANNY *stroll out of ruins.*

LILIAN. Come, you shall have the lesson all to yourself.

BROWN. I'm afraid you won't have time to finish it. I am obliged to run away from Cleve Abbey to-day.

LILIAN. Leave us so soon?

BROWN. You forget I've been here three weeks. The days have gone like a dream, somehow.

LILIAN. You see, it's pleasant to be idle sometimes.

BROWN. Yes—sometimes. All depends on the circumstances.

LILIAN. Thank you. [*Aside.*] I wonder if I'm one of the circumstances.

BROWN. I never thought I could have so enjoyed three weeks doing nothing.

LILIAN. And you really must go?

BROWN. Yes, my partners are peremptory. Thanks to the game of speculation that's now being played on all sides, there's a prospect of what we call at Liverpool very dirty weather on 'Change.

LILIAN. I'm sorry for that.

BROWN. Oh, there's a pleasure in storm, too—with a good ship under one, and plenty of sea-room! I rather like battling with a bad time.

LILIAN. If I were a man, I think I should like it too. Oh, look, Mr. Brown! there's that horrid Mr. Blasenbalg.

BROWN. With his rod and creel, as usual.

LILIAN. I wish papa hadn't given him leave to fish our river. He's always fishing, and I don't think he ever catches anything.

BROWN. I think I know where he would be pretty sure to catch something.   [*Looking at her.*

LILIAN. Oh, yes! I've no mercy on him. Now, shouldn't you say he wanted to give us the slip? He shan't though. Here! Hi! Mr. Blasenbalg!

BROWN. [*Half to himself.*] Well, he does look uncommonly like a cat that knows he's been after the chickens.

Enter BLASENBALG, *with his rod in his hand and his creel on his shoulders. At the same time enter* SERVANT; *he moves table and two chairs to* L., *and then takes up croquet mallets and hoops, and goes off with them.*

BLASENBALG. Good morning, Miss Vavasour. Morning, Brown.

LILIAN. I hope you've had good sport, for once.

BLASENBALG. H'm! so—a leetle.
                    [*Easing his creel, as though he felt the weight.*

LILIAN. A little? Why, I declare you can scarcely carry your basket! You never caught that weight yourself?

BLASENBALG. Ja! I always fish by mine zelf.

BROWN. [*Looking at his rod.*] I should think you had been spearing them, with that uncommon stiff spud at your butt.

BLASENBALG. [*Slightly confused.*] De spike is a plan of my own, zo I can stick him in de grass and wait.

BROWN. Yes, I've watched you.

BLASENBALG. [*Suspiciously.*] Eh! Vatched?

BROWN. At the water, I mean. I never saw you throw a line straight yet.

BLASENBALG. Aha! I have mein own vays to make de fish bite.

LILIAN. Oh, I know—it's ground bait.

BLASENBALG. Ja, ja! It is ground bait! Ha, ha!

LILIAN. But that isn't fair fishing. [*To* BROWN.] Is it? Let us look at your catch.   [*Tries to take creel off his shoulders.*

BLASENBALG. [*Trying to prevent her.*] No, no! Excuse me, Miss Vavasour. Mein fish are too leetle.

LILIAN. Oh, we never allow anything to be killed under half a pound. Come, turn them out.

BLASENBALG. [*Still struggling to prevent the opening of his creel.*] Leetle—dat is—for salmon, but big for drout. So ganz big for drout. Himmel! I must go—I must go in de drain.

LILIAN. In de drain?

BROWN. Wants to run to earth like a fox.

BLASENBALG. Nein, nein! In de drain—de railway, you know —back to Herr Bunter's haus.

BROWN. Oh, you've plenty of time. Come, lady's will is law here, you know!
[*Takes creel, opens it, and throws out lumps of ironstone.*

LILIAN. Weeds and stones! But where are the fish? [*Looks into creel.*] Not so much as a tittlebat.

BROWN. [*Picking up lump of ironstone.*] I didn't know you were a geologist—eh?

BLASENBALG. Ach, zo! A leetle! I look for de vlints and de vlakes as was de tools and de arms of de vor-historisch mensch. De men who was before de vorld.

BROWN. [*Handling lump of ironstone.*] Hum! I should say the men must have been decidedly behind the world who used tools like these. Let me help you to put them back.
[*In aiding* BLASENBALG *to refill creel,* BROWN *retains some of the ironstone, unobserved.*

BLASENBALG. You know, Miss Vavasour, de German is vot you call 'in de cloud'—always for study, study, not so for sport or moneymaking as de Englanders. Goot day! Now must I into de drain. [*Aside.*] All is safe! I have blind dem!
[*Exit.*

LILIAN. Now who but a benighted foreigner would ever waste his time in picking up stones in that way?

BROWN. [*Weighing ironstone in his hand.*] Some people have no idea of the relative value of time and stones. [*To himself thoughtfully.*] As heavy as lead! [*Looking off.*] See, here comes your mamma.

LILIAN. How bright she looks! Isn't she a dear, kind mamma?

BROWN. A model for mothers.

Enter LADY MATILDA.

LADY MATILDA. Ah, Mr. Brown! Such news, Lilian. Fitz-Urse passed with flying colours!

LILIAN. Then give me joy, everybody, for I coached him.

LADY MATILDA. [*Kissing* LILIAN.] How happy this must make you! [*To* BROWN.] Fitz-Urse owes everything to her.

LILIAN. And all the payment I ask is that I may be allowed to take him the good news.

LADY MATILDA. Go, my love.

BROWN. Allow me first. [*Plucks a sprig of laurel, and places it in* LILIAN's *hat.*] In the old times, when there were coaches, I've heard my father say they used always to stick laurels about the coach that carried news of a victory.

LILIAN. Oh, mamma! [*Laughing and singing.*] 'See where the conquering hero comes.' [*Running off.*] Here, Bertie, I want you!   [*Exit, laughing.*

LADY MATILDA. [*Looking proudly after her.*] You can understand how a mother must cling to such a daughter.

BROWN. I should think you would quite hate the man who would rob you of such a treasure.

LADY MATILDA. Luckily, Lilian is still heart-whole—let me hope she may long remain so.

BROWN. Then you don't think she has any—[*Pausing.*] I mean —she hasn't told you—that is—I mean. I beg your pardon, I'm afraid I can't say what I *do* mean.

LADY MATILDA. For the first time, I should think. Come, what is it?

BROWN. I'm obliged to leave you to-day.

LADY MATILDA. Leave us?

BROWN. You've made me only too much at home among you.

LADY MATILDA. Could we do less in return for your forbearance? You have laid us under obligations we can never discharge.

BROWN. Yes, you can—you can pay any debt you owe me ten times over.

LADY MATILDA. Indeed! Only tell me how.

BROWN. Let me ask your daughter to be my wife.
          [*He looks down as if surprised at his own audacity.*

LADY MATILDA. [*Aside.*] At last! [*Aloud.*] Lilian, your wife?

BROWN. You may well be startled.

LADY MATILDA. I must own the proposal does take me by surprise.

BROWN. Yes, I feel how monstrous it must sound, but don't decide against me too hastily. I think I have some reasons in my favour——

LADY MATILDA. One word, before you urge them. Have you said anything to Lily?

BROWN. Well, no; but I fancy in these cases men can express a good deal more without saying——

LADY MATILDA. Lilian is so innocent; so much what I was at her age. She has had so little of the hard schooling of the world. But the reasons you spoke of?

BROWN. I'm afraid they are of a kind to be best appreciated by a man of business.

LADY MATILDA. Suppose for once that I am a man of business.

BROWN. Then I should say it's true I am a plain Liverpool merchant whose father made his own way in the world, and your daughter is a young lady of old family and high connexions; that I am an ordinary man of thirty-three, with my life settled in its grooves, and she's a charming girl of eighteen with all the world before her to choose from. But on the other hand—[*Pauses.*] Really, I don't like to blow my own trumpet.

LADY MATILDA. Oh, be as candid with me as I should be with you under the same circumstances.

BROWN. If I know myself—I can give my wife a whole and loving heart, and it will be the happiness of my life to make her happy.

LADY MATILDA. From all I have seen of you, I quite believe it; I do indeed.

B R O W N. Thank you for that. Then, looking at the thing from a business point of view——

L A D Y M A T I L D A. Oh no, no, really—a mother can't look at marriage in that way.

B R O W N. Even marriage has its business side.

L A D Y M A T I L D A. Well—go on—though I protest——

B R O W N. There's a good deal to be said in favour of my offer— profits average fifteen thousand a year, and the house is as safe as the bank. I'm your mortgagee. So long as I don't absolutely want the money, I should never insist on principal or interest, or even say I bought Cleve Abbey. I should settle it on my wife, and you could go on living here as if nothing had happened.

  [L A D Y M A T I L D A, *during this speech, requires an effort to conceal her satisfaction, as each of her objects is realized.*
Well, don't you think there is something in what I've said— from a business point of view, you know?

L A D Y M A T I L D A. And you call that a business point of view?

B R O W N. What do you call it?

L A D Y M A T I L D A. One of the most unselfish and generous offers ever made for a woman.

B R O W N. Well, it never struck me there was anything out of the way in my proposition.

L A D Y M A T I L D A. In point of fortune you are all we could desire in a son-in-law, and your generosity has swept away every objection I should, naturally, have raised on the score of position or family.

B R O W N. Then I have your consent to speak to Lilian?

L A D Y M A T I L D A. Yes, and my best wishes. I fear Mr. Vavasour will have a strong prejudice against the marriage, chiefly on social grounds, but I hope to satisfy him that these present no really insuperable difficulty.

B R O W N. I'm glad you think that.

L A D Y M A T I L D A. Yes; I have little doubt, with the aid of my experience and our family connection—of course you would live in town during the season—

BROWN. Eh?

[*Looking keenly at her, as if about to interrupt her, but on second thoughts refrains and lets her go on.*

LADY MATILDA. With a good house in the right situation, and the entrée into society we could secure for you, and a circle of acquaintances judiciously chosen. Oh, by the way, have you ever thought of getting into Parliament?

BROWN. Is there any man with a head on his shoulders, and a good balance at his bankers, who has not sometimes thought of getting into Parliament?

LADY MATILDA. [*Regretfully.*] Ah, the House is within the range of most ambitions now. Bearholm is a family seat—or we might fall back on the Shortlands interest at Muckinfield. I've no doubt we could bring you in for—let's say two thousand. There's a purity party in the place, so I'm afraid it couldn't be managed for less.

BROWN. I should call that dirt cheap.

LADY MATILDA. Once in the House, you are too sensible a man to be always chattering about what you do not understand.

BROWN. Well, that's not my theory of a member's duty. I believe it's the practice with a great many, though.

LADY MATILDA. You would speak seldom, and only on questions of trade or commerce—subjects you may be supposed to comprehend.

BROWN. I'm glad there's something I've a right to an opinion on. What a pity you can't be a member.

LADY MATILDA. Our turn may come. Then, in a few sessions, with the Bearholm and Shortlands influence, it's quite on the cards that we might manage for you one of the commercial offices—say the Board of Trade, or the Civil Lordship of the Admiralty. They're always calling out for men of business there.

BROWN. Ah! that coming man—who never seems to be forth-coming.

LADY MATILDA. Lilian will do the honours of her house charmingly.

BROWN. That she will.

LADY MATILDA. That gives immense prestige to a rising man. [LILIAN *sings without.*] Look, here comes Lilian. Good-bye and good-speed! [*Gives him her hand.*] You have my full sanction, and I think I may even venture to answer for her father's.

BROWN. You're sure you're not answering for too much?

LADY MATILDA. Oh, you may rely upon it, I never take more upon my self than I can carry out!   [*Exit.*

BROWN. Don't you, my lady? Well, considering all you've just promised and vowed in my name, I should say godfathers and godmothers were superfluities.

Enter LILIAN.

LILIAN. There, I've left Bertie so happy, and Fanny seemed as pleased as he was. Do you know, I think that's a case. I'm so glad—for Bertie's sake. It'll take the selfishness out of him.

BROWN. Or multiply it by two. I sometimes think, when two people are very fond of each other, they don't care a bit about anybody else.

LILIAN. Oh, that's not my idea of love! I should think it ought to be the most unselfish of feelings. Its greatest joy the giving up of one's own life to be absorbed and guided by another! The right man, of course——   [*Pauses.*

BROWN. Lilian! [LILIAN *starts.*] I beg your pardon, Miss Vavasour.

LILIAN. I like Lilian better.

BROWN. I told you I was going to-day?

LILIAN. Yes, and I told you that I was very sorry.

BROWN. I believe that. Will you believe me as I believe you?

LILIAN. I have always believed you. You never chaff, as most men do now.

BROWN. I like serious things said seriously. I've a very serious thing to say to you—the most serious a man can say to a woman. Lilian, I love you! [*She turns away.*] You may well turn away. Tell me it's out of the question, and put me out of my misery.

LILIAN. [*Slily.*] Is it such misery?

BROWN. To feel that I've made you uncomfortable, and myself ridiculous?

LILIAN. To know that you have made me very proud and very happy.

BROWN. Now, don't play with me. [*Sits quickly by her side.*] Is it true? [LILIAN *is about to answer.*] Don't speak hastily. You are kind and generous. You have seen how my heart was growing to you—only as a man's can grow whose capital of love has never been dribbled away in the small change of flirtation. Because I love you very much, you are ready to love me a little. I am old, compared to you, not bred in your world. You may repent.

LILIAN. Oh no, I should never do that!   [*Gives him her hand.*

BROWN. [*Taking her fondly in his arms, and kissing her.*] My darling!

LILIAN. [*After a long pause.*] Now tell me—when did you begin to love me?

BROWN. The day I came here.

LILIAN. Oh, you old darling!

BROWN. I wanted to see the property before I bid for it——

LILIAN. [*Looks at him.*] Eh?

BROWN. Oh, I don't mean you, dearest! I felt a kind of remorse; and when you so sweetly confided to me the old place, and the old people, and the old peacock, and then at last fairly broke down, those tears showed your heart and won mine.

LILIAN. Oh, I did struggle so hard to keep them under! But I'm glad I cried now. Have you spoken to mamma?

BROWN. Yes—I've her full consent. In fact, she's been kind enough to plan our married life for us. My trade mark is to be got rid of, as burglars punch the cypher out of plate. I'm to be recast into a fine gentleman, with a seat in Parliament and a post under Government.

LILIAN. But I don't want you recast. I like you better in the rough.

BROWN. I'm glad of that. I'm proud, Lilian, and so was my father before me. I'd rather see my name at the head of the

Liverpool Exchange list than at the tail of fashionable intelligence in any newspaper whatever.

LILIAN. I like to hear you say that.

BROWN. It isn't that I value money for money's sake, Lilian. But I think of its nobler uses. To relieve suffering and to comfort sorrow—to feed the lamp of learning, and to strengthen the hand of art—to foster into fruit the seeds of promise that neglect might kill—and to crown with comfort the head grown gray in worthy service.

LILIAN. I never so wanted to be rich before.

BROWN. I warn you—you'll have a rival.

LILIAN. A rival!

BROWN. The office. However much I love you, I feel I must stick to business still.

LILIAN. But we should be in London part of the year, shouldn't we?

BROWN. Our home would be in Liverpool.

LILIAN. But you would like to be in Parliament, wouldn't you?

BROWN. Yes, as soon as my own business can spare me for that of the nation; but if I did go into the House it would be to forward the public work, not my private interest. Lily, you know now what you will have to expect with me—an honest man's love, a fortune that will enable me to help your parents, and a home as happy as affection can make it. I'm proud of the name of a British merchant, and married or single I mean to hold to it.

LILIAN. I'm not afraid to share the life you offer me. I can bring you nothing but myself. I know you will bear with me till I become what your wife should be.

[*He clasps her in his arms.*

BROWN. My own sweet Lilian! At last! Oh, I am so happy; I feel as if I had jumped from the rock of Gibraltar and come down on a sea of feather beds. I'm the proudest, happiest— hang it, here's somebody coming!

LILIAN. Bertie and Fanny.

BROWN. We don't want anybody just now.

LILIAN. No! How stupid of them to go spooning about in that way.   [*Exeunt quickly.*

Enter FITZ-URSE *and* FANNY.

FITZ-URSE. Yes. I hope old Bearholm's interest will get me into the F.O.

FANNY. What is the F.O.?

FITZ-URSE. The Foreign Office—*the* thing in offices. None but swells at the F.O.—come at one and go at seven. Asked everywhere—up to everything. There's only one thing: F.O. is so deucedly expensive. Salary won't keep a fellow in cigars and eau-de-cologne. I say, Miss Bunter, I've just been thinking——

FANNY. Oh, do tell me.

FITZ-URSE. I sometimes wish I was one of those other fellows.

FANNY. What other fellows?

FITZ-URSE. The fellows that make the things in the commercial intelligence. The cotton twist, you know, and the grey shirtings.

FANNY. Mr. Fitz-Urse, I detest the commercial intelligence, and I don't even know what grey shirtings are.

FITZ-URSE. No more do I; haven't an idea—only I see they seem generally 'lively' in the papers, you know. I mean I wish I was a money-making fellow myself.

FANNY. Oh no, no. What inspiration can there be in 'Sugar is going down,' and 'Lead is getting up,' and 'Money is tight?'

FITZ-URSE. Oh, yes, it's a curious fact; money always *is* tight. One can't screw any of it out of anybody without an awful amount of pressure.

FANNY. Oh, if you knew how I loathe money.

FITZ-URSE. Do you though?

FANNY. I've seen so much of it.

FITZ-URSE. Ah, I haven't, you know.

FANNY. I have been so made to feel its miserable insufficiency.

FITZ-URSE. I've been made to feel that too.

FANNY. Give me art and intellect, sweetness and light, you know—a cottage and a crust—a lovely landscape and the 'Stones of Venice.' Oh, I could live upon Ruskin!

FITZ-URSE. By Gad! That would come cheaper than the co-operative stores. I say, Fanny—you don't mind my saying Fanny—do you, Fanny?

FANNY. [*Softly.*] No.

FITZ-URSE. Then I say, Fanny, look here; if a fellow without a rap, just going in about ninety pounds a year, you know, with nothing but his brains to look to in the world, was to say, 'Will you marry me Fanny?' What would *you* say?

FANNY. Oh, Mr. Fitz-Urse.

FITZ-URSE. If *I* said so, Fanny, what would you say?

FANNY. Oh, I really don't know how to answer 'ifs'.

FITZ-URSE. Well, then, I do say so without an 'if,' and now what do you say?

FANNY. Oh, Mr. Fitz-Urse.   [*Blushing and turning away.*

FITZ-URSE. I say, say Bertie!

FANNY. Bertie!

FITZ-URSE. That's 'Yes?'

FANNY. [*Softly.*] Yes!

FITZ-URSE. There's nobody in sight—if you wouldn't mind it. [*Kisses her.*] Oh, that's awfully jolly, give us another. [*Kisses her.*] You'll never leave me for another fellow?

FANNY. Never!

FITZ-URSE. Oh, but I say, what will your governor say?

FANNY. I think I could coax papa.

FITZ-URSE. Tell him I've passed. Say it's awfully difficult— takes no end of brains, and such lots of cram. And, I say, it can't do any harm if you tell him I've a chance of a handle to my name—a title, you know.

FANNY. Oh, how very interesting!

FITZ-URSE. Yes, I may be Lord Bearholm one of these days.

FANNY. Papa's a great Radical; the title will go a long way with him. I expect him here to-day to take me home.

FITZ-URSE. Oh, hang it! Don't go to-day.

FANNY. You will be sorry?

FITZ-URSE. Oh, awful!

FANNY. [*Very tenderly.*] Will you gather me a flower—one little flower?

FITZ-URSE. Are you particular what it is?

FANNY. No.

FITZ-URSE. Will you have it wild or—tame?

FANNY. Wild!

FITZ-URSE. [*Gathers flower from bed.*] There—there's a dandelion. Now, what is it for?

FANNY. That I may place it next my heart, as a sweet souvenir of the place—the time——

FITZ-URSE. And the party—eh, Fanny?   [*Insinuatingly.*

FANNY. Oh, my beloved!

FITZ-URSE. Oh, give me another kiss!
                    [*Kisses her, and exeunt lovingly.*

Enter LADY MATILDA *and* VAVASOUR.

LADY MATILDA. You may rely upon me, Marmaduke. Isn't that Bertie with Fanny?

VAVASOUR. Yes, they seem very confidential. By Jove!

LADY MATILDA. [*Calmly.*] Eh?

VAVASOUR. Why, he's got his arm round her waist!

LADY MATILDA. [*Looking through her eye-glass.*] So I see.

VAVASOUR. By George! He's kissed her.

LADY MATILDA. Twice. I think, my dear, it's hardly fair to watch them.

VAVASOUR. Well, I don't know, considering that the girl's here on a visit.

LADY MATILDA. And what else do you suppose I allowed Lilian to ask her for?

VAVASOUR. What! Invite a girl to your house, that she may take shady walks, with a young fellow's arm round her waist? Well!

LADY MATILDA. I brought her here that she might act as a buffer between Bertie and Lilian. The prospect of the title's uncertain, and even if Bertie came into it, he's too silly and the property too small to trust Lilian's happiness to.

VAVASOUR. I see. What one may call natural selection. Money and rank—Brown and Lilian; rank and money—Bertie and Fanny Bunter. Well, I suppose you know best.

LADY MATILDA. A few things, perhaps, I do. Marriage is one of them. What other combination could fulfil all the requirements so perfectly? Your extrication from difficulties—Lilian's settlement—our credit in the county—all secured at one coup, and an excellent husband for Lilian. Come, come, Marmaduke, smile.

VAVASOUR. No, hang it, Matilda! I'm willing to swallow the black draught—brown, I should say—if you insist on it, but don't ask me to look as if I liked it.

LADY MATILDA. I like it, Marmaduke. Now go; give them your consent and your blessing, and don't look so wretched about it.

Enter SECKER.

Ah, Mr. Secker.

SECKER. Good morning. I thought I should find Brown here. Here are some letters for him.

VAVASOUR. [*Taking letters.*] From Liverpool, and marked 'Important' and 'Immediate', I see. Why, the postmark's three days old!

SECKER. Yes, those idiots at the Fleece never thought of forwarding them. Luckily, I saw them in the bar.

LADY MATILDA. Mr. Vavasour was just going to look for Mr. Brown. But first, Mr. Secker, I must ask you to congratulate us.

SECKER. I do congratulate you, heartily. What for?

LADY MATILDA. All our difficulties are at an end. Mr. Brown has proposed for Lilian.   [VAVASOUR *groans.*

SECKER. [*Aside.*] Hooked him, by George! [*Aloud.*] And you've consented in spite of the business blemish, eh?

VAVASOUR. Yes. Lilian is very fond of him, and this is no
common man, let me tell you. To say nothing of his money,
he has—— [*Glancing at* LADY MATILDA.

LADY MATILDA. Fine temper——

VAVASOUR. And a generous disposition; you must allow that.

SECKER. I don't know a man of more worth, or worth more.
He comes out both ways. I said if anybody could set things
straight, you would—and you've done it beautifully. He's a
lucky fellow. He'll have a charming wife.

VAVASOUR. And an incomparable mother-in-law.
[*Exeunt* SECKER *and* VAVASOUR.

Enter GANTRY.

GANTRY. Mr. and Mrs. Bunter, my lady, come to fetch Miss
Bunter home, and the German gentleman.

LADY MATILDA. Show them here. [*Exit* GANTRY.] There's
some pleasure in receiving these people now—one can enjoy
their vulgarity in the pleasant assurance that Cleve Abbey is
safe from their clutches.

Enter MR. *and* MRS. BUNTER *and* BLASENBALG.

[*Affably.*] So glad to see you.

MRS. BUNTER. How do you do, Lady Matilda, this beautiful
day?

LADY MATILDA. So sorry you are going to rob us of dear
Fanny.

BUNTER. Yes, Lady Matilda, punctuality is my principle.
Fanny is due at Beaumanor Park by 4.30 sharp; that's the
time I fixed, and that's the time to be kep'. So, Maria, if you
see that she's packed——

LADY MATILDA. She has just gone for a stroll in the Park with
my nephew. Suppose we went in search of them?

MRS. BUNTER. Proud, my lady. B., why don't you hoffer my
Lady Matilda your harm?

BUNTER. Maria, I was a going to. [*Offers his arm.*] Will you
allow me, Lady Matilda?

BLASENBALG. [*Aside to him.*] Stay—telegrams—look!

BUNTER. [*Looking off.*] Ah, that's the worst of a position, my lady; it's always a following you in deppytations, or testimonials, or telegrams, or something.

Enter MESSENGER *with telegrams.*

For me, my good man? [MESSENGER *hands several telegrams to* BUNTER.] Bother them wires, they're down on you like a flash of lightning. You can wait, my man.

[*Gives telegrams to* BLASENBALG.

MESSENGER. I've some dispatches here for Mr. Brown, my lady.

LADY MATILDA. Then follow me. Come, Mrs. Bunter.

MRS. BUNTER. [*Who has been looking at garden.*] I can 'ardly drag myself away from this sweet spot. I've often said to B., 'Why don't you have our place laid out in ruins like the Habbey,' haven't I, B?

BUNTER. You 'ave Maria, and my regular answer to the remark has been, 'Maria, don't be ridikalous.'

LADY MATILDA. Ah, there are things money cannot buy: old trees, old ruins, old family pictures, and old family pride. You must leave us poor county folks something to set against your overwhelming advantages. This way, Mrs. Bunter.

[*Exeunt* MRS. BUNTER *and* LADY MATILDA, *followed by* MESSENGER.

BUNTER. I don't like that woman. Sometimes I feel as if she was insulting of me, and sometimes as if she was an 'umbugging of me, and 'umbug is my aversion. Now, B., what's the news?

BLASENBALG. [*Who has opened telegram.*] 'From the Manager. Diddlesex Joint Stock. Received forty thousand. Price of shares in Underhand and Goldney. Asks direction for investment.' [*Looks at another telegram.*] Himmel! Sturm-wetter!

BUNTER. [*Severely.*] Mr. B., I've reason to believe that's profane swearing, though in the German language. I must beg you won't indulge in it afore me; swearing, even in unknown tongues, 'urts my feelings as a Cheristian.

BLASENBALG. I was only swearing for thankfulness. You shall swear for thank your luck when you hear this. [*Reads.*] 'Stock Exchange, 3.10. Great excitement. Underhand and Goldney reported shaky. Bears at vork.'

BUNTER. The devil!

BLASENBALG. That's English! [*Reads.*] 'Reported liabilities—four millions. Awful panic. Nothing like it since '28.'

BUNTER. How providential I'd sold out the day before. I'm tiled—nothing can hit me very hard.

BLASENBALG. How lucky we closed our speculative account for last settling day. [*Reads another telegram.*] 'Panic spread to Manchester and Liverpool. Ten brokers stopped. Brown, Jones Brothers hard hit and reported groggy.'

BUNTER. Brown, Jones Brothers! Why, that's Sam Brown, their mortgagee—the party as they've been bottling here for that girl of theirs—the party that stands between me and this magnificent iron-field.

BLASENBALG. Say between us, Herr Bunter; I vound him.

BUNTER. Yes, you found it, and I'll finance it, and we'll share the profits. [BLASENBALG *appears absorbed in calculations— holding his fingers up.*] What do you mean by that?
[Imitating him.

BLASENBALG. I was thinking out the prospectus of the 'Cleve Abbey Hematite Mining and Smelting Company, Limited. Inexhaustible supply of de raw material.'

BUNTER. 'Enormous demand for the manufactured article.'

BLASENBALG. 'De Great Midland Coal-field in de immediate nachbarhood.'

BUNTER. 'Railway and Canal carriage within easy distance.'

BLASENBALG. Oh, beautiful! Hush, here's Brown!

BUNTER. Oh, Brown!   [*They retire behind pillar.*

Enter BROWN, *excited, letter and telegrams in his hand.*

BROWN. Am I awake or asleep? Which can be true: what I was saying, seeing, and hearing half-an-hour since, or the terrible news of the last few minutes? Ruin hanging over our house by a thread! Had these letters reached me in due time, I should have been there in the midst of it all. And what could I have done? I couldn't have stemmed the panic, but I might have done my best to hold the old house against it—I fear it's too late now. [*Looks at telegram.*] They must have twenty or thirty thousand within twenty-four hours to save the concern, and that was twelve hours ago. My poor Lily, good-bye to you and all my hopes.

[*Sits on chair, and hides his face in his hands.*

BLASENBALG. [*To* BUNTER.] That forty thousand in de bank— make him a bid for the mortgage deed. Vavasours can't pay off. Cleve Abbey is yours!

BUNTER. [*Squeezing* BLASENBALG's *hand.*] Bless you, my German. [*Comes down and sits by* BROWN's *side.*] This is awful news, Brown, awful! It should teach us how unstable are the foundations of earthly prosperity. An 'ouse of sand, my friend —an 'ouse of sand. They tell me you're hard hit.

BROWN. Very hard.

BUNTER. You have my sympathy, sir—my Cheristian sympathy.

BROWN. Thank you for your sympathy. But what we want is ready money, precisely what nobody will advance at such a moment.

BUNTER. Don't undervalue your species. There's them that always 'as an 'and for the distressed, and an 'eart for the 'elpless. What do you want?

BROWN. Do you mean to say that you'll help us?

BUNTER. What do you want? 'Ow much? Give it a name.

BROWN. They tell me forty thousand pounds might tide us over the worst. But it must be had at once.

BUNTER. And money is worth anything just now. I'll let you have the forty thousand pounds if you'll transfer the Cleve Abbey mortgage to me.

BROWN. As an advance, you mean?

BUNTER. No, a price. I never lend—I buys.

BROWN. It's a dead loss of five thousand pounds. But I've no choice. Minutes are worth millions just now. I accept your terms.

BUNTER. Benjamin Bunter ain't the man to let a friend go down without flinging him a rope.

BLASENBALG. [*Aside.*] And charging him five thousand pounds for the accommodation.

BUNTER. I want no thanks. Tools, B. [BLASENBALG *gives him portable inkstand and pen*; BUNTER *fills up cheque from his cheque book.*] The consciousness that I've done my duty by a fellow creature is its own reward.

BLASENBALG. [*Aside.*] And the man half believes it himself. It's vonderful, vonderful!

BUNTER. Ah, it ain't many at such a moment that can look into their 'earts and their banker's books, and ask the one if the other can stand forty thousand to help a fellow creature.

[*Gives cheque to* BROWN.

BROWN. If Mr. Blasenbalg will come with me to Secker, I'll give him the deeds. You have made a hard bargain, but what's five thousand pounds for salvage of our good name—if only we can save it. [*Exit.*

BUNTER. [*Exultant.*] I've done the trick, my boy, and a good action into the bargain!

BLASENBALG. Yes, you have made a first-rate operation. And drawn against Providence for an act of charity. Talk of the Jews! It's only you Christians manage to get interest like dat. [*Exit.*

Enter LADY MATILDA.

LADY MATILDA. I'm going to see about some of our rare plants for Fanny.

BUNTER. Thank you. I 'ope Fanny's been all she should be during her wisit at the Abbey?

LADY MATILDA. Oh yes! I like her extremely, and Lilian and she are great friends.

BUNTER. Ah! I dare say they understand each other. Now, I don't profess to understand Fanny. It seems 'ard a man shouldn't understand his own child—don't it? I've spared nothing on that girl's education. Governesses, finishing schools, the most expensive masters—and the hupshot of it all is, she's quite beyond me. She's taken to what they call 'igh art, and 'igh church, and 'igh other things till she gets that 'igh you would sometimes think she was never coming down again.

LADY MATILDA. Ah! I'm afraid Fanny does run a little into rhodomontade now and then.

BUNTER. That's the word, my lady. To tell you the truth, I was afraid of the Abbey for her. It's astonishing 'ow an old 'ouse, or an old pictur', or an old ruin will get into that girl's head. But if ever we were to live here, I'd 'ave them ruins down pretty sharp.

LADY MATILDA. Thank you. As the ruin is a very old friend of mine, I'm happy to think you're not going to live here.

BUNTER. Well, things quite as unlikely have happened. Estates will change hands you know, and I think it's on the cards that Cleve Abbey might be in the market one of these days.

LADY MATILDA. Mr. Bunter!

BUNTER. Come, between you and me and the post, I know.
[*Puts his finger to his nose.*

LADY MATILDA. Mr. Bunter, I don't understand you.

BUNTER. Yes, you do. You're a deal too wide awake not to— bless you, it's no secret. All the county knows it.

LADY MATILDA. Perhaps all the county does not know that, whatever may have been Mr. Vavasour's temporary embarrasments, Mr. Brown, who has proposed for Miss Vavasour, is to clear them all off.

BUNTER. Brown is, is he? Ah, such is life. Poor Brown.

LADY MATILDA. What do you mean by poor Brown?

BUNTER. I mean just what I say, that Brown hasn't a brown left to bless himself with. Brown, Jones Brothers have gone to smash in the panic; or, if they pull through, Brown may thank the money I've paid him for the Cleve Abbey mortgage deed.

LADY MATILDA. Mr. Bunter, are you mad, or intoxicated?

BUNTER. Me intoxicated? Lady Matilda, I'm not in the 'abit of drinking afore dinner.   [*Exit.*

LADY MATILDA. The mortgage in this man's hands! Brown

ruined! If this is true, the marriage must be broken off at once. Lilian's chance must be kept open. Poor fellow! I must manage it with as little pain to him as possible.

Enter BROWN.

I hope you got your letters and telegrams?

BROWN. I did.

LADY MATILDA. I trust you have not been inconvenienced by their delay?

BROWN. Inconvenienced! That's not the word; give it it's right name—say ruined.

LADY MATILDA. Ruined! Then Bunter's terrible news is true.

BROWN. Yes, it's the old story in three chapters: speculation—panic—ruin! At such a time the innocent suffer for the guilty. It's hard lines—hard lines.

LADY MATILDA. It is indeed; I feel for you.

BROWN. When I proposed to your daughter, I was a rich man. Now I shall have to begin the world again; and the best I can hope will be to reconquer the ground, inch by inch. Worst of all, I can't do what I had hoped here for you. That pains me almost as much as losing Lilian.

LADY MATILDA. Losing Lilian! You ought to say Lilian losing you. [*Sighs.*] Her loss is the greater—I feel it—honestly I do. But you are quite right—this marriage is out of the question now.

BROWN. You think so then?

LADY MATILDA. Yes. I am very, very sorry. I began by looking on this marriage as a painful sacrifice. You had brought me to look on it as a blessing for my girl—an honour for her family.

BROWN. Thank you for that.   [*Shakes her hand warmly.*

LADY MATILDA. But you are quite right. Will you tell Lilian, or shall I?

BROWN. Is she to have any choice?

LADY MATILDA. [*Pausing, then giving* BROWN *her hand.*] You shall ask her. She shall be free to answer. I see her coming.

I will leave you. [*Aside.*] I hope—I think I have acted for the best.   [*Exit.*

Enter LILIAN.

LILIAN. Oh, you truant! I've caught you at last. Papa was so long hugging me, I do believe you were jealous of him. And I'm jealous, sir—very jealous—of all those letters and telegrams.

BROWN. Lilian! [*She looks startled at his manner.*] You may well be jealous of them. They have built a wall between you and me—for they tell me I am a ruined man.

LILIAN. Ruined? You?

BROWN. By the chances of the time—no fault of mine.

LILIAN. No fault of yours? I should think not!

BROWN. You accepted a rich man's offer—a poor man has no right to insist upon that acceptance.

LILIAN. [*Impetuously.*] Rich or poor! [*Suddenly pausing.*] Oh, mamma, mamma!

BROWN. I understand your looks—your words—your hesitation, as if I were sitting inside your heart.

LILIAN. You are—you know you are!

BROWN. Shall I tell you what I hear there? [*Taking her hand tenderly.*] 'I do not care for money—and I do care for this man.'

LILIAN. I do, I do!

BROWN. 'But I am not free to follow my own inclination. My mother looks to my marriage to restore the family fortunes. I must sacrifice myself.'

LILIAN. Oh, no, no!

BROWN. Yes, I hear that. It's only whispered, but it makes itself very clearly heard.

LILIAN. Oh, must I listen to it?

BROWN. Yes, for it is in your heart, with the other voices. You must decide which you will listen to, but your whole heart must speak if it is to be 'Yes.'

LILIAN. Oh, I cannot, I cannot!   [*Sinks into chair.*

BROWN. Then good bye, Lily! It's better you should say no
more, nor I. Heaven bless you!
  [*Kisses her on the forehead, then signals to* LADY MATILDA,
  who enters and goes to LILIAN.

LILIAN. Oh, mamma, mamma!   [*Tableau.*

ACT III

SCENE. *At the Seat of the* BUNTERS, *Beaumanor Park. A cheerful, large, expensively, but flashily furnished room. Range of French windows,* R., *opening at the back on a conservatory, by large glazed doors. The conservatory is filled with tree ferns, palms, exotics, and statues; modern pictures, in costly frames, on the walls, some landscapes, some historical pictures; rich gold cornices and mouldings; bright chintzes and brilliant draperies, portières, &c. Everything in as marked a contrast as possible with Cleve Abbey in the* 1st *Act.*

SECKER *and* BUNTER *discovered at table,* L., *with bottle of Maraschino on silver plateau,* BUNTER *pouring out to* SECKER.

BUNTER. You must try my Maraschino. It's a splendid article. Stands me in fifteen pounds the dozen. Give me a good thing, I say. [SECKER *tastes and smacks his lips.*] And hang the expense!

SECKER. Hang the expense! [*Finishes glass.*

BUNTER. Now let's review the situation. Notice expires at twelve to-day. Brown has transferred his mortgage to me. If Cleve Abbey goes into the market, it's worth but seventy thousand—outside price. But I've a fancy for it, and I can afford to pay for my fancy! So I say to you, 'Here's eighty thousand down.' You say to your client, 'Take Benjamin Bunter's liberal offer'—and [*Confidentially.*] I shouldn't at all wonder if you found a five hundred pound note under your plate the next time you tucked your legs under B. B.'s mahogany.

SECKER. Well, I must say you great capitalists have ways with you.

BUNTER. And means, Mr. Secker. Give a man ways and means and Cheristian principles, and there ain't many things that'll stop him.

SECKER. I should like to know what would stop you. Well, Mr. Vavasour will be here by twelve——

BUNTER. And Brown has promised to be down with the title deeds, by the express, at 11.30.

SECKER. Meanwhile, I'll see my client and take his final instructions.

BUNTER. Exactly. After giving him yours.   [*Winks at him.*

SECKER. [*Returning the wink.*] Ha, ha! And I've no doubt we shall finish to-day's business pleasantly for everyone concerned.

BUNTER. Not a word of this to Lady Matilda. I don't like that woman; she's too sharp and too civil by half. Would you believe it? She's driven herself and Miss Vavasour over in the pony-carriage, and invited herself to lunch—to-day of all days.

SECKER. Ah! there's no accounting for ladies' tastes.

BUNTER. Mind, I don't want any fuss about title! Short and sharp is my motto. Money down—conveyance executed— parchments handed over.

SECKER. In fact, everything hurried through in the most unlawyer-like manner.

BUNTER. Exactly. So I think you and me may say 'done.'
                                        [*Giving him his hand.*

SECKER. [*Taking his hand, heartily.*] Done!

BUNTER. And 'done' and 'done' is enough between two gentlemen.   [*Exit* SECKER.
I've bottled the agent. Bravo! Cleve Abbey's as good as mine! [*Rubbing his hands.*] Iron-field and all—at one-fourth the value! I like bringing these county folks on their marrow-bones. They turn up their noses at honest industry. They look down on B. B.—do they? B. B.'s growing too big to be looked down upon.

        Enter BLASENBALG, *with travelling bag and wrapper.*

Ah, Blasey, my boy! Safe back from the great Babylon?

BLASENBALG. [*Getting rid of bag and wraps.*] Safe as de Bank. With your leave. [*Helps himself to Maraschino.*] Ah!
                                        [*Smacks his lips.*

BUNTER. You've got the analysis of our ironstone? [BLASEN-BALG *nods.*] Satisfactory?

BLASENBALG. Beautiful! Seventy-five per cent. of iron! Near ten over what I reckon.

BUNTER. Bravo!

BLASENBALG. And I've had my rough map of de lodes made out by a regular mining draughtsman, and it looks beautiful. Hundreds and hundreds of acres of de stuff.

BUNTER. While you've been looking after them in London, I've been squaring the agent here. Now, 'and 'em over.

BLASENBALG. [*Innocently.*] Vot?

BUNTER. The analysis and the map, to be sure.

BLASENBALG. Stop! Hadn't we better settle de terms first?

BUNTER. Terms? [BLASENBALG *nods.*] Between you and me, Blasey my boy? After the years we've known each other? After the many good things we've been in together? After all our experiences of the blessings of mutual confidence——

BLASENBALG. And united capital! That sort of thing was all very well while we were blowing bubbles: I start my speculation, and I take my chance! But dis is no bubble; dis is good solid pudding, and I vant my slice of it.

BUNTER. And this is gratitude? Do you remember what you were when I took you up?

BLASENBALG. Vot I vos? Do you remember vot you vos yourself? A poor, crawling, commonplace contractor, mit no idea beyond a lucky job and a paying profit—no higher standpoint than de brute forces of hard work and hard money. Who taught you financing? [BUNTER *groans.*] Who revealed to you de modern philosopher's stone—a bill-stamp? De alchemy dat transmutes fools' hopes into wise men's profits, and condenses de puffs of a prospectus into golden showers. Dat is vot I taught you. And now he vont pay for de lesson!

BUNTER. What of my peace of mind? Have I not paid for it? Quiet sleep, and a calm conscience—that's what I've paid you, Blasenbalg, and it's a heavy price for all I've got by you—if it was ten times as much.

BLASENBALG. Ah! vords, vords—but I vant hard cash.

BUNTER. I thought you didn't believe in it.

BLASENBALG. I believe in other people's. In plain English—I'm tired of being de cat and you de monkey. I leave you to burn your fingers mit your own chestnuts, or I vill be paid for getting dem out of de fire.

BUNTER. How dare you call me a monkey? What's your figure?

BLASENBALG. Two thousand pounds down on de nail for the find. If we work de iron, half de profits; if we sell, half de purchase money. I have here de agreement.

BUNTER. But the price of the estate is to come out of my pocket.

BLASENBALG. Well, I'll owe you half de money.

BUNTER. Thank you for nothing!

BLASENBALG. As you please. It is like it or lump it! I vind de iron. I vollow de lodes. I've got de analysis and de map in my pocket. I can go into de market myself. Dere's lots of capitalists who outbid you by fifty tousens.

BUNTER. This is 'ard! It ain't that I grudge you your share in a good thing, Blasey my boy, but it's this deplorable want of confidence between man and man. [*About to write cheque—pauses.*] Stop! I've never seen the analysis!

BLASENBALG. [*Laughing sardonically.*] 'Want of confidence between man and man!' But I will show you.
    [*Takes analysis from his pocket, and shows it to* BUNTER.

BUNTER. Yes, it's all right!   [*Chuckling—is about to take it.*

BLASENBALG. [*Drawing it back—shaking his head.*] Ah! a bird in hand, you know——

BUNTER. No—how can you? Well, if I must I must. [*Filling up cheque.*] But it's taking a mean advantage of one whose conduct to you has always been that of a brother.

BLASENBALG. And ain't my conduct to you that of a brother? D'ye tink I'd give my brother money's worth, without de money? Nein!

BUNTER. [*Giving cheque.*] There's your cheque, sir.

BLASENBALG. [*Reads cheque to himself.*] 'Pay to Berthold Blasenbalg, or bearer, &c.' [*Aloud.*] All right! Now for a vash after my journey. I always likes to keep my hands clean.
    [*Exit, with bag, &c.*

BUNTER. Then you'd better give me back that cheque! If there was ever an ungrateful rascal! I wish to goodness I'd never seen his face. But I'm so far in the maze that I can't find my way out by myself.

Enter SERVANT.

SERVANT. The Clerk of the Works, sir.

Enter CLERK OF WORKS. SERVANT *takes plateau and bottle off table, and exit with it.*

BUNTER. Ah, Turbit! How are you? How is Mrs. Turbit? Though I didn't see her at chapel last Sabbath.

CLERK. She has her little ones, you know, sir—keeps her at home.

BUNTER. Ah, Turbit, neglect of Cheristian privileges ain't the way to bring a blessing on a family.

CLERK. I've come to ask what's to be done with that clamp of bricks that turned out so bad in the north field, you know, sir.

BUNTER. Turned out bad? What, they're no good for the market, eh?

CLERK. [*Shaking his head.*] Very little I'm afraid, sir. The contractor for Sir Charles Tangent's model cottages has sent them back on our hands.

BUNTER. That's very 'ard on me, Turbit, very 'ard! Let's see. I'll tell you what you can do with those bricks. They're building a chapel at Squash End; send those bricks to the Committee of that chapel, as a contribution from me, with my blessing on the good work.

CLERK. [*Aside—going.*] And the bad bricks! He's a nice 'un, he is. [*Exit.*

BUNTER. Yes, wealth always prospers with those that knows how to use it.

Enter MRS. BUNTER, *with a parcel.*

MRS. BUNTER. [*Radiant.*] 'Ere it is at last! [*Playfully.*] Now, open your mouth and shut your eyes.

BUNTER. [*Impatiently.*] Perhaps, Maria, you call that playfulness. I call it ridikalousness. What is it?

MRS. BUNTER. [*Opening case, and taking out pedigree, em-blazoned on vellum.*] It's our pedigree—straight from the 'Erald's College.

BUNTER. Nonsense, Maria—all vanity. 'Ow often must I remind you we ought not to be puffed up?

MRS. BUNTER. But do look at it, B. [*Spreading it out.*] Ain't it a duck of a pedigree?

BUNTER. If it is a duck, I'll be bound it's brought its bill with it.

MRS. BUNTER. Oh, a bagatelle, quite a bagatelle—only a hundred and thirty.

BUNTER. Only a hundred and thirty! Here, I've just been robbed of two thousand, given away a lot of beautiful bricks—and you must pick my pocket of a hundred and thirty besides!

[MRS. BUNTER *spreads out pedigree on table so that* BUNTER *can read it.*

You're always doing it, Maria. [*Impatiently.*] It's the last load of straws that breaks the camel's back.

MRS. BUNTER. Nonsense, B., it's cheap at the money. Why, the 'Eralds College has been and found our arms.

BUNTER. And I've been and found their 'ands in my pockets. A hundred and thirty pounds for a bit of parchment and a lot of stuff and 'umbug!

MRS. BUNTER. Stuff and 'umbug. Why, they prove the Bunters was Anglo-Saxons before the Conquest!

BUNTER. Well, I'm glad they've found that out. It's pleasant to know other people had ancestors as well as them aristocrats at the Abbey. [*Taking it.*] As I shall have to pay for it, I may as well take the benefit. Hollo! What's the meaning of them painted Dutch ovens?

MRS. BUNTER. Perhaps it'll tell you if you read it.

BUNTER. [*Reads.*] 'The Bunters, an ancient Anglo-Saxon Family, settled originally about Wethering Sett, County of Suffolk.' I wonder 'ow they knew that; I didn't. 'Their lands were probably confiscated by the Conqueror.' Very likely; you see the aristocracy was down on us, Maria, even that early—'owing no doubt, to the stubborn resistance of the Saxon landowner'. I'm glad we resisted. It was 'ighly creditable to us under the circumstances. I dare say most people of property knocked under. 'The family were not prominent under the Plantagenets.' No, I never heard we were. A poor lot them Plantagenet Bunters. 'Nor are we accurately informed which side they espoused during the Wars of the Roses.' That's a pity. Let's 'ope it was the side that came uppermost. 'At the Revolution we find a Bunter parish constable of Wimmering.' You see, Maria, we'd come down by that time—'and the name occurs frequently in Suffolk registers under the first three Georges, but without public function.' No, we didn't seem to care for public functions—a retiring family, the Bunters.

MRS. BUNTER. But ain't there anything about you, B?

BUNTER. Ain't there? What do you think of this, Maria? 'The present representative of the family is Benjamin Bunter, Esquire, honourably known in connection with extensive public works, and financial operations in all parts of the world.' That's very neatly put. 'He is the only son of the late eminent Nonconformist divine, the Rev. Boanerges Bunter, of Ball's Pond, Islington.' Ah, how proud the old man would have been, if he could have read all that, in the coal and 'tatur shed where he worked all the week, afore taking the pulpit at the Sniggs Rents, Ebenezer.

MRS. BUNTER. You don't grudge the money now, B?

BUNTER. Well, considering all the trouble they must have taken to find out all them facts about the Bunters, from the Anglo-Saxon before the Conquest down to Ball's Pond, I don't mind. But you really must go back to my Lady Matilda.

MRS. BUNTER. I say, B., she's been at me again about her nephew and Fanny.

BUNTER. It won't do, I tell you. The young fellow hasn't a rap.

MRS. BUNTER. But suppose he was to come into the title, B?

BUNTER. Suppose his aunt's baby should be a boy?

MRS. BUNTER. We shall soon know. Whatever it may be, it's expected every day, I'm told.

BUNTER. Between you and me, Maria, I've tipped the doctor's confidential man to telegraph the result.

MRS. BUNTER. If it's a girl——

BUNTER. Time enough to talk about that when the little event comes off. Look, there's my lady, looking as pleasant as if nothing more than luncheon was hanging over her head.

MRS. BUNTER. I must show her them new Bignonias.
    [*Exit into conservatory, where enter* LADY MATILDA, LILIAN *and* FANNY.

BUNTER. Ah, my lady's uncommonly civil since she knew I held the mortgage deed. She'll find I'm not so easy 'umbugged as Brown.

Enter SERVANT, *with telegram on salver.*

SERVANT. Telegram, sir, and no answer.
                    [*Gives telegram, and exit.*

BUNTER. [*Reading envelope of telegram.*] 'You are requested not to give the messenger any gratuity.' Well, I wasn't going to. [*Opens telegram and reads.*] 'Fashionable Intelligence. Births. The Honourable Mrs. Reginald Fitz-Urse, twins.' [*Starts.*] Eh? [*Reads.*] 'Girls.' Girls? Then I don't mind how many there is of them. They can't sit in the House of Lords, at least not yet. My son-in-law, Lord Bearholm! It does sound imposing. Next to being a lord oneself is having a lord in the family. The ladies.

Enter LADY MATILDA *and* MRS. BUNTER. LILIAN *and* FANNY *remain conversing in conservatory.*

LADY MATILDA. [*Looking round her.*] Very gorgeous indeed. Such a brilliant gloss of newness upon everything.

MRS. BUNTER. Yes, Bunter likes to see things spick and span. Bless you! He'd order a new coat of paint every year for every article in the place, if I'd let him.

LADY MATILDA. [*Superciliously looking at the pictures through eye-glass.*] Including the pictures?

MRS. BUNTER. [*Anxiously.*] I hope you admire them, Lady Matilda? They're all B.'s taste.

LADY MATILDA. So I should have guessed. Very fine, very fine indeed.

BUNTER. Does your ladyship mean the landscapes, or the history subjects?

LADY MATILDA. No, I meant the frames.

BUNTER. [*Angrily, aside.*] Admiring the frames! These aristocrats have no taste for art! [*Aloud.*] Yes, that's my style. None of your smoky old Italian and Flemish 'umbugs for me. Give me the she-doovers of our own school.

LADY MATILDA. Ah, you prefer young pupils to old masters.

BUNTER. Of course I do. There's R.A.'s! This is what you may call a magnificent ar-ray of first-class talent. Ha, ha!

[*Laughs triumphantly.*

LADY MATILDA. [*Blankly.*] I beg your pardon.

BUNTER. Ar-ray—Royal Academy! [*Aside.*] What a damn'd fool this woman is!

LADY MATILDA. Ah, very neat indeed—when it's explained.

BUNTER. [*Aside.*] Confound her impudence!

LADY MATILDA. And your statues, Mr. Bunter—pray do you have them done by contract?

BUNTER. Contract? Carrara, every one of them Carrara!

LADY MATILDA. Ah! I fancied there was a sort of family likeness about them. At all events, I am pretty certain I recognize some old friends.

BUNTER. No, I bought them all fresh made.

MRS. BUNTER. Hot and hot, as you may say, from the studio.

LADY MATILDA. Ah, I thought I remembered some of them in the neighbourhood of the New Road. The arts are a great deal to you men of business.

BUNTER. Yes, we're a treading in the steps of the Venetians and the Florentines. It was the merchant princes employed the artists there, you know, my lady.

LADY MATILDA. And here, thanks to financing and falsification, trade is rising into an art. [*Sniffs at her flaçon.*] Really, I'm so used to the dullness of Cleve Abbey, your bran-new splendour quite gives me a headache.

BUNTER. Ah, we're used to it. We never have no 'eadaches. It's nothing when you're used to it.

MRS. BUNTER. But my lady, you haven't seen half round the place yet.

LADY MATILDA. You call it 'Beaumanor Park,' I think? Now I should christen it 'Bunter House,' if I were you.

MRS. BUNTER. Well, Beaumanor Park does sound old fashioned——

LADY MATILDA. [*Aside.*] And does not sufficiently identify the place with the people. [*Aloud.*] I'm quite at your service.

MRS. BUNTER. This way, my lady. Come, B.

> [*Exeunt* LADY MATILDA *and* MRS. BUNTER.

BUNTER. That woman sets by blood a b'iling. Egad, you would think to look at her that she meant to buy us up, instead of vicé versà! But we're all dust of the earth, 'igh and 'umble—'igh and 'umble.   [*Exit after ladies.*

LILIAN *and* FANNY *have entered during this dialogue, and now come down.*

LILIAN. The worst thing about your house, Fanny, is that it is all too bright—too gay. I haven't seen a single corner where I could fancy you reading Tennyson and enjoying a good cry.

FANNY. Ah, you should see my oratory—all black draperies, ebony furniture, and the sweetest death's head in ivory. Do come over some morning, and let's revel in 'In Memoriam' together. One long sigh, interspersed with sobs.

LILIAN. I'm afraid I shouldn't appreciate that style of amusement; I'm so dreadfully light-hearted.

FANNY. You should mortify yourself, dear. Keep the fasts and vigils—try bread and water twice a week, and you've no idea how low-spirited you'll soon feel.

LILIAN. I'm afraid I should relapse into coffee and rolls, fish and a cutlet, on the slightest provocation. I've an awfully healthy appetite, as well as a dreadfully light heart; and yet I've reason enough to be sad.   [*Sighs.*

FANNY. You said 'No' to Mr. Brown, didn't you?

LILIAN. Yes, I said 'No,' but it wasn't from my heart.

FANNY. I said 'Yes' to Bertie, and it was from my heart. It was papa said 'No' and meant it, and that's a deal worse than saying 'No' oneself, and not meaning it.

LILIAN. Shall I give your love to Bertie when I see him?

FANNY. Thank you, dear, but I see him every day myself. He's looking out for my signal now, at the old oak in the park—the 'talking oak', as I call it.

LILIAN. Ah, you're a happy girl—you can see the man you love.

MRS. BUNTER. [*Outside.*] Fanny!

FANNY. Yes, mamma. [*To* LILIAN.] Come, dear.

Enter BROWN; *deposits his bag on chair.*

BROWN. Miss Vavasour!

LILIAN. You here?

FANNY. Mr. Brown! I'll see you are not interrupted.   [*Exit.*

BROWN. I am here on a business appointment with Mr. Bunter. I came in through the conservatory. You are the last person I expected to see.

LILIAN. Mamma is here. Don't be surprised if she treats you coldly—you have not treated her, or any of us kindly—you have given us no news of yourself.

BROWN. No news is good news. We've pulled through. Do you remember my saying I liked to battle with a bad time? It was a rash thing to say. This has been an awful three weeks. I've sometimes looked in the glass of a morning to see if my hair hadn't turned white over-night. [*With affected gaiety.*] It hasn't, has it?

LILIAN. Oh, don't laugh; it pains me. We have all thought of you very much. But you will come to see us at the Abbey? [*Looks round her.*] In this house somehow——

BROWN. Everything seems in keeping with the purse-proud snobs, its owners, nothing with you. Yes, I will venture over to the Abbey once more.

LILIAN. Once more?

BROWN. To bid you all good-bye, before I leave England.

LILIAN. Before you leave England?

MRS. BUNTER. [*Outside.*] Miss Vavasour!

LILIAN. I'm coming! I must see you again. I have so much to say to you. Watch till you can speak with me alone.

MRS. BUNTER. [*Outside.*] Miss Vavasour!

LILIAN. I'm coming, Mrs. Bunter. [*Exit.*

BROWN. Heaven bless her bright face! I don't know whether the sight of it has done more to quicken or kill my courage. To leave England is little, but to leave Lilian—here comes that snob. I cannot face him so soon after her!

[*Exit, taking his bag.*

Enter BUNTER *and* FANNY.

BUNTER. Look here, Fanny, while your mamma is showing her ladyship our chany, I want to know what's the matter with you—you are as dull as a mute at a funeral. Do look a little lively, can't you, at least afore visitors?

FANNY. Do not ask me for smiles, papa, unless it be the smiles that mask a broken heart.

BUNTER. Broken fiddlestick! All because I've said no to your silly fancy for this young Fitz-Urse.

FANNY. [*Tragically.*] Beware, papa, how you drive two young hearts to extremity!

BUNTER. Now do be calm, Fanny.

FANNY. [*Suddenly turning on him.*] Calm! [*Crosses her hands on her bosom, à la Mater Dolorosa.*]

'And in my breast, if calm at all,
 If any calm—a calm despair.'

BUNTER. Pooh, pooh! None of them pre-raffe-le-tite attitudes here. Suppose I was to tell you I'd thought better of it?

FANNY. Papa!

BUNTER. You seem very fond of him—I'm very fond of you. My happiness is in making other people happy. I'm told he's clever.

FANNY. Oh, so clever! Look how he passed that Civil Service examination.

BUNTER. Ah, I never passed one myself, so I don't know what sort of a passage it is. But it shows he's fit for the service of his country. And therefore I say, take him, Fanny, and make the best of him.

FANNY. And you mean that, papa? [*With a gush of emotion.*] Bless you! Very much bless you!   [*Kisses him twice.*

BUNTER. Ditto—very much ditto.   [*Kisses her twice.*

FANNY. [*Disgusted.*] What do you mean by 'very much ditto,' papa?

BUNTER. Bless you, I mean—and take notice I gave you my blessing before the post came in. [FANNY *rushes to the window.*] Nobody'll suspect the telegram. [FANNY *jumping up and waving her handkerchief.*] What do you mean by that?   [*Imitates her signal.*

FANNY. [*Blushing.*] That's for Bertie, papa.

BUNTER. Why, do you mean to tell me he's there, on the look out?

FANNY. Yes, papa.

BUNTER. And that you've been in the habit of doing that sort of thing?   [*Imitating her.*

FANNY. Yes, papa.

BUNTER. And that you would have gone on doing that sort of thing, if I hadn't given my consent?

FANNY. Yes, papa.

BUNTER. [*Severely.*] Well, Fanny, if this is what you call honouring your father and mother——

FANNY. How could I honour my father and my mother more than by giving them such a son-in-law?

BUNTER. But how about his principles—his principles and his piety? How about them, Fanny?

FANNY. He will have me, papa, to guide him to the sweet symbolism of Nature, and the chastening discipline of the Early Church.

BUNTER. Well, I hope he'll like it.

FANNY. I must tell mamma. If Bertie comes, papa, say I'll be back directly.   [*Exit.*

Enter FITZ-URSE.

FITZ-URSE. The governor! Oh, I say, I didn't expect to see you, you know.

BUNTER. No, sir; you expected to see Miss Bunter. [*With affected sternness.*] The sight of an indignant parent may well startle you. I know all—your signals and your rendez-vous-ing. You weren't far off, it seems.

FITZ-URSE. Only in the Park, sir, under the big oak, like— what's his name—Charles the 12th, you know. Always am there at twelve, looking out for this sort of thing. [*Waves his handkerchief.*] One for 'come,' two for 'don't.'

Enter SERVANT.

SERVANT. Mr. Brown, sir, by appointment.   [*Exit.*

BUNTER. [*With dignity, to* FITZ-URSE.] Go, young man, and join the ladies. No more of these clandestical proceedings. You have my permission to address Miss Bunter as an accepted suitor.

FITZ-URSE. No—have I though? I wish you'd told me before. It's been very damp under that tree, and doosed slow, waiting for this sort of thing. [*Waving handkerchief.*] One for 'come,' and two for 'don't.' By, by, Bunter!   [*Exit.*

Enter BROWN, *with bag, shown in by* SERVANT.

BUNTER. Ah, my dear friend. Glad to see you! You've had an early journey. I suppose you'd like a little breakfast. We mustn't quite neglect the carnal man. Montmorency! Breakfast for Mr. Brown, in my study. [SERVANT *bows, and exit.*] You'll be snuggest there. Well, I was glad to see you'd escaped the 'Gazette.'

BROWN. Yes, that forty thousand saved us. It was worth the five thousand I paid you for it.

BUNTER. Ah! I might have made cent. per cent. of the money then, but I never grudged it.

BROWN. It was a scrape for life—but we've saved our credit, at the cost of our capital.

BUNTER. Quite right. What is wealth? Dross, Mr. Brown, except as used for something better than mere worldliness.

BROWN. Other-worldliness, for example.

BUNTER. Exactly. You've brought the title deeds?

BROWN. Here they are.
[*Takes deeds from bag on table, and hands them to him.*

BUNTER. I shall have to get the mortgage money out of the estate. There is nothing for it but a sale.

BROWN. Have you thought of the family?

BUNTER. Though of them? My 'eart's been bleeding for them this month past. But I can't lie out of my money. I am ready to give them a fancy price——

BROWN. Ah! You mean to bid, then?

BUNTER. A sale by private contract won't hurt their feelings so much. My wife and daughter like the place, though it's too old-fashioned for me. When we've settled there——

Enter BLASENBALG. BROWN *and he exchange bows.*

Ah, Blasenbalg! I was just going to tell Brown how happy we should be to see him at Cleve Abbey—whether it's for shooting or fishing——

BROWN. Fishing! Mr. Blasenbalg ought to know something about that.

BLASENBALG. Ja, dere is good fishing at de Abbey.

BROWN. Especially among the potholes of the mountain lime-stone. I remember you preferred your fish in a fossil state.

BLASENBALG. Ah, I remember you used to laugh at my vlints.

BROWN. I did once—but I know better now.

BLASENBALG. What do you mean?

BROWN. You remember when I and Miss Vavasour emptied your creel? [BLASENBALG *nods.*] I kept back some bits of your vlints, as you call them.

BLASENBALG. You kept dem back—for what?

BROWN. Mere idle curiosity. [BLASENBALG *gives a sigh of relief.*] It struck me they felt heavy.

BLASENBALG. Ja, de vlints is heavy.

BROWN. But these turned out to be no more flints than they

were nuggets. In fact it seems they were nuggets—if not of gold, of iron.

BUNTER. [*Startled.*] Iron? Pooh, pooh!

BLASENBALG. Nonsense! What do you know about iron?

[*Enter* SERVANT, *with breakfast on tray, and carries it off into the study.*

BROWN. Nothing, but I have a friend who knows a good deal. He saw the stones knocking about my office, and recommended me to have them analyzed.

BLASENBALG. But you vos not vool enough to waste your money?

BROWN. Yes, I was. And you'll both be interested to know that the stone turns out to be hematite, containing seventy-five per cent. of iron. Here's the analysis, if you've any curiosity about it.

BUNTER. Oh, I don't care about it.   [*Takes it.*

BROWN. It's of some importance though. If the stone exists in quantity, the estate is of enormous value.

BLASENBALG. Ah, dese analysts are always finding out mares' nests for fools to lay their eggs in.

BUNTER. I wouldn't give a fig for scientific opinions—you may buy as many as you like at a guinea apiece. Give me practical men, sir—practical men.

BROWN. At all events the matter deserves consideration. It should be mentioned to Vavasour.

BUNTER. [*Horrified.*] Mentioned to Vavasour! Are you mad?

BROWN. Then you believe the iron's there?

BUNTER. [*Confused.*] It's better not to unsettle people's minds, when they're made up to sell. What can be the good of your spoiling the market?

BROWN. I was thinking it might improve the market for the vendor. [BUNTER *is about to tear paper.*] I'll trouble you for that analysis.

BLASENBALG. [*Aside to* BUNTER *as* BROWN *puts up paper.*] He vants a slice—offer him one.

BUNTER. [*To* BROWN.] Keep this dark, and we don't mind giving you a share of our luck—say a fourth.

BLASENBALG. Say—in drittel—dat's share and share alike.

BUNTER. I don't know what he means, but he says you're to have some 'drittel'—oh yes, share and share alike.

BROWN. It's a tempting offer, but——

BUNTER. [*Eagerly.*] No buts—take it, my boy, take it, and my blessing go along with it.

BROWN. I've some doubts whether it isn't stealing a march on Vavasour.

BUNTER. Nonsense, there's no reservation of minerals in the conveyance. He can't claim a penny more on account of the iron, if he knew nothing about it.

BLASENBALG. Dat's de law.

BROWN. But is it justice? Is it honesty? Is it fair dealing between gentlemen?

BUNTER. What's that got to do with us? Keep on the right side of the law and don't fly in the face of Providence. It's sinful! If people went on your tack, how do you think business would go on ? How would fortunes be made?

BROWN. As fortunes should be made, by fair dealing and hard work. If the world went on my tack, thousands of families wouldn't be ruined to enrich a few score of successful speculators, and British enterprise would not stand in the pillory as it does now, with 'Lie' branded on its forehead!

BUNTER. I didn't expect to hear such very coarse language from you; but if you like to fly in the face of Providence, go and fly—fly away—but don't say as I didn't offer 'andsome.

Enter SERVANT.

SERVANT. Mr. Brown's breakfast is served.

BUNTER. Montmorency, go away; get out! [*Exit* SERVANT. *Very earnestly.*] I say, Brown, honour bright—you ain't in the market yourself?

BROWN. [*In the same tone.*] Honour bright, Mr. Bunter, I am not. You are mortgagee now. I've handed over the deeds. I wash my hands of the whole business, and I leave you to reconcile your week-day practice with your Sunday profession.

[*Exit into study.*

BLASENBALG. The fool! [*Locks door on him.*] Better keep him safe. Vy, if you ain't blushing!

BUNTER. I thought as Brown does—once.

BLASENBALG. Luckily you know better now.

Enter LADY MATILDA.

LADY MATILDA. Now Mr. Bunter, my husband and Mr. Secker are waiting. I think there's nothing to interfere with the settlement of this morning's business. The sooner the better.

BUNTER. Perhaps you are right. Unpleasant things can't be got over too soon.

LADY MATILDA. I quite agree with you. Here come the gentlemen. Shall we take our seats?

[VAVASOUR *and* SECKER *appear in conservatory.*

BUNTER. [*To* BLASENBALG.] She's a game 'un! Does your ladyship intend to be present?

LADY MATILDA. If you have no objection. I rather pique myself upon being a woman of business, you know.

Enter VAVASOUR *and* SECKER; *bows interchanged.*

VAVASOUR. [*Rubbing his hands.*] Good morning, Bunter, good morning! Fine, cheery weather!

BUNTER. Be seated, gentlemen. [*Aside to* BLASENBALG.] The Squire looks very lively, considering. [*Formally.*] We needn't go into the circumstances which have driven things to this painful point.

VAVASOUR. Not the least necessary, I should say.

BUNTER. Mr. Secker has told you of my offer for Cleve Abbey.

VAVASOUR. Yes. An extremely handsome offer I think it is.

BUNTER. We none of us want to give the lawyers a job—no offence to you, Mr. Secker. We'll have no long-winded investigation of title.

LADY MATILDA. Where every parchment harbours a question, and every question a note of interrogation and five pounds. Perfectly unnecessary, I think.

BUNTER. It's quite a privilege to have to deal with a head like your ladyship's. Here's my cheque for eighty thousand. Here's the mortgage deed to be cancelled—the conveyance of Cleve Abbey to be executed.

[*Gives cheque and parchments to* SECKER *as he speaks.*

VAVASOUR. [*Pushing parchment over to* BUNTER.] I beg your pardon. If you will execute this release——

BUNTER. [*Startled.*] Release!

VAVASOUR. [*Prompted by* SECKER.] And sign this receipt for mortgage—principal and interest.

[*Points to paper attached to release.*

BUNTER. What do you mean?

LADY MATILDA. Simply that we have great satisfaction in clearing off our encumbrances, and no intention at present of selling Cleve Abbey.

VAVASOUR. [*Brings his hand down on table, emphatically.*] Not an acre of it!

BUNTER.   ⎞ The devil you haven't!
BLASENBALG. ⎠ Potz tausend!

VAVASOUR. I am sure, as a neighbour, you will be glad to hear that thanks to the accidental discovery of a magnificent field of hematite iron on the property [BUNTER *and* BLASENBALG *astonished.*] Mr. Secker has been enabled, not only to pay off the mortgage, but to secure five times the former income of the estate, in the shape of mineral rents and royalties— mineral rents and royalties!

LADY MATILDA. I begged Mr. Secker to leave us the pleasure of giving you this information.

BUNTER. So that accounts for your being in such a hurry.

VAVASOUR. Exactly—we wanted to give you an agreeable surprise.

BUNTER. That's why you're all looking so lively?

LADY MATILDA. Yes—we felt, by anticipation, how much your

kind and Christian heart, which has sympathized so much in our difficulties, would rejoice in the removal of them.

BUNTER. [*Aside.*] That woman is a disgustin' hippercrit! [*Aloud.*] I know who told you of this.   [*Jumps up.*

LADY MATILDA. [*Eagerly.*] Who?

BUNTER. It was that fellow Brown! [*Aside to* BLASENBALG.] I thought he was up to some villainy of his own, or he'd have stood in with us.

LADY MATILDA. No, we have heard nothing from Mr. Brown. But if you can worm the name of his informant out of Mr. Secker——

SECKER. [*Shaking his head.*] That's my secret. I couldn't tell you—not if you were to put a five hundred pound note under my dinner plate.   [*With a meaning look at* BUNTER.

BUNTER. Whoever told you only wanted to 'umbug you.

LADY MATILDA. Whoever does that will find us a match for them.

VAVASOUR. [*Emphatically.*] I should think they would!

BUNTER. Or if there is anything that looks like ironstone, it ain't worth a rap——

LADY MATILDA. Pardon me, here's the analysis, made by the same high, scientific authority who analysed some of precisely the same ore for Mr. Blasenbalg.

BLASENBALG. Blown!

BUNTER. Done brown! Lady Matilda, you won't be surprised if I feel rather hurt at this. I don't think I've been 'andsomely treated—I ain't clear I've been legally treated. I'm pretty sure there was an agreement to sell, and that would be held as good as a sale, in equity.

                [SECKER *returns cheque to* BUNTER.

LADY MATILDA. I think the less we invoke equity in this transaction the better. Now Mr. Bunter, I haven't seen half your fine things yet. May I ask you to show Mr. Vavasour over your greenhouses?

VAVASOUR. Yes, I should like to borrow a hint or two for some improvements we're contemplating at the Abbey. That's one use of these new places—*fiat experimentum in corpore vili*, you know. No, I daresay you don't know—it's Latin.

BUNTER. [*Aside.*] They shan't see me down in the mouth. [*Aloud.*] That way. [*Pointing off.*]

[*Exeunt* VAVASOUR *and* SECKER.

You will find my gardeners, but you must excuse me; I must talk to my lawyer. We'll see if the law allows people to be choused in this 'eartless way. Yes, my lady, I repeat the word—choused! [*Exit in a rage.*

BLASENBALG. Dis cheque what Herr Bunter gave me for two thousand pounds, I think I'd better lose no time to get him cashed at de County Bank! [*Exit.*

LADY MATILDA. [*Walking up and down in triumph.*] This is triumph! To trick these tricksters—to watch their insolent hopes growing and growing, and to crush them at their ripest. Our fortune is increased five fold. No need now of Lilian falling to a position equally below her merits and her family. Poor Brown, I pity him! He was a noble fellow, but what a mercy it is that affair was broken off in time! Lilian can do so much better now.

Enter LILIAN.

LILIAN. Mamma, Mrs. Bunter is asking for you.

LADY MATILDA. Let her ask. I'm too happy for her just now.

LILIAN. What's the matter, mamma? You look quite radiant.

LADY MATILDA. [*With a sigh.*] Ah, joy is a great beautifier! [*Takes* LILIAN *in her arms.*] Let me kiss my own darling and tell her this good news: that we are rich again, richer than ever we were—our position in the county prouder than before. That in shaping my Lilian's future, we need no longer consult anything but her heart and her deserts.

LILIAN. Oh, this is news! But what good fairy has wrought this transformation?

LADY MATILDA. It's all through a discovery of ironstone on the estate.

LILIAN. Oh, if that discovery had been made a month ago!

LADY MATILDA. Better as it is, or Mr. Brown's sudden change

of fortune would not have made it so clearly your duty to break with him.

LILIAN. But, mama, are you quite sure it was my duty?

LADY MATILDA. I know it sounds very worldly—but I say now, as I said then, 'Yes.'

LILIAN. Ah, mamma, he did not say 'No' to his heart because we were poor!

LADY MATILDA. This is unwise. You have been saved from a sacrifice, and you seem to regret it, even to reproach me with it. But come, poor Mrs. Bunter has been condoling with us all the morning; we ought to give her the opportunity of congratulating us. Let us hope she'll do it less clumsily.

[*Exit.*

LILIAN. Ah, why will mamma insist on my being happy in her way, instead of my own? But she is right. All is over between us now. But he is here. He promised to see me once more, to say good-bye. Oh, must it be for ever?

BROWN. [*Within study.*] Lilian!

LILIAN. That's his voice!

BROWN. I'm locked in; the key's on your side. Let me out.

LILIAN. [*Unlocking door;* BROWN *comes out.*] How very strange! What was that for?

BROWN. [*Laughing.*] For fear I might spoil sport. Your mamma has done that most effectually. I couldn't resist the temptation to assist at the scene through the keyhole.

LILIAN. Then you know this wonderful change in our fortunes.

BROWN. Yes. I congratulate you. My fortunes have changed too—unhappily for the worst. I shall have to begin the world again.

LILIAN. And alone, too?

BROWN. Yes. Pioneers and forlorn hopes must carry nothing but their implements and arms. I am glad to have this opportunity of saying good-bye. I have very little time to spare. I sail at the end of the month.

LILIAN. Going to leave England?

BROWN. Yes. England's a capital place to spend a fortune, but one wants elbow-room and a new country to make one. I'm going to establish a new connection in Australia.

LILIAN. So far away! It will be a hard struggle for you there. Oh, if good wishes could help you——

BROWN. I shall have yours, I'm sure. It will be pleasant to know I leave all so changed for the better at the Abbey, that your mamma is free to carry out her plans for you.

LILIAN. I preferred yours.

BROWN. But everything is altered since then. I've torn that chapter out of my book; you had better tear it out too.

LILIAN. Did you find it so easy to tear out?

BROWN. Sailors on a lee shore have enough to do with the ship. I've thought as little as I could of Cleve Abbey.

LILIAN. But this breaking up of old habits, associations, friendships!

BROWN. Trees can be transplanted with the roots—but the less they are uncovered, the better. Remember—even when I thought myself a rich man there was a great river between us; now 'tis an ocean.

LILIAN. We were both poor then. It might have been my duty not to increase the family difficulties by an imprudent marriage—even to relieve them, if I could, by a worldly one. But this is all changed now. We are rich——

BROWN. And I am poor.

LILIAN. Not so poor as I was when you asked me to be your wife. [*Holds out her arms.*] I now ask to share your struggle with poverty and privation. You shall see if I falter. Oh, will you not have mercy on a woman's heart?

BROWN. My own brave girl! Mine for ever now. Let who will say 'No!'

Enter LADY MATILDA *and* VAVASOUR.

LADY MATILDA. Lilian! Mr. Brown! You in this house!

VAVASOUR. Very unexpected indeed. Everything is unexpected to-day.

LADY MATILDA. I thought it was understood when you left us

a month ago that all intercourse between Miss Vavasour and yourself was at an end. I felt full confidence in that understanding.

LILIAN. He never broke it, mamma. It was I—I who, when he put me from him with cold words and proud looks, would not be thrust away. He never asked me to be his wife. It was I asked him to be my husband.

LADY MATILDA. [*Severely*.] And so forgot that guiding principle of your sex—a woman's dignity.

BROWN. But obeyed her sex's safer guide—a woman's heart.

LADY MATILDA. I appeal to your generosity, sir. Will you take advantage of her weakness?

LILIAN. Papa—will you plead for me?

VAVASOUR. Well really, my dear, I'm afraid your mamma knows so much the best what's good for everybody.

Enter SECKER.

SECKER. Ah, Brown, I've found you at last. I positively decline to carry my bagged fox any longer. Now, Lady Matilda, I can tell you to whom you owe your iron El Dorado.

LADY MATILDA. I'm so glad. The burden of gratitude was too heavy to be pleasant. Who is it?

SECKER. There he stands. [*Points to* BROWN.] Bunter has betrayed you—don't deny it.

BROWN. I never deny the truth. I am sorry you had not the good taste to hold your tongue. I never meant them to know this.

LILIAN. They know you did not. Oh, mamma! What wealth could be like poverty with this man? What rank like his nobleness?

VAVASOUR. Really I think, my dear—mind, I only say I think—considering what we owe him——

LADY MATILDA. He may claim his own payment.

[BROWN *takes* LILIAN's *hand.*

VAVASOUR. Eh, my lady, don't say no [*Rubbing his hands.*] Egad! this is as good as another iron mine.

LADY MATILDA. You have won her fairly, sir. I had dreamt of a very different lot for her. But she has made her choice. I hope she has chosen wisely.

VAVASOUR. Hope, my lady! I'll lay my head—and that's no trifling bet—she has chosen well. Heaven bless you, darling. [*Kisses* LILIAN.] And you too, Mr. Brown, as my lady has no objection.   [*Shakes* BROWN's *hand heartily.*

Enter BUNTER *and* BLASENBALG.

BUNTER. [*Aside to* BLASENBALG.] The law won't help us— it never will when it ought to. Hallo, Brown, out! [*Confused.*] I hope you had a comfortable breakfast.

BROWN. As comfortable as could be expected in a lock-up.

BUNTER. Ah, that was Blasenbalg's doings. It was of no use after all.

BROWN. Not the slightest. I had taken your own wise precaution.

BUNTER. What do you mean?

BROWN. I made it all right beforehand with the agent—eh, Secker?   [SECKER *chuckles and rubs his hands.*

BLASENBALG. I like dat man, though he has done me out of the best ting I was ever in for.

Enter MRS. BUNTER, FANNY *and* FITZ-URSE.

LADY MATILDA. Ah, here come your turtle-doves, Mr. Bunter. Let me present mine. [*Presenting* LILIAN *and* BROWN.] She has proposed—he has accepted her.

VAVASOUR. No, no, my dear, you mean——

LADY MATILDA. I mean what I say, Marmaduke—I generally do.

FANNY. Oh, this is delightful! Do let us all be married together!

FITZ-URSE. Yes, as they say at Newman's, 'One pair wedding greys out—another to follow.' I'll enter the two matches together for the same day, over the St. George's T. Y. E.

BUNTER. Well, I don't know. One must observe distinctions of rank. Considering what my son-in-law is——

FITZ-URSE. Eh?

BUNTER. Yes, you'll be glad to know, my lady, that the Honorable Mrs. Reginald Fitz-Urse has been brought to bed of two girls.

LADY MATILDA. Ah, I condole with you most sincerely on your disappointment.

BUNTER. What! That my son-in-law is a nobleman?

LADY MATILDA. That he isn't.

BUNTER. What d'ye mean?

LADY MATILDA. Oh, you can't be expected to know these things. Will you explain, my dear.

VAVASOUR. Ah, I'm always called on in any difficulty. Don't you see, Mr. Bunter, that as Bearholm is a barony by writ, the title falls into abeyance between the co-heiresses, instead of going to the next male.

BUNTER. Then he ain't a nobleman?

VAVASOUR. Certainly not—unless he's one of nature's.

LADY MATILDA. Luckily you don't care about family. You have his principles to fall back upon, you know, and his talents.

BUNTER. [*Aside.*] That woman is a disgustin' hippercrit! [*Fiercely to* BLASENBALG.] What are you sniggering at? I'll give you something to snigger for on the wrong side of your ugly mouth! I've sent to stop that cheque.

BLASENBALG. I guessed you vould—so I vent and got it cashed first.

BUNTER. Done brown again! I should like to know if there's any part of me left that can be done browner.

MRS. BUNTER. Let me comfort you, dear.   [*Embraces him.*

LADY MATILDA. Marmaduke, will you order the carriage for the Abbey? [*To* BROWN.] You may claim your place in it now, as in everything belonging to us.

BROWN. Including your hearts, I hope?

VAVASOUR. And the old acres, of course.

LADY MATILDA. Yes, the dear old acres—saved! Thanks to you.   [*Giving* BROWN *her hand.*

PLATE 4

New Men and Old Acres. The end of Act III

LILIAN. Don't thank him, mamma; he couldn't help it. Noblesse
  oblige.   [*Fondly turning to* BROWN.

LADY MATILDA. Mr. Brown, you have taught us all a lesson.

BROWN. [*Simply.*] Have I?

LILIAN. Yes. That it doesn't need the Old Acres to make New
  Men gentlemen!   [*Slightly bowing to* BROWN.

ENGAGED

AN ENTIRELY ORIGINAL FARCICAL COMEDY
IN THREE ACTS

BY

WILLIAM SCHWENCK GILBERT

(1836–1911)

---

*First performed at the Haymarket Theatre
3 October 1877*

CAST

CHEVIOT HILL, a young man of property	Mr. George Honey
BELVAWNEY, his friend	Mr. Harold Kyrle
MR. SYMPERSON	Mr. Howe
ANGUS MACALISTER, a Lowland peasant lad	Mr. Dewar
MAJOR McGILLICUDDY	Mr. Weathersby
BELINDA TREHERNE	Miss Marion Terry
MINNIE, Symperson's daughter	Miss Lucy Buckstone
MRS. MACFARLANE, a Lowland widow	Miss Emily Thorne
MAGGIE, her daughter, a Lowland lassie	Miss Julia Stewart
PARKER, Minnie's maid	Miss Julia Roselle

Three months' interval is supposed to elapse between the First
and Second Act. Three days' interval is supposed to elapse
between the Second and Third Acts.

PREFACE TO *ENGAGED*

By 1877, Gilbert, who had already been a practising barrister and journalist with over ten years of writing for the theatre behind him, was making a considerable reputation as a comic satirist. He began in extravaganza, burlesque, and farce: *Dulcamara, or The Little Duck and the Great Quack* (1866); *Harlequin Cock Robin and Jenny Wren* (1867), a pantomime; *The Merry Zingara, or The Tipsey Gipsey and the Pipsey Wipsey* (1868); and *The Pretty Druidess, or The Mother, the Maid, and the Mistletoe* (1869) are early works. Gilbert also contributed farcical and burlesque musical entertainments to the repertoire of the German Reeds at their Gallery of Illustration, such as *Ages Ago* (1869), *Our Island Home* (1870), *A Sensation Novel* (1871), and *Happy Arcadia* (1872). Two 'fairy' comedies, *The Palace of Truth* (1870) and *The Wicked World* (1873), the first showing what happens when the court of King Phanor is forced, through inhabiting a magic palace, to speak only the truth, and the second, set in fairyland on a cloud high above the earth, and depicting with greater intensity the clash between real mortal love and the fairies' idealized conception of love, foreshadow not only the satirical content but also the fantastic element of several Gilbert and Sullivan operas. Classical legend is the subject of the comedy-drama *Pygmalion and Galatea* (1871), the same year as the first collaboration with Sullivan, *Thespis, or The Gods Grown Old*, a classical burlesque. Over the next few years Gilbert continued prolific: burlesques, dramas, comedies, farces, and operas quickly followed one another. *Trial by Jury* came in 1875, and after *Engaged* Gilbert focused his attention primarily upon comic opera.

Gilbert's work outside extravaganza, burlesque, and opera was proportionately much smaller than his output in those forms. Like Robertson and Byron he always had a taste for strong melodrama, which he satisfied in plays like *Charity* (1874), *Dan'l Druce* (1876), and *Brantinghame Hall* (1888). One of his most successful pieces was the bitter-sweet *Sweethearts* (1874), written for the Prince of Wales's, in which a young

woman who heedlessly lets her lover go to India without offering him the smallest encouragement meets him thirty years later
on his return to discover that he has virtually forgotten a
relationship which she has treasured all these years. Delicate,
gently sentimental, and with a satisfyingly happy ending,
Sweethearts provided Mrs. Bancroft with one of her finest roles.
Gilbert wrote two or three farces, an indifferent comedy,
Randall's Thumb (1871), and adapted Labiche and Michel's *Un
Chapeau de Paille d'Italie* as *The Wedding March* (1873), but his
best non-musical comic work before *Engaged* was another 'farcical
comedy', *Tom Cobb* (1875); *Foggerty's Fairy* (1881), another
fairy comedy, followed. Here again the ideas of transformation
and reversal are paramount: Foggerty, harassed by another
woman in the very hour before his wedding, invokes his
guardian fairy to obliterate her from his history. Since all the
consequences of knowing her are also obliterated, Foggerty
finds several years of his past life completely changed, and the
fairy has to rescue him from an even more painful predicament
than before.

The content and tone of *Engaged* owed much to the irony and
'topsy-turvydom' already considerably developed in the burlesques, musical entertainments, early operas, and fairy comedies; similarities of characterization and attitude can also be
found in *Tom Cobb*. Nonetheless, *Engaged* is the acme of Gilbert's
comic writing before the Opera Comique and Savoy operas, a
play by a mature ironist and master craftsman. It is surely the
best nineteenth-century comedy before *The Importance of Being
Earnest*, and Wilde's debt to it is very great. The combination
of exaggerated romantic feeling and hard-headed calculation
in the heroines, the candid revelation of motives, the blithe
unawareness on the part of any character that he or she is
transgressing accepted social and moral limits, the fusion of
farcical and melodramatic complications in an elegant, graceful,
witty, and highly ironic comedy—these features of *Engaged* are
also characteristics of *The Importance of Being Earnest*.[1] Wilde's
more specific borrowings from Gilbert—Miss Treherne's eating
of tarts in a moment of crisis, 'Belvawneying', the mourning
clothes that Symperson dons prematurely in expectation of the

---

[1] On Wilde's debt to *Engaged*, see Lynton Hudson, *The English Stage 1850–
1950* (1951), pp. 101–5.

much-desired death of Cheviot Hill and his unpleasant surprise in finding Cheviot still alive—are also woven into the fabric of his comedy and are comically valuable in themselves.

Engaged is more important in its own right, however, than as an influence upon *The Importance of Being Earnest*. Although its spirit was that of the destructive irony of contemporary burlesque, it was a spirit generally alien to nineteenth-century comedies, which certainly contained satirical characters, scenes, and points of view, but always accompanied them with sentimental characters, scenes, and points of view, subordinating them to an overall and eventually triumphant morality that was domestically and socially acceptable. On the contrary, Gilbert exposed the selfishness underlying all human actions without depicting any redeeming qualities, not even a sense of humour, and in so doing deliberately slaughtered several sacred cows of nineteenth-century comedy. The continuous profession of worthy sentiments is one of them, and another is comedy's frequently idyllic conception of rural life and the virtue inevitably resident therein: the sweetly bucolic opening of *Engaged* lulls the audience into the belief that Angus, Maggie, and Mrs. Macfarlane are rather overdone representatives of perfect pastoral innocence. The idealized heroine, romantically and domestically motivated, the quietly happy inferior to dominant man, is brilliantly satirized in the characters of Maggie, Miss Treherne, and Minnie Symperson. The hero's devotion to a single adored object without thought of financial advantage or disadvantage (a common situation in nineteenth-century comedy), together with the necessary assertion of male authority, is ironically reversed in Angus, Cheviot Hill, and Belvawney. In fact all the 'romantic' characters are concerned with 'pecuniary settlements'; Gilbert pursues comedy's satirical treatment of the theme of money to its logical extreme. Even the powerful bond between tender father and doting daughter and the popular stage figure of the kindly, protective parent with only his child's best interests at heart are exploded in the relationship between Symperson and Minnie.

Its satirical frankness unsoftened by music or the pleasing light diversions of burlesque, *Engaged* was found unpleasant by many critics, although it was by no means a failure, with 110 performances on its first run. It was not often revived: in 1878

George Honey again took the role of Cheviot Hill at the Strand;
H. J. Byron played him in 1881 at the Court, and in 1886
Beerbohm Tree acted the same part at the Haymarket. The
text used is that in the Chatto and Windus *Original Plays*,
Second Series (1881), collated with the privately printed 1877
edition, *French's Acting Edition*, v. 117, and the Lord Chamberlain's copy. The *Original Plays* text shows only a few slight
changes from the 1877 edition; the stage directions in the latter
are somewhat fuller and have been incorporated here. The
French is the only acting edition that I could discover; it is
virtually identical with the 1877.

NOTE

It is absolutely essential to the success of this piece that it should
be played with the most perfect earnestness and gravity
throughout. There should be no exaggeration in costume,
make-up, or demeanour; and the characters, one and all, should
appear to believe, throughout, in the perfect sincerity of their
words and actions. Directly the characters show that they are
conscious of the absurdity of their utterances the piece begins to
drag.

W. S. GILBERT

ACT I

SCENE. *Garden of a humble but picturesque cottage, near Gretna, on the border between England and Scotland. The cottage, R., is covered with creepers, and the garden is prettily filled with flowers. The door faces audience. A wooden bridge leads off L. The whole scene is suggestive of rustic prosperity and content.* MAGGIE MACFARLANE, *a pretty country girl, is discovered spinning at a wheel, L., and singing as she spins. A rustic stool, R.* ANGUS MACALISTER, *a good-looking peasant lad, appears at back and creeps softly down to* MAGGIE *as she sings and spins, and places his hands over her eyes.*

ANGUS. Wha is it?

MAGGIE. Oh, Angus, ye frightened me sae! [*He releases her.*] And see there—the flax is a' knotted and scribbled—and I'll do naething wi' it!

ANGUS. Meg! My Meg! My ain bonnie Meg!

MAGGIE. Angus, why, lad, what's wrang wi' 'ee? Thou hast tear-drops in thy bonnie blue een.

ANGUS. Dinna heed them, Meg. It comes fra glowerin' at thy bright beauty. Glowerin' at thee is like glowerin' at the noon-day sun!

MAGGIE. Angus, thou'rt talking fulishly. I'm but a puir brown hill-side lassie. I dinna like to hear sic things from a straight honest lad like thee. It's the way the dandy toun-folk speak to me, and it does na come rightly from the lips of a simple man.

ANGUS. Forgive me, Meg, for I speak honestly to ye. Angus Macalister is not the man to deal in squeaming compliments. Meg, I love thee dearly, as thou well knowest. I'm but a puir lad, and I've little but twa braw arms and a straight hairt to live by, but I've saved a wee bit siller—I've a braw housie and a scrappie of gude garden-land—and it's a' for thee, lassie, if thou'll gie me thy true and tender little hairt!

MAGGIE. Angus, I'll be fair and straight wi' ee. Thou askest me for my hairt. Why, Angus, thou'rt tall and fair and brave. Thou'st a gude, honest face, and a gude, honest hairt, which is mair precious than a' the gold on earth! No man has a word to say against Angus Macalister—no, nor any woman neither. Thou hast strong arms to work wi', and a strong hairt to help thee work. And wha am I that I should say that a' these blessings are not enough for me? If thou, gude, brave, honest man, will be troubled wi' sic a puir little humble mousie as Maggie Macfarlane, why, she'll just be the proudest and happiest lassie in a' Dumfries!

ANGUS. My ain darling!   [*They embrace.*

Enter MRS. MACFARLANE, *from cottage.*

MRS. MACFARLANE. Why, Angus—Maggie, what's a' this?

ANGUS. Mistress Macfarlane, dinna be fasht wi' me; dinna think worse o' me than I deserve. I've loved your lass honestly these fifteen years, but I never plucked up the hairt to tell her so until noo; and when she answered fairly, it wasna in human nature to do aught else but hold her to my hairt and place one kiss on her bonnie cheek.

MRS. MACFARLANE. Angus, say nae mair. My hairt is sair at losing my only bairn, but I'm nae fasht wi' ee. Thou'rt a gude lad, and it's been the hope of my widowed auld heart to see you twain one. Thou'lt treat her kindly—I ken that weel. Thou'rt a prosperous, kirk-going man, and my Mag should be a happy lass indeed. Bless thee, Angus; bless thee!

[*Kisses him.*

ANGUS. [*Wiping his eyes.*] Dinna heed the water in my ee—it will come when I'm ower glad. Yes, I'm a fairly prosperous man. What wi' farmin' a bit land, and gillieing odd times, and a bit o' poachin' now and again; and what wi' my illicit whusky still—and throwin' trains off the line, that the poor distracted passengers may come to my cot, I've mair ways than one of making an honest living—and I'll work them a' nicht and day for my bonnie Meg!

MRS. MACFARLANE. D'ye ken, Angus, I sometimes think that thou'rt losing some o' thine auld skill at upsetting railway trains. Thou hast not done sic a thing these sax weeks, and the cottage stands sairly in need of sic chance custom as the poor delayed passengers may bring.

MAGGIE. Nay, mither, thou wrangest him. Even noo, this very day, has he not placed twa bonnie braw sleepers across the up-line, ready for the express from Glaisgie, which is due in twa minutes or so?

MRS. MACFARLANE. Gude lad! Gude thoughtfu' lad! But I hope the unfortunate passengers will na' be much hurt, puir unconscious bodies!

ANGUS. Fear nought, mither. Lang experience has taught me to do my work deftly. The train will run off the line, and the traffic will just be blocked for half a day, but I'll warrant ye that, wi' a' this, nae mon, woman, or child amang them will get sae much as a bruised head or a broken nose.

MAGGIE. My ain tender-hearted Angus! He wadna hurt sae much as a blatherin', buzzin' bluebottle flee!

[Railway whistle heard.

ANGUS. Nae, Meg, not if takin' care and thought could help the poor dumb thing. [Wiping his eyes.] There, see lass, [Looking off.] the train's at a standstill, and there's nae harm done. I'll just go and tell the puir distraught passengers that they may rest them here in thy cot, gin they will, till the line is cleared again. Mither, get thy rooms ready, and put brose i' the pot, for mebbe they'll be hungry, puir souls. Farewell, Meg; I'll be back ere lang, and if I don't bring 'ee a full half-dozen o' well-paying passengers, thou may'st just wed the red-headed exciseman!   [Exit.

MAGGIE. Oh, mither, mither, I'm ower happy! I've nae deserved sic a good fortune as to be the wife o' yon brave and honest lad!

MRS. MACFARLANE. Meg, thine auld mither's hairt is sair at the thought o' losin' ye, for hitherto she's just been a' the world to 'ee; but now thou'lt cleave to thine Angus, and thou'lt learn to love him better than thy puir auld mither! But it mun be—it mun be!

MAGGIE. Nay, mither, say not that. A gude girl loves her husband wi' one love and her mither wi' anither. They are not alike, but neither is greater nor less than the ither, and they dwell together in peace and unity. That is how a gude girl loves.

MRS. MACFARLANE. And thou art a gude girl, Meg?

MAGGIE. I am a varra gude girl indeed, mither—a varra, varra gude girl!

MRS. MACFARLANE. I'm richt sure o' that. Well, the puir belated passengers will be here directly, and it is our duty to provide for them sic puir hospitality as our humble roof will afford. It shall never be said o' Janie Macfarlane that she ever turned the weary traveller fainting from her door.

MAGGIE. My ain gentle-hearted mither!

[*Exeunt together into cottage.*

Enter ANGUS *with* BELVAWNEY *and* MISS TREHERNE, *over bridge. She is in travelling costume, and both are much agitated and alarmed.*

ANGUS. Step in, sir—step in, and sit ye doun for a wee. I'll just send Mistress Macfarlane to ye. She's a gude auld bodie, and will see to your comforts as if she was your ain mither.

BELVAWNEY. Thank you, my worthy lad, for your kindness at this trying moment. I assure you we shall not forget it.

ANGUS. Ah, sir, wadna any mon do as muckle? A dry shelter, a bannock and a pan o' parritch is a' we can offer ye, but sic as it is ye're hairtily welcome.

BELVAWNEY. It is well—we thank you.

ANGUS. For wha wadna help the unfortunate?

BELVAWNEY. [*Occupied with* MISS TREHERNE.] Exactly—every one would.

ANGUS. Or feed the hungry?

BELVAWNEY. No doubt.

ANGUS. It just brings the tear-drop to my ee' to think——

BELVAWNEY. [*Leading him off.*] My friend, we would be alone, this maiden and I. Farewell. [*Exit* ANGUS *into cottage.*] Belinda—my own—my life! Compose yourself. It was in truth a weird and gruesome accident. The line is blocked—your parasol is broken, and your butterscotch trampled in the dust, but no serious harm is done. Come, be cheerful. We are safe—quite safe.

MISS TREHERNE. Safe! Ah, Belvawney, my own own Belvawney—there is, I fear, no safety for us so long as we are liable to be overtaken by that fearful Major to whom I was to have been married this morning!

BELVAWNEY. Major McGillicuddy? I confess I do not feel comfortable when I think of Major McGillicuddy.

MISS TREHERNE. You know his barbaric nature, and how madly jealous he is. If he should find that I have eloped with you, he will most surely shoot us both!

BELVAWNEY. It is an uneasy prospect. [*Suddenly.*] Belinda, do you love me?

MISS TREHERNE. With an impetuous passion that I shall carry with me to the tomb!

BELVAWNEY. Then be mine to-morrow! We are not far from Gretna, and the thing can be done without delay. Once married, the arm of the law will protect us from this fearful man, and we can defy him to do his worst.

MISS TREHERNE. Belvawney, all this is quite true. I love you madly, passionately; I care to live but in your heart; I breathe but for your love; yet, before I actually consent to take the irrevocable step that will place me on the pinnacle of my fondest hopes, you must give me some definite idea of your pecuniary position. I am not mercenary, heaven knows, but business is business, and I confess I should like a little definite information about the settlements.

BELVAWNEY. I often think that it is deeply to be deplored that these grovelling questions of money should alloy the tenderest and most hallowed sentiments that inspire our imperfect natures.

MISS TREHERNE. It is unfortunate, no doubt, but at the same time it is absolutely necessary.

BELVAWNEY. Belinda, I will be frank with you. My income is £1000 a year, which I hold on certain conditions. You know my friend Cheviot Hill, who is travelling to London in the same train with us, but in the third class?

MISS TREHERNE. I believe I know the man you mean.

BELVAWNEY. Cheviot, who is a young man of large property, but extremely close-fisted, is cursed with a strangely amatory disposition, as you will admit when I tell you that he has contracted a habit of proposing marriage, as a matter of course, to every woman he meets. His haughty father (who comes of a very old family—the Cheviot Hills had settled in this part of the world centuries before the Conquest) is compelled by his health to reside in Madeira. Knowing that I exercise an all but supernatural influence over his son, and fearing that his affectionate disposition would lead him to contract an undesirable marriage, the old gentleman allows me £1000 a year so long as Cheviot shall live single; but at his death or marriage the money goes over to Cheviot's uncle Symperson, who is now travelling to town with him.

MISS TREHERNE. Then so long as your influence over him lasts, so long only will you retain your income?

BELVAWNEY. That is, I am sorry to say, the state of the case.

MISS TREHERNE. [*After a pause.*] Belvawney, I love you with an imperishable ardour which mocks the power of words. If I were to begin to tell you now of the force of my indomitable passion for you, the tomb would close over me before I could exhaust the entrancing subject. But, as I said before, business is business, and unless I can see some distinct probability that your income will be permanent, I shall have no alternative but to weep my heart out in all the anguish of maiden solitude— uncared for, unloved, and alone!

[*Exit* MISS TREHERNE *into cottage.*

BELVAWNEY. There goes a noble-hearted girl indeed! Oh for the gift of Cheviot's airy badinage—oh for his skill in weaving a net about the hearts of women! If I could but induce her to marry me at once before the dreadful Major learns our flight! Why not? We are in Scotland. Methinks I've heard two loving hearts can wed, in this strange country, by merely making declaration to that effect. I will think out some cunning scheme to lure her into marriage unawares.

Enter MAGGIE, *from cottage.*

MAGGIE. Will ye walk in and rest a wee, Maister Belvawney?

There's a room ready for ye, kind sir, and ye're heartily welcome to it.

BELVAWNEY. It is well. [MAGGIE *going*.] Stop! Come hither, maiden.

MAGGIE. Oh, sir! You do not mean any harm towards a puir, innocent, unprotected cottage lassie?

BELVAWNEY. Harm! No, of course I don't. What do you mean?

MAGGIE. I'm but a puir, humble mountain girl; but let me tell you, sir, that my character's just as dear to me as the richest and proudest lady's in the land. Before I consent to approach ye, swear to me that you mean me no harm.

BELVAWNEY. Harm? Of course, I don't. Don't be a little fool! Come here.

MAGGIE. [*Aside*.] There is something in his manner that reassures me. It is not that of the airy trifler with innocent hairts. [*Aloud*.] What wad ye wi' puir, harmless Maggie Macfarlane, gude sir?

BELVAWNEY. Can you tell me what constitutes a Scotch marriage?

MAGGIE. Oh, sir, it's nae use asking me that, for my hairt is not my ain to give. I'm betrothed to the best and noblest lad in a' the bonnie Borderland. Oh, sir, I canna be your bride!

BELVAWNEY. My girl, you mistake. I do not want you for my bride. Can't you answer a simple question? What constitutes a Scotch marriage?

MAGGIE. Ye've just to say before two witnesses, 'Maggie Macfarlane is my wife;' and I've just to say, 'Maister Belvawney is my husband,' and nae mon can set us asunder. But, sir, I canna be your bride, for I am betrothed to the best and noblest——

BELVAWNEY. I congratulate you. You can go.

MAGGIE. Yes, sir.   [*Exit* MAGGIE.

BELVAWNEY. It is a simple process; simple, but yet how beautiful! One thing is certain—Cheviot may marry any day, despite my precautions, and then I shall be penniless. He may die, and equally I shall be penniless. Belinda has £500 a year; it is not much, but it would at least save me from starvation.
                                                                [*Exit*.

Enter SYMPERSON *and* CHEVIOT HILL, *over bridge. They both show signs of damage—their hats are beaten in and their clothes disordered through the accident.*

SYMPERSON. Well, here we are at last——

CHEVIOT. Yes; here we are at last, and a pretty state I'm in, to be sure.

SYMPERSON. My dear nephew, you would travel third class, and this is the consequence. After all, there's not much harm done.

CHEVIOT. Not much harm? What d'ye call that? [*Showing his hat.*] Ten and ninepence at one operation! My gloves split— one and four! My coat ruined—eighteen and six! It's a coarse and brutal nature that recognizes no harm that don't involve loss of blood. I'm reduced by this accident from a thinking, feeling, reflecting human being, to a moral pulp—a mash— a poultice. Damme, sir, that's what I am! I'm a poultice!

SYMPERSON. Cheviot, my dear boy, at the moment of the accident you were speaking to me on a very interesting subject.

CHEVIOT. Was I? I forget what it was. The accident has knocked it clean out of my head.

SYMPERSON. You were saying that you were a man of good position and fortune, that you derived £2000 a year from your bank, that you thought it was time you settled. You then reminded me that I should come into Belvawney's £1000 a year on your marriage, and I'm not sure, but I rather think you mentioned, casually, that my daughter Minnie is an Angel of Light.

CHEVIOT. True, and just then we went off the line. To resume —Uncle Symperson, your daughter Minnie is an Angel of Light, a perfect being, as innocent as a new-laid egg.

SYMPERSON. Minnie is indeed all that you have described her.

CHEVIOT. Uncle, I'm a man of few words. I feel and I speak. I love that girl, madly, passionately, irresistibly. She is my whole life, my whole soul and body, my Past, my Present, and my To Come. I have thought for none but her; she fills my mind, sleeping and waking; she is the essence of every

hope—the tree upon which the fruit of my heart is growing—
my own To Come!

SYMPERSON. [*Who has sunk overpowered on to stool during this
speech.*] Cheviot, my dear boy, excuse a father's tears. I won't
beat about the bush. You have anticipated my devoutest wish.
Cheviot, my dear boy, take her; she is yours!

CHEVIOT. I have often heard of rapture, but I never knew what
it was till now. Uncle Symperson, bearing in mind the fact
that your income will date from the day of the wedding, when
may this be?

SYMPERSON. My boy, the sooner the better! Delicacy would
prompt me to give Belvawney a reasonable notice of the
impending loss of his income, but should I, for such a mere
selfish reason as that, rob my child of one hour of the happiness that you are about to confer upon her? No! Duty to my
child is paramount!

CHEVIOT. On one condition, however, I must insist. This must
be kept from Belvawney's knowledge. You know the strange,
mysterious influence that his dreadful eyes exercise over me.

SYMPERSON. I have remarked it with astonishment.

CHEVIOT. They are much inflamed just now, and he has to wear
green spectacles. While this lasts I am a free agent, but under
treatment they may recover. In that case, if he knew that I
contemplated matrimony, he would use them to prevent my
doing so—and I cannot resist them—I cannot resist them!
Therefore, I say, until I am safely and securely tied up,
Belvawney must know nothing about it.

SYMPERSON. Trust me, Cheviot, he shall know nothing about
it from *me*. [*Aside.*] A thousand a year! I have endeavoured,
but in vain, to woo Fortune for fifty-six years, but she smiles
upon me at last; she smiles upon me at last!   [*Exit.*

CHEVIOT. At length my hopes are to be crowned! Oh, my own
—my own—the hope of my heart—my love—my life!

Enter BELVAWNEY, *who has overheard these words.*

BELVAWNEY. Cheviot! Whom are you apostrophizing in those
terms? You've been at it again, I see.

CHEVIOT. Belvawney, that apostrophe was private; I decline to admit you to my confidence.

BELVAWNEY. Cheviot, what is the reason of this strange tone of defiance? A week ago I had but to express a wish to have it obeyed as a matter of course.

CHEVIOT. Belvawney, it may not be denied that there was a time when, owing to the remarkable influence exercised over me by your extraordinary eyes, you could do with me as you would. It would be affectation to deny it; your eyes withered my will; they paralyzed my volition. They were strange and lurid eyes, and I bowed to them. Those eyes were my Fate— my Destiny—my unerring Must—my inevitable Shall. That time has gone—for ever!

BELVAWNEY. Alas for the days that are past and the good that came and went with them!

CHEVIOT. Weep for them if you will. I cannot weep with you, for I loved them not. But, as you say, they are past. The light that lit up those eyes is extinct—their fire has died out— their soul has fled. They are no longer eyes; they are poached eggs. I have not yet sunk so low as to be the slave of two poached eggs.

BELVAWNEY. Have mercy. If any girl has succeeded in en- slaving you—and I know how easily you are enslaved— dismiss her from your thoughts; have no more to say to her, and I will—yes, I will bless you with my latest breath.

CHEVIOT. Whether a blessing conferred with one's latest breath is a superior article to one conferred in robust health we need not stop to inquire. I decline, as I said before, to admit you to my confidence on any terms whatever. Begone! [*Exit* BELVAWNEY.] Dismiss from my thoughts the only woman I ever loved! Have no more to say to the tree upon which the fruit of my heart is growing! No, Belvawney, I cannot cut off my tree as if it were gas or water. I do not treat women like that. Some men do, but I don't. I am not that sort of man. I respect women; I love women. They are good; they are pure; they are beautiful; at least many of them are.

Enter MAGGIE; *he is much fascinated.*

This one, for example, is very beautiful indeed!

PLATE 5

Engaged. Harold Kyrle as Belvawney. Act I

MAGGIE. If ye'll just walk in, sir, ye'll find a bannock and a pan o' parritch waitin' for ye on the table.

CHEVIOT. This is one of the loveliest women I ever met in the whole course of my life!

MAGGIE. [*Aside.*] What's he glowerin' at? [*Aloud.*] Oh, sir, ye mean no harm to a poor Lowland lassie?

CHEVIOT. Pardon me; it's very foolish. I can't account for it— but I am arrested, fascinated.

MAGGIE. Oh, gude sir, what's fascinated ye?

CHEVIOT. I don't know; there is something about you that exercises a most remarkable influence over me; it seems to weave a kind of enchantment around me. I can't think what it is. You are a good girl, I am sure. None but a good girl could so powerfully affect me. You *are* a good girl, are you not?

MAGGIE. I am a varra gude girl indeed, sir.

CHEVIOT. I was quite sure of it.
[*Gets his arm round her waist.*

MAGGIE. I am a much better girl than nineteen out of twenty in these pairts. And they are all gude girls too.

CHEVIOT. My darling! [*Kisses her.*

MAGGIE. Oh, kind sir, what's that for?

CHEVIOT. It is your reward for being a good girl.

MAGGIE. Oh, sir, I did na look for sic a recompense; you are varra varra kind to puir little Maggie Macfarlane.

CHEVIOT. I cannot think what it is about you that fascinates me so remarkably.

MAGGIE. Maybe it's my beauty.

CHEVIOT. Maybe it is. It is quite possible that it may be, as you say, your beauty.

MAGGIE. I am remarkably pretty, and I've a varra neat figure.

CHEVIOT. There is a natural modesty in this guileless appreciation of your own perfection that is, to me, infinitely more charming than the affected ignorance of an artificial town-bred beauty.

MAGGIE. Oh, sir, can I close my een to the picture that my

looking-glass holds up to me twenty times a day? We see the rose on the tree, and we say that it is fair; we see the silver moon sailing in the braw blue heavens, and we say that she is bright; we see the brawling stream purling over the smooth stanes i' the burn, and we say that it is beautiful; and shall we close our een to the fairest of nature's works—a pure and beautiful woman? Why, sir, it wad just be base ingratitude! No, it's best to tell the truth about a' things: I am a varra, varra, beautiful girl!

CHEVIOT. Maggie Macfarlane, I'm a plain, blunt, straightforward man, and I come quickly to the point. I see more to love in you than I ever saw in any woman in all my life before. I have a large income, which I do not spend recklessly. I love you passionately; you are the essence of every hope; you are the tree upon which the fruit of my heart is growing—my Past, my Present, my Future—you are my own To Come. Tell me, will you be mine—will you join your life with mine?

Enter ANGUS, *who listens.*

MAGGIE. Ah, kind sir, I'm sairly grieved to wound sae true and tender a love as yours, but ye're ower late. My love is nae my ain to give ye; it's given ower to the best and bravest lad in a' the bonnie Borderland!

CHEVIOT. Give me his address that I may go and curse him!

MAGGIE. Ah, ye must not curse him. Oh, spare him, spare him, for he is good and brave, and he loves me, oh, sae dearly, and I love him, oh, sae dearly too. Oh, sir, kind sir, have mercy on him, and do not—do not curse him, or I shall die!

[*Throwing herself at his feet.*

CHEVIOT. Will you, or will you not, oblige me by telling me where he is, that I may at once go and curse him?

ANGUS. [*Coming forward.*] He is here, sir, but dinna waste your curses on me. Maggie, my bairn, [*Raising her.*] I heard the answer ye gave to this man, my true and gentle lassie. Ye spake well and bravely, Meg—well and bravely! Dinna heed the water in my ee—it's a tear of joy and gratitude, Meg—a tear of joy and gratitude!

CHEVIOT. [*Touched.*] Poor fellow! I will *not* curse him! [*Aloud.*] Young man, I respect your honest emotion. I don't want to distress you, but I cannot help loving this most charming girl. Come, is it reasonable to quarrel with a man because he's of the same way of thinking as yourself?

ANGUS. Nay, sir, I'm nae fasht, but it just seems to drive a' the bluid back into my hairt when I think that my Meg is loved by anither! Oh, sir, she's a fair and winsome lassie, and I micht as justly be angry wi' ye for loving the blue heavens. She's just as far above us as they are!

[*Wiping his eyes and kissing her.*

CHEVIOT. [*With decision.*] Pardon me, I cannot allow that.

ANGUS. Eh?

CHEVIOT. I love that girl madly—passionately—and I cannot possibly allow you to do that—not before my eyes, I beg. You simply torture me.

MAGGIE. [*To* ANGUS.] Leave off, dear, till the puir gentleman's gone, and then ye can begin again.

CHEVIOT. Angus, listen to me. You love this girl?

ANGUS. I love her, sir, a'most as weel as I love mysel'.

CHEVIOT. Then reflect how you are standing in the way of her prosperity. I am a rich man. I have money, position, and education. I am a much more intellectual and generally agreeable companion for her than you can ever hope to be. I am full of anecdote, and all my anecdotes are in the best possible taste. I will tell you some of them some of these days, and you can judge for yourself. Maggie, if she married me, would live in a nice house in a good square. She would have wine—occasionally. She would be kept beautifully clean. Now, if you really love this girl almost as well as you love yourself, are you doing wisely or kindly in standing in the way of her getting all these good things? As to compensation—why, I've had heavy expenses of late—but if—yes, if thirty shillings——

ANGUS. [*Hotly.*] Sir, I'm puir in pocket, but I've a rich hairt. It is rich in a pure and overflowing love, and he that hath love hath all. You canna ken what true love is, or you wadna dare to insult a puir but honest lad by offering to buy his treasure for money.

MAGGIE. My ain true darling!   [*They embrace.*

CHEVIOT. Now, I'll not have it! Understand me, I'll not have it. It's simple agony to me. Angus, I respect your indignation, but you are too hasty. I do not offer to buy your treasure for money. You love her; it will naturally cause you pain to part with her, and I prescribe thirty shillings, not as a cure, but as a temporary solace. If thirty shillings is not enough, why, I don't mind making it two pounds.

ANGUS. Nae, sir, it's useless, and we ken it weel, do we not, my brave lassie? Our hearts are one as our bodies will be some day; and the man is na born and the gold is na coined that can set us twain asunder!

MAGGIE. Angus, dear, I'm varra proud o' sae staunch and true a love; it's like your ain true self, an' I can say nae more for it than that. But dinna act wi'out prudence and forethought, dear. In these hard times twa pound is twa pound, and I'm nae sure that ye're acting richtly in refusing sae large a sum. I love you varra dearly—ye ken that right weel—an' if ye'll be troubled wi' sic a poor little mousie I'll mak' ye a true an' loving wife, but I doubt whether, wi' a' my love, I'll ever be worth as much to ye as twa pound. Dinna act in haste, dear; tak' time to think before ye refuse this kind gentleman's offer.

ANGUS. Oh, sir, is not this rare modesty? Could ye match it amang your toun-bred fine ladies? I think not! Meg, it shall be as you say. I'll tak' the siller, but it'll be wi' a sair and broken hairt! [CHEVIOT *gives* ANGUS *money*.] Fare thee weel, my love—my childhood's—boyhood's—manhood's love! Ye're ganging fra my hairt to anither, who'll gie thee mair o' the gude things o' this world than I could ever gie 'ee, except love, an' o' that my hairt is full indeed! But it's a' for the best; ye'll be happier wi' him—and twa pound is twa pound. Meg, mak' him a gude wife, be true to him, and love him as ye loved me. Oh, Meg, my poor bruised hairt is well nigh like to break! [*Rushes out in great agony.*

MAGGIE. [*Looking wistfully after him.*] Puir laddie, puir laddie! Oh, I did na ken till noo how weel he loved me!

CHEVIOT. Maggie, I'm almost sorry I—poor lad, poor fellow! He has a generous heart. I am glad I did not curse him. [*Aside.*] This is weakness! [*Aloud.*] Maggie my own—ever and for always my own, we will be very happy, will we not?

MAGGIE. Oh, sir, I dinna ken, but in truth I hope so. Oh, sir, my happiness is in your hands noo; be kind to the puir cottage lassie who loves ye sae weel. My hairt is a' your ain, and if ye forsake me my lot will be a sair one indeed! [*Exit, weeping.*

CHEVIOT. Poor little Lowland lassie! That's my idea of a wife. No ridiculous extravagance; no expensive tastes. Knows how to dress like a lady on £5 a year; ah, and does it too! No pretence there of being blind to her own beauties; she knows that she is beautiful, and scorns to lie about it. In that respect she resembles Symperson's dear daughter, Minnie. My darling Minnie. [*Looks at miniature.*] My own darling Minnie. Minnie is fair, Maggie is dark. Maggie loves me! That excellent and perfect country creature loves me! She is to be the light of my life, my own To Come! In some respects she is even prettier than Minnie—my darling Minnie, Symperson's dear daughter, the tree upon which the fruit of my heart is growing; my Past, my Present, and my Future, my own To Come! But this tendency to reverie is growing on me; I must shake it off.

Enter MISS TREHERNE.

Heaven and earth, what a singularly lovely girl!

MISS TREHERNE. A stranger! Pardon me, I will withdraw.
[*Going.*

CHEVIOT. A stranger indeed, in one sense, inasmuch as he never had the happiness of meeting you before—but, in that he has a heart that can sympathize with another's misfortune, he trusts he may claim to be regarded almost as a friend.

MISS TREHERNE. May I ask, sir, to what misfortunes you allude?

CHEVIOT. I—a—do not know their precise nature, but that perception would indeed be dull, and that heart would be indeed flinty, that did not at once perceive that you are very very unhappy. Accept, madam, my deepest and most respectful sympathy.

MISS TREHERNE. You have guessed rightly, sir! I am indeed a most unhappy woman.

CHEVIOT. I am delighted to hear it—a—I mean I feel a pleasure, a melancholy and chastened pleasure, in reflecting that, if your distress is not of a pecuniary nature, it may perchance lie in my power to alleviate your sorrow.

MISS TREHERNE. Impossible, sir, though I thank you for your respectful sympathy.

CHEVIOT. How many women would forego twenty years of their lives to be as beautiful as yourself, little dreaming that extraordinary loveliness can co-exist with the most poignant anguish of mind! But so too often we find it, do we not, dear lady?

MISS TREHERNE. Sir! This tone of address, from a complete stranger!

CHEVIOT. Nay, be not unreasonably severe upon an impassionable and impulsive man, whose tongue is but the too faithful herald of his heart. We see the rose on the tree, and we say that it is fair; we see the bonnie brooks purling over the smooth stanes—I should say stones—in the burn, and we say that it is beautiful, and shall we close our eyes to the fairest of nature's works, a pure and beautiful woman? Why, it would be base ingratitude, indeed!

MISS TREHERNE. I cannot deny that there is much truth in the sentiments you so beautifully express, but I am, unhappily, too well aware that whatever advantages I may possess personal beauty is not among their number.

CHEVIOT. How exquisitely modest is this chaste insensibility to your own singular loveliness! How infinitely more winning than the bold-faced self-appreciation of under-bred country girls!

MISS TREHERNE. I am glad, sir, that you are pleased with my modesty. It has often been admired.

CHEVIOT. Pleased! I am more than pleased—that's a very weak word. I am enchanted. Madam, I am a man of quick impulse and energetic action. I feel and I speak—I cannot help it. Madam, be not surprised when I tell you that I cannot resist the conviction that you are the light of my future life, the essence of every hope, the tree upon which the fruit of my heart is growing—my Past, my Present, my Future, my own

To Come! Do not extinguish that light, do not disperse that essence, do not blight that tree! I am well off; I'm a bachelor; I'm thirty-two; and I love you, madam, humbly, truly, trustfully, patiently. Paralyzed with admiration, I wait anxiously and yet hopefully for your reply.

MISS TREHERNE. Sir, that heart would indeed be cold that did not feel grateful for so much earnest, single-hearted devotion. I am deeply grieved to have to say one word to cause pain to one who expresses himself in such well-chosen terms of respectful esteem; but, alas, I have already yielded up my heart to one who, if I mistake not, is a dear personal friend of your own.

CHEVIOT. Am I to understand that you are the young lady of property whom Belvawney hopes to marry?

MISS TREHERNE. I am, indeed, that unhappy woman!

CHEVIOT. And is it possible that you love him?

MISS TREHERNE. With a rapture that thrills every fibre of my heart—with a devotion that enthralls my very soul! But there's some difficulty about his settlements.

CHEVIOT. A difficulty! I should think there was. Why, on my marrying, his entire income goes over to Symperson! I could reduce him to penury to-morrow. As it happens, I *am* engaged, I recollect, to Symperson's daughter; and if Belvawney dares to interpose between you and me, by George, I'll do it!

MISS TREHERNE. Oh, spare him, sir! [*Falls on her knees.*] You say that you love me? Then, for my sake, remain single for ever—it is all I ask; it is not much. Promise me that you will never, never marry, and we will both bless you with our latest breath!   [*Rises.*

CHEVIOT. There seems to be a special importance attached to a blessing conferred with one's latest breath that I entirely fail to grasp. It seems to me to convey no definite advantage of any kind whatever.

MISS TREHERNE. Cruel, cruel man!   [*Weeps.*

Enter BELVAWNEY, *in great alarm, over bridge.*

BELVAWNEY. We are lost! We are lost!

MISS TREHERNE. What do you mean?

CHEVIOT. Who has lost you?

BELVAWNEY. Major McGillicuddy discovered your flight, and followed in the next train. The line is blocked through our accident, and his train has pulled up within a few yards of our own. He is now making his way to this very cottage! What do you say to that?

MISS TREHERNE. I agree with you; we are lost!

CHEVIOT. I disagree with you; I should say you are found.

BELVAWNEY. This man is a reckless fire-eater; he is jealous of me. He will assuredly shoot us both if he sees us here together. I am no coward—but—I confess I am uneasy.

MISS TREHERNE. [*To* CHEVIOT.] Oh, sir, you have a ready wit; help us out of this difficulty, and we will both bless you——

BELVAWNEY. With our latest breath!

CHEVIOT. That decides me. Madam, remain here with me. Belvawney, withdraw. [BELVAWNEY *retires.*] I will deal with this maniac alone. All I ask is, that if I find it necessary to make a statement that is not consistent with strict truth, you, madam, will unhesitatingly endorse it?

MISS TREHERNE. I will stake my very existence on its veracity, whatever it may be.

CHEVIOT. Good. He is at hand. Belvawney, go.

[*Exit* BELVAWNEY.

Now, madam, repose upon my shoulders, place your arms around me so—is that comfortable?

MISS TREHERNE. It is luxurious.

CHEVIOT. Good.

MISS TREHERNE. You are sure it does not inconvenience you?

CHEVIOT. Not at all. Now we are ready for him.

Enter, over bridge, MCGILLICUDDY, *with two* FRIENDS *dressed as for a wedding, with white favours, and carrying a large wedding cake.* MCGILLICUDDY *has pistols. All greatly excited.*

MCGILLICUDDY. Where is the villain? I'll swear he is concealed somewhere. Search every tree, every bush, every

PLATE 6

Engaged. The end of Act I, and other scenes

geranium. [*Sees* CHEVIOT *and* MISS TREHERNE.] Ha! they are here. Perjured woman! I've found you at last.

MISS TREHERNE. [*To* CHEVIOT.] Save me!

Enter BELVAWNEY, *listening.*

MCGILLICUDDY. Who is the unsightly scoundrel with whom you have flown—the unpleasant-looking scamp whom you have dared to prefer to me? Uncurl yourself from around the plain villain at once, unless you would share his fate.

Enter MAGGIE *and* ANGUS.

MISS TREHERNE. Major, spare him!

CHEVIOT. Now, sir, perhaps you will be so good as to explain who the deuce you are, and what you want with this lady?

MCGILLICUDDY. I don't know who you may be, but I'm McGillicuddy. I am betrothed to this lady; we were to have been married this morning. I waited for her at the church from ten till four; then I began to get impatient.

CHEVIOT. I really think you must be labouring under some delusion.

MCGILLICUDDY. Delusion! Ha, ha! Here's the cake!

CHEVIOT. Still, I think there's a mistake somewhere. This lady is my wife.

MCGILLICUDDY. What! Belinda, oh, Belinda! Tell me that this unattractive man lies; tell me that you are mine and only mine, now and for ever!

MISS TREHERNE. I cannot say that. This gentleman is my husband!

[MCGILLICUDDY *falls sobbing on seat*; BELVAWNEY *tears his hair in despair*; MAGGIE *sobs on* ANGUS's *shoulder.*

ACT II

SCENE. *Double Drawing-room in* SYMPERSON's *House in London. Door,* R.C., *open at back. Another door,* L. *Chair and stool,* R.C. *Piano,* R. *Sofa,* L.C. *Indications that a wedding is about to take place. A plate of tarts and a bottle of wine on table,* R., *against flat.*

Enter MINNIE SYMPERSON, *in wedding dress, followed by* PARKER, *her maid, holding her train.*

MINNIE. Take care, Parker—that's right. There! How do I look?

PARKER. Beautiful, miss; quite beautiful.

MINNIE. [*Earnestly.*] Oh, Parker, am I really beautiful? Really, *really* beautiful, you know?

PARKER. Oh, miss, there's no question about it. Oh, I do so hope you and Mr. Cheviot Hill will be happy.

MINNIE. Oh, I'm sure we shall, Parker. He has often told me that I am the tree upon which the fruit of his heart is growing; and one couldn't wish to be more than *that*. And he tells me that his greatest happiness is to see me happy. So it will be my duty—my *duty*, Parker—to devote my life, my whole life, to making myself as happy as I possibly can.

Enter SYMPERSON, *dressed for wedding.*

SYMPERSON. So, my little lamb is ready for the sacrifice. You can go, Parker. [*Exit* PARKER.] And I am to lose my pet at last; my little dickey-bird is to be married to-day! Well, well, it's for her good. I must try and bear it—I must try and bear it.

MINNIE. And as my dear old papa comes into £1000 a year by it, I hope he won't allow it to distress him too much. He must try and bear up. He mustn't fret.

SYMPERSON. My child, I will not deny that £1000 a year is a consolation. It's quite a fortune. I hardly know what I shall do with it.

MINNIE. I think, dear papa, you will spend a good deal of it on brandy, and a good deal more on billiards, and a good deal more on betting.

SYMPERSON. It may be so; I don't say it won't. We shall see, Minnie; we shall see. These simple pleasures would certainly tend to soothe your poor old father's declining years. And my darling has not done badly either, has she?

MINNIE. No, dear papa; only fancy! Cheviot has £2000 a year from shares in the Royal Indestructible Bank.

SYMPERSON. And don't spend £200. By-the-bye, I'm sorry that my little bird has not contrived to induce him to settle anything on her; that, I think, was remiss in my tom-tit.

MINNIE. Dear papa, Cheviot is the very soul of honour; he's a fine, noble, manly, spirited fellow, but if he *has* a fault, it is that he is very, oh very, *very* stingy. He would rather lose his heart's blood than part with a shilling unnecessarily. He's a noble fellow, but he's like that.

SYMPERSON. Still I can't help feeling that if my robin had worked him judiciously——

MINNIE. Papa, dear, Cheviot is an all but perfect character, the very type of knightly chivalry; but he *has* faults and among other things he's one of the worst tempered men I ever met in all my little life. Poor simple little Minnie thought the matter over very carefully in her silly childish way, and she came to the conclusion, in her foolish little noddle, that, on the whole, perhaps she could work it better after marriage, than before.

SYMPERSON. Well, well, perhaps my wren is right.

MINNIE. Don't laugh at my silly little thoughts, dear papa, when I say I'm sure she is.

SYMPERSON. Minnie, my dear daughter, take a father's advice, the last he will ever be entitled to give you. If you would be truly happy in the married state, be sure you have your own way in everything. Brook no contradictions. Never yield to outside pressure. Give in to no argument. Admit no appeal. However wrong you may be, maintain a firm, resolute, and determined front. These were your angel mother's principles through life, and she was a happy woman indeed. I neglected those principles, and while she lived I was a miserable wretch.

MINNIE. Papa, dear, I have thought over the matter very carefully in my little baby-noddle, and I have come to the conclusion—don't laugh at me, dear papa—that it is my duty—my *duty*—to fall in with Cheviot's views in everything *before* marriage, and Cheviot's duty to fall into my views in everything *after* marriage. I think that is only fair, don't you?

SYMPERSON. Yes, I dare say it will come to that.

MINNIE. Don't think me a very silly little goose when I say I'm sure it will. Quite, quite sure, dear papa. Quite.   [*Exit.*

SYMPERSON. Dear child—dear child! I sometimes fancy I can see traces of her angel mother's disposition in her. Yes, I think—I *think* she will be happy. But poor Cheviot! Oh lor, poor Cheviot! Dear me, it won't bear thinking of!

Enter MISS TREHERNE, *unobserved. She is dressed in stately and funereal black.*

MISS TREHERNE. Come here, manservant. Approach. I'm not going to bite you. Can I see the fair young thing they call Minnie Symperson?

SYMPERSON. Well really, I can hardly say. There's nothing wrong, I hope?

MISS TREHERNE. Nothing wrong? Oh, thoughtless, frivolous, light-hearted creature! Oh, reckless old butterfly! Nothing wrong! You've eyes in your head, a nose on your face, ears on each side of it, a brain of some sort in your skull, haven't you, butler?

SYMPERSON. Undoubtedly, but I beg to observe I'm not the——

MISS TREHERNE. Have you or have you not the gift of simple apprehension? Can you or can you not draw conclusions? Go to, go to, you offend me.

SYMPERSON. [*Aside.*] There *is* something wrong, and it's *here*. [*Touching his forehead.*] I'll tell her you're here. Whom shall I say?

MISS TREHERNE. Say that one on whose devoted head the black sorrows of a long lifetime have fallen, even as a funeral pall, craves a minute's interview with a dear old friend. Do you think you can recollect that message, butler?

SYMPERSON. I'll try, but I beg, I *beg* to observe, I'm not the butler. [*Aside.*] This is a most surprising young person!

[*Exit.*

MISS TREHERNE. At last I'm in my darling's home, the home of the bright blythe carolling thing that lit, as with a ray of heaven's sunlight, the murky gloom of my miserable school-days. But what do I see? Tarts? Ginger wine? There are rejoicings of some kind afoot. Alas, I am out of place here. What have I in common with tarts? Oh, I am ill-attuned to scenes of revelry! [*Takes a tart and eats it.*

Enter MINNIE.

MINNIE. Belinda! [*They rush to each other's arms.*

MISS TREHERNE. Minnie! My own long-lost lamb! This is the first gleam of joy that has lighted my darksome course this many and many a day! And in spite of the change that time and misery have brought upon me, you knew me at once!

[*Eating the tart all this time.*

MINNIE. Oh, I felt sure it was you, from the message.

MISS TREHERNE. How wondrously fair you have grown! And this dress! Why, it is surely a bridal dress! Those tarts—that wine! Surely this is not your wedding-day?

MINNIE. Yes, dear, I shall be married in half an hour.

MISS TREHERNE. Oh, strange chance! Oh, unheard-of coincidence! Married! And to whom?

MINNIE. Oh, to the dearest love—my cousin, Mr. Cheviot Hill. Perhaps you know the name?

MISS TREHERNE. I have heard of the Cheviot Hills somewhere. Happy—strangely happy girl! You, at least, know your husband's name.

MINNIE. Oh yes, it's on all his pocket-handkerchiefs.

MISS TREHERNE. It is much to know. I do not know mine.

MINNIE. Have you forgotten it?

MISS TREHERNE. No; I never knew it. It is a dark mystery. It may not be fathomed. It is buried in the fathomless gulf of the Eternal Past. There let it lie.

MINNIE. Oh, tell me all about it, dear.

MISS TREHERNE. It is a lurid tale. Three months since I fled from a hated one who was to have married me. He pursued me. I confided my distress to a young and wealthy stranger. Acting on his advice, I declared myself to be his wife; he declared himself to be my husband. We were parted immediately afterwards, and we have never met since. But this took place in Scotland, and by the law of that remarkable country we are man and wife, though I didn't know it at the time.

MINNIE. What fun!

MISS TREHERNE. Fun! Say, rather, horror—distraction—chaos! I am rent with conflicting doubts! Perhaps he was already married; in that case I am a bigamist. Maybe he is dead; in that case I am a widow. Maybe he is alive; in that case I am a wife. What am I? Am I single? Am I married? Am I a widow? Can I marry? Have I married? May I marry? Who am I? Where am I? What am I? What is my name? What is my condition in life? If I am married, to whom am I married? If I am a widow, how came I to be a widow, and whose widow came I to be? Why am I his widow? What did he die of? Did he leave me anything? If anything, how much, and is it saddled with conditions? Can I marry again without forfeiting it? Have I a mother-in-law? Have I a family of step-children, and if so, how many, and what are their ages, sexes, sizes, names and dispositions? These are questions that rack me night and day, and until they are settled, peace and I are not on terms!

MINNIE. Poor dear thing!

MISS TREHERNE. But enough of my selfish sorrows. [*Goes up to table and takes a tart.* MINNIE *is annoyed at this.*] Tell me about the noble boy who is about to make you his. Has he any dross?

MINNIE. I don't know. [*Secretly removes tarts to another table.*] I never thought of asking—I'm such a goose. But papa knows.

MISS TREHERNE. Have those base and servile things called settlements been satisfactorily adjusted? [*Eating.*

MINNIE. I don't know. It never occurred to me to inquire. But papa can tell you.

MISS TREHERNE. The same artless little soul!

MINNIE. [*Standing so as to conceal tarts from* BELINDA.] Yes, I am quite artless—quite, quite artless. But now that you *are* here you will stay and see me married.

MISS TREHERNE. I would willingly be a witness to my darling's joy, but this attire is, perhaps, scarcely in harmony with a scene of revelry.

MINNIE. Well, dear, you're not a cheerful object, and that's the truth.

MISS TREHERNE. And yet these charnel-house rags may serve to remind the thoughtless banqueters that they are but mortal.

MINNIE. I don't think it will be necessary to do that, dear. Papa's sherry will make *that* quite clear to them.

MISS TREHERNE. Then I will hie me home, and array me in garments of less sombre hue.

MINNIE. I think it would be better, dear. Those are the very things for a funeral, but this is a wedding.

MISS TREHERNE. I see very little difference between them. But it shall be as you wish, though I have worn nothing but black since my miserable marriage. There is breakfast, I suppose?

MINNIE. Yes, at dear Cheviot's house.

MISS TREHERNE. That is well. I shall return in time for it. Thank heaven I can still eat!
      [*Takes a tart from table and exit, followed by* MINNIE.

Enter CHEVIOT HILL. *He is dressed as for a wedding.*

CHEVIOT. Here I am at last—quite flurried and hot after the usual row with the cabman, just when I wanted to be particularly calm and self-contained. I got the best of it though. Dear me, this is a great day for me—a great day. Where's Minnie, I wonder? Arraying herself for the sacrifice, no doubt. Pouf! This is a very nervous occasion. I wonder if I'm taking a prudent step. Marriage is a very risky thing; it's like Chancery: once in it you can't get out of it, and the costs are enormous. There you are—fixed. Fifty years hence, if we're both alive, there we shall both be—fixed. That's the devil of it. It's an unreasonably long time to be responsible for another person's expenses. I don't see the use of making it for as long as that. It seems greedy to take up half a century of another person's attention. Besides—one never knows—one might come across somebody else one liked better—that uncommonly nice girl I met in Scotland, for instance. No, no, I shall be true to my Minnie—quite true. I am quite determined that nothing shall shake my constancy to Minnie.

Enter PARKER.

What a devilish pretty girl!

PARKER. [*Aside.*] He's a mean young man, but he ought to be good for half-a-crown to-day.

CHEVIOT. Come here, my dear; a—how do I look?

PARKER. Very nice indeed, sir.

CHEVIOT. What, really?

PARKER. Really.

CHEVIOT. What, tempting, eh?

PARKER. Very tempting indeed.

CHEVIOT. Hah! The married state is an enviable state, Parker.

PARKER. *Is* it, sir? I hope it may be. It depends.

CHEVIOT. What do you mean by 'it depends?' You're a member of the Church of England, I trust? Then don't you know that in saying 'it depends' you are flying in the face of the marriage service? Don't go and throw cold water on the married state, Parker. I know what you're going to say—it's expensive. So it is, at first, very expensive, but with economy you soon retrench that. By a beautiful provision of Nature, what's enough for one is enough for two. This phenomenon points directly to the married state as our natural state.

PARKER. Oh, for that matter, sir, a tigress would get on with you. You're so liberal, so gentle, so—there's only one word for it—dove-like.

CHEVIOT. What, you've remarked that, eh? Ha, ha! But dove-like as I am, Parker, in some respects, yet [*Getting his arm round her.*] in other respects—[*Aside.*] deuced pretty girl!—in other respects I am a man, Parker, of a strangely impetuous and headstrong nature. I don't beat about the bush; I come

quickly to the point. Shall I tell you a secret? There's something about you, I don't know what it is, that—in other
words, you are the tree upon which—no, no, damn it, Cheviot
—not to-day, not to-day.

PARKER. What a way you have with you, sir!

CHEVIOT. What, you've noticed that, have you? Ha, ha! Yes, I
have a way, no doubt; it's been remarked before. Whenever I
see a pretty girl—and you are a very pretty girl—I can't help
putting my arm like that. [*Putting it round her waist.*] Now,
pleasant as this sort of thing is—and you find it pleasant,
don't you? [PARKER *nods.*] Yes, you find it pleasant—pleasant
as it is, it is decidedly wrong.

PARKER. It is decidedly wrong in a married man.

CHEVIOT. It is decidedly wrong in a married man. In a married
man it's abominable, and I shall be a married man in half an
hour. So, Parker, it will become necessary to conquer this
tendency, to struggle with it, and subdue it—in half an hour.
[*Getting more affectionate.*] Not that there's any real harm in
putting your arm round a girl's waist. Highly respectable
people do it, when they waltz.

PARKER. Yes, sir, but then a band's playing.

CHEVIOT. True, and when a band's playing it don't matter, but
when a band is *not* playing, why it's dangerous, you see. You
begin with this, and you go on from one thing to another,
getting more and more affectionate, until you reach *this* stage.
[*Kissing her.*] Not that there's any real harm in kissing, either;
for you see fathers and mothers, who ought to set a good
example, kissing their children every day.

PARKER. Lor, sir, kissing's nothing; everybody does that.

CHEVIOT. That is your experience, is it? It tallies with my own.
Take it that I am your father, you are my daughter—or take
it even that I am merely your husband, and you my wife, and
it would be expected of me.   [*Kissing her.*

PARKER. But I'm not your wife, sir.

CHEVIOT. No, not yet, that's very true, and of course makes a
difference. That's why I say I must subdue this tendency;
I must struggle with it; I must conquer it—in half an hour.

MINNIE. [*Without.*] Parker, where's Mr. Cheviot?

CHEVIOT. There is your mistress, my dear—she's coming. Will you excuse me? [*Releasing her.*] Thank you. Good day, Parker.

PARKER. [*Disgusted.*] Not so much as a shilling, and that man's worth thousands! [*Exit.*

Enter MINNIE.

CHEVIOT. My darling Minnie—my own, own To Come!

[*Kissing her.*

MINNIE. Oh, you mustn't crush me, Cheviot; you'll spoil my dress. How do you like it?

CHEVIOT. It's lovely. It's a beautiful material.

MINNIE. Yes; dear papa's been going it.

CHEVIOT. Oh, but you're indebted to me for that beautiful dress.

MINNIE. To you! Oh, thank you—thank you!

CHEVIOT. Yes. I said to your papa, 'Now do for once let the girl have a nice dress; be liberal; buy the very best that money will procure; you'll never miss it. So, thanks to me, he bought you a beauty. Seventeen and six a yard if it's a penny. Dear me! To think that in half an hour this magnificent dress will be *my* property!

MINNIE. Yes. Dear papa said that as you had offered to give the breakfast at your house, he would give me the best dress that money could procure.

CHEVIOT. Yes, I *did* offer to provide the breakfast in a reckless moment; that's so like me. It was a rash offer, but I've made it, and I've stuck to it. Oh, then there's the cake.

MINNIE. Oh, tell me all about the cake.

CHEVIOT. It's a very pretty cake. Very little cake is eaten at a wedding breakfast, so I've ordered what's known in the trade as the three-quarter article.

MINNIE. I see; three-quarters cake, and the rest wood.

CHEVIOT. No; three-quarters wood, the rest cake. Be sure, my dear, you don't cut into the wood, for it has to be returned to the pastrycook to be filled up with cake for another occasion. I thought at first of ordering a seven-eighths article; but one isn't married every day—it's only once a year—I mean it's only now and then. So I said, 'Hang the expense; let's do the thing well.' And so it's a three-quarters.

MINNIE. How good you are to me! We shall be very happy, shall we not?

CHEVIOT. I—I hope so—yes. I *hope* so. Playfully happy, like two little kittens.

MINNIE. That will be delightful.

CHEVIOT. Economically happy, like two sensible people.

MINNIE. Oh, we must be very economical.

CHEVIOT. No vulgar display; no pandering to a jaded appetite. A refined and economical elegance; that is what we must aim at. A simple mutton chop, nicely broiled, for you; and *two* simple mutton chops, *very* nicely broiled, for me—

MINNIE. And some flowery potatoes—

CHEVIOT. A loaf of nice household bread—

MINNIE. A stick of celery—

CHEVIOT. And a bit of cheese, and you've a dinner fit for a monarch.

MINNIE. Then how shall we spend our evenings?

CHEVIOT. We'll have pleasant little fireside games. Are you fond of fireside games?

MINNIE. Oh, they're great fun.

CHEVIOT. Then we'll play at tailoring.

MINNIE. Tailoring? I don't think I know that game.

CHEVIOT. It's a very good game. You shall be the clever little jobbing tailor, and I'll be the particular customer who brings his own materials to be made up. You shall take my measure, cut out the cloth (real cloth, you know), stitch it together, and try it on; and then I'll find fault like a real customer, and you shall alter it until it fits, and when it fits beautifully that counts one to you.

MINNIE. Delightful!

CHEVIOT. Then there's another little fireside game which is great fun. We each take a bit of paper and a pencil and try who can jot down the nicest dinner for ninepence, and the next day we have it.

MINNIE. Oh, Cheviot, what a paradise you hold open to me!

CHEVIOT. Yes. How's papa?

MINNIE. He's very well and very happy. He's going to increase his establishment on the strength of the £1000 a year, and keep a manservant.

CHEVIOT. I know. I've been looking after some servants for him; they'll be here in the course of the morning. A cook, a housemaid, and a footman. I found them through an advertisement. They're country people, and will come very cheap.

MINNIE. How kind and thoughtful you are! Oh, Cheviot, I'm a very lucky girl!   [*Exit.*

CHEVIOT. Yes, I think so too, if I can only repress my tendency to think of that tall girl I met in Scotland. Cheviot, my boy, you must make an effort; you are going to be married, and the tall girl is nothing to you.

Enter PARKER.

PARKER. Please, sir, here's a gentleman to see you.

CHEVIOT. Oh, my solicitor, no doubt. Show him up.

PARKER. And please, some persons have called to see you about an advertisement.

CHEVIOT. Oh, Symperson's servants. To be sure. Show up the gentleman, and tell the others to wait.   [*Exit* PARKER.

Enter BELVAWNEY. *He looks very miserable.*

CHEVIOT. [*Much confused.*] Belvawney! This is unexpected.

BELVAWNEY. Yes, Cheviot. At last we meet. Don't, oh don't frown upon a heartbroken wretch.

CHEVIOT. Belvawney; I don't want to hurt your feelings, but I will not disguise from you that, not having seen you for three months, I was in hopes that I had got rid of you for ever.

BELVAWNEY. Oh, Cheviot, don't say that; I am so unhappy. And you have it in your power to make me comfortable. Do this, and I will bless you with my latest breath.

CHEVIOT. It is a tempting offer; I am not proof against it. We all have our price, and that is mine. Proceed.

BELVAWNEY. Miss Treherne—Belinda, whom I love so dearly, won't have anything to say to me.

CHEVIOT. It does her credit. She's a very superior girl.

BELVAWNEY. It's all through you, Cheviot. She declares that the mutual declaration you made to protect her from Mc-Gillicuddy amounts to a Scotch marriage.

CHEVIOT. What!

BELVAWNEY. She declares she is your wife. She professes to love me as fondly as ever, but a stern sense of duty to you forbids her to hold any communication with me.

CHEVIOT. Oh, but this is absurd, you know!

BELVAWNEY. Of course it is, but what's to be done? You left with Symperson immediately after making the declaration. As soon as she found you were gone she implored me to tell her your name and address. Of course I refused, and she quitted me, telling me that she would devote her life to finding you out.

CHEVIOT. But this is simple madness. I can't have it! This day, too, of all others! [*Aside.*] If she'd claimed me last week, or even yesterday, I wouldn't have minded, for she's a devilish fine woman; but if she were to turn up now—! [*Aloud.*] Belvawney, my dear friend, tell me what to do—I'll do anything.

BELVAWNEY. It seems that there's some doubt whether this cottage, which is just on the border, is in England or Scotland. If it is in England, she has no case; if it is in Scotland, I'm afraid she has. I've written to the owner of the property to ascertain, and if, in the meantime, she claims you, you must absolutely decline to recognize this marriage for a moment.

CHEVIOT. Not for one moment!

BELVAWNEY. It was a mere artifice to enable her to escape from McGillicuddy.

CHEVIOT. Nothing more!

BELVAWNEY. It's monstrous—perfectly monstrous—that that should constitute a marriage. It's disgraceful—it's abominable. Damme, Cheviot, it's immoral.

CHEVIOT. So it is—it's immoral. That settles it in *my* mind. It's immoral.

BELVAWNEY. You're quite sure you'll be resolute, Cheviot?

CHEVIOT. Resolute? I should think so! Why, hang it all, man, I'm going to be married in twenty minutes to Minnie Symperson!

BELVAWNEY. What!

CHEVIOT. [*Confused at having let this out.*] Didn't I tell you? I believe you're right; I did *not* tell you. It escaped me. Oh, yes, this is my wedding-day.

BELVAWNEY. Cheviot, you're joking—you don't mean this! Why, I shall lose £1000 a year by it, every penny I have in the world! Oh, it can't be—it's nonsense!

CHEVIOT. What do you mean by nonsense? The married state is an honourable estate, I believe? A man is not looked upon as utterly lost to all sense of decency because he's got married, I'm given to understand. People have been married before this, and have not been irretrievably tabooed in consequence, unless I'm grossly misinformed? Then what the dickens do you mean by saying 'nonsense' when I tell you that I'm going to be married?

BELVAWNEY. Cheviot, be careful how you take this step. Beware how you involve an innocent and helpless girl in social destruction.

CHEVIOT. What do you mean, sir?

BELVAWNEY. You cannot marry; you are a married man.

CHEVIOT. Come, come, Belvawney, this is trifling.

BELVAWNEY. You are married to Miss Treherne. I was present, and can depose to the fact.

CHEVIOT. Oh, you're not serious.

BELVAWNEY. Never more serious in my life.

CHEVIOT. But as you very properly said just now, it was a mere artifice—we didn't mean anything. It would be monstrous to regard that as a marriage. Damme, Belvawney, it would be immoral!

BELVAWNEY. I may deplore the state of the law, but I cannot stand tamely by and see it deliberately violated before my eyes.

CHEVIOT. [*Wildly.*] But Belvawney, my dear friend, reflect; everything is prepared for my marriage, at a great expense. I love Minnie deeply, devotedly. She is the actual tree upon which the fruit of my heart is growing. There's no mistake about it. She is my own To Come. I love her madly— rapturously. [*Going on his knees to* BELVAWNEY.] I have prepared a wedding breakfast at a great expense to do her honour. I have ordered four flys for the wedding party. I have taken two second-class Cook's tourists' tickets for Ilfracombe, Devon, Exeter, Cornwall, Westward Ho! and Bideford Bay. The whole thing has cost me some twenty or twenty-five pounds, and all this will be wasted—utterly wasted—if you interfere. Oh, Belvawney, dear Belvawney, let the recollection of our long and dear friendship operate to prevent your shipwrecking my future life.   [*Sobbing hysterically.*

BELVAWNEY. I have a duty to do. I must do it.   [*Going.*

CHEVIOT. But reflect, dear Belvawney; if I am married to Miss Treherne, you lose your income as much as if I married Minnie Symperson.

BELVAWNEY. No doubt, if you could prove your marriage to Miss Treherne. But you can't——
         [*With melodramatic intensity.*
CHEVIOT. Those eyes!

BELVAWNEY. You don't know where she is——
         [*With fiendish exultation.*
CHEVIOT. Oh, those eyes!

BELVAWNEY. The cottage has been pulled down, and the cottagers have emigrated to Patagonia——

CHEVIOT. Oh, those eyes!

BELVAWNEY. I'm the only witness left. *I* can prove your marriage, if I like; but you can't. [CHEVIOT *falls sobbing into a chair.*] Ha, ha, ha, ha! [*With Satanic laugh.*] It's a most painful and unfortunate situation for you; and, believe me, dear Cheviot, you have my deepest and most respectful sympathy.   [*Exit.*

CHEVIOT. This is appalling, simply appalling! The cup of happiness dashed from my lips just as I was about to drink a life-long draught. The ladder kicked from under my feet just as I was about to pick the fruit of my heart from the tree upon which it has been growing so long. I'm a married man! More than that, my honeymoon's past, and I never knew it! Stop a moment, though. The bride can't be found; the cottage is pulled down, and the cottagers have emigrated. What proof is there that such a marriage ever took place? There's only Belvawney, and Belvawney isn't a proof. Corroborated by the three cottagers, his word might be worth something; uncorroborated, it is worthless. I'll risk it. He can do nothing; the bride is nowhere; the cottagers are in Patagonia, and——

> *At this moment enter* MRS. MACFARLANE, MAGGIE, *and* ANGUS. *They stand bobbing and curtseying in rustic fashion to* CHEVIOT, *whom they do not recognize. He stares aghast at them for a moment, then staggers back to sofa.*

CHEVIOT. The man, the woman, and the girl, by all that's infernal!

MRS. MACFARLANE. Gude day, sir. We've just ca'd to see ye about the advertisement.   [*Producing paper.*

CHEVIOT. I don't know you—I don't know you. Go away.
> [CHEVIOT *buries his head in a newspaper, and pretends to read.*

MAGGIE. Ah, sir, ye said that we were to ca' on ye this day at eleven o'clock, and sae we've coom a' the way fra Dumfries to see ye.

CHEVIOT. I tell you I don't know you. Go away. I'm not at all well. I'm very ill, and it's infectious.

ANGUS. We fear no illness, sir. This is Mistress Macfarlane, the gude auld mither, who'll cook the brose and boil the parritch, and sit wi' ye, and nurse ye through your illness till the sad day ye dee!   [*Wiping his eye.*
> [CHEVIOT *pokes a hole with his finger through newspaper, and reconnoitres unobserved.*

MRS. MACFARLANE. And this is Meg, my ain lass Meg!

CHEVIOT. [*Aside.*] Attractive girl, very. I remember her perfectly.

MRS. MACFARLANE. And this is Angus Macalister, who's going to marry her, and who'll be mair than a son to me!

ANGUS. Oh, mither, mither, dinna say it, for ye bring the teardrop to my ee, and it's no canny for a strong man to be blithering and soughing like a poor weak lassie!

> [*Wiping his eye.*
> [MAGGIE *advances to hole in newspaper and peeps through.*

MAGGIE. Oh, mither, mither!

> [*Staggers back into* ANGUS's *arms.*

MRS. MACFARLANE. What is it, Meg?

ANGUS. Meg, my weel lo'ed Meg, my wee wifie that is to be, tell me what's wrang wi' 'ee.

MAGGIE. Oh, mither, it's him, the noble gentleman I plighted my troth to three weary months agone! The gallant Englishman who gave Angus twa golden pound to give me up!

ANGUS. It's the coward Sassenach who well nigh broke our Meg's heart!

MRS. MACFARLANE. My lass, my lass, dinna greet; maybe he'll marry ye yet.

CHEVIOT. [*Desperately.*] Here's another! Does anybody else want to marry me? Don't be shy. You, ma'am, [*To* MRS. MACFARLANE.] *you're* a fine woman—perhaps *you* would like to try your luck?

MAGGIE. Ah, sir! I dinna ken your name, but your bonnie face has lived in my twa een, sleeping and waking, three weary, weary months! Oh, sir, ye should na ha' deceived a trusting, simple Lowland lassie. 'Twas na weel done—'twas na weel done!

> [*Weeping on his shoulder*; *he puts his arm round her waist.*

CHEVIOT. [*Softening.*] My good girl, what do you wish me to do? I remember you now perfectly. I *did* admire you very much—in fact, I do still; you're a very charming girl. Let us talk this over, calmly and quietly. [MAGGIE *moves away.*] No, you needn't go; you can stop there if you like. There,

there, my dear, don't fret. [*Aside.*] She *is* a very charming girl, I almost wish I—I really begin to think I—no, no, damn it, Cheviot! not to-day.

MAGGIE. Oh, mither, he told me he loved me!

CHEVIOT. So I did. The fact is, when I fell in love with you— don't go my pretty bird—I quite forgot that I was engaged. There, there! I thought at the time that you were the tree upon which the fruit of my heart was growing, but I was mistaken. Don't go; you needn't go on that account. It was another tree—

MAGGIE. Oh, mither, it was anither tree!

[*Weeping on* CHEVIOT'*s shoulder.*

MRS. MACFARLANE. Angus, it was anither tree!

[*Weeping on* ANGUS'*s shoulder.*

ANGUS. Dinna, mither, dinna; I canna bear it!   [*Weeps.*

CHEVIOT. Yes, it was another tree—you can remain there for the present—in point of fact, it was growing on both trees. I don't know how it is, but it seems to grow on a great many trees—a perfect orchard—and you are one of them, my dear. Come, come, don't fret, you are one of them!

Enter MINNIE *and* SYMPERSON.

MINNIE. Cheviot!

SYMPERSON. What is all this?

CHEVIOT. [*Rapidly referring to piece of paper given to him by* MRS. MACFARLANE, *as if going over a washerwoman's bill.*] 'Twenty-four pairs socks, two shirts, thirty-seven collars, one sheet, forty-four nightshirts, twenty-two flannel waistcoats, one white tie.' Ridiculous—quite ridiculous—I won't pay it.

MINNIE. Cheviot, who is this person who is hanging on your neck? Say she is somebody—for instance, your sister or your aunt. Oh, Cheviot, say she is your aunt, I implore you!

[*The three cottagers curtsey and bow to* MINNIE.

SYMPERSON. Cheviot, say she is your aunt, I command you.

CHEVIOT. Oh, I beg your pardon. I didn't see you. These ladies are—are my washerwomen. Allow me to introduce them. They have come—they have come for their small account. [MAGGIE, *who has been sobbing through this, throws herself hysterically on to* CHEVIOT's *bosom.*] There's a discrepancy in the items—twenty-two flannel waistcoats are ridiculous, and, in short, some washerwomen are like this when they're contradicted—they can't help it—it's something in the suds; it undermines their constitution.

SYMPERSON. [*Sternly.*] Cheviot, I should like to believe you, but it seems scarcely credible.

MAGGIE. Oh, sir, he's na telling ye truly. I'm the puir Lowland lassie that he stole the hairt out of three months ago, and promised to marry; and I love him sae weel—sae weel, and now he's married to anither!

CHEVIOT. Nothing of the kind. I—

SYMPERSON. You are mistaken, and so is your mith—mother. He is not yet married to anith—nother.

MAGGIE. Why, sir, it took place before my very ain eyes, before us a', to a beautiful lady, three months since.

MINNIE. Cheviot, say that this is not true. Say that the beautiful lady was somebody—for instance, your aunt. Oh, say she was your aunt, I implore you!

SYMPERSON. [*Sternly.*] Cheviot, say she was your aunt, I command you!

CHEVIOT. Minnie, Symperson, don't believe them—it was no marriage. I don't even know the lady's name—I never saw her before—I've never seen her since. It's ridiculous—I couldn't have married her without knowing it—it's out of the question!

SYMPERSON. Cheviot, let's know exactly where we are. I don't much care whom you marry, so that you marry someone— that's enough for me. But please be explicit, for this is business and mustn't be trifled with. Tell me all about it.

CHEVIOT. [*In despair.*] I cannot!

Enter BELVAWNEY.

BELVAWNEY. I can.

SYMPERSON. Belvawney!

BELVAWNEY. I was present when Cheviot and a certain lady declared themselves to be man and wife. This took place in a cottage on the border—in the presence of these worthy people.

SYMPERSON. That's enough for me. It's a Scotch marriage! Minnie, my child, we must find you someone else. Cheviot's married. Belvawney, I am sorry to say I deprive you of your income.

BELVAWNEY. I beg your pardon, not yet.

SYMPERSON. Why not?

BELVAWNEY. In the first place, it's not certain whether the cottage was in England or in Scotland; in the second place, the bride can't be found.

SYMPERSON. But she *shall* be found. What is her name?

BELVAWNEY. That I decline to state.

SYMPERSON. But you shall be made to state. I insist upon knowing the young lady's name.

Enter MISS TREHERNE, *in a light and cheerful dress.*

BELVAWNEY. [*Amazed.*] Belinda Treherne!

MISS TREHERNE. [*Rushing to* MINNIE.] Minnie, my own old friend!

CHEVIOT. 'Tis she!

MISS TREHERNE. [*Turns and recognizes* CHEVIOT.] My husband!

CHEVIOT. My wife!
[MISS TREHERNE *throws herself at* CHEVIOT's *feet, kissing his hands rapturously.* BELVAWNEY *staggers back.* MINNIE *faints in her father's arms.* MAGGIE *sobs on* ANGUS's *breast. Picture.*

ACT III

BELVAWNEY. [*Sings.*]

> Says the old Obadiah to the young Obadiah,
> I am drier, Obadiah, I am drier.
> I am drier.

> Says the young Obadiah to the old Obadiah,
> I'm on fire, Obadiah, I'm on fire.
> I'm on fire.

MINNIE. Oh, thank you, Mr. Belvawney. How sweetly pretty that is. Where can I get it?

MISS TREHERNE. How marvellous is the power of melody over the soul that is fretted and harassed by anxiety and doubt. I can understand how valuable must have been the troubadours of old, in the troublous times of anarchy. Your song has soothed me, sir.

BELVAWNEY. I am indeed glad to think that I have comforted you a little, dear ladies.

MINNIE. Dear Mr. Belvawney, I don't know what we should have done without you. What with your sweet songs, your amusing riddles, and your clever conjuring tricks, the weary days of waiting have passed like a delightful dream.

MISS TREHERNE. It is impossible to be dull in the society of one who can charm the soul with plaintive ballads one moment, and the next roll a rabbit and a guinea-pig into one.

BELVAWNEY. You make me indeed happy, dear ladies. But my joy will be of brief duration, for Cheviot may return at any moment with the news that the fatal cottage was in Scotland, and then—oh, Belinda, what is to become of me?

MISS TREHERNE. How many issues depend on that momentous

question? Has Belvawney a thousand a year, or is he ruined? Has your father that convenient addition to his income, or has he not? May Maggie marry Angus, or will her claim on Cheviot be satisfied? Are you to be his cherished bride, or are you destined to a life of solitary maidenhood? Am I Cheviot's honoured wife, or am I but a broken-hearted and desolate spinster? Who can tell? Who can tell?

BELVAWNEY. [*Goes to window.*] Here is a cab with luggage—it is Cheviot! He has returned with the news! Ladies—one word before I go. One of you will be claimed by Cheviot; that is very clear. To that one (whichever it may be) I do not address myself—but to the other (whichever it may be), I say I love you (whichever you are) with a fervour which I cannot describe in words. If you (whichever you are) will consent to cast your lot with mine, I will devote my life to proving that I love you and you only (whichever it may be) with a single-hearted and devoted passion, which precludes the possibility of my ever entertaining the slightest regard for any other woman in the whole world. I thought I would just mention it. Good morning!   [*Exit.*

MISS TREHERNE. How beautifully he expresses himself. He is indeed a rare and radiant being.

MINNIE. [*Nervously.*] Oh, Belinda, the terrible moment is at hand.

MISS TREHERNE. Minnie, if dear Cheviot should prove to be my husband, swear to me that that will not prevent your coming to stop with us—with dear Cheviot and me—whenever you can.

MINNIE. Indeed I will. And if it should turn out that dear Cheviot is at liberty to marry me, promise me that that will not prevent you looking on our house—on dear Cheviot's and mine—as your home.

MISS TREHERNE. I swear it. We will be like dear, dear sisters.

Enter CHEVIOT, *as from journey, with bag and rug.*

MISS TREHERNE. Cheviot, tell me at once—are you my own—husband?

MINNIE. Cheviot, speak—is poor, little, simple Minnie to be your bride?

CHEVIOT. Minnie, the hope of my heart, my pet fruit tree! Belinda, my Past, my Present, and my To Come! I have sorry news, sorry news.

MISS TREHERNE. [*Aside.*] Sorry news! Then I am *not* his wife.

MINNIE. [*Aside.*] Sorry news! Then she *is* his wife.

CHEVIOT. My dear girls—my very dear girls, my journey has been fruitless—I have no information.

MISS TREHERNE *and* MINNIE. No information!

CHEVIOT. None. The McQuibbigaskie has gone abroad!
        [*Both ladies fall weeping into chairs.*

MISS TREHERNE. More weary waiting, more weary waiting!

MINNIE. Oh, my breaking heart; oh, my poor bruised and breaking heart!

CHEVIOT. We must be patient, dear Belinda. Minnie, my own, we must be patient. After all, is the situation so very terrible? Each of you has an even chance of becoming my wife, and in the mean time I look upon myself as engaged to both of you. I shall make no distinction. I shall love you both, fondly, and you shall both love me. My affection shall be divided equally between you, and we will be as happy as three little birds.

MISS TREHERNE. [*Wiping her eyes.*] You are very kind and thoughtful, dear Cheviot.

MINNIE. I believe, in my simple little way, that you are the very best man in the whole world.

CHEVIOT. [*Deprecatingly.*] No, no.

MINNIE. Ah, but do let me think so; it makes me so happy to think so!

CHEVIOT. Does it? Well, well, be it so. Perhaps I am. And now tell me, how has the time passed since I left? Have my darlings been dull?

MISS TREHERNE. We should have been dull indeed but for the airy Belvawney. The sprightly creature has done his best to make the lagging hours fly. He is an entertaining rattlesnake —I should say, rattletrap.

CHEVIOT. [*Jealous.*] Oh, *is* he so? Belvawney has been making the hours fly, has he? I'll make *him* fly, when I catch him!

MINNIE. His conjuring tricks are wonderful.

CHEVIOT. Confound his conjuring tricks!

MINNIE. Have you seen him bring a live hen, two hair brushes, and a pound and a half of fresh butter out of his pocket-handkerchief?

CHEVIOT. No, I have not had that advantage.

MISS TREHERNE. It is a thrilling sight.

CHEVIOT. So I should be disposed to imagine. Pretty goings on in my absence! You seem to forget that you two girls are engaged to be married to *me*!

MISS TREHERNE. Ah, Cheviot, do not judge us harshly. We love you with a reckless fervour that thrills us to the very marrow—don't we, darling? But the hours crept heavily without you, and when, to lighten the gloom in which we were plunged, the kindly creature swallowed a live rabbit and brought it out, smothered in onions, from his left boot, we could not choose but smile. The good soul had promised to teach *me* the trick.

CHEVIOT. Has he? That's his confounded impudence. Now, once for all, I'll have nothing of this kind. One of you will be my wife, and until I know which, I will permit no Belvawney-ing of any kind whatever, or anything approaching thereto. When that is settled, the other may Belvawney until she is black in the face.

MISS TREHERNE. And how long have we to wait before we shall know which of us may begin Belvawneying?

CHEVIOT. I can't say. It may be some time. The McQuibbi-gaskie has gone to Central Africa. No post can reach him, and he will not return for six years.

MISS TREHERNE. Six years! Oh, I cannot wait six years! Why, in six years I shall be eight-and-twenty!

MINNIE. Six years! Why, in six years the Statute of Limitations will come in, and he can renounce us both.

MISS TREHERNE. True; you are quite right. [*To* CHEVIOT.] Cheviot, I have loved you madly, desperately, as other woman never loved other man. This poor inexperienced child, [*Embracing* MINNIE.] who clings to me as the ivy clings to the oak, also loves you as woman never loved before. Even that poor cottage maiden, whose rustic heart you so recklessly enslaved, worships you with a devotion that has no parallel in the annals of the heart. In return for all this unalloyed affection, all we ask of you is that you will recommend us to a respectable solicitor.

CHEVIOT. But, my dear children, reflect—I can't marry all three. I am most willing to consider myself engaged to all three, and that's as much as the law will allow. You see I do all I can. I'd marry all three of you with pleasure if I might; but, as our laws stand at present, I'm sorry to say—I'm very sorry to say—it's out of the question.   [*Exit.*

MISS TREHERNE. Poor fellow. He has my tenderest sympathy; but we have no alternative but to place ourselves under the protecting ægis of a jury of our countrymen.

Enter SYMPERSON, *with two letters.*

SYMPERSON. Minnie—Miss Treherne—the post has just brought me two letters; one of them bears a Marseilles post-mark, and is, I doubt not, from the McQuibbigaskie. He must have written just before starting for Central Africa.

MINNIE. From the McQuibbigaskie? Oh, read, read!

MISS TREHERNE. Oh, sir, how can you torture us by this delay? Have you no curiosity?

SYMPERSON. Well, my dear, very little on this point; you see it don't much matter to me whom Cheviot marries. So that he marries some one, that's enough for me. But, however, *your* anxiety is natural, and I will gratify it. [*Opens letter and reads.*] 'Sir—In reply to your letter, I have to inform you that Evan Cottage is certainly in England. The deeds relating to the property place this beyond all question.'

MINNIE. In England!

MISS TREHERNE. [*Sinking into chair.*] This blow is indeed a crusher. Against such a blow I cannot stand up!   [*Faints.*

MINNIE. [*On her knees.*] My poor Belinda—my darling sister— love—oh, forgive me—oh, forgive me! Don't look like that! Speak to me, dearest—oh, speak to me—speak to me.

MISS TREHERNE. [*Suddenly springing up.*] Speak to you? Yes, I'll speak to you! All is *not* yet lost! True, he is not married to me, but why should he not be? I am as young as you! I am as beautiful as you! I have more money than you! I will try— oh, how hard I will try!

MINNIE. Do, darling, and I wish—oh, how I wish you may get him!

MISS TREHERNE. Minnie, if you were not the dearest little friend I have in the world I could pinch you!   [*Exit.*

SYMPERSON. [*Who has been reading the other letter.*] Dear me— how terrible!

MINNIE. What is terrible, dear papa?

SYMPERSON. Belvawney writes to tell me the Indestructible Bank stopped payment yesterday, and Cheviot's shares are waste paper.

MINNIE. Well, upon my word. There's an end of *him*!

SYMPERSON. An end of him. What do you mean? You are not going to throw him over?

MINNIE. Dear papa, I am sorry to disappoint you, but unless your tom-tit is very much mistaken, the Indestructible was not registered under the Joint-Stock Companies Act of sixty-two, and in that case the shareholders are jointly and severally liable to the whole extent of their available capital. Poor little Minnie don't pretend to have a business head, but she's not *quite* such a little donkey as *that*, dear papa.

SYMPERSON. You decline to marry him? Do I hear rightly?

MINNIE. I don't know, papa, whether your hearing is as good as it was, but from your excited manner I should say you heard me perfectly.   [*Exit.*

SYMPERSON. This is a pretty business! Done out of a thousand a year, and by my own daughter! What a terrible thing is this incessant craving after money! Upon my word, some people seem to think that they're sent into the world for no other purpose but to acquire wealth; and, by Jove, they'll sacrifice their nearest and dearest relations to get it. It's most humiliating—most humiliating!

Enter CHEVIOT, *in low spirits.*

CHEVIOT. [*Throwing himself into a chair*; *sobs aloud.*] Oh, Uncle Symperson, have you heard the news?

SYMPERSON. [*Angrily.*] Yes, I *have* heard the news; and a pretty man of business *you* are to invest all your property in an unregistered company!

CHEVIOT. Uncle, don't *you* turn against me! Belinda is not my wife. I'm a ruined man; and my darlings—my three darlings, whom I love with a fidelity, which, in these easy-going days, is simply Quixotic—will have nothing to say to me. Minnie, your daughter, declines to accompany me to the altar. Belinda I feel sure will revert to Belvawney, and Maggie is at this present moment hanging round that Scotch idiot's neck, although she knows that in doing so she simply tortures me. Symperson, I never loved three girls as I loved those three—never! never! and now they'll all three slip through my fingers—I'm sure they will.

SYMPERSON. Pooh, pooh, sir. Do you think nobody loses but you? Why, I'm done out of a thousand a year by it.

CHEVIOT. [*Moodily.*] For that matter, Symperson, I've a very vivid idea that you won't have to wait long for the money.

SYMPERSON. What d'you mean? Oh—of course—I understand.

CHEVIOT. Eh?

SYMPERSON. Mrs. Macfarlane! I have thought of her myself. A very fine woman for her years; a majestic ruin, beautiful in decay. My dear boy, my very dear boy, I congratulate you.

CHEVIOT. Don't be absurd. I'm not going to marry anybody.

SYMPERSON. Eh? Why, then how—? I don't think I quite follow you.

CHEVIOT. There is another contingency on which you come into the money. My death.

SYMPERSON. [*Delighted.*] To be sure! I never thought of that! And, as you say, a man can die but once.

CHEVIOT. I beg your pardon. I didn't say anything of the kind —*you* said it; but it's true, for all that.

SYMPERSON. I'm very sorry, but of course, if you have made up your mind to it——

CHEVIOT. Why, when a man's lost everything, what has he to live for?

SYMPERSON. True, true. Nothing whatever. Still——

CHEVIOT. His money gone, his credit gone, the three girls he's engaged to gone.

SYMPERSON. I cannot deny it. It is a hopeless situation. Hopeless, quite hopeless.

CHEVIOT. His happiness wrecked, his hopes blighted; the three trees upon which the fruit of his heart was growing—all cut down. What is left but suicide?

SYMPERSON. True, true! You're quite right. Farewell.

[*Going.*

CHEVIOT. Symperson, you seem to think I *want* to kill myself. I don't want to do anything of the kind. I'd much rather live—upon my soul I would—if I could think of any reason for living. Symperson, can't you think of *something* to check the heroic impulse which is at this moment urging me to a tremendous act of self-destruction?

SYMPERSON. Something! Of course I can! Say that you throw yourself into the Serpentine—which is handy. Well, it's an easy way of going out of the world, I'm told—rather pleasant than otherwise, I believe—quite an agreeable sensation, I'm given to understand. But you—you get wet through, and your—your clothes are absolutely ruined.

CHEVIOT. [*Mournfully.*] For that matter, I could take off my clothes before I went in.

SYMPERSON. True, so you could. I never thought of that. You could take them off before you go in—there's no reason why you shouldn't, if you do it in the dark—and *that* objection falls to the ground. Cheviot, my lion-hearted boy, it's impossible to resist your arguments; they are absolutely convincing.

[*Shakes his hand. Exit.*

CHEVIOT. Good fellow, Symperson—I like a man who's open to conviction. But it's no use—all my attractions are gone—and I can *not* live unless I feel I'm fascinating. Still, there's one chance left—Belinda! I haven't tried her. Perhaps, after all, she loved me for myself alone. It isn't likely—but it's barely possible.

Enter BELVAWNEY, *who has overheard these words.*

BELVAWNEY. Out of the question; you are too late. I represented to her that you are never likely to induce any one to marry you now that you are penniless. She felt that my income was secure, and she gave me her hand and her heart.

CHEVIOT. Then all is lost; my last chance is gone, and the irrevocable die is cast! Be happy with her, Belvawney; be happy with her!

BELVAWNEY. Happy! You shall dine with us after our honeymoon and judge for yourself.

CHEVIOT. No, I shall not do that; long before you return I shall be beyond the reach of dinners.

BELVAWNEY. I understand—you are going abroad. Well, I don't think you could do better than try another country.

CHEVIOT. [*Tragically.*] Belvawney, I'm going to try another world!   [*Drawing a pistol from his pocket.*

BELVAWNEY. [*Alarmed.*] What do you mean?

CHEVIOT. In two minutes I die!

BELVAWNEY. You're joking, of course?

CHEVIOT. Do I look like a man who jokes? Is my frame of mind one in which a man indulges in trivialities?

BELVAWNEY. [*In great terror.*] But my dear Cheviot, reflect—

CHEVIOT. Why should it concern you? You will be happy with Belinda. You will not be well off, but Symperson will, and I dare say he will give you a meal now and then. It will not be a nice meal, but still it will be a meal.

BELVAWNEY. Cheviot, you mustn't do this; pray reflect; there are interests of magnitude depending on your existence.

CHEVIOT. My mind is made up.   [*Cocking the pistol.*

BELVAWNEY. [*Wildly.*] But I shall be ruined!

CHEVIOT. There is Belinda's fortune.

BELVAWNEY. She won't have me if I'm ruined! Dear Cheviot, don't do it—it's culpable—it's wrong!

CHEVIOT. Life is valueless to me without Belinda.
           [*Pointing the pistol to his head.*

BELVAWNEY. [*Desperately.*] You shall have Belinda; she is much—very much to me, but she is not everything. Your life is very dear to me, and when I think of our old friendship—— Cheviot, you shall have anything you like, if you'll only consent to live!

CHEVIOT. If I thought you were in earnest, but no—no.
[*Putting pistol to head.*

BELVAWNEY. In earnest? Of course I'm in earnest! Why, what's the use of Belinda to me if I'm ruined? Why, she wouldn't look at me.

CHEVIOT. But perhaps if I'm ruined, she wouldn't look at *me*.

BELVAWNEY. Cheviot, I'll confess all, if you'll only live. You—you are *not* ruined!

CHEVIOT. Not ruined?

BELVAWNEY. Not ruined. I—I invented the statement.

CHEVIOT. [*In great delight.*] You invented the statement? My dear friend! My very dear friend! I'm very much obliged to you! Oh, thank you, thank you a thousand times! Oh, Belvawney, you have made me very, very happy! [*Sobbing on his shoulder, then suddenly springing up.*] But what the devil did you mean by circulating such a report about me? How dare you do it, sir? Answer me that, sir.

BELVAWNEY. I did it to gain Belinda's love. I knew that the unselfish creature loved you for your wealth alone.

CHEVIOT. It was a liberty, sir; it was a liberty. To put it mildly, it was a liberty.

BELVAWNEY. It was. You're quite right—that's the word for it—it was a liberty. But I'll go and undeceive her at once.
[*Exit.*

CHEVIOT. Well, as I've recovered my fortune, and with it my tree, I'm about the happiest fellow in the world. My money, my mistress, and my mistress's money, all my own. I believe I could go mad with joy!

Enter SYMPERSON, *in deep black; he walks pensively, with a white handkerchief to his mouth.*

CHEVIOT. What's the matter?

SYMPERSON. [*Disappointed*]. Hallo! You're still alive?

CHEVIOT. Alive? Yes; why, [*Noticing his dress.*] is anything wrong?

SYMPERSON. No, no, my dear young friend, these clothes are symbolical; they represent my state of mind. After your terrible threat, which I cannot doubt you intend to put at once into execution——

CHEVIOT. My dear uncle, this is very touching; this unmans me. But, cheer up, dear old friend, I have good news for you.

SYMPERSON. [*Alarmed.*] Good news? What do you mean?

CHEVIOT. I am about to remove the weight of sorrow which hangs so heavily at your heart. Resume your fancy check trousers—I have consented to live.

SYMPERSON. Consented to live? Why, sir, this is confounded trifling. I don't understand this line of conduct at all. You threaten to commit suicide; your friends are dreadfully shocked at first, but eventually their minds become reconciled to the prospect of losing you; they become resigned, even cheerful; and when they have brought themeslves to this Christian state of mind, you coolly inform them that you have changed your mind and mean to live. It's not business, sir— it's not business.

CHEVIOT. But my dear uncle, I've nothing to commit suicide for; I'm a rich man, and Belinda will, no doubt, accept me with joy and gratitude.

SYMPERSON. Belinda will do nothing of the kind. She has just left the house with Belvawney, in a cab, and under the most affectionate circumstances.

CHEVIOT. [*Alarmed.*] Left with Belvawney? Where have they gone?

SYMPERSON. I don't know. Very likely to get married.

CHEVIOT. Married?

SYMPERSON. Yes, before the registrar.

CHEVIOT. [*Excitedly.*] I've been sold! I see that now! Belvawney has done me! But I'm not the kind of man who stands such treatment quietly. Belvawney has found his match.

Symperson, they may get married, but they shall not be happy; I'll be revenged on them both before they're twenty-four hours older. She marries him because she thinks his income is secure. I'll show her she's wrong. I won't blow out my brains; I'll do worse.

SYMPERSON. What?

CHEVIOT. I'll marry.

SYMPERSON. Marry?

CHEVIOT. Anybody. I don't care who it is.

SYMPERSON. Will Minnie do?

CHEVIOT. Minnie will do; send her here.

SYMPERSON. In one moment, my dear boy—in one moment!
                                    [*Exit hurriedly.*

CHEVIOT. Belinda alone in a cab with Belvawney! It's maddening to think of it! He's got his arm round her waist at this moment, if I know anything of human nature! I can't stand it —I cannot and I will not stand it! I'll write at once to the registrar and tell him she's married. [*Sits at writing table and prepares to write.*] Oh, why am I constant by disposition? Why is it that when I love a girl I can think of no other girl but that girl, whereas when a girl loves me she seems to entertain the same degree of affection for mankind at large? I'll never be constant again; henceforth I fascinate but to deceive!

Enter MINNIE.

MINNIE. Mr. Cheviot Hill, papa tells me that you wish to speak to me.

CHEVIOT. [*Hurriedly, writing at table.*] I do. Miss Symperson, I have no time to beat about the bush; I must come to the point at once. You rejected me a short time since—I will not pretend that I am pleased with you for rejecting me—on the contrary, I think it was in the worst taste. However, let bygones be bygones. Unforeseen circumstances render it necessary that I should marry at once, and you'll do. An early answer will be esteemed, as this is business.
                                    [*Resumes his writing.*

MINNIE. Mr. Hill, dear papa assures me that the report about the loss of your money is incorrect. I hope this may be the case, but I cannot forget that the information comes from dear papa. Now dear papa is the best and dearest papa in the whole world, but he has a lively imagination, and when he wants to accomplish his purpose, he does not hesitate to invent—I am not quite sure of the word, but I think it is 'bouncers'.

CHEVIOT. [*Writing.*] You are quite right, the word is bouncers. Bouncers or bangers—either will do.

MINNIE. Then forgive my little silly fancies, Mr. Hill; but before I listen to your suggestion I must have the very clearest proof that your position is, in every way, fully assured.

CHEVIOT. Mercenary little donkey! I will not condescend to proof. I renounce her altogether.   [*Rings bell.*

Enter MAGGIE *with* ANGUS *and* MRS. MACFARLANE. ANGUS *has his arm round* MAGGIE'*s waist.*

CHEVIOT. [*Suddenly seeing her.*] Maggie, come here. Angus, do take your arm from round that girl's waist. Stand back, and don't you listen. Maggie, three months ago I told you that I loved you passionately; to-day I tell you that I love you as passionately as ever; I may add that I am still a rich man. Can you oblige me with a postage-stamp? [MAGGIE *gives him a stamp from her pocket—he sticks it on to his letter.*] What do you say? I must trouble you for an immediate answer, as this is not pleasure—it's business.

MAGGIE. Oh sir, ye're ower late. Oh, Maister Cheviot, if I'd only ken'd it before! Oh sir, I love ye right weel; the bluid o' my hairt is nae sae dear to me as thou. [*Sobbing on his shoulder.*] Oh Cheviot, my ain auld love! My ain auld love!

ANGUS. [*Aside.*] Puir lassie, it just dra's the water from my ee to hear her. Oh, mither, mither! My hairt is just breaking.
                    [*Sobs on* MRS. MACFARLANE'*s shoulder.*

CHEVIOT. But why is it too late? You say that you love me. I offer to marry you. My station in life is at least equal to your own. What is to prevent our union?

MAGGIE. [*Wiping her eyes.*] Oh, sir, ye're unco guid to puir little Maggie, but ye're too late; for she's placed the matter in her solicitor's hands, and he tells her that an action for breach will just bring damages to the tune of a thousand pound. There's a laddie waiting outside noo, to serve the bonnie writ on ye.

[*Turns affectionately to* ANGUS.

CHEVIOT. [*Falls sobbing on to sofa.*] No one will marry me. There is a curse upon me—a curse upon me. No one will marry me—no, not one!

MRS. MACFARLANE. Dinna say that, sir. There's mony a woman—nae young, soft, foolish lassie, neither, but grown women o' sober age who'd be mair a mither than a wife to ye; and that's what ye want, puir laddie, for ye're no equal to takin' care o' yersel'.

CHEVIOT. Mrs. Macfarlane, you are right. I am a man of quick impulse. I see, I feel, I speak. I—you are the tree upon which—that is to say—no, no, damn it, I can't, I can't! One must draw the line somewhere.

[*Turning from her with disgust.*

Enter MISS TREHERNE *and* BELVAWNEY. *They are followed by* SYMPERSON *and* MINNIE.

Belinda! Can I believe my eyes? You have returned to me; you have not gone off with Belvawney after all? Thank heaven, thank heaven!   [*Getting hysterical.*

MISS TREHERNE. I thought that as I came in I heard you say something about a tree.

CHEVIOT. You are right. As you entered I was remarking that I am a man of quick impulse. I see, I feel, I speak. I have two thousand a year, and I love you passionately. I lay my hand, my heart, and my income, all together, in one lot, at your feet!

MISS TREHERNE. Cheviot, I love you with an irresistible fervour that seems to parch my very existence. I love you as I never loved man before, and as I can never hope to love man again. But in the belief that you were ruined I went with my own adored Belvawney before the registrar, and that registrar has just made us one! [*Turns affectionately to* BELVAWNEY.

BELVAWNEY. [*Embraces* BELINDA.] Bless him for it—bless him for it!

CHEVIOT. [*Deadly calm.*] One word. I have not yet seen the

letter that blights my earthly hopes. For form's sake, I trust I may be permitted to cast my eye over that document? As a matter of business—that's all.

BELVAWNEY. Certainly. Here it is. You will find the situation of the cottage described in unmistakable terms.

[*Hands the letter to* CHEVIOT.]

CHEVIOT. [*Reads.*] 'In reply to your letter I have to inform you that Evan Cottage is certainly in England. The deeds relating to the property place this beyond all question.' Thank you; I am satisfied.   [*Takes out pistol.*

BELVAWNEY. Now, sir, perhaps you will kindly release that young lady. She is my wife!

[CHEVIOT'*s arm has crept mechanically round* MISS TREHERNE'*s waist.*

MISS TREHERNE. Oh, Cheviot, kindly release me—I am his wife!

CHEVIOT. Crushed! Crushed! Crushed!

SYMPERSON. [*Looking over his shoulder at letter, reads.*] 'Turn over.'

CHEVIOT. [*Despairingly.*] Why should I? What good would it do? Oh, I see. I beg your pardon. [*Turns over the page.*] Hallo!

ALL. What?

CHEVIOT. [*Reads.*] 'P.S. I may add that the border line runs through the property. The cottage is undoubtedly in England, though the garden is in Scotland.'

MISS TREHERNE. And we were married in the garden!

CHEVIOT. [*Amorously.*] Belinda, we were married in the garden!

[BELINDA *leaves* BELVAWNEY, *and turns affectionately to* CHEVIOT, *who embraces her.*

BELVAWNEY. Belinda, stop a bit! Don't leave me like this!

MISS TREHERNE. Belvawney, I love you with an intensity of devotion that I firmly believe will last while I live. But dear Cheviot is my husband now; he has a claim upon me which it could be impossible—nay, criminal—to resist. Farewell, Belvawney; Minnie may yet be yours! [BELVAWNEY *turns sobbing to* MINNIE, *who comforts him.*] Cheviot—my husband —my own old love—if the devotion of a lifetime can atone for the misery of the last few days, it is yours, with every wifely sentiment of pride, gratitude, admiration, and love.

CHEVIOT. [*Embracing her.*] My own! My own! Tender blossom of my budding hopes! Star of my life! Essence of happiness! Tree upon which the fruit of my heart is growing! My Past, my Present, my To Come!

[*Picture.* CHEVIOT *is embracing* MISS TREHERNE. BELVAWNEY *is being comforted by* MINNIE. ANGUS *is solacing* MAGGIE, *and* MRS. MACFARLANE *is reposing on* SYMPERSON'*s bosom.*

APPENDIX

CRITICISM OF *ENGAGED*

Reaction to *Engaged* in 1877 ranged between keen appreciation and delight on one hand and horror and disgust on the other. The first-night audience enjoyed itself but was distinctly uneasy; murmurs of disapproval and hisses were largely drowned out by bursts of spontaneous laughter. Later audiences—the play ran until 1 February 1878—appeared to mellow and receive the play more enthusiastically. Reviewers were generally agreed on the merits of the staging and acting: Marion Terry as Belinda Treherne and Harold Kyrle as Belvawney were judged the performers who carried off most perfectly the unconscious absurdity of their roles, but George Honey, a low-comedy actor of some repute (the original Eccles of *Caste*), was considered too broad and out of harmony with the rest of the ensemble in the part of Cheviot Hill. What the reviewers could not agree on was the merits or defects of the play itself, or the degree of praise or blame to be attached to Gilbert.

Few expressed unqualified praise. The *Morning Post* (4 October) said that *Engaged* was as witty a play as Gilbert had ever written, with 'a strong didactic purpose' and 'by no means without a certain truth to human nature'. Its purpose was 'mockery of the selfish and heartless of both sexes'. *John Bull* (13 October) termed it 'a fine piece of irony. . . . the humour is undeniable and the writing brilliant', and the play 'thoroughly original in treatment'. The *Daily Telegraph* (6 October) compared *Engaged* with *Gulliver's Travels*, and declared itself shaken by the power of Gilbert's satire: 'he strips off the outward covering concealing our imperfections, and makes us stand shivering. The failings we are aware of, the thoughts we scarcely dare utter are proclaimed to the world and diagnosed by this merciless surgeon.' Gilbert, however, 'must expect the rebuke of such as go to the theatre for the peace of oblivion, and not for the agony of dissection. There are many who would rather be soothed at the play in a fool's paradise than be taunted with the humbug of society and the meanness of human nature.' The *Athenaeum* (13 October) also compared Gilbert with Swift (as well as Aristophanes), but saw 'no purpose beyond provoking our laughter. . . . no moral aim whatever. The lesson, if any, to be extracted from his plays is that our nature is too pitiful to be redeemed.' Although *Engaged* offers 'a picture of humanity more cynical than has perhaps been painted since the days of Swift', Gilbert's audacity is triumphantly successful:

The experiment has rarely, if ever before, been made of supplying a drama in three acts in which there is not a single human being who does not proclaim himself absolutely detestable. In the present instance it has been made, and it is a success. So witty is the treatment that the piece, to those who are prepared to accept the author's standpoint, is one of the most mirthful and original that has, during late years, been seen on the stage.

The most rapturous praise of *Engaged* came from the *Evening Standard* (5 October), which did more than approve of the 'ingenious complications' and 'singularly witty' dialogue:

Mr. W. S. Gilbert's new play *Engaged* is in many respects one of the most remarkable pieces the stage has produced for many years. Wildly extravagant and fantastic in every detail; full of that peculiar humour for which the author of the 'Bab Ballads' is famous; and without a semblance of even such probability as is found in an ordinary farce, there yet appears to be a purpose beneath the surface of altogether irresistibly comic incident. *Engaged* satirises with ruthless and scathing sarcasm the selfishness which is so often hidden under the loftiest sentiment, and with the bitterest irony exposes the real motives of those who in the great race for love or money give themselves up wholly to the influences of true and pure affection—but only after having ascertained that the money question is satisfactory beyond possibility of doubt. Falsehood and fickleness are to be scorned, except indeed, when there is anything to be got by exercising them; and unshaken fidelity is to be the guiding principle of every one who can make it pay. Visitors to the Haymarket who do not care to trouble themselves about the moral of a play, however, need not do so here, and will find ready at hand a piece which, written in the vein which characterised *Trial by Jury*, is a gem of comic and original writing; and they may enjoy it to their heart's content and to the vigorous expansion of their lungs.

A larger category of reviewers praised the wit, cleverness, and keen sense of the ludicrous in *Engaged*, but also found the play overlong, repetitive, heartless, and disagreeable. The *Morning Advertiser* (6 October), for instance, described it as 'a violent burlesque upon everyday existence and a fantastic mockery of life as we know it'. While highly commending the acting, staging, and sense of ridiculous extravagance in 'this mad play', the reviewer worried that this was not 'the kind of thing old-fashioned people might expect to see at the Haymarket.' After a time, one suffers from a 'surfeit of absurdity' and 'begins to wish for something solid, and for some slight appearance of heart and honesty'. The *Sunday Times* (7 October) believed that 'this is the wittiest piece Mr. Gilbert has yet written' and expressed acute enjoyment of the dialogue; 'there is, indeed, an absolute carnival of satire and mirth.' The play 'deserves a visit from all who can relish an entertainment that outrages common sense while it gratifies senses that are anything but common'. However, there is a serious deficiency:

Carried away by his cleverness, Mr. Gilbert has forgotten to make any appeal to sympathy. . . . if there is one thing obvious to the student of dramatic art it is that a play cannot succeed on the strength of a purely intellectual interest, but that some display of sympathy must be elicited. . . . In *Engaged* Mr. Gilbert is more cold-bloodedly cynical than any human being has ever shown himself in the drama. Thus, though as an intellectual exercise his new play is admirable, we doubt whether it will ever be thoroughly and lastingly popular.

The response of the *Globe and Traveller* (4 October) was equally mixed. It also applied 'carnival' to Gilbert's humour—'a carnival of absurdity'—but doubted whether *Engaged* would become a general favourite, since 'the frank, outspoken cynicism which constitutes its greatest recommendation to a certain class of minds renders it wholly intolerable to another class.' Merits predominate over defects, and the comedy is 'very clever, one may say almost intolerably clever'. Like other reviewers who confessed to being puzzled and bewildered by *Engaged*, this one admitted to his share of uncertainty and perplexity:

The piece, indeed, overleaps all canons and defies all criticism. Very easy would be the task of dwelling upon its ingenuity, which is absolutely unsurpassable, and scarcely more difficult would be that of condemning its extravagance. . . . Our verdict is that the result thus obtained is excellent farce. It is, however, difficult to confute those who maintain it is rank and absolute nonsense.

The *Echo* (10 October) was much more disturbed. *Engaged* is 'a curious production—weird, cynical, spiteful, ridiculous, and clever in turn'. The characters should have been placed in the fairyland world of *The Palace of Truth* and *The Wicked World* where 'they might have passed muster', but set in the everyday world they are 'distortions of daily life' and 'the actions and speeches seem those of a few gleanings from the ward of one of our great lunatic asylums'. After praising the acting, the reviewer concluded:

It is not often that a piece is received with so mingled an outburst of cheers and dissatisfaction, and this was not surprising considering the opposite qualities it possesses; for Mr. Gilbert seemed to have given his audience a draught of champagne of the finest vintage, which was no sooner to their lips than they found it was marred with dashes of sulphuric acid and the most nauseous bitter he could find. . . . That the piece is clever and original must be granted, for it displays power of no mean order, but that it is a good comedy, or likely to elevate the stage or the minds of those who witness the play, must be most strenuously denied.

An example of fluctuations of opinion in the same paper is provided by the *Theatre*, which commented on *Engaged* several times over the course of four months. Its first review (9 October) declared that because of its extravagance the play was 'beyond the reach of the serious analysis which we may desire to bestow upon it', being a 'deliberate caricature', 'a grotesque skit upon sham love and friendship; a sally directed against social selfishness and against young ladies' eagerness to secure for themselves "good matches"; a joke perpetrated at the expense of the pretended *ingenue*, of the melodramatic lover, and of the sentimental maiden'. Although the reviewer was uncertain whether *Engaged* would suit public taste, 'its cleverness and wealth of humour cannot be denied.' The author of the column 'En Passant' the following week (16 October) was more forthright; he called *Engaged* 'a premeditated insult'. There the matter rested until the first number of 1878 (2 January) when the *Theatre* decided that 'this amusing piece, which has in some quarters been much too seriously canvassed, and has had attributed to it a great deal of cynical meaning which it was never intended to carry, still wins abundant appreciation from its laughing audiences, and proves a timely protest against the favourite theory of managers, that our laughs must always be borrowed from across the Channel.' A few weeks later, however (30 January), 'A Lowland Scot' savaged *Engaged* in the correspondence column for being untrue to the people, character, and language of the Lowlands, for violating all dramatic probability in plot and characterization, and for being 'out of conformity with the order of nature'. In conclusion, 'I take *Engaged* to be, on the whole, the worst play put upon the boards of any London theatre since the production of Johnson's *Irene*. There is no truth, no verisimilitude, in the whole of it.'

In judging so sternly, 'A Lowland Scot' was only agreeing with the tenor of much of the criticism of four months before. *The Times* (8 October) said that 'the action consists but of a series of scenes of the most whimsical and grotesque nature, in which common sense and probability are alike set at defiance'. Although allowing that their very absurdity made some of these scenes 'irresistibly comic', and that the play was unquestionably clever, the reviewer believed that 'it is a cleverness not altogether wholesome or pleasant', and that 'there are subjects on which the jester must be prepared to find that his audience can scarcely separate the laughter he may excite from a feeling of distaste'. Satire against human selfishness and littleness is too hackneyed a theme, 'a theme of which the world has perhaps for the present grown somewhat tired, at least in so undiluted a form'. Furthermore, the play is too long—the jest 'is something too elaborate'—and 'if intended as a satire on human selfishness it loses its point through the absence of all relief or contrast. If taken as a bit of fooling, excellent as some of the fooling is, there is altogether too much of it.' The *Saturday Review* (13 October) called *Engaged* 'a long-drawn-out skit upon the false stage sentiment which may be found . . . in almost every stage play in which sentiment plays a part. . . . The joke of making everybody turn the usual sentiments of the stage into practical ridicule can hardly be sustained for more than the space of one act at most.' For the reviewer of the *World* (10 October) the pleasure derived from 'amusing passages' was vitiated 'if the spectator can hardly rise from the entertainment with any respect for it; inevitably by such productions plays and players alike are brought into contempt'. In fact he was bored by the whole thing:

Mr. Gilbert develops his theme after a very laborious and prolix fashion. One act should have been sufficient for his purpose: but he has occupied three acts by repeating his incidents to a wearisome extent, and by hammering his humour into so thin a tissue that it falls into holes at last upon the slightest touch. Burlesque should be served in liqueur-glasses, as it were; only very gross appetites can require a quart-measure of the cordial, even when its strength has been reduced much below proof. . . . the Haymarket company might surely find more congenial and profitable occupation than they obtain in illustrating the tiresome triviality of Mr. Gilbert's new extravaganza.

Another review, whose source and date I have been unable to identify, but which appears to have been written a few weeks after the first night of *Engaged*, decided upon reflection that Gilbert's purpose was 'not to enlighten but puzzle an audience', a serious mistake because 'a play too deep for instant comprehension misses its main object. Wit too complicated and involved to be understood on the instant has to sacrifice its brightest charm.' Additionally, *Engaged*, despite meritorious acting, lacks common humanity and fails on that account; 'the dramatist who writes "simplicity" and "humanity" on his standard will win more to his side than the crotchety author who elects to succeed with "mystification" and "cynicism."'

The Gilbert who emerged from the more hostile reviews was indeed a 'crotchety author', cold, bitter, cynical, and mercilessly misanthropic. One of the mildest of these reviews is in the *Illustrated London News* (13 October). Its critic thought that Gilbert had made a fundamental error in his conception of satire:

Instead of showing how inferior motives interfere with and qualify the noblest intentions, he sacrifices the latter entirely to the former, and makes the only real impulse to consist in selfishness. . . . The satirist has no right to belie humanity, and instead of correcting certain faults or frailties, to condemn it altogether as wholly despicable and bad. . . . We could have wished that Mr. Gilbert had treated us with a genuine comedy, in which there had been less burlesque and more of true dramatic life and character. We confess that to us the piece is unsatisfactory, and leaves behind a disagreeable impression.

The author of another review whose source I have not been able to trace was even more severe. *Engaged* is 'an elaborate piece of mockery, the object of which appears to be to sneer at every sentiment of honour, decency, and virtue that ordinary people are brought up to look upon with respect'. Distortion and scorn are two of the playwright's principal characteristics, scorn 'not only of the weaknesses but of the honest beliefs of ordinary men and women'. Satire of this kind was tolerable in the *Bab Ballads*, but in a three-act play it becomes 'offensive cynicism'. The dialogue admittedly 'compels laughter, but mostly of the unwholesome sort'; all the characters are 'monsters', in spite of the funny things they say. But the laughter they evoke 'is of the order that quaintly-dressed foreigners excite among a rude mob, and that malformations give rise to on the lips of the vulgar'. The actors fully enter into the spirit of the play; indeed, if 'a select company of intelligent monkeys' could choose a play to perform, it would be *Engaged*. Finally, 'Mr. Gilbert is heartily welcome to his views of life. His talents are undeniably brilliant, and in his power of provoking mirth he is almost without a living rival. But speaking only of "Engaged", we should prefer mirth that did not appear to be the result of an imperfect digestion acting upon a cynical disposition.' The critic of the *Hornet* (10 October) was just as upset. The play is merely a 'snarling mockery', and its author's sense of humour hideously warped; 'you do not naturally expect good taste from Mr. Gilbert, for grapes do not grow on briars; but the sort of man who attempts to extract humour from the subject of wilful attempts to upset railway trains may well be left to enjoy his funereal fancies.' It is fortunate that *Engaged* is 'entirely original' and that Gilbert had not imitated another playwright, 'for we cannot think that any other man could be found who would so deliberately insult the audience of the oldest comedy theatre in town. For heartless, coldblooded, brutal cynicism, the play has perhaps never been equalled.'

If this seems harsh comment, it is nothing to the abuse heaped on Gilbert and his play by the *Figaro* (10 October). Its critic began calmly enough with a thoughtful paragraph reviewing Gilbert's career in the theatre to date, praising the fairy comedies and *Trial by Jury*, but pointing out that although Gilbert had been very successful 'one enormous blemish' mars all his plays and poems: 'in the quality of sympathy they were all painfully deficient. Clever, bizarre, witty, they undoubtedly were; but they failed to touch the heart.' This deficiency could be overlooked in the plays 'laid in some imaginary region, beyond the pale of human experience', but as soon as Gilbert 'condescended to treat of the life which men and women actually live, his failure was painfully complete'. When he came to consider *Engaged* itself, the reviewer warmed to his task. It would have been much better, he thought, if Gilbert had written a play 'wholesome in its moral tone, powerful in its construction, genial in its humour, and manly in its sentiment'.

Instead of that, he has elected to vindicate his originality at the expense of every quality which any writer, possessed of a grain of self-respect, would seek to cultivate; and, unless we are much mistaken, at a cost which laughter, extorted from his audience in spite of their sense of honour or of decency, however loud and hearty it may sound in his ears, will scarcely repay. The flattery of injudicious admirers, who confuse impudence with courage, and brutality with strength, may titillate the nostrils of his vanity with incense pleasant enough for the time; but such a reward is dearly bought, if it be accompanied by the utter repugnance of everyone who has the sense to detect, and the honesty to denounce, the complete degradation to author, actor, and spectator alike, involved in the production of such a work as this entirely original farcical comedy.

To tell the story of 'Engaged' is more than can be expected of anyone who assisted at its first representation. One does not care to relate the details of a rough passage across the Channel, if one is not proof against sea-sickness. The recapitulation of the symptoms of nausea is neither pleasant to the sufferer, nor edifying to his audience. Let our readers conceive a play in three acts, during which every character only opens his or her mouth to ridicule, in the coarsest manner, every feeling that is generally held in respect by any decent man or woman. The hero is a combination of mental imbecility, vulgar cunning, paltry mendacity, greedy stinginess, shameless cowardice, and unctuous sensuality. A Scotch peasant girl is introduced, with her betrothed, of whom this hero buys her for two pounds, in consequence of her own graceful intercession; her betrothed is delighted with the bargain, and complacently looks on while the purchaser caresses his modest acquisition. Later in the piece, this girl's mother approves the contract, and when her daughter has changed her mind offers to supply her place. There are two other young girls introduced, who vie with one another in the sentimental utterance of such mercenary principles as the most degraded woman might possibly feel, but would be ashamed to confess. From beginning to end of this nauseous play not one of the characters ever says a single word or does a single action that is not inseparable from the lowest moral degradation; while, much to the delight of that portion of the audience who believe that to scoff at what is pure and noble is the surest sign of intellectual pre-eminence, speeches in which the language ordinarily employed by true feeling is used for the purpose of deriding every virtue which any honest man reverences, even if he does not possess, are tediously re-iterated by actresses whom one would wish to associate only with what is pure and modest. Nor is there any dramatic end, as far as we can see, served by all this. The story, such as it is, might well be detached from this sickening atmosphere; for vice is never satirised in this work in order that it may be laughed at, much less that it may be rebuked. To answer that 'all this is a burlesque' seems to us but a poor defence; the characters are dressed in the ordinary costume of the present day; the language, as we have said, is precisely that which would be employed in serious drama; there are few if any of those amusing exaggerations which, in true burlesque, dispel, almost before it has time to form, any idea that the speaker is really in earnest. We do not believe that, except among the most repulsive comedies of the seventeenth century, or in the very lowest specimens of French farce, can there be found anything to equal in its heartlessness Mr. Gilbert's latest original work.

To speak of the acting of such a play is hardly necessary. Everyone who has any respect for the stage must have felt grieved and sick at heart to see such grace, such energy, such charm of manner and voice, such perfect self-forgetfulness, as Miss Terry displayed, wasted on such abominable material. Mr. Kyrle will, we hope, escape soon from a part which must, if persevered in, prejudice the career of one who promises to fill a great void among our actors. . . . Miss Lucy Buckstone, had she been less charming, could hardly have dared to speak the lines set down for her. Deeply do we regret that she ever should have been compelled to waste so much attractiveness on what is in itself so repulsive. Mr. Howe was, in spite of all he had to say or do, a perfect gentleman in demeanor; that he seemed to enjoy his part we should not like to say. Mr. Honey must not be discouraged; the public will soon forget the degradation to which he has had to submit; they will easily pardon him if he ap-peared, occasionally, to forget words which he well might be ashamed to remember.

In concluding his attack, the *Figaro* critic protested that he was not destitute of a sense of humour, nor did he insist that every entertain-ment must inculcate a moral lesson. If *Engaged* had been a burlesque whose characters were dressed in fantastic costumes and spoke exag-gerated bombast, if there had also been 'light and delicate touches of pure and wholesome fun', he might have disliked the subject but found the play more acceptable. However, this had not been the case:

It is because the cynicism is so coarse, the satire so inartistic, the wit so unrefined, while the representation of the characters, admitting them to be caricatures, is so free from any exaggeration or extravagance, that to ordinary people they can appear nothing but real types of human nature; it is because the tendency of such practical joking with the principles of right and wrong cannot but be to corrupt the general public who frequent theatres, that we feel pained at seeing such a piece produced on our stage, and that we honestly express that feeling with all the earnestness in our power.[1]

All this fuss and bother baffled Our Captious Critic of the *Illustrated Sporting and Dramatic News* (20 October) who declared prophetically that Gilbert 'has produced a work that must influence English comedy in a palpable way'. His review is perhaps the most considered and intelligent defence of *Engaged*, and seems a fitting one with which to conclude. Almost all of it appears here:

It seldom falls to the lot of a comic drama to evoke such diverse critical opinions as have generally been passed upon W. S. Gilbert's new and original piece *Engaged*, at the Haymarket Theatre. The fact that this farcical comedy has had the effect of initiating a certain kind of playgoer into the strongest expressions of condemnation, and of arousing in another kind of spectator the liveliest admiration and eulogy is the surest proof that it is an unique and remarkable production.

For my own part I will say at once that I consider *Engaged* the cleverest comic work that has proceeded from Mr. Gilbert's brilliant pen. Having begun by this admission, I must also confess that I have been altogether puzzled by the serious denunciations which have been levelled by critics against what they call the 'heartless cynicism' of one of the most riotously humorous, whimsically incongruous, utterly comical burlesques it has ever been my lot to see or read. Indeed, when some of the critics of *Engaged* deduced from its three acts of grotesque drollery awful evidences of a mind diseased, a lacerated heart, more bitterly sceptical of human good than Dean Swift's *sava indignatio*, more terrible than his against the human race, I protest I was fairly mystified. I went and saw the piece a second time, thinking that perchance upon my first visit I might not have sufficiently studied it to apprehend fully the import of its conception and its dialogue. But my impressions remained the same. I had an extra chuckle or so, perhaps, over one or two touches of grave banter that had previously escaped my notice. But after a careful consideration of the whole case I was quite unable to regard *Engaged* as anything more serious than a whimsical, satirical, exquisitely humorous extravaganza. Where is this bitter, heartless cynicism they talk so much about? I cannot find it. And although I appear before you in the character of a Captious Critic, I am not by any means an individual of misanthropical proclivities. On the contrary, I am, as a rule, inclined to think better of my species than by their general behaviour they warrant one in thinking. Then I believe I also know correctly what the term cynicism means in the drama. To go back in stage history, I think the comedies of Congreve and

[1] In 1882 William Archer, in a chapter on Gilbert that generally awarded him high praise, excepted *Engaged* from his favour. Although he found it 'extremely amusing' and 'ingenious', it is also 'repulsive, vulgar', and 'leaves a bitter taste in the mouth. It is as unpleasant and degrading as "Gulliver's Travels" without their deep human truth. Its cynicism is as irrelevant as it is exaggerated.' (*English Dramatists of To-day*, pp. 172–6.)

Wycherley, for example, as diabolically cynical, as they are grossly impure. To come to our own time, I consider the libretti of three-fourths of the French opéras-bouffes which have been translated with sufficient plainness into English, practically and palpably cynical, and they are indecent withal. I may say the same of some Palais Royal pieces, mightily popular amongst us, against which, although they did not escape unblamed, no charge of heartless cynicism has been brought.

I compare Mr. W. S. Gilbert's fanciful farce, *Engaged*, with the productions thus indicated, in all respects. And it seems to me that, while upon artistic grounds it is equal to the best of them, it is less heartlessly cynical than any of them; it is as amusing as the most amusing of them; and it is untainted by a tinge of the indecent suggestiveness upon which all of them, ancient or modern, largely depend for their humour. Therefore I ask again why this talk of diseased minds, deformed imagination, wicked scepticism, sardonic hatred of the entire human race in connection with the new Haymarket piece?

That the satirical vein is characteristic of Gilbert's humour we are all aware. That there lives not a writer for our stage who has such a lively sense of the ironical and incongruous in social customs and ethics few will attempt to deny. But (from my point of view at all events) his cynicism being altogether intellectual and artistic, serves his dramatic purpose excellently, without doing violence to the feelings of the humane, or assisting the sneers of the vicious. It is your sensually cynical writer who does mischief and deserves reprobation. Yet he is generally applauded as a warm-hearted sort of person, whose scoffs at virtue, howsoever devilish, are the outcome of a full-blooded and hilarious nature.

It is not my habit to detail the plot of any piece that I may discuss in this place. The plot of *Engaged* is very slight and episodical. But the balance of incident in the three acts is carefully preserved, and the episodes of the farce are arranged with artistic skill. When the play opens, the mock seriousness and realism of the events at first deceives the unwary spectator, who is about to prepare himself for domestic comedy. And the sudden surprise that jerks one into a consciousness of the drollery of the burlesque is a shock as exhilarating to an appreciative spectator as the first plunge into cold water is to an early riser. Angus MacAlister's allusion to his honest calling, which consists chiefly in poaching, but is supplemented by the occasional upsetting of a tourist's train, is a purposely extravagant touch of burlesque, that ought to supply at the very outset, to any intelligent spectator, the key-note of the humour of the farce. Yet I was astonished to find one critic quoting it as an evidence of the author's utter and diabolical heartlessness. 'The man who will make a pun will pick a pocket', remarked the learned lexicographer. The critic in question evidently argues upon equally sound premises, that the comic writer who can make a joke about the upsetting of a railway train must be guilty of something infinitely more criminal than petty larceny. Lord preserve us, we live in grave and parlous times.

THE TYRANNY OF TEARS

A COMEDY IN FOUR ACTS

BY

CHARLES HADDON CHAMBERS (1860–1921)

─────

First performed at the Criterion Theatre
6 April 1899

─────

CAST

Mr. Parbury	Mr. Charles Wyndham
Mr. George Gunning	Mr. Frederick Kerr
Colonel Armitage, Mrs. Parbury's father	Mr. Alfred Bishop
Evans, Parbury's butler	Mr. Stanley Pringle
Mrs. Parbury	Miss Mary Moore
Miss Hyacinth Woodward	Miss Maude Millett

PREFACE TO *THE TYRANNY OF TEARS*

HADDON CHAMBERS was an Australian of Irish parentage who arrived in England in 1880, published his first short story in 1884, and had his first play performed in 1886. Before *The Tyranny of Tears* he wrote seven more and collaborated on five others, mostly dramas with the occasional comedy. His first success was *Captain Swift* (1888), produced by Tree at the Haymarket, a play about an Australian bushranger and bandit who escapes to England, moves in good society, falls in love with a beautiful heiress, is tracked down by a detective, and shoots himself to avoid capture and a revelation of the past that could only hurt others. Like *Captain Swift*, Chambers's next play to attract attention, *The Idler* (1890), is a heavily emotional drama with an upper middle-class setting, and concerns a man expiating his bad past abroad by marrying a good girl; she is also loved by the hero, who takes the decent way out by agreeing to lead an expedition to the North Pole.[1] *The Idler* was a St. James's piece, and the morose hero was played by George Alexander: Chambers was fortunate in that several of his plays were taken up by the leading actor-managers of the day. Beerbohm Tree also produced the drama *John-a-dreams* (1894),[2] and in the same decade Chambers collaborated on two Adelphi melodramas, *The Fatal Card* (1894) with B. C. Stephenson, and *Boys Together* (1896) with Comyns Carr. He also tried his hand at the romantic cloak-and-sword drama then much in vogue with *In the Days of the Duke* (1897), another Adelphi play done in collaboration with Comyns Carr.

After *The Tyranny of Tears* Chambers wrote nine more plays, the most noteworthy being *Passers-by* (1911), with leading roles for Gerald du Maurier and Irene Vanbrugh, and *The Saving*

---

[1] In the 1890s such a device was a not uncommon way of morally extricating a hero from the consequences of a scandal involving a socially prominent wife. Henry Arthur Jones uses it in *The Liars*, when the *raisonneur* persuades Falkner to choose a heroic African expedition rather than elopement with Lady Jessica. At the end of Jones's drama *The Masqueraders* (1894), the astronomer-hero, despite winning the suffering Lady Skene from her boorish husband, chastely leaves her and embarks on a scientific expedition to Africa.

[2] See Volume Two, p. 21.

Grace (1917). The former depicts the indolent, whimsical, and impulsive hero's interest in the life of the street outside his front door, his reunion with the unmarried mother of his child, and the breaking of his engagement with an understanding fiancée. The principal character of the latter play is the patriotic, impecunious, and lovable ex-officer Binns, who with only a few shillings in the house schemes to marry his daughter to an empty-headed aviator with a rich mother. Any moral difficulty is resolved by the young couple falling in love, and Binns goes off happily to war, unaware that his wife has secured his commission by a secret telegram to a friendly general. As in *The Tyranny of Tears*, the plot and characters are managed with considerable economy, deftness, and simple charm; both humour and idealism are warm, gentle, and unstrained. *The Saving Grace* is one of the best comedies of its period.

Considering the lack of subtlety and the strongly melodramatic nature of Chambers's theatrical writing before *The Tyranny of Tears*, that comedy's lightness of touch is surprising. In fact the play is an excellent example of what comic dramatists had learned over the years. From the French they absorbed the planned management of plot structure, the elimination of irrelevant material, and the careful subordination of means to ends. In Pinero and Jones French skills are generally applied to plays with many characters, a substantial plot, and an elaborate social setting. *The Tyranny of Tears* goes further: the characters are remarkably few in number; the plot is slight; and the setting is many miles, both literally and figuratively, from Mayfair. The comic distance travelled from *John Bull* is immense, but not so far that one cannot see the way back. Both plays are intended for middle-class audiences and occupy themselves with middle-class domestic concerns; the Englishman's fireside is as much the subject of the later play as the earlier. Like Colman, Chambers was not a playwright to forgo mixing in a significant proportion of seriousness and sentiment with clever banter and comic situation; *The Times*, indeed, commented, in words that one could easily use of the comedy of a hundred years before, 'that occasionally it becomes too serious for a comedy'.[1] But of course *The Tyranny of Tears* is a late Victorian play and shows it, not only in the skill of construction and technique, but also in the

[1] *The Times*, 7 April 1899.

domestic middle-class realism of both situation and setting, and the restraint, quietness, and control exercised in dialogue and characterization.[1] The Victorian domestic ideal, including the rightful exercise of a husband's authority over a wife who learns her lesson, burns brightly through the vicissitudes of the Parburys and is ingeniously counterpointed by the anti-idealistic though still somewhat romantic relationship between Gunning and Miss Woodward. In this relationship too the man asserts himself at the end: 'perhaps she wants a master', he says, and like many a heroine and dutiful wife before her, she agrees. The hereditary process by which a comedy like *The Tyranny of Tears* descends from a comedy like *John Bull* is a long and involved one and has been the main theme of the Introduction to this volume. It will suffice to say in conclusion that Chambers's play represents a hundred years of development, refinement, and social readjustment in comedy, and can be seen as the quintessential distillation of the comic experience of the nineteenth-century stage.

The Tyranny of Tears received 113 performances on its first run at the Criterion. Wyndham revived it twice: at Wyndham's Theatre in 1902 and at the Comedy in 1914; the second revival seems to have been the last in the West End. The text used here is that of the first edition of 1900, published by Heinemann, with occasional corrections, and collated with the Lord Chamberlain's copy. The play was reprinted six times and became *French's Acting Edition*, no. 1050; these reprints and the *French* text are identical with the first edition.

---

[1] If one admires these qualities, Chambers is superior to his contemporaries in these respects: Jones, Pinero, Wilde, and Shaw can hardly be praised for a combination of simplicity, quiet restraint, and gentle charm. (Pinero's *Trelawney of the 'Wells'* is a possible exception.)

ACT I

SCENE. MR. CLEMENT PARBURY's *study at his house in the neighbourhood of Hampstead Heath. The main entrance leading from the hall is* L. *A door,* R., *leads to the dining-room. A glass door,* R.C., *opens into a garden. The fireplace is* C. *The room is comfortably and not severely furnished. The furniture is made up of odds and ends selected with taste. The couch down* L. *is a deep and cosy one; the desk or writing-table about* R.C. *is a large and serviceable one. There is a smaller desk higher up, and near it on wall,* R., *a telephone apparatus. The apartment altogether represents the workshop of a literary man of careless good taste. There is a touch, too, of femininity in its decorations, and a portrait of* MRS. PARBURY *is the only picture on the walls, which otherwise are mostly hidden by bookcases.*

For a few moments before and when the curtain rises the noise of street singers is heard. MISS WOODWARD *and* EVANS *are discovered.* MISS WOODWARD *is dressed with severe simplicity in a costume of dark colour, with linen collar and cuffs; her dark hair is drawn back from her forehead. Her costume, being well cut, does not conceal the graceful outline of her figure. She is a handsome, innocent, yet determined-looking girl of twenty. She is at the window looking out.*

EVANS. [*Raising his voice above the outside singers.*] They wouldn't listen to me, Miss Woodward. [*Suddenly the music stops. A pause.*] Ah, they've listened to Mr. Parbury. [MISS WOODWARD *goes to desk, sits.*] Mr. Parbury's a very masterful man—outside his house—isn't he, miss? [MISS WOODWARD *favours* EVANS *with a cold stare, then resumes work at desk.*] [*Aside.*] What an iceberg that young woman is!
     [*Telephone bell rings. Exit* EVANS. MISS WOODWARD *goes to telephone and takes line.*

MISS WOODWARD. [*Speaking into telephone—very sweetly.*] Yes, are you there? Yes—who are you? Speak a little louder, please. Oh! Well? Yes—I don't know—Mr. Parbury's just coming in now—he'll speak to you—keep the line.
     [*She returns to the desk.*

Enter PARBURY *from garden. His hair is untidy; he is flustered and cross. He is an agreeable-looking man of about forty.*

PARBURY. Thank heaven, they're gone! This house is a mistake! With the nerve force one expends in swearing at street singers one might do some good work. Make a note, please— look for house in secluded part of country. [MISS WOODWARD *makes note.*] And make a note—write *Times re* Street Music; suggest Local Option.

MISS WOODWARD. The *Saturday Sentinel* is waiting to speak to you on the telephone.

PARBURY. Oh, worrying about the article, I suppose. [*Goes to telephone.*] Hullo! hullo! [*Gives them a ring up.*] Are you there? [*Crossly.*] Are you there? Well? [*Pause; he listens.*] Oh, of course, still harping on my article. I suppose that's you, Jackson? Oh, well, if you'll keep this confounded telephone quiet, and send a man to clear the neighbourhood of street singers, you'll have a chance of receiving the copy in half an hour. What? All right, old man. Yes, yes. I'll send it by special messenger. Yes. Good-bye! [*Rings off, and hangs up tube.*] That is another mistake—that telephone.

MISS WOODWARD. I was afraid you would find it so.

PARBURY. You were right! You are always right! But my wife thought it would save me a lot of correspondence and a lot of going out. [*Aside, with a sigh.*] I always liked going out. [*Aloud.*] Make a note, please—get rid of the telephone. [MISS WOODWARD *makes note.*] Now we'll get on, please. I've promised the article in half an hour. [*Looks at his watch.*] They go to press this afternoon.

MISS WOODWARD. [*Sits at desk, note-book before her.*] Shall I read the last sentence?

PARBURY. Please.

MISS WOODWARD. [*Reading.*] 'The pity of it is that Mr. Theodore Bellevue seems to enjoy a positively huge content-ment of his own achievement——'

PARBURY. [*Thinking.*] The pity of it—yes—yes, of his own achievement. Yes. [*Walks the stage.*] Achievement. [*Under his breath.*] Damn the street singers! Damn the telephone!

[*Aloud.*] What is it? Oh—ah! Contentment of his own achievement—er—er—. [*Dictates.*] 'One gathers from the complacency of his manner—[*Pause.*]—that his iconoclasm is its own reward—' Er—'What follows in the approval of the unthinking—the applause of the uncultured—' [*Pause.*] What's that?

MISS WOODWARD. The applause of the uncultured.

PARBURY. 'Makes up—makes up—' Er—[*Pulls his hair.*] Er——

Enter MRS. PARBURY. *She is a pretty, fragile, little woman of about twenty-eight, and is charmingly dressed.*

MRS. PARBURY. I'm not interrupting, am I, darling?

PARBURY. [*Concealing his irritation.*] No, darling, but——

MRS. PARBURY. I'll be ever so quiet.   [*Comes to couch; sits.*

PARBURY. Yes, I know, dear—but I fear—I fear you'll be rather bored. I'm dictating an article that *must* be finished this afternoon——

MRS. PARBURY. Oh, I shall like it! Go on as if I were not in the room. But oh, how tumbled your hair is. [*Rises, goes to him.*] I must put it straight. Then you'll be able to think better. There! Now I can see his clever forehead again!
     [*Goes to couch and sits.* PARBURY *walks up and back, trying to collect his thoughts; then he looks at* MRS. PARBURY *with the wish in his face that she were not there; finally he goes over to* MISS WOODWARD *and speaks in a lowered voice.*

PARBURY. What was that last?

MISS WOODWARD. [*Reading in a lowered voice.*] 'What follows in the approval of the unthinking, the applause of the uncultured makes up—'

PARBURY. Yes, yes. Makes up! [*Fidgeting.*] Makes up— [*Vaguely.*] What does it make up? I'm damned if I know what it does make up now. I've forgotten.

MISS WOODWARD. [*Looking up at him with discreet sympathy after a glance at* MRS. PARBURY.] Shall I go back a little?

PARBURY. Please do. Cut the other; it doesn't make up any-thing.

MISS WOODWARD. [*Reading.*] 'One gathers from the complacency of his manner that his iconoclasm is its own reward.'

PARBURY. Thanks. Where's his article?
[MISS WOODWARD *rises, gives him an open magazine, and resumes her seat. After glancing at the magazine, and still in a low voice.*
'His smug self-sufficiency——'   [*Pause.*

MRS. PARBURY. Darling! I can't hear you.
[*Pause.* PARBURY'S *and* MISS WOODWARD'S *eyes meet.*

PARBURY. Can't you, dear? I suppose I must unconsciously have lowered my voice.

MRS. PARBURY. I'm sure you did.

PARBURY. I've an idea. [*Comes behind her and touches her shoulders caressingly.*] Suppose I finish the article quickly and give it to you to read before sending it away?

MRS. PARBURY. Yes, do.
[PARBURY *looks at her, expecting her to move, but she doesn't.*

PARBURY. Well, dear?

MRS. PARBURY. [*Wonderingly.*] Well?

PARBURY. You—you're not going?

MRS. PARBURY. Going!

PARBURY. Yes, dear. I thought——

MRS. PARBURY. [*With great reproach, and looking as if about to cry.*] Clement!
[*She rises, and with trembling hands begins to gather up her fancy work.*

PARBURY. [*Relenting.*] Don't go, dear, unless you wish to.

MRS. PARBURY. [*More tremblingly and tearfully.*] I certainly don't wish to remain where I am unwelcome.

PARBURY. [*Reproachfully.*] Mabel!

MRS. PARBURY. I thought I had a right to be where my husband was—that the privileges of a wife were at least equal to those of a secretary.

PARBURY. [*In a low voice.*] Hush, dear! [*Turns to* MISS WOODWARD, *who has been a secret but attentive observer of the scene.*]

Miss Woodward, would you kindly run what we have done into type? We'll finish presently.

[MISS WOODWARD *rises, takes her notes, and crosses to door. She pauses a moment, shrugs her shoulders, and exit.* PARBURY *passes his arm round* MRS. PARBURY.

MRS. PARBURY. [*Freeing herself.*] Oh, no; you wished me to go, and I'm going.

PARBURY. It doesn't matter now. [*Grimly.*] The article hasn't a million to one chance of being finished this afternoon.

MRS. PARBURY. Why did you send Miss Woodward away?

PARBURY. Frankly?

MRS. PARBURY. Of course.

PARBURY. Because I hate scenes before other people.

MRS. PARBURY. Scenes! What do you mean?

PARBURY. What! Isn't there to be a scene! How splendid!

MRS. PARBURY. I don't understand the humour you are in.

PARBURY. I'm in a capital humour, dear. You've saved me for the moment from a savage attack on the work of a man whom I respect and admire.

MRS. PARBURY. You mean simply that I've interrupted your work. You will not have reason to complain again.

[*Is going.*

PARBURY. Wait, dear.

MRS. PARBURY. No, no. There are things one can't get over. Perhaps you can explain why it is that Miss Woodward's presence doesn't disturb you, while mine does?

PARBURY. Easily. Miss Woodward is a mouse.

MRS. PARBURY. I hate mice!

PARBURY. I mean she is a table—a chair—a desk—a dictionary —a something useful that is always in the right place at the right moment, and yet of whose presence one is pleasantly unconscious. She is a triumph of the negative.

MRS. PARBURY. And I?   [*Her face is not turned to him.*

PARBURY. Positive, my love—quite positive; you bristle with emotions. When you are in the room, one knows it. [MRS.

PARBURY *takes out her handkerchief and begins to cry. Pause.*
PARBURY, *who has gone to desk, looks round inquiringly, then
comes down gently and sees what she is doing. Aside.*] Exactly!

MRS. PARBURY. [*Wiping her eyes.*] Of course I quite understand
now that you don't love me.

PARBURY. [*Comes to her, concealing his impatience.*] But I do! I do!

MRS. PARBURY. Oh no, you don't! When we were first married
you didn't object to my being in the room when you were
working.

PARBURY. I admit I didn't *say* so then; I was younger, and had
more patience and stronger nerves.

MRS. PARBURY. [*Turning to him with a gleam of anger.*] Then
you admit you have always objected to my presence in your
study?

PARBURY. [*Smoothly.*] I admit I have always felt that a writing
man's writing hours are sacred hours.

MRS. PARBURY. They shouldn't be sacred from his wife.

PARBURY. [*Gently.*] They should be sacred *to* his wife, dear.
[*Slight pause.*] If you were a writing woman you would
understand what I mean.

MRS. PARBURY. I'm sure I'm very sorry I'm not a genius, but
you understood that when you married me, didn't you?

PARBURY. Yes, darling, I quite understood that! [*He appears to
say this quite unconsciously.* MRS. PARBURY *turns to him deeply
offended; then suddenly goes up to leave the room. He quickly
meets her. Taking her hands.*] I only knew you were the best
little woman in the world!

MRS. PARBURY. [*Struggling to free her hands.*] Don't, please.
I'm going!

PARBURY. Where?

MRS. PARBURY. To send Miss Woodward to you, since you
prefer her society to mine.

PARBURY. But I tell you I'm scarcely conscious of the girl's
existence; anyway, it was you who brought her here. You
may remember I proposed having a male secretary.

MRS. PARBURY. Yes; to make a companion of at my expense. You were always a man's man! If I had had more experience I would have known that by the host of men friends you had when we married.

PARBURY. [*Cheerily.*] I haven't them now, dear.

MRS. PARBURY. You mean—that I—[*Struggling to release her hands.*] You are most brutal. Let me go!

PARBURY. Not while you are angry, dear.
  [*Gently forces her into a chair. There is another slight pause. She is certainly angry, but she doesn't attempt to leave the chair. He looks down at her, and lays a hand lightly on her hair.*

MRS. PARBURY. [*Brushing his hand away.*] Please don't do that. I am not a child! [PARBURY *takes a chair and sits next to her. Pause.*] Perhaps you will tell me why you have used your superior strength to keep me here against my will?

PARBURY. [*Taking her hand.*] Do you know that I'm very much in love with you?

MRS. PARBURY. You in love with me! You don't know what love is! All you feel at this moment is the sort of insolent pity the strong have for the weak.

PARBURY. You weak, darling! Oh, come! You know better than that! You can't be unconscious of your power!

MRS. PARBURY. I really don't understand you.

PARBURY. I only meant to remind you that after all you do always get your own way. I'm really very glad, for I'm sure your way must always be the best way. Oh, the power and determination of this little hand! [*Holding her hand.*] Do let me, with the deepest submission, kiss 'The Mailed Fist.'
  [*He kisses her hand.*

MRS. PARBURY. As it pleases you to be rude to me I shall try to bear it patiently.

PARBURY. I don't mean to be rude. It's my unfortunate way of putting things. I kissed your hand because of the real tender love my heart holds for you, and for the same reason I put back this dear, rebellious little lock of hair which has escaped from over your ear. And what a perfect ear! It's as delicate and fragile as a shell, and it's just the daintiest pink possible.

MRS. PARBURY. [*Mollified.*] I know my ears are all right, though I think you are making fun of me.

PARBURY. I think I'm making love to you.

MRS. PARBURY. [*Suddenly taking one of his hands in hers.*] Oh, if you only loved me in the way I love you!

PARBURY. I love you in a most excellent way.

MRS. PARBURY. But it's different—you don't understand. I love to breathe the air you breathe, to hear your voice even when it's dictating a dry article, to listen to your footsteps, to watch the changing expressions on your face. I live by the warmth your life gives me; you don't grudge me that, do you?

PARBURY. Why, of course not, darling!

MRS. PARBURY. I love this room because it is yours; the surroundings are yours; the atmosphere is yours. When you are out——

PARBURY. [*Gently patting her hand.*] Which is not often, dear.

MRS. PARBURY. When you are out I always stay here, because here I get most of you; even the thin odour of cigarette smoke is dear to me. Smoke now.

PARBURY. Shall I?

MRS. PARBURY. [*Gives him a cigarette from his case on table, and lights it.*] That's delightful! [*Sniffs the smoke.*] But only because it's you! I used to detest tobacco.

PARBURY. [*Smiling.*] You dear!   [*Puts his arm around her.*

MRS. PARBURY. You understand a little now, don't you?
[*Putting her head on his shoulder.*

PARBURY. Perfectly!

MRS. PARBURY. And you are not angry any more?

PARBURY. Was I angry?

MRS. PARBURY. Horribly!

PARBURY. I'm sorry.

MRS. PARBURY. Not vexed about the article?

PARBURY. Bother the article. I knew it hadn't a million to one chance.

MRS. PARBURY. And it doesn't matter?

PARBURY. Not in the least!

MRS. PARBURY. Then we may have tea in here?

PARBURY. Rather! Let's go the pace.

MRS. PARBURY. [*Goes to him, standing before him, her hands by her sides.*] Kiss me! [*He kisses her. She throws her arms round him and whispers to him. He whispers a word in reply. They both laugh slightly, and he playfully pinches her cheek.*] Brute! [*She smooths her hair and goes to door; blows him a kiss, to which he responds. Exit.*

PARBURY. [*Standing for moment, a whimsical look on his face.*] Dear little woman! What a pity she cries so much! [*Goes to desk and turns over pages of magazine, still continuing his thought.*] What a pity! What a pity!

    Enter MISS WOODWARD, *carrying loose type-written* MS.
Oh, thanks.

MISS WOODWARD. Do you wish to finish the article now?

PARBURY. Impossible! Tea will be taken here in a few minutes.

MISS WOODWARD. [*With a touch of indignant surprise.*] Here? Oh, I beg your pardon.

PARBURY. Not at all. I said here. [MISS WOODWARD *permits a slight groan to escape her.*] Eh?

MISS WOODWARD. Nothing; I didn't speak.
    [*Sits and bends over desk.* PARBURY *looks at her suddenly and keenly as though he had never noticed her before. Slight pause. She arranges papers at desk. He is leaning against the mantelpiece.*

PARBURY. Do you know, Miss Woodward, I believe you are more disappointed about that article than I am.

MISS WOODWARD. I was certainly very interested.

PARBURY. Why?

MISS WOODWARD. It was so strong! I admire strength.

PARBURY. [*Smiling.*] You are not then quite the machine one gets into the habit of imagining one's secretary to be?

MISS WOODWARD. [*Meeting his eye calmly and fearlessly for a moment.*] I should like to be what you wish me to be.

PARBURY. [*A little disconcerted.*] Humph! [*Stands with his hands in his pockets looking at her, while she is busy at the desk. The door suddenly opens.* PARBURY *starts almost violently.* MRS. PARBURY *puts her head into the room.*

MRS. PARBURY. Darling, I've got rid of a would-be intruder for you. I thought you'd like to know.

PARBURY. Thank you, dear; who was it?

MRS. PARBURY. A horrid person named Gunning. There's the creature's card. [*Throws card into room on to chair by door.*] I knew you'd be pleased, darling. Tea in five minutes. [*Exit.*

PARBURY. Gunning! Not George surely? [*Quickly gets the card.*] It is! My dear old friend; I wouldn't miss seeing him for worlds! [*Rushes to window, opens it, and bends out.*] Why, there he is, going across the lawn! [*Shouts.*] George! George! Hi! Gunning!   [*Runs off.*

GUNNING. [*Outside, very distant.*] Hullo, Clement!

PARBURY. [*Outside.*] Wait a moment, old chap!
    [MISS WOODWARD *goes up and looks through window, comes down, and with her handkerchief carefully dusts a photograph of* PARBURY *which stands on book-case; then looks at the portrait of* MRS. PARBURY, *shrugs her shoulders slightly, returns to desk.*

Enter PARBURY *and* GUNNING, *through window.*

PARBURY. Quite a mistake! I assure you, my dear fellow, my wife gave orders that I was not to be disturbed, thinking I was engaged upon an important piece of work.

GUNNING. [*Looking at* MISS WOODWARD.] Won't you present me to Mrs. ——

PARBURY. [*Hastily.*] To Miss Woodward, my secretary— certainly! Mr. Gunning, Miss Woodward. [*They bow.* MISS WOODWARD *moves to go.*] Don't go, Miss Woodward. You might very kindly get rid of some of this correspondence for me. [*Takes a bundle of letters from desk.*] 'Dear Sir—I would esteem it a great favour if you would send me your photograph, together with your autograph.' [*Throws letter aside, and reads another.*] 'My dear Sir—I have read with the deepest interest and the highest pleasure your deservedly successful novel, "The Overthrow of Harvey Masterton," and feel convinced that if you knew the story of my life—.' No one can deal with these people like Miss Woodward.

GUNNING. [*Taking off his gloves.*] What is your method, Miss Woodward?

MISS WOODWARD. It is Mr. Parbury's—perfect civility, consistent with finality. [*Sits at desk and writes letters.*

GUNNING. Excellent! I suppose being a popular author entails a lot of correspondence?

PARBURY. Awful!

GUNNING. For my part, my correspondence is practically nil.

PARBURY. I have noticed it with pain.

GUNNING. Oh, I'd have written to you, but what was the good of it? I'm not literary, and I'm not married.

PARBURY. And so you've kept away for five years.

GUNNING. About that.

PARBURY. Five years and three months—for I've been married all that time, and you neither came to the wedding nor called on me afterwards.

GUNNING. I was discreet.

PARBURY. Discreet! Damned unfriendly, I call it, considering the years we had been pals.

GUNNING. Well, the rest of our old set stuck to you, anyway. What has become of them? Take Wybrow, for instance—an awful good chap.

PARBURY. Wybrow, Wybrow—what *has* become of Wybrow?

GUNNING. Never comes here, eh?

PARBURY. Well, he did a few times some years ago, but——

GUNNING. I understand—a little too Bohemian.

PARBURY. [*Quickly.*] Not for me, George, I assure you.

GUNNING. No, no, of course not, my dear chap. Exit Bohemian Wybrow. Then there was Carson—one of the best.

PARBURY. [*Warmly.*] Wasn't he a good fellow?

GUNNING. Capital! Where is he?

PARBURY. Married, you know.

GUNNING. So I heard. You meet constantly, of course?

PARBURY. No, we met them at Brighton one winter some years ago, but I don't think our wives quite—you understand, don't you?

GUNNING. Yes, yes, I understand. You dropped the Carsons. But Burleigh——

PARBURY. Burleigh—ah!   [*Laughs.*

GUNNING. There was a great spirit if you like. He was your best man.

PARBURY. Yes; he gave me this watch.

GUNNING. Which you still wear. Touching constancy! When did you see him last?

PARBURY. Wait a moment. What is all this interrogation for?

GUNNING. Idle curiosity if you like—study of life if you like. Come, out with it, when did you last have dear old Tom Burleigh to dinner?

PARBURY. [*Almost defiantly.*] The day we returned from our honeymoon.   [*Slightly awkward pause.*

GUNNING. [*Musingly.*] About five years and six weeks ago.

PARBURY. Of course, I see a lot of him at the clubs. That is to say, I used to when I was still a club man.

GUNNING. Which now you are not?

PARBURY. Which now I am not. What does a man want with a club when he has a home of his own?

GUNNING. Excellent sentiment, but neither the sentiment nor the words are your own, Clement. [*Their eyes meet and they burst into laughter.*] I know, I know; 'and what does a man want with men friends when he has a wife of his own,' and 'the husband's old friends are the wife's worst enemies,' and 'what I say about clubs is, down with them!'   [*Laughs.*

PARBURY. [*Suddenly serious.*] What the devil are you laughing at, George? You don't presume——

GUNNING. I—why, of course not, my dear chap. Only now you see how wise I was not to intrude after your marriage, not to wait for my congé as the other poor boys did! I knew something.

PARBURY. You always did, you brute! I believe you were born knowing something. But seriously, [*Lowers his voice.*] George, I assure you she's the best little woman in the world!

GUNNING. Why, of course; it would be impious to suggest otherwise. [*Exit* MISS WOODWARD. *His eyes follow her off.*] A perfect wife, and a charming secretary! You're a lucky fellow, Clement!

PARBURY. Is Miss Woodward charming? On my word, I hadn't noticed it, but I'm in love with my wife, you see.

GUNNING. Of course you would be the last to discover that your secretary was personally pleasing.

PARBURY. You're a sinister scoundrel, George, and coarse to a fault. Now, tell me what you've been doing all these years— shedding your illusions apparently.

GUNNING. I've had none to lose since I grew up. I got rid of mine about the time of measles and whooping-cough.

PARBURY. It's a pity.

GUNNING. Not at all. One can't attain the proper philosophical attitude towards life while one nourishes illusions; one can never gain perspective.

PARBURY. Great man! How beautifully you talk! I suppose you have quite a nice thing in perspectives about with you now.

GUNNING. Pretty well.

PARBURY. So much for the journey of the soul. What of the body? Where have you been?

GUNNING. Round the world twice since I saw you.

PARBURY. What did you see on the other side?

GUNNING. Just what one sees on this side; there is always a man—and a woman.

PARBURY. I know you were adventuring in Upper India last year, for the papers were full of a rather fine thing you did— saved a lot of miserable lives—an ordinary, manly, commonplace, heroic, English sort of thing.

GUNNING. Oh, don't mention that; one was carried away by impulse.

PARBURY. And so we keep our impulses even when we lose our illusions; I'm glad of that anyway. [*Then he comes behind* GUNNING's *chair, takes him by the shoulder, and shakes him.*] Old fool! I can't help liking you as much as ever!

GUNNING. [*Looking up with genuine pleasure.*] Really?

PARBURY. Honestly!

GUNNING. [*Rises*; *puts his hands on* PARBURY's *shoulders.*] Well, I'm glad, because I've often been weak enough to regret not seeing you. As for your literary successes, I suppose I ought to congratulate you; but I always knew you'd be a great man, because you never bored me.

PARBURY. [*Drily.*] Thanks so much. Now tell me how you found me.

GUNNING. By means of the illustrated press—interview with Mr. Clement Parbury—copyright. The author of the 'Overthrow of Harvey something' at his pretty retreat at Hampstead—copyright. Snapshot of Mr. Parbury at work—copyright. View of the study from the garden—view of the garden from the study—copyright.

PARBURY. Shut up! You make me blush.

GUNNING. Forgive me—it's only envy. It's the envious people who call this a vulgar age, I suppose.

Enter EVANS; *places occasional table for tea in front of sofa, and exit.*

PARBURY. Now you are to see my wife. How do you imagine her? Large, I suppose, with huge hands and feet and a beetling brow?

GUNNING. I'm content to wait.

Re-enter EVANS *with tea service.*

PARBURY. When you have had tea, you will go away to dress. You will return here to dinner at eight.

GUNNING. I think not.

PARBURY. One moment. You will probably meet only my wife's

father, Colonel Armitage, and your dinner will be a fairly plain one, but I promise that your palate will not be outraged.

GUNNING. I really think not, old man. I remember the fate of old Burleigh. And I never even gave you a watch.

PARBURY. George, you hurt me. [*Slight pause.*] Then you refuse?

GUNNING. I make conditions.

PARBURY. What are they?

GUNNING. That you come yachting with me from to-morrow till the end of the week. I've hired a charming little twenty-tonner, one after your own heart—that is, if your heart or my memory hasn't entirely changed.

PARBURY. [*Enthusiastic.*] Splendid! There's nothing I should like so much, and I've no special work on hand just now.

GUNNING. Then it's agreed.

PARBURY. Certainly.

GUNNING. Good; we'll drink of the Cuvée '36, brush up our swearing vocabulary, and I'll teach you to gain perspective!

PARBURY. [*His face suddenly falling.*] Oh, the deuce!

GUNNING. What's the matter? What are you afraid of?

PARBURY. Of nothing in the world.

GUNNING. [*Slapping him on the back.*] Hero!

Enter MRS. PARBURY, *wearing a bright smile, which fades when she sees* GUNNING.

PARBURY. Mabel, I want to present you to my dear old friend, George Gunning. My wife, George.

MRS. PARBURY. How do you do? I'm very pleased.
[*She gives him simultaneously a cold smile and a stiff hand-shake.*

GUNNING. I'm very delighted to meet Clement's wife.

MRS. PARBURY. You'll let me give you some tea?

GUNNING. Thank you. [*Aside to* PARBURY.] She's charming!
[PARBURY *digs him in the ribs.*

MRS. PARBURY. [*Handing* GUNNING *tea-cup.*] I've given you no sugar.

GUNNING. I'll take one piece.

Enter MISS WOODWARD, *with* MS., *which she hands to* PARBURY.

PARBURY. Thank you.   [*He reads and signs letters.*

MRS. PARBURY. Clement, come for your tea.

PARBURY. In one moment, dear.

MRS. PARBURY. Miss Woodward, you will take tea?

MISS WOODWARD. Thank you, yes.

GUNNING. [*To* MRS. PARBURY.] Allow me.
    [*Takes* MISS WOODWARD'*s cup to her, and offers her bread and butter, &c.*

MISS WOODWARD. Thank you.

PARBURY. You've often heard me speak of Gunning, Mabel; we were at Cambridge together.

MRS. PARBURY. Oh yes, I remember. [*To* GUNNING.] You were very great friends?

GUNNING. Inseparables!

PARBURY. I should say so!

MRS. PARBURY. [*Uneasily.*] Indeed!

PARBURY. [*Comes over and takes his tea.*] You see, Gunning had been my fag at Harrow, and my ill-treatment of him inspired a dog-like devotion. [*To* MISS WOODWARD.] Let me take your cup. [*Adds in a lower voice.*] I've an idea!
    [MISS WOODWARD *goes to desk;* PARBURY *follows her.*

GUNNING. Let me. [*Assists* MRS. PARBURY *with the tea service.*

PARBURY. [*To* MISS WOODWARD *in a low voice.*] I think I can finish the article in three sentences. Take your notes into the other room; I'll join you in a moment.
    [MISS WOODWARD *gathers her notes and exit.*

MRS. PARBURY. [*Pouring out a fresh cup of tea for* GUNNING.] But of course it's not in the nature of things that college friendships, however strong, can last always. Time estranges, doesn't it, Mr. Gunning, and fate drives people into different —well, different ways of life, doesn't it? Some men marry soon. Are you married, Mr. Gunning?

GUNNING. Alas, no, Mrs. Parbury!

PARBURY. He has too much respect for your sex, dear. Forgive me for three minutes.   [*Exit.*

MRS. PARBURY. Not married? Well, I should have thought——

GUNNING. That I'm old enough to know better. I admit it.

MRS. PARBURY. Well, I was going to say that in marriage a man changes so much. He becomes more—more——

GUNNING. [*Gently.*] Respectable?

MRS. PARBURY. Well, I wasn't going to say quite that; though, as you suggest it, no doubt it is true. I was going to say more responsible. He enters into a broader, a fuller life; he gains in nobility, don't you think?

GUNNING. [*Amused.*] Oh, no doubt. Clement has improved enormously!

MRS. PARBURY. I'm so glad you recognize that. You may smoke, Mr. Gunning, if you care to.

GUNNING. Thank you. I'll steal one of Clement's cigarettes if I may.   [*Takes cigarette from box on desk.*

MRS. PARBURY. Of course Clement was always good and strong and clever. It only wanted marriage to—to——

GUNNING. To perfect him?

MRS. PARBURY. Well, I was going to say to complete him; but it comes to the same thing, doesn't it?

GUNNING. Quite, quite!

MRS. PARBURY. I found my happiness when I married Clement.

GUNNING. You had been looking for it?

MRS. PARBURY. Of course; isn't that every woman's duty?

GUNNING. Yes, yes; and every man's.

MRS. PARBURY. [*Less confidently.*] Well, yes, I should think so.

GUNNING. And one's happiness once found is worth fighting for?

MRS. PARBURY. [*Firmly.*] Worth fighting very hard for!

GUNNING. [*Drily.*] Of course. [*Aside.*] Poor Burleigh!

MRS. PARBURY. You, I suppose, have never met a woman who could make you happy?

GUNNING. I have never met a woman whom I was sure of being able to make happy.

MRS. PARBURY. [*Slightly embarrassed.*] Oh!

GUNNING. And, anyway, the state of marriage has always appeared to me to be a state of warfare.

MRS. PARBURY. Mr. Gunning, you little know——

GUNNING. I admit the case of you and Clement to be an exceptional one. I'm talking of ordinary cases—the average marriage; there you will find, according to my observation, an endless war—a war of self-interests, a war of opposing emotions, a war of irreconcilable nervous organisations——

MRS. PARBURY. Oh, Mr. Gunning!

GUNNING. Viewed from the hill-tops rather a pitiful sort of war, in which can be won neither the full joys of love nor the complete glories of battle.

MRS. PARBURY. Oh, Mr. Gunning!

GUNNING. I remain single, Mrs. Parbury, quite without happiness—except in the reflection that I am neither an oppressor exercising a daily tyranny, nor a slave rightly struggling to be free.

MRS. PARBURY. Of course I don't in the least agree with you. [*The telephone bell rings.*] There's some one on the telephone—forgive me. [*Goes to telephone.*] Are you there? Yes—who are you? The article—yes—no, you can't have it to-day—no, it hasn't a million to one chance of being finished. [*To* GUNNING, *with a smile.*] That's Clement's slang, not mine. [*Again into telephone.*] What?

Enter PARBURY *and* MISS WOODWARD.

I say it hasn't a million to one chance of being finished.

PARBURY. What? Who is it?

MRS. PARBURY. It's the *Saturday Sentinel.*

PARBURY. But my dear, the article is finished. [*Rushes to telephone.* MISS WOODWARD *and* GUNNING *are laughing secretly.* MRS. PARBURY *stands rather confused.*] Hullo! Hullo! Are you there? [*Rings violently.*] Hullo—oh, is that you, Jackson? What's the matter? [*Rather a long pause. He smiles while listening.*] No, no, not at all, my dear chap. What was said was, 'It's a million to one you'll have the copy in half an hour'—eh? Yes, those were the very words . . . no, quite a mistake, you don't listen properly. A messenger has just gone off in a cab with it. What? Yes. [*Laughs.*] All right. Good-bye.

MRS. PARBURY. I really don't know what there is to laugh at, Miss Woodward.

MISS WOODWARD. I was only smiling at the messenger in the cab.   [*Folds MS. and puts it in envelope.*

PARBURY. Yes, send some one at once, please, Miss Woodward.
                                                  [*Exit* MISS WOODWARD.

MRS. PARBURY. It wasn't my fault, dear. You know you did use those words.

PARBURY. My fault entirely. [*Aside to* GUNNING.] Have you told her?

GUNNING. What?

PARBURY. About the yachting?

GUNNING. Why, of course not. That's your affair, my dear fellow.

PARBURY. [*His hand on* GUNNING's *shoulder.*] Mabel, dear, we're going yachting for a few days. I think I want a little change.

MRS. PARBURY. [*Coming towards them, brightly.*] Oh, what a good idea! When do we go? [PARBURY *and* GUNNING *look at each other.*] Are you coming, Mr. Gunning?
    [PARBURY *presses* GUNNING *forward.* GUNNING *looks round at* PARBURY *reproachfully.*

GUNNING. [*Embarrassed.*] Well, it's my yacht, Mrs. Parbury, but she's very small—only a little tub of a thing, and— [*Looks at his watch.*] By Jove! I'll never be able to dress and get back for dinner if I don't hurry. [*Gets his hat and gloves.*]

I need only say *au revoir*; don't trouble, Clement, I'll find my way out—*au revoir*!

        [*Exit.* MRS. PARBURY, *who is puzzled, sits on sofa.*

PARBURY. [*Calling after* GUNNING.] Dinner at eight, remember.

GUNNING. [*Outside.*] All right!

PARBURY. Capital fellow, George Gunning!

MRS. PARBURY. What does he mean by a little tub of a thing? Surely we're not——

PARBURY. No, dear, certainly not. You're quite right. I wouldn't think of letting you run any risks.

MRS. PARBURY. Then we're not going?

PARBURY. No, dear; that is to say, Gunning and I are going.

MRS. PARBURY. [*Rising, aghast.*] Without me?

PARBURY. Only for a few days, of course.   [*Laughing feebly.*

MRS. PARBURY. You are not serious?

PARBURY. Quite!   [*His laugh becomes feebler.*

MRS. PARBURY. But—but you never go away without me!

PARBURY. I haven't hitherto, but——

MRS. PARBURY. Well?   [*Appears about to cry.*

PARBURY. I've been working very hard, you know, lately. I feel I want a change.

MRS. PARBURY. [*Tearfully.*] It doesn't occur to you that I might want a change.

PARBURY. Well, have one, dear. Aunt Martha would be delighted to have you at Oaklands.

MRS. PARBURY. I don't want to go to Aunt Martha. How would you like to go to Aunt Martha?

PARBURY. [*Suppressing a groan.*] What is it you *do* want?

MRS. PARBURY. [*Quickly.*] You! I want to be with you! It's very simple—it's not asking very much. If you don't like my being with you, why did you marry me?

        [*Taking out her handkerchief.*

PARBURY. Now, dear, please don't cry! [*Aside.*] If she does,

I'm done for! [*Aloud.*] It's only common sense that you can't go knocking about with a couple of men in a tub of a boat.

MRS. PARBURY. Of course I quite know now that you don't love me.   [*Bursts into tears. Sits on sofa.*

PARBURY. [*With real irritation.*] Oh, damn it! 'Pon my soul, you make me almost hate——

MRS. PARBURY. Of course you hate me. Your old friend has done that for me. You are breaking my heart!

PARBURY. [*Who has recovered control of his temper and resumed his natural bantering tone.*] Not at all, dear. [*Sits at his desk and affects to be busy.*] I was only going to say that I hated—now, what the deuce was it I hated? Oh, I know—to see a woman cry. I do think a woman is wise who does her crying in private, and yet—I wonder—they know best—millions to one they know best. I must write something about it.

MRS. PARBURY. [*Rises, wiping her eyes, her back to him.*] Of course, you're going all the same?

PARBURY. [*Affecting great pre-occupation.*] Going? Going where?

MRS. PARBURY. With Mr. Gunning.
                    [*Pause. She continues to cry gently.*

PARBURY. Gunning—Gunning! Who's Gunning? Oh—George—yachting, you mean! Not I! I'm staying here.

MRS. PARBURY. [*Comes towards him gladly, her arms extended.*] Clement!

PARBURY. Eh? Oh, forgive me for a few minutes.   [*Writes.*

MRS. PARBURY. [*Reproachfully.*] I was only going to kiss you.

PARBURY. [*Writing.*] All right, dear—presently—presently, there's a dear girl! [MRS. PARBURY *has a slow silent exit, looking back at him. He doesn't look up, but goes on writing. When the door closes, he puts down his pen.*] Oh, the tyranny of it! The tyranny of it!   [*Slow curtain.*

ACT II

SCENE. *The same as Act I. Evening after dinner, the same day.
The room is lighted with lamps, but as it is a still warm evening, the
curtains are not drawn over the glass door which leads into the
garden and is open.*

Enter EVANS. *He places cigars and cigarettes on occasional table,
and lights a small spirit cigar-lamp. Exit. Voices of ladies and
a ripple of laughter heard from the drawing-room, and for a
moment the sound made by fingers running lightly and
irresponsibly over the keys of the piano. Enter* COLONEL
ARMITAGE, *followed by* GUNNING *and* PARBURY. ARMI-
TAGE *goes to mantelpiece.* GUNNING *selects the easiest chair
in the room.* PARBURY *goes to occasional table.* ARMITAGE *is
a well-preserved man of sixty-five, very carefully dressed—
something of an elderly dandy.*

PARBURY. Cigarette or cigar, George?

GUNNING. Thanks, I have a cigarette.
[*Takes one from his case and lights it.*

PARBURY. Colonel?

ARMITAGE. Thank you, I'll take a cigar. I think, however, I'll
—er—smoke it in the garden. Mabel's limited appreciation
of tobacco——

PARBURY. Oh, Mabel won't mind—she's quite educated.

ARMITAGE. Not beyond the cigarette, I fancy.
[*He strolls to the glass door, lights his cigar, and steps out.
For a few moments he is still seen; then he wanders away.*

GUNNING. Nice old chap, your father-in-law.

PARBURY. Isn't he? I'm quite fond of him. [*Pause. They smoke
in silence.*] What are you thinking of?

GUNNING. I'm not thinking. I'm digesting. I had an excellent
dinner.

Enter EVANS *with coffee, &c.* GUNNING *takes coffee.*

EVANS. Cognac, sir, or green chartreuse?

GUNNING. Cognac. [*He takes glass.*] Thank you.

PARBURY. Colonel, here's your coffee.

ARMITAGE. [*Outside.*] I'll have it out here, if I may.

PARBURY. Serve Colonel Armitage's coffee in the garden.

EVANS. Yes, sir. [*Exit.*

GUNNING. I've wired for the champagne.

PARBURY. [*Uneasily.*] Oh, yes! [*Slight pause.*

GUNNING. I notice the glass keeps up well.

PARBURY. Really? Good! [*Slight pause.*

GUNNING. Yes, we ought to have capital weather.

PARBURY. Capital! [*He is very embarrassed.*] If it doesn't rain it'll be pretty—er—fine.

GUNNING. [*Favours him with a slow stare.*] What's the matter, old man?

PARBURY. Nothing in the world. Why?

GUNNING. Oh, it doesn't matter. But I think the change will do you good. [*Slight pause.*] By the way, would to-morrow afternoon suit you for a start?

PARBURY. [*Standing with his back to the fireplace, looking up at the ceiling.*] I'm not going, old man.

GUNNING. [*Indifferently.*] Oh!

Re-enter EVANS *from garden, and exit. Silence till he has gone.*

PARBURY. Well, you don't seem surprised.

GUNNING. [*Effecting a yawn.*] I never permit myself to be surprised.

PARBURY. Or disappointed.

GUNNING. Oh yes, I own I'm disappointed. I looked for a good time for a few days. You were the only one of the old lot available, and you were the best of them. I can't bear the new lot. They wear strange colours, drop their 'g's,' and get on one's nerves.

PARBURY. I'm really sorry, George.

GUNNING. Don't bother. One simply goes alone. [*Discreetly.*] The calls of business are often irresistible.

PARBURY. Don't rot. You know what the situation is.

GUNNING. Mine is one of those poor intelligences that never know without information.

PARBURY. I'll supply it.

GUNNING. Don't, if it matters.

PARBURY. I will, though it does matter. [*Grimly.*] My wife wept.

GUNNING. Unanswerable argument.

PARBURY. Quite. George, what the devil is a man to do?

GUNNING. I knew a man who once interfered between a husband and wife who were disagreeing. The husband and wife each got a black eye. The man got two.

PARBURY. You might at least talk.

GUNNING. Oh, certainly.

PARBURY. You know the situation.

GUNNING. Well, if one dare say so, I fancy you are suffering from the tyranny of a fascinating egoism.

PARBURY. I'm suffering from the tyranny of tears.

GUNNING. What I can't understand is how a man of your strong nature arrived where you are.

PARBURY. I'll make an effort to tell you. To begin with, I suppose I'm fairly good-natured.

GUNNING. Oh yes!

PARBURY. Or say, if you like, of indolent habit, which after all often passes for the same thing. Then of course I was in love— I am still. One drifted. It's so easy to give way in little things—really not unpleasant when you're in love. And then there's one's work, which fills the mind and makes the little things appear smaller than they are. I say one drifted.

GUNNING. Sometimes, if I know you, you rebelled. What then?

PARBURY. [*Promptly.*] Tears! And over such absurdly paltry things! Oh, the farcical tragedy of it all! I wished to go shooting for a few days. Tears! I fancied dining and spending the evening with an old chum. Tears! I would go on a walking tour for a week. Tears! Some one would ask me for three days' hunting. Tears! Tears, you understand, always on hand. Tears—tears—tears *ad*—— [*Pulling himself up.*] No.

GUNNING. [*Quietly.*] No—not *ad nauseam.*

PARBURY. No, that would be too low a thing to say.

GUNNING. Do you know, Clement, I really like you tremendously.

PARBURY. Thanks, old man. Have some more brandy?

GUNNING. No thanks. [*Pause.*] Don't stop. I'm interested.

PARBURY. That's all. I drifted, almost unconsciously, right up to to-day, for all the world like the man in the moral storybook one read as a child on Sundays, who drifted in his boat on the Erie River towards Niagara. To-night I'm conscious— I'm awake—I can feel the water gliding along the boat's keel. I can see Niagara. I don't like it. What the devil's one to do?

GUNNING. Get out and walk. [*Pause. They smoke.*

PARBURY. Of course, I shall change it all. I must, but it will be beastly work.

GUNNING. Beastly. When do you begin?

PARBURY. When occasion serves. I can't go back over this yachting business. I've said I'm not going.

GUNNING. Quite right. [*Slight pause.*

PARBURY. Oh, if the *exigeant* women only knew—if they only knew!

Enter ARMITAGE *from garden.*

Talking of brandies, this is Hennessy '63. Have some, Colonel?

ARMITAGE. Perhaps half a glass. [*Takes brandy and sits.*

Enter MRS. PARBURY *from drawing-room.*

MRS. PARBURY. Miss Woodward and I are boring each other. Shall we come to you, or will you come to us? [GUNNING *and* ARMITAGE *rise.*] There, the question's answered.

Enter MISS WOODWARD. *She goes to the desk.*

GUNNING. [*To* MRS. PARBURY.] You were playing the piano just now?

MRS. PARBURY. Yes, but I play wretchedly nowadays. I gave up practising when we married.

GUNNING. One should never give up an accomplishment.

ARMITAGE. You used to play charmingly, Mabel.

MRS. PARBURY. You thought so, dear, and that was enough for me. Why don't we sit in the garden? It's a perfect night. [ARMITAGE *strolls off to garden.* MRS. PARBURY *goes to* PARBURY *and takes his arm. In a low voice.*] Are you still angry?

PARBURY. [*As they go out to the garden.*] I angry with you! Nonsense. [*He pats her hand.*] Poor little woman! Poor little woman! [*Exeunt.*

GUNNING. Are you not coming, Miss Woodward?

MISS WOODWARD. No, thank you. I have some work to do.

GUNNING. But you seem to me to be always working.

MISS WOODWARD. I needn't, you know. I do it because I like it.

GUNNING. What are you doing now?

MISS WOODWARD. Correcting proof sheets of a new novel. It will save Mr. Parbury the trouble of doing it to-morrow.

GUNNING. I wanted you to talk to me.

MISS WOODWARD. What about?

GUNNING. Yourself.

MISS WOODWARD. I'm not interesting.

GUNNING. On the contrary.

MISS WOODWARD. What do you wish to know?

GUNNING. All about you. May I?

MISS WOODWARD. Will you go away and leave me to work if I tell you?

GUNNING. Yes.

MISS WOODWARD. [*Putting down her pen, and resting her cheek on her hand.*] I'm the thirteenth daughter of a parson. Why my parents had thirteen daughters, I don't know, but I suppose it was because they are very poor. We were all given the names of flowers—Rose, Lily, Tulip, Mignonette— I can't remember them all—but Hyacinth fell to my lot. Why

we were called after flowers, I don't know; but I suppose it
was because we are none of us the least like flowers. My eldest
sister married my father's curate. I don't know why, but I
suppose it was because she came first and is the plainest in the
family.

GUNNING. [*Laughing.*] Yes, well?

MISS WOODWARD. [*Speaking in an even, emotionless way.*] Two
other of my sisters run a Kindergarten, and one other is a
governess. Personally I would rather be a domestic servant.
The others remain at home, help in the house, and await
husbands. I fear they will wait in vain, because there are so
many women in our part of the country and so few men. For
my part I seized an early opportunity of learning shorthand
and typewriting—and—well, here I am. Now you know the
story of my life.   [*She returns to her work.*

GUNNING. I'm afraid it was deuced impertinent of me to ask.

MISS WOODWARD. Not at all—only eminently man-like.
                            [*Pause. She works; he smokes.*

GUNNING. And so you have found your happiness.

MISS WOODWARD. Oh no. I've only just started to look for it.

GUNNING. Oh ho! Ambitious!

MISS WOODWARD. Very. Have you ever been poor?

GUNNING. Yes, at one time—had to pawn things.

MISS WOODWARD. I mean being one of fifteen in a family—
large inferior joints to last for days—hot, cold, hashed,
minced, shepherd's pie—[GUNNING *shudders at this.*]—too
much potatoes—too much boiled rice—too much bread and
dripping—too much weak tea—too much polishing up of
things not worth polishing up—too much darning on too
little material—and for ever giving thanks out of all proportion to the benefits received. I wish some one would write
the history of a hat or a frock—I mean a hat or a frock that
has marched steadily and sullenly under various guises
through an entire family such as ours, from the mother down
to the youngest girl. What might be written of the thoughts
that had been thought under such a hat, or of the hearts that
had felt under such a frock!

GUNNING. Why don't you write the story?

MISS WOODWARD. Perhaps some day I shall try. [*Returns to her work.*] In the meantime you ought to go. You promised, you know. You have nothing more to learn. I don't think in all my life I've talked so much about myself as I have to you, a stranger.   [*She keeps her eyes on her work.*

GUNNING. You have been engagingly frank. I do hope I shall have another opportunity——

MISS WOODWARD. Not at all likely, Mr. Gunning. [*Pause.*] Good-night.

[*Still without looking up.* GUNNING *looks at her, goes up to the window, turns, looks at her again.*

GUNNING. Good-night, Miss Woodward.

[*Exit to garden.* MISS WOODWARD *goes on with her work for a few moments; then drops her face on her hand in her favourite attitude.*

MISS WOODWARD. Rather than go back, I—well, I know I'd rather die. [*She looks over the pages for a moment or two, then yawns slightly; she gathers her pages together, and places a paperweight over them.*] That will have to do. [*She rises, looks off.*] There was actually a man ready to take a sort of languid interest in me. Quite a new experience. [*She takes up* PARBURY*'s photograph and speaks to it.*] You don't take an interest in me of any kind, do you? [*To the photograph.*] You never will, and I don't think I want you to. But I do want to stay near you because you are so strong—

Enter MRS. PARBURY *from garden, carrying* ARMITAGE*'s coffee cup and saucer.*

—and so weak, and so kind, and so foolish.

[MRS. PARBURY *has come down and is watching her unobserved.* MISS WOODWARD *slowly raises the photograph to her lips. The cup and saucer drop from* MRS. PARBURY*'s hand to the floor and are broken.* MISS WOODWARD, *much startled, slowly turns towards* MRS. PARBURY, *and their eyes meet. There is a pause. Suddenly, with a quick movement,* MRS. PARBURY *snatches the photograph from* MISS WOODWARD.

MRS. PARBURY. How dare you! How dare you! [*Long pause.*

She is almost breathless. Then she partly regains self-control.]
What train do you intend taking?

MISS WOODWARD. I don't understand you.

MRS. PARBURY. I mean for your home, of course.

MISS WOODWARD. [*Moves as if she had received a blow, and clasps her hands together.*] I am not going home.

MRS. PARBURY. Oh, indeed you are. You don't suppose you can stay here, do you?

MISS WOODWARD. Why shouldn't I?

MRS. PARBURY. How dare you ask that when I have just caught you in the act of kissing my husband's photograph?

MISS WOODWARD. That was in a moment of abstraction. I wasn't even thinking of Mr. Parbury.

MRS. PARBURY. Oh! And you are the daughter of a clergyman! [*She goes up and fetches the A.B.C. from bookcase, and offers it to* MISS WOODWARD.] Here is the A.B.C.

MISS WOODWARD. [*Turning away.*] I have no use for it just now, thank you.

MRS. PARBURY. Then I'll look you out an early morning train myself. Let me see—[*turning over leaves.*]—Carfields, Worcestershire, isn't it? Here it is. 7.20. I suppose that's too early. 9.35; that will do. Please understand you are to take the 9.35 from Paddington in the morning.

MISS WOODWARD. [*Firmly.*] I shall do nothing of the kind.

MRS. PARBURY. [*Ignoring the remark.*] In the meanwhile there is no necessity that my husband should know the reason of your going. You can make some excuse. I wouldn't have him know for worlds.

MISS WOODWARD. Of course he shall never know from me— but I want you to quite understand, Mrs. Parbury, that I am *not* going to Carfields to-morrow. Rather than go home under the circumstances I would starve in the gutter.

MRS. PARBURY. Well, you must find a lodging till you get other employment. You will have a month's salary, of course. Anyway, I'm determined you leave this house in the morning.

MISS WOODWARD. Is there any real occasion for my leaving?

MRS. PARBURY. Haven't you sufficient delicacy of feeling left
to teach you that?

MISS WOODWARD. [*Warmly.*] I don't think I need lessons of
delicacy of feeling from you. [*Slight pause.*] I'm sorry I said
that, and it means a great deal for me to say I'm sorry. I'm
sorry too about the photograph. I think it all might be
forgotten.

MRS. PARBURY. Forgotten!

MISS WOODWARD. After all, I'm only a girl, and I've worked
very hard for Mr. Parbury. I think you might be more lenient.

MRS. PARBURY. I'm very sorry for you, Miss Woodward, but
I owe a duty to myself and to my husband. You must go in
the morning.   [*She moves to return to garden.*

MISS WOODWARD. Mrs. Parbury!

MRS. PARBURY. Well?

MISS WOODWARD. I suppose I ought to be a lady and go,
because you, the mistress of the house, wish me to. But I
don't feel a bit like a lady just now. I only feel like a poor girl
whose chances in life are being ruined for a very small and
innocent folly.

MRS. PARBURY. Well, what does all this mean?

MISS WOODWARD. [*Fiercely.*] It means that I am in Mr.
Parbury's employment, not yours, and that I will take my
dismissal from him only.

MRS. PARBURY. Oh, I can promise you that. [*She calls into the
garden.*] Clement!

[*Exit to garden.* MISS WOODWARD *throws a hard look after
her. Then her eyes fall on the broken cup and saucer. She stoops,
collects the fragments, and puts them in waste-paper basket.
Then she goes to desk, sits and works on proof sheets as before.*

Enter PARBURY *and* MRS. PARBURY.

PARBURY. Working again, Miss Woodward! Really, you are
indefatigable!

MISS WOODWARD. I'm only correcting these proof sheets.

MRS. PARBURY. No doubt Miss Woodward wishes to finish
the work to-night, as she is leaving to-morrow.

PARBURY. Leaving to-morrow?

MISS WOODWARD. I think Mrs. Parbury is mistaken.

PARBURY. What do you mean, dear?

MRS. PARBURY. I wish her to go.

PARBURY. Why?

MRS. PARBURY. I can't tell you. It is not a thing you would understand. It is simply impossible for her to remain. In her heart she knows I am right.

> [*Slight pause.* PARBURY *goes to* MISS WOODWARD.

PARBURY. Are you satisfied here?

MISS WOODWARD. Perfectly.

PARBURY. You have no wish to go away?

MISS WOODWARD. Not while you wish me to remain.

PARBURY. Do you know why my wife wishes you to go?

MISS WOODWARD. Yes.

PARBURY. Will you kindly tell me?

MISS WOODWARD. I'm sorry I can't. I've promised. But—[*With a look at* MRS. PARBURY.]—I don't think that Mrs. Parbury's reasons are adequate.   [*Pause.* PARBURY *is thoughtful.*

PARBURY. [*To* MRS. PARBURY.] Have you anything more to say?

MRS. PARBURY. I have only to repeat that it is quite impossible for Miss Woodward to stay.

PARBURY. Well, I have made up my mind that there is something very foolish under all this, and I shall not allow it to deprive me of Miss Woodward's services. [MRS. PARBURY *looks surprised.*] I don't mind saying in her presence that she is invaluable to me. I should never be able to replace her. [*Sense of relief on* MISS WOODWARD'*s part.*] Now, come. [*Looking from one to the other.*] What is it? A tiff—a stupid misunderstanding? Oh, you women, why will you fuss about little things? Make it up, do. Think of 'The Roll of Ages.' Shake hands, cry, embrace, kiss, or whatever your pet method may be. Weep if you like, though personally I'd rather you didn't. Anyway, as far as I am concerned, the incident is closed.

> [*He turns to go.*

MRS. PARBURY. [*Doggedly.*] Miss Woodward leaves this house in the morning.

PARBURY. [*Looks at his wife for a moment; then turns to* MISS WOODWARD.] Miss Woodward, would you be so very kind—
[*He opens the door for her with great courtesy.* MISS WOODWARD *bows and exit.*

MRS. PARBURY. [*Turning to him with assumed brightness.*] Now, darling, it will be different. Of course, I couldn't say much before her. You were quite right to be nice and courteous to her now she is going.

PARBURY. But I assure you she is not.
[MRS. PARBURY *takes his arm caressingly.*

MRS. PARBURY. But she is—believe me, she is. Of course, we don't want to be hard on her, and she shall have a month's salary and a strong recommendation.

PARBURY. [*Disengaging his arm.*] My dear Mabel, I absolutely refuse to act in the dark. I hate mysteries. If you care to tell me what all this bother is about, I'll judge for myself what's the right thing to do.   [*Sits on sofa.*

MRS. PARBURY. I can't—it's impossible. There are some things that men can't be trusted to know about. You must leave this matter to me.   [*Sits next to him.*

PARBURY. That I quite decline to do.
[*She again takes his arm and talks rapidly, gradually rather hysterically, towards the end appearing about to cry.*

MRS. PARBURY. Darling, do listen. You don't understand. You have never been like this with me before. I'm sure I'm not asking very much. You can easily get another secretary. Another time you shall have a man one, as you originally wanted to. You were right, dear—you often are. [PARBURY *rises and crosses.* MRS. PARBURY *follows him.*] Darling, do be reasonable. I've been a good wife to you, haven't I? I've always respected your wishes, and not bothered you more than I could help. This is only a little thing, and you must let me have my own way. You must trust me absolutely, dear. You know anything I would do would only be for your good, for you know that I love you. [*She takes out her handkerchief.*] I adore you, darling. You must give way—you must—you must!

PARBURY. [*Stepping back from her.*] If you cry I shall leave the
room.   [*Sits. Begins to write.*

MRS. PARBURY. [*In a low voice.*] I wasn't going to cry.

PARBURY. I'm glad to hear it.

MRS. PARBURY. [*Puts her handkerchief away.*] I had no intention of crying, dear. [PARBURY *still writes. Pause. She
comes to desk.*] Shall I write out an advertisement for you,
dear?

PARBURY. What for?

MRS. PARBURY. For a new secretary—a man.

PARBURY. No. My mind's made up. I shall not change my
secretary.

MRS. PARBURY. Clement!

PARBURY. [*Rises and goes to her.*] Listen, my dear Mabel.
Perhaps I'm a good deal to blame for the pain you are going
to suffer now, and I'm very sorry for you; in many ways you
are the best little woman in the world. I've been weak and
yielding, and I've gradually allowed you to acquire a great
deal more power than you know how to use wisely.

MRS. PARBURY. Really, Clement, you must be raving.

PARBURY. Listen, my dear, listen. What's been the result?
You've taken from me my habits. You've taken from me my
friends. You've taken from me my clubs. You've taken from
me my self-esteem, my joy in life, my high spirits, the cheery
devil that God implanted in me—but damn it, you must leave
me my secretary.

MRS. PARBURY. [*Excitedly walking the stage.*] Oh, I understand
now. You use this exaggerated language, you make these
cruel accusations, you work yourself into a passion, because
you have grown to think more of Miss Woodward than of me.

PARBURY. Now you know that to be a purely fantastic interpretation of what I said. [*She takes out handkerchief.*] I observe
with pain, too, that you are about to cry again.

MRS. PARBURY. [*Puts handkerchief up her sleeve, controls her
anger, and becomes very determined.*] You are quite wrong.
Probably I shall never again know the relief of tears. Your
callousness and obstinacy seem to have dried up all the

tenderness in me. Miss Woodward leaves this house in the morning, or *I* leave it to-night.

PARBURY. Oh, come, come, Mabel, that is too ridiculous.

MRS. PARBURY. I'm very, very serious. Please, for your own sake, understand that. Which is it to be?

PARBURY. There, dear, let's drop it now. Don't you think domestic squabbles like this, besides being boring, are just a little—may one say it, vulgar? Let's go back to the garden.

MRS. PARBURY. Which is it to be?

PARBURY. [*Shrugs his shoulders.*] Of course, you know I'm decided. Miss Woodward stays.

MRS. PARBURY. Very well. [*She goes to bell and rings.* PARBURY *goes up, takes a book, and negligently turns over the leaves, secretly, however, watching his wife. Pause.*

Enter EVANS.

MRS. PARBURY. Where is Caroline?

EVANS. She's in her room, ma'am.

MRS. PARBURY. Send her to me, please.

EVANS. Yes, ma'am.   [*Exit.*

MRS. PARBURY. I needn't keep you from your friend Mr. Gunning any longer.

PARBURY. I'm all right here, dear; I'm perfectly contented. [*He turns over leaves.*] There is such a wise passage here. I'd like to read it to you. [*She makes a gesture of irritation.*] No? Well, it must keep.

Enter CAROLINE.

MRS. PARBURY. Caroline, I shall want you to pack a few things for me.

CAROLINE. What shall you want, ma'am?

MRS. PARBURY. I'll come upstairs and show you.

CAROLINE. Yes, ma'am.   [*Exit. Slight pause.*

PARBURY. [*Rising from his leaning attitude against table up stage, putting down the book, and coming down two steps.*] You foolish little woman. You know this is impossible. Be reasonable.

MRS. PARBURY. [*Firmly.*] Which is it to be?

PARBURY. [*With a gesture conveys that the subject is closed and returns to his former attitude.*] I think I have a right to ask what you propose doing.

MRS. PARBURY. I propose going home with my father.

ARMITAGE's *laugh is heard in the garden. Then he appears at the entrance, still laughing.* GUNNING *appears behind him.* ARMITAGE *enters.* GUNNING *remains at the window, smoking.*

ARMITAGE. [*To* PARBURY.] That's really the funniest thing I've heard for years. Have you heard that story, Clement?

PARBURY. What story?

ARMITAGE. Story of—[*Then he sees* MRS. PARBURY.] Oh, quite a drawing-room story, believe me, dear.

MRS. PARBURY. Father, I wish to speak to you.

ARMITAGE. Certainly, dear. What is it?
                    [PARBURY *exchanges a look with* GUNNING.

GUNNING. Mrs. Parbury, I must reluctantly say good-night. Your charming house is almost in the country, and I've to get back to London. I thank you for——

MRS. PARBURY. [*Interrupting.*] Please don't go, Mr. Gunning. It's quite early, and Clement and you, as such *very old* friends, must still have a great deal to talk about.

PARBURY. [*Taking* GUNNING's *arm.*] No, George, you really mustn't go.   [*Leads him up to window.*

GUNNING. I assure you, my dear chap——

PARBURY. [*Interrupting.*] But I make it a personal favour. Dear student of life, stay and observe.   [*They remain up at window.*

MRS. PARBURY. Dear father, I wish you to take me home with you to-night.

ARMITAGE. [*Surprised.*] Certainly, dear, but——

MRS. PARBURY. Don't question me. [*Puts her hand on his shoulder.*] You love me, don't you?

ARMITAGE. Naturally, my dear. But nowadays, of course, I take second place.

MRS. PARBURY. I thought so too, but I was wrong. Wait for me a few minutes.

ARMITAGE. [*Hesitatingly, after glancing at* PARBURY *and again at his daughter.*] One moment, Mabel. This is all so sudden.

MRS. PARBURY. Father, do you hesitate to receive me?

ARMITAGE. Good heavens, no! But Clement——

MRS. PARBURY. Shhh!   [*Puts her hand over his mouth.*

ARMITAGE. Oh! I was thinking, my dear, that unfortunately there is no mother to receive you now. I'm only an old bachelor, and you'll be—er—give me a word.

MRS. PARBURY. [*Kisses him, and goes to door. She looks across the room at her husband, and then whispers to herself.*] He'll never let me go.   [*Exit.*

PARBURY. [*To* GUNNING.] She'll not go, my dear fellow.

GUNNING. Humph! You think not? Anyway, *I* must.

PARBURY. Don't.

GUNNING. The domestic atmosphere is volcanic, and I feel remorseful.

PARBURY. Nonsense, it had to come. You must see me through it now.

GUNNING. How beastly selfish you married men are !

ARMITAGE. Clement, I'm in a difficulty.

PARBURY. You mean about Mabel, Colonel?

ARMITAGE. Yes.

PARBURY. She proposes going home with you.

ARMITAGE. Yes.

PARBURY. [*Smiling confidently.*] I don't think she'll go.

Enter EVANS.

EVANS. [*To* ARMITAGE.] Your carriage, sir. [PARBURY *looks uneasy. Exit* EVANS.

ARMITAGE. [*Whistles. Looks at his watch.*] I think she means it. I ordered my man to wait in the Avenue till he was called. Mabel has evidently had him called.

PARBURY. [*Is thoughtful.*] Humph!

ARMITAGE. I don't wish to be in the least degree meddlesome, but well, there it is!

PARBURY. The question, I suppose, is what's it all about?

ARMITAGE. Well, yes. I suppose that's it; although I don't in the least wish to know.

PARBURY. You hear, George; what's it all about?

GUNNING. [*Almost angrily.*] Now how the deuce should I know? Colonel, you would be very kind if you would use your authority to prevent Clement dragging me into his domestic difficulties. Married men have a cowardly way of endeavouring to involve their friends. Perhaps you have noticed it.

ARMITAGE. I have, Mr. Gunning. My experience of married life extended over a period of twenty-six years.

GUNNING. May one discreetly express the hope that they were very happy years?

ARMITAGE. Very happy years—with, however, I must admit, intermittent troubles. Mabel's mother was one of the best women in the world, but if I may say so without disloyalty, she was just a little—a little—er—give me a word.

PARBURY. Would the word *exigeant* apply?

ARMITAGE. Admirably. Perhaps you have noticed in Mabel the slightest tendency—eh?

PARBURY. Well, well!

ARMITAGE. Her mother's jealousy, too, was something amazing. I hope I'm not conceited, but in those days I was just a little—er—popular, and perhaps I ought not to confess it, a little—er—give me a word.

GUNNING. Human. [*They laugh slightly.*

ARMITAGE. [*With affected severity.*] Clement, I hope you are not too human?

PARBURY. Quite the contrary, I assure you, Colonel.

ARMITAGE. Then why—I suppose, after all, it is my duty to ask—why does Mabel come home with me to-night?

PARBURY. She is simply using pressure to get her own way in a matter in which I think her way the wrong way.

ARMITAGE. Gad! they do like their own way, don't they? Well, no doubt she'll be more reasonable to-morrow. I think I may trust you.

PARBURY. You may—absolutely.

Enter MRS. PARBURY. *She has put on a hat and a cloak.*

MRS. PARBURY. You'll forgive me, I'm sure, Mr. Gunning. Good-night. You'll have Clement all to yourself.

GUNNING. Good-night, Mrs. Parbury.   [*They shake hands.*

PARBURY. [*In a low voice.*] Don't go, Mabel. It's very foolish.

MRS. PARBURY. [*Softening.*] You could prevent me if you wished.

PARBURY. I'm opposed to all violence.

MRS. PARBURY. [*Hard again.*] Which way is it to be?

PARBURY. [*Firmly.*] My way, dear.   [*Goes up to fireplace.*

MRS. PARBURY. Good heavens! He'll really let me go. [*Hesitates for a moment; then draws herself up.*] Come, father.

ARMITAGE. Good-night, Mr. Gunning. Good-night, Clement.

PARBURY *and* GUNNING. Good-night, Colonel.

[*Exeunt* MRS. PARBURY *and* ARMITAGE.

PARBURY. [*Comes down, a little astonished.*] By Jove, she's really going!

[GUNNING *sits.* PARBURY *stands listening. Pause. Then there is the noise of a carriage door being shut.*

EVANS. [*Outside.*] Home!

[PARBURY *somewhat unsteadily lights a cigarette. He then catches* GUNNING'*s eye. They look at each other. Slow curtain.*

ACT III

SCENE. *The Rose Garden at* PARBURY's *house. A garden table, seat, and chairs. The next morning.*

Enter MISS WOODWARD. *She is dressed simply, but less severely than before. Her hair is dressed more loosely. She carries a little basket full of roses. She places some roses upon the table, which is laid for two for breakfast. She plucks more roses and fastens them in her dress. Meanwhile she hums an air and conveys the impression of being happier than in the previous Acts.*

Enter GUNNING. *He wears a light morning suit, a round hat and brown boots, and carries a stick and gloves.*

GUNNING. Good-morning, Miss Woodward.

MISS WOODWARD. Good-morning.   [*They shake hands.*

GUNNING. Shall I resist the temptation to pay you a compliment?

MISS WOODWARD. [*Gathering more roses.*] Yes, please.

GUNNING. I thought you would say so. All the same, I feel it to be a deprivation.

MISS WOODWARD. Isn't that remark itself the cloven foot of compliment?

GUNNING. Eh—well, perhaps it is. I'm sorry.

MISS WOODWARD. And therefore unlike you.

GUNNING. Unlike me? What does that mean?

MISS WOODWARD. That it isn't much in your way to pay women compliments.

GUNNING. I hope you are doing me an injustice.

MISS WOODWARD. I don't think so. You haven't a very lofty opinion of women as a sex, have you?

GUNNING. Pretty well—pretty well. But what makes you think so?

MISS WOODWARD. I heard you talk, you know, yesterday afternoon.

GUNNING. Oh yes; one does talk a lot of rot sometimes, doesn't one?

MISS WOODWARD. Yes.   [*Embarrassed pause.*

GUNNING. Is Mr. Parbury down yet?

MISS WOODWARD. No. But he is sure to be in a few minutes. He is generally early. Breakfast, as you see, will be served here. Perhaps—perhaps you would rather wait indoors.

GUNNING. No, I'll stay here if I may. . . . I'm afraid we made rather a late night of it.   [*He sits.*

MISS WOODWARD. Really?

GUNNING. Three o'clock.

MISS WOODWARD. You had much to talk of. I envy people with pleasant memories.

GUNNING. I don't remember that we talked much of old times. I think we talked of the present.

MISS WOODWARD. [*Rather hardly.*] Then my envy has flown.

GUNNING. You are right. This affair is rather boring.

MISS WOODWARD. [*Innocently.*] What affair, Mr. Gunning?

GUNNING. Miss Woodward, you are a triumph of the inscrutable.

MISS WOODWARD. I'm sure that is very clever, because I can't quite understand it.

GUNNING. Quite seriously, Miss Woodward, you interest me more than any person I have ever met.

MISS WOODWARD. Do you always say that to girls, Mr. Gunning?

GUNNING. No. Why?

MISS WOODWARD. You ought to. I'm sure it's very encouraging.   [*She picks another rose.*

GUNNING. [*Doubtfully.*] Ahem!

MISS WOODWARD. Are you quite sure you wouldn't rather wait indoors?

GUNNING. Oh, quite. I like being here.

MISS WOODWARD. But I'm sure you find it difficult getting

down to one's level. I often think that the very wise must be very lonely.

GUNNING. [*Rising.*] What an extremely unpleasant remark!

MISS WOODWARD. I'm sorry. [*She sighs.*] We don't seem to get on very well, do we?

GUNNING. [*With sincerity, and coming close to her.*] I'd like to get on well with you. [*Pause. They look in each other's faces.*] Will you give me a rose?

MISS WOODWARD. No, Mr. Gunning.

PARBURY. [*Outside.*] Are you there, George?

GUNNING. Yes.

PARBURY. [*Outside, to* EVANS.] Serve breakfast.

Enter PARBURY.

Good-morning. I hope I haven't kept you waiting. Oh, you are here, Miss Woodward. Good-morning. [*Looks at the table.*] And you have managed to find us some roses. How very kind of you! [MISS WOODWARD *gives him letters. He runs them over.*] No, no, no, no! Will you kindly see what they're all about? [*She is about to go.*] Oh, not now—after breakfast will do.

MISS WOODWARD. I have breakfasted, thank you.

PARBURY. Really! I suppose I'm horribly late. [*Looks at his watch. Then, noticing the roses she carries in her hand.*] How very beautiful they are! Look, George. [*She selects one and hands it to him.*] For me? Thank you. [*He fastens it in his buttonhole.*] [*Exit* MISS WOODWARD. Lovely, isn't it?

GUNNING. [*Gruffly.*] Yes, it's all right.

PARBURY. What's the matter? Cross?

GUNNING. Not at all. But really, you married men are very tiresome.

PARBURY. Oh, I see—wanted a rose yourself. Shall I call Miss Woodward back and ask for you?

GUNNING. Don't trouble. I've done that myself.

PARBURY. You have? Ha, ha! [*Begins to laugh, but stops*

suddenly.] Oh! [*Holding his head.*] Dear, dear, what a head I have!

GUNNING. You haven't asked after *my* head.

PARBURY. [*Sits at table.*] Your pardon. How is it?

GUNNING. [*Sits at table.*] I'd like to sell it this morning. Do you know, Clement, I'm not quite certain about that whisky of yours.

PARBURY. I am. It's fifteen years old.

Enter EVANS, *with breakfast-tray.*

But you always had a way of mixing your drinks over-night and growling in the morning.

GUNNING. Put it at that, if you like. I do know that I always had a way of disliking you particularly in the morning. I regret I don't appear to have grown out of it.

PARBURY. I'm so glad. I hate being too popular. [EVANS *offers bacon to* PARBURY. *He pushes the dish away.*] Take it away. Have some bacon, George?
     [*Takes a piece of toast, looks at it; then puts it down.*

GUNNING. Thank you.
     [*Helps himself to bacon. Exit* EVANS *with bacon dish.*

PARBURY. I must say I think your display of temper is in the worst possible taste under the circumstances.

GUNNING. [*Buttering toast.*] What do you mean by 'under the circumstances'?

PARBURY. You know what I mean. How much sleep do you think I've had?

GUNNING. I'm sure I don't know. What concerns me is that you detained me in this outlandish place—what county is it?— till past three o'clock, and then insisted, with alcoholic tears in your eyes, on my returning to breakfast.

PARBURY. Tea or coffee?

GUNNING. Tea—no; coffee—no, neither.

PARBURY. Have some hot milk?   [*Offers him the jug.*

GUNNING. Ugh! Don't.   [*Takes an egg. Shells it.*

PARBURY. [*Lifts the lid of the tea-pot, then of the coffee-pot, and closes them gently with a look of distaste.*] No, not this morning. Still, we must drink something. What shall it be?

GUNNING. I am your guest.

PARBURY. Perhaps we had better split a bottle.

GUNNING. Please be frank. Do you mean Bass or champagne?

PARBURY. Champagne, of course. [*He calls loudly.*] Evans! Evans!

EVANS. [*Outside.*] Yes, sir.

Enter EVANS.

PARBURY. Bring a bottle of champagne.

EVANS. [*Starting ever so slightly.*] Cham——

PARBURY. [*Irritably.*] Champagne and glasses.

EVANS. [*Recovering his composure.*] Yes, sir.

[*Exit* EVANS, *wearing a discreet smile.*

PARBURY. It's a thing I haven't done for years—taken wine in the morning.

GUNNING. Five years.

PARBURY. Exactly.

GUNNING. In what I may venture to describe as the pre-domestic period, it was rather a way of yours.

PARBURY. You mean ours.

GUNNING. Ours, if you prefer it. Where's the salt?

PARBURY. There it is, right before your eyes. Why don't you look?

GUNNING. Pass the mustard, please. What a good chap you were in those days.

PARBURY. Yes. Strange, you were always——

GUNNING. Always what?

PARBURY. Toast?

GUNNING. Thanks, I've got some. Always what?

PARBURY. It's quite pleasant out here, isn't it?

GUNNING. Delightful. You were saying I was always——

PARBURY. Oh, it doesn't matter.

GUNNING. Of course, being about me it wouldn't matter.

PARBURY. I'm afraid of offending you.

GUNNING. You couldn't do that.

PARBURY. Well, I was going to say you were always rather sour-natured.

GUNNING. Really!

[*He takes up a daily paper and glances through it, continuing to do so while* PARBURY *speaks.*

PARBURY. And that has, I fancy, quite unconsciously to you, I am sure, a disturbing influence on others of happier nature.

[*Taking an egg.*

GUNNING. [*Drawlingly.*] Yes.   [*He continues to read.*

PARBURY. Take yesterday, for instance. Of course, you didn't intend it. I wouldn't suggest that for a moment. But damn it, look at the result!

GUNNING. [*In the same manner as before.*] Yes.   [*He reads.*

PARBURY. [*Taking the top off his boiled egg.*] Simply deplorable. I've broken loose from my moorings. I'm at the mercy of every breeze. I feel that I've lost moral stability. Confound it, why doesn't that champagne come?

Enter EVANS *with champagne; pours out two glasses and hands them to* GUNNING *and* PARBURY.

PARBURY. I'm not quite certain that for a man like me— [GUNNING *groans and returns to his newspaper.*]—a man, if I may say so, of generous instincts and large sympathies—a groove isn't a good thing, even if it be a little narrow. Of course, for a man of your nature, it's a different matter.

GUNNING. [*Suddenly puts down the paper, draws his chair closer to the table, and takes an egg with apparent cheerfulness.*] What were you saying, old man?

PARBURY. Nothing.

GUNNING. [*Affecting heartiness.*] Let's talk about you.

PARBURY. [*Fingering the rose in his buttonhole.*] Dear, dear, how cross you are to-day!

EVANS. Excuse me, sir, may I speak to you?

PARBURY. Yes—what is it?

EVANS. It's about cook, sir.

PARBURY. What's the matter with her?

EVANS. Well sir, so to speak, she wants to know where she stands.

PARBURY. [*Looks at* EVANS, *then at* GUNNING.] How can I help her?

EVANS. I mean, sir, or rather she means, now mistress has gone away——

PARBURY. I presume my wife has a right to go away for a few days without cook's permission.

EVANS. Yes, sir, certainly. But excuse me, sir; there's been gossip. Emma, the 'ousemaid, accidentally overheard something between Mrs. Parbury and her maid. Servants is as nervous as race-horses, sir, and cook's nerves is particularly sensible. So to speak, dismoralisation's set up in the kitchen.

PARBURY. Well, you had better go and set it down again, Evans, and don't bother me any more.

EVANS. Yes, sir, certainly. Excuse me, sir, I was to ask you who cook is to take her orders from.

PARBURY. In my wife's absence, from me, of course.

EVANS. Not from Miss Woodward, sir?

PARBURY. [*Starting slightly.*] Why, has Miss Woodward given any orders?

EVANS. No, sir, but cook thought——

PARBURY. That will do, Evans.

EVANS. Yes, sir.
[*Exit. There is a pause.* PARBURY *and* GUNNING *exchange looks.*

GUNNING. Devilish awkward.

PARBURY. What bores servants are!
[PARBURY *slowly drinks a glass of wine.* GUNNING *also drinks.* PARBURY *refills the glasses.*

Enter ARMITAGE.

ARMITAGE. Am I an intruder?

PARBURY. Good-morning, Colonel. [*He rises and shakes hands.*] Not in the least.

ARMITAGE. Good-morning, Mr. Gunning.

GUNNING. Good-morning, Colonel.   [*They shake hands.*

PARBURY. Have you breakfasted?

ARMITAGE. Thanks, yes, but poorly. I didn't get to bed till four.

PARBURY. Nor did I.

GUNNING. Nor I.

ARMITAGE. And then I had but little sleep.

PARBURY. The same with me.

GUNNING. And with me.

ARMITAGE. [*With a touch of asperity.*] Your troubles, Clement, you have, of course, brought upon yourself, but I think it's a little hard on your friends that they should be made to suffer with you.

GUNNING. Hear, hear!

Enter EVANS *with fruit.* GUNNING *and* PARBURY *each take an apple.*

ARMITAGE. [*Tapping the champagne bottle with his stick.*] What's this? Some new kind of table water, I suppose.

PARBURY. Champagne.

ARMITAGE. Champagne at this hour! Well, I suppose you know best how to regulate your life. Have you an extra glass?

PARBURY. Another glass, Evans.

EVANS. Yes, sir.   [*Exit.*

ARMITAGE. It's a thing I haven't done for many years.

PARBURY. I trust, Colonel, you won't accuse me of leading you from the path of morning abstinence.

ARMITAGE. Really, Clement, I think this display of ill-humour is scarcely in—er—give me a word.

GUNNING. Good taste.

ARMITAGE. Exactly! Good taste, considering that we are suffering from the effects of your domestic—er—er—

GUNNING. Maladministration.

ARMITAGE. Maladministration—exactly.

GUNNING. I quite agree with you, Colonel.

ARMITAGE. Look at your friend there. If he'll allow me to say so, he's put on ten years since yesterday. Look at me! Last evening, I suggest—I hope I'm not conceited—I suggest I didn't look a day over forty-seven.

GUNNING. Not an hour.

ARMITAGE. While to-day—what would you say, Mr. Gunning?

GUNNING. [*Looks at him critically, then falls back in his chair.*] Fifty-two.

[PARBURY *looks savagely at* GUNNING, *throws his apple on table, and turns away.*]

ARMITAGE. I feared so, but I like you for your frankness.

[*He cuts a cigar.*

Enter EVANS, *with tumbler on tray; he places tumbler on table, and collects the breakfast things. Pause.* ARMITAGE *lights his cigar with a match* EVANS *hands him.*

ARMITAGE. You haven't asked me if I have a message for you.

PARBURY. Prenez-garde!

GUNNING. [*Loudly.*] You mean about Newmarket.

ARMITAGE. [*After a glance at* EVANS.] Yes; Allerton doesn't run any of his horses. Death in the family, you know.

PARBURY. So I heard. That will do, Evans. You may leave the champagne.

EVANS. Yes, sir.   [*Exit with breakfast tray.*

PARBURY. [*Watches* EVANS *off; then to* ARMITAGE.] Of course, you know, I'm really most anxious about Mabel. How is she?

ARMITAGE. I think I told you that I was up practically all night with her.

PARBURY. Was she ill?

ARMITAGE. Bodily, no. We supped in the kitchen at two. It's amazing how emotion stimulates the appetite. No, Clement, her indisposition is of the mind. She wept.

PARBURY. All the time?

ARMITAGE. All the time. [*Slight pause. Then he adds with a sigh.*] I had rather a trying night.

> [*They all drink champagne*; GUNNING *rises, bends over a rosebush, and hums the air of the music-hall song,* ' '*E 'as my sympathy.*'

ARMITAGE. I'm not without experience. Poor dear Mabel's mother, for instance—one of the best women in the world—*she* would cry at times, and if she got well off the scratch, she was—er—hard to beat. Mind you, I'll be fair; I was much to blame—very much to blame. But as for Mabel, bless you, that dear child could have given her poor mother a stone and —er—what's the expression?

GUNNING. Romped home.

ARMITAGE. That's it—romped home.

PARBURY. Come, Colonel, give me the message.

ARMITAGE. I have no message for you. I may tell you, you are not in very great favour. [GUNNING *smiles.*] You're not well spoken of, Clement.

PARBURY. Oho! Perhaps my wife had a good word for my old friend, Gunning.

ARMITAGE. In regard to Mr. Gunning, I think the word 'serpent' was employed. [PARBURY *laughs quietly*; GUNNING *becomes serious.*] All the same, I have a message for him.

GUNNING. Really.

PARBURY. [*Rising.*] In that case, I'll get out of the way. I shall be in my study if I'm wanted.

ARMITAGE. Very well. But I must say, Clement, that I find you, very much to my surprise and regret, just a little—a little—er—give me a word.

GUNNING. Callous?

ARMITAGE. Thanks, yes—callous; and, dearly fond as I am of my daughter, I think I have a right to ask how long you intend leaving your wife on my hands.

GUNNING. Perfectly reasonable—perfectly——

PARBURY. Shut up, George! [*He goes to* ARMITAGE.] My dear old friend——

ARMITAGE. [*Interrupting.*] Hear me out, please. My dear daughter is, of course, always more than welcome to my home, but I trust you will not misunderstand me when I say that I require notice. Since I regained my liberty—I mean, since the death of your wife's dear mother, I've drifted into my own— er—little ways. This affair has deranged my plans. Without being indiscreet, I may tell you that I've had to send telegrams.

GUNNING. Deuced hard lines!

PARBURY. Send her back to me, Colonel. Consult at once your happiness and mine by using your authority. Tell her that cook is in revolt, and that Evans is impertinent. Tell her that I only want my own way when I know I am absolutely right, as in this case. And above all, tell her that I prefer her society to that of a second-class cynic who bellows for champagne at ten o'clock in the morning. [*Exit.*

GUNNING. In regard to your son-in-law, Colonel, you have my respectful sympathy.

ARMITAGE. A good fellow, but inconsiderate. [*He lowers his voice.*] I may tell you in confidence, Gunning, that I had been looking forward to keeping a rather pleasant appointment to-night——

GUNNING. [*Falling into the confidential manner.*] Really?

ARMITAGE. Yes, rather pleasant—rather pleasant.
[*He takes a miniature from his pocket and looks at it.*

GUNNING. [*Leaning towards him.*] Might one venture to——

ARMITAGE. [*Keeping the miniature away from him.*] Oh, no, no, no, no—wouldn't be fair. Oh, no. Besides, you might know her hus—you might—er——

GUNNING. Yes, yes, of course; one can't be too discreet.

ARMITAGE. [*Quickly.*] Not, mind you, that there's anything the whole world mightn't know, only she—er—she's not happy at home, and a quiet evening at a theatre—you understand?

GUNNING. Quite, quite!

ARMITAGE. Now you, my dear fellow, can do me a friendly turn.

GUNNING. I should be delighted to, but—I don't see——

ARMITAGE. I'll explain. My daughter wishes to see you. She seems to think that you hold the key of the situation.

GUNNING. But I don't. I should very much object to.

ARMITAGE. Never mind—never mind! See her and do your utmost to make it up between her and Clement.

GUNNING. It's no business of mine.

ARMITAGE. To put it bluntly, I shall not be able to keep my appointment to-night if I still have my daughter on my hands.

GUNNING. That would be a pity.

ARMITAGE. In which case my friend will be vexed—*very vexed.* I should have mentioned that on her mother's side my friend is Spanish.

GUNNING. [*Smiling. Shakes hands.*] That decides me. Where is your daughter now?

ARMITAGE. She's there, my boy, quite close. We walked over the Heath together. One moment. [*He brings a chair forward.*] Would you kindly lend me your arm? [*With* GUNNING'*s assistance he mounts a chair; then he raises his hat on his stick.*] That's the signal the coast is clear. Trust an old campaigner. There she is! I say, put that wine away! [GUNNING *puts the bottle under table, and places the glasses on table and covers them over with serviette.*] It's all right. Thank you, thank you! [*As* GUNNING *helps him down.*] Remember, my dear fellow, that I've trusted you implicitly. My happiness is in your hands. If we men didn't stand shoulder to shoulder in these little matters, society would—er—would——

GUNNING. Crumble to dust.

ARMITAGE. Exactly.

Enter MRS. PARBURY. *Advancing cautiously, she bows very stiffly to* GUNNING, *who takes his hat off.*

GUNNING. Good-morning, Mrs. Parbury.

MRS. PARBURY. [*Coldly.*] Good-morning.

ARMITAGE. Well, I'll leave you. There's nothing further I can do for you at present, dear?

MRS. PARBURY. You might stay in the garden and give me a signal if Clement is coming. I have no intention of meeting him under the circumstances.

ARMITAGE. Very well, I'll give you an unmistakable signal. 'I'll sing thee songs of Araby.' [*Exit.*

MRS. PARBURY. [*Grimly.*] Well, Mr. Gunning, I hope you're satisfied with your work.

GUNNING. My work, Mrs. Parbury—come, come!

MRS. PARBURY. Oh, I hope you won't dispute that. Clement and I were living together in perfect harmony, in perfect happiness, until you turned up yesterday.

GUNNING. Like a bad penny, eh?

MRS. PARBURY. I was going to say like the snake in the garden.

GUNNING. Better still. Our conversation doesn't open propitiously. Don't you think it would conduce to the comfort of us both if we didn't pursue it any further?

MRS. PARBURY. Isn't that a little cowardly?

GUNNING. I acknowledge cowardice in regard to other people's affairs.

MRS. PARBURY. Yesterday you were a hero.

GUNNING. Believe me, Mrs. Parbury, you are mistaken. I didn't interfere in any way.

MRS. PARBURY. You did worse.

GUNNING. How?

MRS. PARBURY. You sneered.

GUNNING. Really, Mrs. Parbury, I——

MRS. PARBURY. You aired opinions to me—pernicious opinions. I have a right to assume that you aired the same opinions to Clement, over whom you have some sort of influence.

GUNNING. I?

MRS. PARBURY. Not, I think, a good influence, Mr. Gunning. I've been thinking things over since midnight. Hitherto I've been obliged to think very little of serious things. Perhaps trouble sharpens the intelligence. I've discovered that your influence over Clement is the influence of ridicule—the ridicule of the untamed for the tamed.

GUNNING. Say of the disreputable for the respectable, if you like, Mrs. Parbury.

MRS. PARBURY. Thank you. That quite expresses my present opinion. Of course it is in your power at least to modify it.

GUNNING. I should be grateful if you would show me the way.

MRS. PARBURY. You are not sincere.

GUNNING. 'Pon my word, I am. [MRS. PARBURY *raises her hand protestingly.*] No, but really—I assure you, dear Mrs. Parbury—I'm not nearly such a bad fellow as you think. What can I do?

MRS. PARBURY. Something—*anything* to remove Miss Woodward from this house.

GUNNING. Miss Woodward! What has she to do with your quarrel with Clement?

MRS. PARBURY. Everything. Sit down. [*He does so. She makes sure that they are unobserved; then takes a chair next to him.*] Mr. Gunning, strange as it may appear after all that has occurred, I am going to trust you.   [*Lowering her voice.*

GUNNING. You are very good.

MRS. PARBURY. That wretched girl is in love with Clement.

GUNNING. [*Starting from his chair as if shot.*] What!

MRS. PARBURY. Sit down! Sit down!

GUNNING. Miss Woodward is in love with——

MRS. PARBURY. Sit down, *please*, Mr. Gunning.

GUNNING. [*Laughs—sitting.*] No, no, no; I simply can't believe it.

MRS. PARBURY. Why not?

GUNNING. It seems such a monstrous absurdity.   [*Laughs.*

MRS. PARBURY. [*Drawing herself up.*] I see nothing monstrously absurd in any one falling in love with my husband. I did!

GUNNING. Oh, of course—a charming chap; but she's such an original girl.

MRS. PARBURY. [*Indignant.*] You infer that I am not?

GUNNING. Not at all, Mrs. Parbury. You are really most interesting.

MRS. PARBURY. I don't think you are very tactful.

GUNNING. I'm a boor—a perfect boor.

MRS. PARBURY. You appear to take an interest in Miss Woodward.

GUNNING. [*Confused.*] Only the interest of the student. I still think you must be mistaken.

MRS. PARBURY. [*Emphatically.*] I caught her in the act of kissing his photograph.

GUNNING. You saw her— [*Laughs.*] My dear Mrs. Parbury, a day-dream!

MRS. PARBURY. A fact. When pressed, she didn't deny it.

GUNNING. Does Clement know?

MRS. PARBURY. No; I thought it wise not to tell him.

GUNNING. [*Heartily.*] You were right—very right.

MRS. PARBURY. I'm glad you think so.

GUNNING. Some men are so weak.

MRS. PARBURY. [*Drawing herself up again.*] Mr. Gunning!

GUNNING. So easily flattered.

MRS. PARBURY. [*With more emphasis.*] Mr. Gunning!

GUNNING. In nine cases out of ten it's vanity that leads men astray.

MRS. PARBURY. [*With growing wrath.*] Mr. Gunning, we are speaking of my husband.

GUNNING. Yes, yes, dear old Clement has his share of vanity, of course. [*Aside.*] Damn him!   [*Rises.*

MRS. PARBURY. [*Rising indignantly.*] How dare you speak like that of my husband! A less vain man doesn't exist, and what small faults he has concern only him and me—and not you in any way.

GUNNING. I beg ten thousand pardons, Mrs. Parbury. Of course you know Clement far better than I do. Please don't go.

MRS. PARBURY. I shall certainly not remain to hear my husband abused.

GUNNING. But I assure you——

MRS. PARBURY. Clement vain indeed!

GUNNING. No, no; a mistake. Do sit down again.

MRS. PARBURY. You might with advantage look for vanity nearer home, Mr. Gunning.

GUNNING. Perfectly true, perfectly true.

[*He places her chair for her.*

MRS. PARBURY. As for the sort of weakness you were good enough to credit my husband with——

GUNNING. Nothing but a slip of the tongue. Do sit down.

MRS. PARBURY. No doubt you have accustomed yourself to judging other men from your own standpoint.

GUNNING. That's it; quite true! You are always right. Won't you sit?

[*She sits. He sighs with relief, then takes a chair himself.*

MRS. PARBURY. What do you propose?

GUNNING. I'm waiting for a suggestion from you.

MRS. PARBURY. This brazen hussy——

GUNNING. That expression seems to me to be unnecessarily harsh, Mrs. Parbury.

MRS. PARBURY. Oh of course, if you defend the girl—

GUNNING. Pardon me, but I have an old-fashioned prejudice against speaking ill of the absent.

MRS. PARBURY. I didn't observe it when you spoke of my husband.

GUNNING. [*Laughing.*] Fairly hit. Come, let's be practical. Miss Woodward must not remain in the house, and Clement must not know the truth. On these points we are quite agreed.

MRS. PARBURY. Quite.

GUNNING. Very well. I'll see Clement. I have an idea.

MRS. PARBURY. You'll not tell him you've seen me.

GUNNING. Certainly not.

MRS. PARBURY. Remember above all, it's most important to our future happiness that Clement should be the first to give way.

GUNNING. Oh, I'll remember that.

MRS. PARBURY. And, Mr. Gunning, if you succeed I'll try to forget the mischief you've created, and will ask you to come and see us—[*Shakes hands with him.*] occasionally.

GUNNING. Thank you so much.

[*Voice of* ARMITAGE *outside singing 'I'll sing thee songs of Araby.'*

MRS. PARBURY. That's father's signal. I am going to walk on the Heath. I'm far too proud to allow myself to be discovered by Clement here. He might think I want to come back.

[*Exit. Voice of* ARMITAGE, *still singing, comes nearer until he enters with* PARBURY, *with the words 'or charm thee to a tear.' Unseen by* PARBURY, GUNNING *points out to* ARMITAGE *the direction in which* MRS. PARBURY *has gone.*

ARMITAGE. [*In a low voice, to* GUNNING.] Will it be all right?

GUNNING. I hope so.

ARMITAGE. Well, I'll finish my constitutional. I'll look in again, Clement, in the hope that you will then be able to tell me how long this extremely uncomfortable state of affairs is to last. [*Exit* ARMITAGE, *singing until he is well off.*

PARBURY. Give me a cigarette, George.

[GUNNING *hands him a cigarette; then takes a cigarette himself. They both smoke. There is a short silence.*

PARBURY. Not a stroke of work. It's absurd!

[*Throws cigarette on ground in a rage.*

GUNNING. You are not happy?

PARBURY. Not particularly.

GUNNING. Then how can you expect to do imaginative work?

PARBURY. Quite so!

GUNNING. I'm afraid you've made a mistake, old chap.

PARBURY. Eh?

GUNNING. You know I'm your friend.

PARBURY. Of course.

GUNNING. Apart from all chaff.

PARBURY. Yes, yes.

GUNNING. Well, you've gone too far.

PARBURY. [*Looks at him.*] You think so?

GUNNING. Yes. By a petulant discontent you've precipitated an awkward crisis.

PARBURY. You see it now in that light?

GUNNING. Yes. I've been thinking things over, Clement. After all, the love of a good woman is a priceless possession.

PARBURY. You appear to have dropped into the platitudinous.

GUNNING. [*With much gravity.*] Don't jest, old man, over so sacred a thing.

PARBURY. [*After eyeing* GUNNING *keenly for a moment.*] You have changed your views since yesterday.

GUNNING. Only the unimaginative never change their views.

PARBURY. You think, then, I've been wrong?

GUNNING. Very!

PARBURY. I should have gone on putting up with the existing conditions?

GUNNING. They might have been worse.

PARBURY. Submitting to the old tyranny?

GUNNING. A wholesome discipline, believe me.

PARBURY. What of our spoilt yachting cruise?

GUNNING. I ought never to have proposed it. Think what a loving wife must suffer under the circumstances—lying awake at night listening to the wind howling in the chimneys and sobbing in the trees. It doesn't bear thinking of.

PARBURY. Quite so—quite so! And about our dear old friends whom I was obliged to drop. You may remember you made some very strong comments on my weakness yesterday.

GUNNING. I was hasty. I admit it.

PARBURY. Wybrow, for instance—an awful good chap.

GUNNING. A tavern wit—a Johnsonian spirit—eminently out of place on the domestic hearth.

PARBURY. Well, take Carson—one of the best.

GUNNING. Foolishly married a woman your wife couldn't get on with. You admitted it.

PARBURY. But Burleigh—a truly great spirit—your own words.

GUNNING. Burleigh? It isn't because a man gives you a watch that you need thrust him down your wife's throat, is it?

PARBURY. What an old fraud you are, George!

GUNNING. Not at all. One sees things more clearly in the morning.

PARBURY. Well, since you've resigned your attitude of non-intervention, what do you advise?

GUNNING. Discreet surrender.

PARBURY. I'm to send for my wife?

GUNNING. Exactly.

PARBURY. Unconditionally?

GUNNING. Of course. Why impose conditions on a weak, loving, trusting woman? [*Going to him.*] Damn it all, old man, show a little heart.

PARBURY. You know it means the sacrifice of my secretary?

GUNNING. Well?

PARBURY. Well?

GUNNING. [*A little embarrassed; he drops the cigarette and places his foot on it.*] It's obvious that Miss Woodward can't stay on here in your wife's absence.

PARBURY. I've thought of that.

GUNNING. You heard what Evans said. The servants are talking already—and if the servants are talking this morning the neighbours will be talking this afternoon, and the entire north-west of London by the evening.

PARBURY. Quite true—quite true.

GUNNING. I suppose you don't wish to compromise the girl?

PARBURY. Certainly not—certainly not. [*He goes slowly over to* GUNNING, *and looks him in the face, smiling.*] And so that's your secret.

GUNNING. What do you mean?

PARBURY. All this solicitude for my happiness—this sudden change of your point of view—this miraculous conversion of the cynic into the peacemaker—all inspired by a pair of blue eyes. An arrow from Cupid's bow has winged its way into this wooden heart—[*Tapping* GUNNING'*s chest.*] and 'Earth has won her child again,' as Goethe puts it.

GUNNING. Don't talk rot!

PARBURY. Don't be offended. I like it. It pleases me. Think of it! One dull evening in a suburban home, one morning's encounter in a rose-garden, and the thing's done—the sage melts into the man, the onlooker into the soldier. I tell you I like it. It's so natural, so human—so splendidly unlike you. Let me help. What can I do? She's coming here now with some letters for me to sign. 'Were it ever so airy a tread, your heart would hear her and beat.' Isn't it so? Shall I speak to her for you? Better still, shall I leave you alone together?

GUNNING. [*Fixing his hat on more firmly and taking his stick.*] I'm going. You bore me.

Enter MISS WOODWARD. *She carries some typewritten letters and pen and ink. She goes to the table and stands waiting for* PARBURY.

PARBURY. One moment, old man. [*He looks in* GUNNING'*s face; then speaks in a lower voice.*] Don't let it pass unrecorded. You have permitted yourself a blush.

GUNNING. [*Trying to pass him.*] Don't be an idiot.

PARBURY. [*Restraining him.*] It's a beautiful, touching truth. The philosopher—the man who has gained perspective—the student who sits perched on a lofty ledge and looks down pityingly on the rest of us, is actually blushing—blushing a poor, simple, human blush!   [*Laughs loudly.*

GUNNING. Go to the devil!   [*Exit.*

PARBURY. [*Turning to* MISS WOODWARD. *He goes to her.*] Forgive my laughter, Miss Woodward, but it isn't often one surprises a philosopher in a blush. Now let us see! [*He sits and takes the letters.* MISS WOODWARD *remains standing by him. He reads. Interrupting himself after a moment, he laughs slightly.*] Dear old George! [*He continues reading; then signs the letter. He looks over another and says 'Excellent!' and signs it. Then he quickly signs the other letters and sits back in his chair.*] Thank you! [MISS WOODWARD *gathers up the letters.*] I'm afraid that's all the work I can do to-day. I'd like to have gone on with the novel, but it seems the mood won't come.

MISS WOODWARD. I'm very sorry.

PARBURY. The day is out of joint.

MISS WOODWARD. I wish I could do something.

PARBURY. No, no, don't you trouble. It'll all come right presently. By the way, what a good fellow Gunning is!

MISS WOODWARD. Is he?

PARBURY. Don't you think so?   [*Looking at her.*

MISS WOODWARD. I've seen so little of him, but I'm sure he must be if you think so.   [*She is going.*

PARBURY. Wait one moment, Miss Woodward. I know there was something else I wanted to say to you. [*She comes back. He rises and paces stage thoughtfully.*] Oh, yes; I know! I'm afraid my domestic complications have made things a little uncomfortable for you here.

MISS WOODWARD. [*Astonished; drops the letters on the table.*] I don't—don't understand.

PARBURY. I mean that you probably feel it rather awkward to actually live—night and day—in the house in my wife's absence?

MISS WOODWARD. [*Blankly.*] Oh, yes, yes; quite, I suppose.

PARBURY. [*Not looking at her.*] I don't know much about these matters, but I do know that you women are very sensitive and apt to worry about what people might say.

MISS WOODWARD. [*In the same manner as before.*] Yes—of course.

PARBURY. I thought so. Well, it has occurred to me that perhaps under present circumstances it would be better if——

MISS WOODWARD. You mean for me to go away.

PARBURY. Yes.   [*Pause.*

MISS WOODWARD. [*In a low voice.*] If I had been wiser I would have expected it.

PARBURY. I mean, of course, to sleep only. Mrs. Howlands at Parkhurst House just down here lets some of her rooms, I know, and probably she has a vacant bedroom now. I'll send down presently and see what can be done. In fact, I'll send Evans now.   [*Is about to go.*

MISS WOODWARD. Mr. Parbury!

PARBURY. [*Stopping.*] Yes.

MISS WOODWARD. Don't send, please.

PARBURY. Oh, I see; you would rather go yourself.

MISS WOODWARD. I would rather go altogether.

PARBURY. [*Amazed.*] You would rather go altogether?

MISS WOODWARD. I mean I *will* go altogether.

PARBURY. Miss Woodward, what is this for? What have I done?

MISS WOODWARD. Nothing that hasn't been perfect kindness to me.

PARBURY. Then why wish to go now? I know I can't expect to have you always, because you will some day get married.

MISS WOODWARD. I shall never get married.

PARBURY. Nonsense! Of course you will, and the man who gets you will, in my opinion, be a very lucky fellow; but until that day I certainly looked forward to having the benefit of your services.

MISS WOODWARD. I'm sorry if I disappoint you. Please forgive me and let me go.

PARBURY. But really, Miss Woodward, I must beg for some sort of explanation. Last night you acknowledged you were perfectly satisfied. You wished to remain.

MISS WOODWARD. You have unconsciously shown me to-day that I was wrong.

PARBURY. Indeed! I would be glad to know how. Oh, how weary one gets of mysteries! [MISS WOODWARD's *head droops lower. He walks the stage; then looks at* MISS WOODWARD *and pauses; he goes to her and speaks more gently.*] I beg your pardon, I fear I spoke impatiently. Do understand that I only wish for your own good. I admit in our relations I've hitherto been rather selfish. I'm afraid writing men are prone to be so. I've allowed you to study my wishes and feelings and nerves all the time, without giving any thought to yours. I'll try to be more considerate in the future if you'll only regard me as an elder brother and tell me what is troubling you now.

MISS WOODWARD. I'm sorry, but I can't. I'm ashamed that you should worry about me at all.

PARBURY. Is it anything to do with Mr. Gunning?

MISS WOODWARD. Nothing at all. How could it be?

PARBURY. Miss Woodward, I don't like to press you, but this general cloud of mystery is seriously affecting my nerves. At least tell me—I make it a personal favour—the cause of the quarrel between my wife and you.

MISS WOODWARD. It's impossible! Mrs. Parbury may tell you after I've gone. I'd rather you despised me then than now.

PARBURY. [*Wonderingly.*] Despise you?

[*Their eyes meet. Pause.*

MISS WOODWARD. [*Passionately.*] Please don't—don't even try to guess.

PARBURY. [*The light breaking in on him slowly.*] I think I understand.

[MISS WOODWARD *turns up stage and stands with head bowed, her back to the audience. There is a long pause. At first* PARBURY *doesn't appear ill-pleased. He looks down at the rose in his button-hole, and begins to raise it half tenderly to his face. Then his face becomes grave, and he slowly removes the flower from his coat, and places it on the table against which* MISS WOODWARD *is standing. He takes one of her hands.*

PARBURY. I don't ask anything—I don't guess anything, my dear child—my little sister. I was wrong to press you to tell me your trouble, for what could a hardened, rough-natured man do with the secrets of a young girl's heart?

MISS WOODWARD. Don't speak like that; only say that I may go.

PLATE 7

The Tyranny of Tears. The end of Act III, and other scenes.
British Museum

PARBURY. Yes.

MISS WOODWARD. Thank you.
[*Sees the rose where he has placed it. After a slight pause she takes it up. During the following, she slowly picks it to pieces, dropping the petals on the ground.*

PARBURY. [*Speaking very gently.*] I suppose there must soon come a time to every girl of heart who goes out alone into the world—a time when life seems to press hardly upon her and weariness of the unaccustomed stress makes her heart falter, and when she longs to take rest for a time in the old childhood, in the home she perhaps once thought to be dull and dreary, in the mother's arms that have always been ready to open with love for her.

MISS WOODWARD. Don't!
[*Sinks into chair, buries her face in her hands.*

PARBURY. Perhaps you feel that that time has come now. If so, go home for a little while, and get rest and fresh strength for the battle of life. Come back to the fight soon. You are bound to succeed, because you have talent and ambition and courage. [*Slight pause. He takes her hand.*] Don't cry. There is nothing you have lost or suffered yet quite worth a tear—

Enter MRS. PARBURY, GUNNING, *and* ARMITAGE.
—nothing quite worth a tear. [*He is bending towards her.* MRS. PARBURY *stops near* MISS WOODWARD *and* PARBURY, *brought up short by seeing their intimate position.* PARBURY *draws back from* MISS WOODWARD, *who remains upright and motionless.* GUNNING *and* ARMITAGE *exchange glances.* MISS WOODWARD *crosses to go.*

MRS. PARBURY. [*In a low voice, speaking slowly, with deep emotion.*] I suppose—I have still a right to ask—for some explanation?

PARBURY. Of what, dear?

MRS. PARBURY. Of this familiarity.

PARBURY. You shouldn't mistake sympathy for familiarity. I was only giving Miss Woodward some advice about her affairs.

MRS. PARBURY. What affairs?

PARBURY. I said *her* affairs, dear, not ours.

MRS. PARBURY. If that is all the explanation——

[*Turns away.*

MISS WOODWARD. Mr. Parbury very kindly and very properly advised me to go home for a time—[*She comes down to* MRS. PARBURY *and speaks to her alone.*] and I—I descended to your level—I cried!   [*Quick curtain.*

ACT IV

SCENE. *Same as Acts I and II. Same day as Act III.*
Upon the curtain rising, MISS WOODWARD *is discovered at the desk. A luncheon gong is immediately heard.* MISS WOODWARD *looks up and listens for a moment; then shrugs her shoulders and resumes her work. She opens a drawer of the desk, glances at its contents, and then writes.*

MISS WOODWARD. [*Writing.*] Drawer four. Reviews favourable of 'Harvey Masterton.' In top corner, tied in bundle, reviews unfavourable. [*She closes and locks that drawer and unlocks another, into which she looks. Writing.*] Drawer five. Proof sheets of new novel corrected to page 180. At back, accounts with publishers. [*The luncheon gong is struck again. She opens another drawer, looks into it for a moment, turns over its contents, then shrugs her shoulders and writes.*] A variety of photographs of Mrs. Parbury and two packets of letters marked 'Private.' How touching! [*She closes the drawer with a bang, and opens another.*

Enter EVANS.

EVANS. Excuse me, miss, but have you heard the luncheon gong?

MISS WOODWARD. Yes, thank you.

EVANS. It's been struck twice, specially for you, miss.

MISS WOODWARD. Who told you to strike it the second time?

EVANS. Mr. Parbury, miss.

MISS WOODWARD. And who sent you now?

EVANS. Mrs. Parbury asked me to tell you they're at lunch. They're the only words that's been spoken since they sat down. It's rather trying to the nerves, miss, waiting on people that only open their mouths to eat.

MISS WOODWARD. You will please say that I don't wish any lunch.

EVANS. Yes, miss.

MISS WOODWARD. Has Emma packed my things?

EVANS. She's packing them now, miss.

MISS WOODWARD. [*Glancing at an A.B.C. which is on the desk.*] Will you please order a cab for me at—let me see—[*Consulting the book.*]—four-twenty—say at half-past three.

EVANS. Yes, miss. Excuse me, miss, but we're all very sorry you're going—particularly cook. Cook's very strong in her attachments.

MISS WOODWARD. [*Looking into a drawer.*] It's very kind of cook.

EVANS. Cook's words was, 'This'll be a dull 'ouse when the little sunbeam's gone.'

MISS WOODWARD. That will do, Evans.

EVANS. Excuse me, miss, it was meant kindly. We was all on your side in this embroglo.

[*A pause.* MISS WOODWARD *is obstinately silent, and goes on working.*]

EVANS. Can't I get you something, miss?

MISS WOODWARD. Yes; ask cook to kindly make me a sandwich, and I'll have a glass of beer.

EVANS. Sandwich of mutton or 'am, miss?

MISS WOODWARD. Ham, please. [*Exit* EVANS.] It's sure to be cold mutton to-night. [*She writes.*] Old manuscripts. [*Closes drawer.*] There, that's all in order for him. [*Rises.*] I know there are some books of mine here. I may as well have them. [*Goes towards book-shelves, but stops when she comes to the occasional table on which is the photo of* PARBURY. *She stretches out her hand and takes the photograph gingerly. Then she looks round to see if she is observed, with an affectation of fear.*] Poor thing! Was it outraged by a kiss? What a shame! But it's all right now! [*Puts it back with care.*] No one shall hurt it. It's perfectly safe—perfectly safe. [*She goes to book-shelf.*] Keats— mine. [*Takes a volume.*] Matthew Arnold—mine.

Enter EVANS *with sandwiches, beer, &c., on a small tray, which he places on the desk.*

'Jane Eyre'—mine. I think that's all. [*Brings the books down and places them on desk.*] Thank you, Evans. [*She sits.*

EVANS. Cook thought you would care for that piece of cake, miss.

MISS WOODWARD. I would. Thank cook for me.

EVANS. Yes, miss. [*He goes to door.*] There's still a hominous silence at the lunch-table, miss.

MISS WOODWARD. [*Taking a sandwich.*] That's all right, Evans. [*Exit* EVANS.] After all, one must have food. [*She takes a respectable bite out of a sandwich.*] And who could over-estimate the consolations of literature?

[*Opens a book and reads.*

'Is the calm thine of stoic souls who weigh
Life well, and find it wanting, nor deplore;
But in disdainful silence turn away,
Stand mute, self-centred, stern, and dream no more?'

Yes, Mr. Arnold, it is.   [*Takes another bite of a sandwich.*

Enter MRS. PARBURY.

MRS. PARBURY. Why won't you come to lunch, Miss Woodward. But oh, I see you're having something here.

MISS WOODWARD. [*For a moment slightly confused.*] I—I— [*Drinks some of her beer.*]—I have a railway journey before me.

MRS. PARBURY. All the more reason you should come and lunch properly.

MISS WOODWARD. You are very kind, but I am in no mood for merriment.

MRS. PARBURY. Merriment!

MISS WOODWARD. Aren't you all merry? I'm so sorry. I thought it would be all right now that I'm going away.

MRS. PARBURY. I'm afraid that won't make any difference. You speak as though you thought you had a grievance against me.

MISS WOODWARD. Oh no; I suppose it's the other way about.

MRS. PARBURY. Perhaps it ought to be, but somehow I don't feel it acutely. I feel only a dull pain. It's a terrible thing, Miss Woodward, for a young married woman to suddenly realise that her happiness is gone. I feel that I have aged many years in the last few hours.

MISS WOODWARD. So do I. I'm sadder, but healthier.

> [*Finishes the beer.*

MRS. PARBURY. It's so much worse for me.

MISS WOODWARD. Oh, of course our own troubles are always the worst. That is what has been called 'the vanity of grief.'

MRS. PARBURY. Well, Miss Woodward, I'll say good-bye. I bear you no ill-will now—really I don't; and I shall always be glad to hear that you are doing well, although naturally under the circumstances I can hold out no hopes of your coming back here.

MISS WOODWARD. [*In amazement.*] You, Mrs. Parbury, hold out hopes of my returning here! Do you think there is enough money in the Bank of England to induce me to do that?

MRS. PARBURY. I didn't mean it unkindly. I was only trying to say a nice womanly thing, and to show you that I didn't blame you so much for falling in love with my husband.

MISS WOODWARD. I never did.

MRS. PARBURY. Oh, Miss Woodward, you know I saw you here. [*Pointing to* PARBURY's *photograph.*] It was the greatest shock of my life.

MISS WOODWARD. You mean I kissed his photograph?

MRS. PARBURY. You know you did.

MISS WOODWARD. [*With a little laugh.*] I suppose I did.

MRS. PARBURY. Then how can you say——

MISS WOODWARD. [*Gravely.*] It was a motherly kiss.

MRS. PARBURY. [*Turning away.*] It seems impossible to talk with you. I used to think you a serious-minded person.

MISS WOODWARD. Please don't go, Mrs. Parbury, I'm quite serious. I'd like to explain. I think I owe it to you.

MRS. PARBURY. [*Turning.*] Well?

MISS WOODWARD. You will let me be quite frank?

MRS. PARBURY. Oh, I shall like it.

MISS WOODWARD. I'm not so sure of that.

MRS. PARBURY. I'll take the risk. Go on, please.

MISS WOODWARD. The interest which I began to take in Mr. Parbury sprang in a way from what has been called the maternal instinct.

MRS. PARBURY. If you go through the world exercising your maternal instinct on other women's husbands, Miss Woodward, you'll end badly.

MISS WOODWARD. I don't propose doing so. I'm going home to try it on my sisters.

MRS. PARBURY. If you had known anything of life, you would have seen that I had sufficient of the maternal instinct for the needs of my husband.

MISS WOODWARD. I'm very, very sorry; please don't be angry, but I didn't think it found the right expression. It was very impudent of me, I know.

MRS. PARBURY. Very.

MISS WOODWARD. It seemed to me that you smoothed his hair when he'd rather it was rough, and roughed it when he'd rather it was smooth. [*Demurely.*] I think that expresses what I mean. I have a beastly sly way of noticing everything, and I began to feel sorry for Mr. Parbury. And being quite as egotistical as most girls, I began to think I should have made him a better wife than you.

MRS. PARBURY. Oh.

MISS WOODWARD. Perhaps in the remotest corner of my heart I think so still.

MRS. PARBURY. [*Indignant.*] Well?

MISS WOODWARD. But I never loved him—never in the least degree.

[MRS. PARBURY, *during the foregoing, has listened with anger gathering in her face, but at the end, after an apparent momentary struggle with herself, she bursts into laughter.*]

MISS WOODWARD. I'm glad you're not angry.

MRS. PARBURY. [*Still laughing.*] It's impossible to be angry. And so because you thought his wife bored him, you gave his photograph a nice motherly kiss. That was very sweet of you, I'm sure.

MISS WOODWARD. It was well meant, Mrs. Parbury; and you must always remember that I didn't know you were looking.

MRS. PARBURY. [*Laughing.*] Why do you make me laugh when you must know that my heart is breaking—that I have lost my happiness for ever. [*Pause. She begins to laugh again.*] And I thought you a designing hussy, when you are only a very quaint and harmless girl.

Enter GUNNING.

GUNNING. I'm afraid I'm in the way.

MRS. PARBURY. Not at all. We have said all we had to say to each other. Oh, how that girl has made me laugh!

[*Exit* MRS. PARBURY, *laughing.*

MISS WOODWARD. Good-bye, Mr. Gunning.

[*Gathering her books together.*

GUNNING. I want a little talk with you.

MISS WOODWARD. I'm sorry I can't give you the time.

GUNNING. Oh yes you will, Miss Woodward.

MISS WOODWARD. Indeed? I admit my position is a lowly one, but that doesn't lessen your presumption.

[*Goes towards the door.*

GUNNING. [*With conviction.*] You won't go.

MISS WOODWARD. But I will.

GUNNING. My dear Miss Woodward, believe me, you will not.

MISS WOODWARD. You don't propose using force, I suppose?

GUNNING. No. I think you would like me to, but unfortunately this is not our house, and one must observe the convenances.

MISS WOODWARD. [*Going to door.*] Good-bye, Mr. Gunning.

GUNNING. Moral force will detain you.

MISS WOODWARD. [*Turning.*] What moral force, pray?

GUNNING. Curiosity. You know you are dying to know what I have to say.

MISS WOODWARD. Indeed I am not.

GUNNING. Oh yes, you are. And further, a certain womanly graciousness will prevent your going. You are saying to yourself, 'Mr. Gunning has evinced a genuine interest in me. It would be cattish of me to refuse him a few minutes' talk.'

MISS WOODWARD. [*Slowly comes to sofa and puts her books down.*] I certainly don't wish to be cattish.

GUNNING. Of course not.

MISS WOODWARD. [*Sits on sofa.*] And anyway I want to eat my piece of cake. Will you pass it, please? [*He passes the plate.*] Thank you. I hope you won't mind my eating.

GUNNING. Not at all. I like it.

MISS WOODWARD. Not that I fear it would make any difference if you did.

GUNNING. No, certainly not. Go on being natural, please. [*Pause. He watches her nibbling the cake.*] Shall I ring for a fresh piece?

MISS WOODWARD. No, thank you. I'm used to this piece now. [*She glances up at him.*] You needn't be disconcerted, Mr. Gunning.

GUNNING. I'm not a bit.

MISS WOODWARD. You look it a little.

GUNNING. Do I?

MISS WOODWARD. And you know you didn't detain me here to watch me eating cake.

GUNNING. No, although you do it very nicely. I want to ask you what you think of me.

MISS WOODWARD. I haven't thought of you.

GUNNING. Well, I'd like you to begin.

MISS WOODWARD. I'm afraid I haven't time now.

GUNNING. It might be to your interest, though I don't say positively that it would be.

MISS WOODWARD. Explain.

GUNNING. I think I ought first to tell you something about myself.

MISS WOODWARD. [*In mock alarm.*] Not the story of your life, surely? My cab will be here soon.

GUNNING. You told me yours last night.

MISS WOODWARD. You asked me to. I haven't asked you.

GUNNING. You needn't reproach me for taking an interest in you.

MISS WOODWARD. I don't; but you make such a fuss about it, as if it were a sort of miracle.

GUNNING. [*Crossly takes plate from her lap and cake from her hand; puts them on table.*] Oh well, I suppose I oughtn't to detain you, Miss Woodward. You are evidently anxious to get back to your twelve sisters and the hat and frock you told me about.

MISS WOODWARD. [*Rises.*] You needn't throw the family poverty in my face, although it serves me right for giving my confidence to a comparative stranger.

GUNNING. Miss Woodward, I humbly beg your pardon.

MISS WOODWARD. Although the home may be grubby, I daresay we are as happy as you. We believe in things, anyway—you don't.

GUNNING. Don't judge me by a hasty remark. Besides, I had an alternative to suggest.

MISS WOODWARD. You? You don't want a secretary, do you?

GUNNING. I—I wanted to tell you in a different way, but you won't let me. I want you as my wife.

MISS WOODWARD. Your wife, Mr. Gunning?

GUNNING. It may appear sudden and cold-blooded—but your cab is coming.

MISS WOODWARD. You've taken my breath away. How exciting it is when it does come. I really don't know what to say. I know there is a usual thing. It isn't 'To what am I indebted for this honour,' is it?

GUNNING. I don't know. I've never asked a girl before.

MISS WOODWARD. We don't know each other in the least.

GUNNING. That's where we would start with a big advantage. We'd have all the pleasure of finding each other out. Anyway, you are not displeased.

MISS WOODWARD. Oh no; either way I score. If I say yes, I suppose I'll make a good match.

GUNNING. Pretty good.

MISS WOODWARD. And if I say no, I shall at least be able to boast of a proposal.

GUNNING. That's so.

MISS WOODWARD. Not that there's much satisfaction in that to a practical mind.

GUNNING. No. [*Goes to her.*] Try the other.

MISS WOODWARD. But we don't love each other.

GUNNING. Another big advantage. Love is the rock upon which so many well-intentioned young persons split. They engage to marry each other while the intelligence is perverted, the reason unbalanced, and the judgment obscured by an overpowering sentiment. They enter into a solemn life-binding contract in a highly emotional and altogether un-normal moral condition. The disastrous results of such folly we see examples of daily. We will escape that snare. [*He comes close to her.*] Of course if the sentiment should subsequently come, if that particular kind of emotion should by chance supervene, we'll deal with it as best we may.

MISS WOODWARD. Still, there must be something in love-making. I remember my sister and the curate seemed to have a very good time. We all thought them fussy, but I know they liked it.

GUNNING. I made love to you in the garden this morning.

MISS WOODWARD. Did you? I thought it was pity, and resented it.

GUNNING. You refused me a rose, and gave one——

MISS WOODWARD. I refused you because I thought you pitied me, and gave one to Mr. Parbury because I pitied him.

GUNNING. I'd like you to pity me.

MISS WOODWARD. I *should* if I said yes. [*Leaves him.*] But I mean to say no.

GUNNING. [*Following her.*] You are afraid.

MISS WOODWARD. Of what?

GUNNING. Of what people call my 'nasty sneering way,' for instance.

MISS WOODWARD. [*Confidently.*] Oh, I could deal with that all right.

GUNNING. I'm sure you could. [*Goes near to her.*] Say yes, Hyacinth.

Enter EVANS.

EVANS. Your cab is here, miss.

GUNNING. [*To* MISS WOODWARD, *in a low voice.*] Send it away. [*She hesitates.*] Do.

MISS WOODWARD. Thank you, Evans. Let it wait.

[GUNNING *moves away with a satisfied smile.*

EVANS. Yes, miss.   [*Exit.*

MISS WOODWARD. Good-bye, Mr. Gunning. If you were entirely different from what you are, I think I could have liked you; or if I were entirely different from what I am, I think I might have married you. But you are hopelessly modern and cold-blooded, and I am only an old-fashioned, healthy English girl, and a healthy English girl doesn't want to make experiments; she wants to be loved.

[*Suddenly* GUNNING *throws his arm round her and bends forward to kiss her. She quickly raises her clenched hand as if to strike him in the face. He looks her in the eyes without flinching.*

GUNNING. Perhaps she wants a master.

MISS WOODWARD. [*Softly.*] Perhaps.

[*Her hand slowly drops*; *he kisses her.*

ARMITAGE. [*Outside.*] No, my dear; I can't wait any longer.

GUNNING. [*In a low voice to* MISS WOODWARD.] The garden. Will you come and find me a rose?

MISS WOODWARD. Yes.

Enter ARMITAGE, MRS. PARBURY, *and* PARBURY. MISS WOODWARD *and* GUNNING *exeunt quickly to garden.* MRS. PARBURY *comes down and sits on sofa.* PARBURY *goes* R. *and sits*; ARMITAGE *remains* C. *They are all silent and uneasy. A considerable pause, during which they are occupied with avoiding each other's eyes.*

ARMITAGE. A cheerful day.

PARBURY. Yes.

MRS. PARBURY. Very.   [*Another uneasy pause.*

ARMITAGE. Well, I must be going.

PARBURY. Don't go.

MRS. PARBURY. Please stay, father.   [*Another pause.*

ARMITAGE. [*With much irritation.*] Well, you see I'm staying.

MRS. PARBURY. Thank you.

PARBURY. Thank you, Colonel.

ARMITAGE. But I should like to know what the devil for?

MRS. PARBURY. Father!

PARBURY. Colonel!

ARMITAGE. I really think I have cause to be angry. A more depressing function than your luncheon party to-day I've never experienced. I think I have a right to a little cheerfulness in my middle age. I'm sure I've earned it. I've had a great deal to put up with in my life.

PARBURY. No doubt, no doubt.

ARMITAGE. Of course I have always accepted my full share of the blame. That I have felt to be only right and manly. [*Pause. He looks at* PARBURY.] As for my late dear wife, her heart was rarely deaf to a proper expression of regret. The memory of her I feel to be a blessing to this day. [*He blows his nose sympathetically.*] One thing I can tell you, Mabel, that when your dear mother and I made it up—well, we *did* make it up. I am not without some very agreeable recollections—most agreeable. [*Pause. He comes to* MRS. PARBURY.] I trust you won't require me tonight, my dear. I have to attend a Masonic Banquet.

MRS. PARBURY. No, father; I shan't want you.

ARMITAGE. Then good-bye. [*Aside to her.*] Be true to your own good heart. Your dear mother was—sometimes. [*He kisses her, and then goes to* PARBURY.] Good-bye, Clement. [*Aside to him.*] Bear up; I've been there myself. [*He goes—aside at door.*] Rather tactful, I think—rather tactful.

> [*Exit. There is a constrained silence.* MRS. PARBURY *is particularly uneasy. After a moment* PARBURY *rises, lights a cigarette, and stands at mantelpiece.*

MRS. PARBURY. Am I in the way, dear? Do you want to work?

PARBURY. No. To-day must be a holiday.

MRS. PARBURY. Holidays are meant to be happy days.

PARBURY. I suppose so.

MRS. PARBURY. [*Very sadly.*] Our happy days have gone. I suppose they will never come back.

PARBURY. It would be wiser to look for new ones than to weep over the old ones.

MRS. PARBURY. I'll not cry, dear; I promise you that. [*Pause. Suddenly rises and turns to him.*] Clement, can't we start again?

PARBURY. Perhaps. But we must consider first where we now are and the direction in which we should go.

MRS. PARBURY. Perhaps in your heart you are blaming me more than I deserve—I mean about Miss Woodward.

PARBURY. You chose to keep the motives of your conduct a secret from me.

MRS. PARBURY. I may have been wrong. I saw her kiss your photograph.

PARBURY. [*Starts slightly.*] Why didn't you tell me? [*Pause.*] Why didn't you tell me?

MRS. PARBURY. I thought—I thought it would be wiser not to.

PARBURY. What have I ever done to earn so low an estimate of my character from you—that I am not to be trusted with the knowledge that a foolish girl had kissed my photograph.

MRS. PARBURY. Nothing, dear; nothing. But I was jealous—furious. I am sorry. [*She is half-turned from him. He smiles very kindly, and half makes a step forward as if to take her in his arms, then restrains himself.*] You are very, very angry with me?　　　　　　　　　　　　　　　　　　　　　[*Drooping.*

PARBURY. I am very, very pained.

MRS. PARBURY. Can't you forgive?

PARBURY. Yes, that is forgiven.

MRS. PARBURY. You say you forgive, but you don't make me feel it. [*Slight pause. He is obviously tempted to come to her, but does not.*] Won't you forget too, and let us go back together?

PARBURY. No, we can never go back.

MRS. PARBURY. Love counts for something, Clement.

PARBURY. [*Comes to her.*] Does love without respect count for very much? Would you like to go back to the old way—the way of petty tyranny—the way of the cowardly, unnecessary tear—the way of gaining your own ends at all costs—the way of being a spoilt child instead of a thoughtful and considerate woman—the way of my own contemptible weakness?

MRS. PARBURY. I never looked upon it in that light. I thought I was happy then.

PARBURY. Because you never dreamed that my love was beginning to wear badly.

MRS. PARBURY. [*Startled.*] Clement! Oh! [*Goes to him.*] Good God!

PARBURY. I don't want ever to think or speak of it again; but to-day I must, for if we are honest with each other, we may be able in time to save ourselves from that most pitiable and hideous of all states of existence—that is called 'a cat and dog life.' Have you never seen it—that domestic flower with the rotten heart? The thin outside petals of courtesy, of hollow words of endearment before others, mask the ugly truth from the casual and unobservant; but the intimate friends know, and the prying eyes of the spiteful are undeceived. That man and woman who appear in public wearing the veneered ghost of a smile are walking in hell. Think of their private lives—the slow death of love; the hearts poisoned with bitterness; the ever-growing rancour; the bandied insolences; the swift thoughts, black as murder; the final dull monotony of aching hatred. Do you think such cases rare? Every rank of society has its examples. Do you think such a couple have deliberately sought their hell? Oh no; they may have started as fairly as we did. Their love has not been slain by a blow; it has been pecked to a cupboard skeleton by littlenesses—little jealousies, little selfishnesses, little insults, little tyrannies, little intolerances.

MRS. PARBURY. Clement, you terrify me. Oh, I am ashamed— ashamed. You have made me shudder at the old way. Dear, if I have lost a particle of your love, I'll win it back. You will show me the new way, won't you?

PARBURY. The new way for us is the old way for the wise. It is a pleasant way strewn with flowers, the flowers of self-abnegation—of sweet reasonableness—of patient tolerance —of enduring trustfulness. Walking in that way we seek diligently for the happiness, not of ourselves, but of each other. Rising in the morning we say, not I will find happiness to-day, but I will give happiness to-day. In that way lie peace, the fulfilment of our better selves, the full golden harvest of love.
[*As he speaks these words with deep sympathy, standing a little away from her, she gradually draws nearer to him.*

MRS. PARBURY. I will walk in that way with you, Clement. [*She stoops, and taking one of his hands kisses it. Pause. He stoops and raises her, and takes her in his arms.*

Enter MISS WOODWARD *and* GUNNING. GUNNING *wears a rose in his coat.*

GUNNING. Really—I beg your pardon.

MRS. PARBURY. Don't trouble about us any more. We're reconciled. [*She remains in her husband's arms.* GUNNING *turns smilingly to* MISS WOODWARD *and takes her hand.*

MISS WOODWARD. [*Smiling back upon* GUNNING.] Don't trouble about us any more. We're engaged.　　　[*Curtain.*